Justiz und Justizverfassung
Judiciary and Judicial System

Rechtshistorische Reihe

Band 446

Zur Qualitätssicherung und Peer Review der vorliegenden Publikation

Die Qualität der in dieser Reihe erscheinenden Arbeiten wird vor der Publikation durch einen Herausgeber der Reihe geprüft.

Notes on the quality assurance and peer review of this publication

Prior to publication, the quality of the work published in this series is reviewed by one of the editors of the series.

Frank L. Schäfer/
Werner Schubert (Hrsg./eds.)

Justiz und Justizverfassung
Judiciary and Judicial System

Siebter Rechtshistorikertag im Ostseeraum,
3.-5. Mai 2012 Schleswig-Holstein

7th Conference in Legal History in the Baltic Sea Area,
3rd-5th May 2012 Schleswig-Holstein

PL ACADEMIC RESEARCH

Bibliografische Information der Deutschen Nationalbibliothek
Die Deutsche Nationalbibliothek verzeichnet diese Publikation in der DeutschenNationalbibliografie; detaillierte bibliografische Daten sind im Internet über http://dnb.d-nb.de abrufbar.

Umschlagabbildung:
Justitia. Allegorie der Gerechtigkeit.
Druck aus dem 17. Jahrhundert.

Gedruckt auf alterungsbeständigem, säurefreiem Papier.

ISSN 1615-0344-290X
ISBN 978-3-631-63912-2 (Print)
E-ISBN 978-3-653-03624-4 (E-Book)
DOI 10.3726/978-3-653-03624-4

PL Academic Research ist ein Imprint der Peter Lang GmbH.

Peter Lang – Frankfurt am Main · Bern · Bruxelles · New York · Oxford · Warszawa · Wien

www.peterlang.de

Vorwort

Der Tagungsband dokumentiert den VII. Rechtshistorikertag im Ostseeraum. Die Veranstaltungsreihe dient seit dem Jahr 2000 zur Förderung der Kooperation und des Gedankenaustauschs zwischen den Rechtshistorikerinnen und Rechtshistorikern in den Anrainerstaaten der Ostsee. Zugleich ist die Veranstaltungsreihe Bestandteil eines größeren Netzwerkes in Nordeuropa sowie im Ostseeraum. Zu nennen sind bei den Historikern die Kooperation „Nordic Spaces: Formation of States, Societies and Regions, Cultural Encounters, and Idea and Identity Production in Northern Europe after 1800“ und bei den Rechtshistorikern die Doktorandenförderung über das Projekt „Legal history on the edge of Europe: Nordic law in the European legal community 1000–2000 a.d. (REUNA)“. Hinzu kommen einzelne Veranstaltungen wie 2010 in Finnland zu „Nordic Legal Traditions and the Changing European Context“ und die thematische Kongressreihe „Carlsberg Academy Conference on Medieval Legal History“ in Kopenhagen.

Der VII. Rechtshistorikertag im Ostseeraum fand vom dritten bis zum fünften Mai 2012 in Schleswig-Holstein statt. Tagungszentrum war das Dr. Otto Bagge-Kolleg der Dr. Otto Bagge-Stiftung der Rechtswissenschaftlichen Fakultät der Christian-Albrechts-Universität zu Kiel in Sehlendorf an der Ostsee. Am vierten und fünften Mai tagten die Teilnehmer an historischen Stätten der Gerichtsbarkeit und der Wissenschaft in Schleswig-Holstein: im Sitzungssaal des Schleswig-Holsteinischen Oberlandesgerichts in Schleswig, im Kuppelsaal des Prinzenpalais des Landesarchivs Schleswig-Holstein in Schleswig sowie im Roten Saal des Rathauses der Hansestadt Lübeck. Dafür gilt unser besonderer Dank Herrn Heinz-Karl Waßmuth, Vizepräsident des Schleswig-Holsteinischen Oberlandesgerichts, Herrn Professor Dr. Dr. Rainer Hering, Direktor des Landesarchivs Schleswig-Holstein, sowie Herrn Bernd Saxe, Bürgermeister der Hansestadt Lübeck.

Mit dem Thema „Justiz und Justizverfassung“ knüpfte der VII. Rechtshistorikertag im Ostseeraum an den IV. Rechtshistorikertag im Ostseeraum in Greifswald über „Gerichtskultur im Ostseeraum“ an. Die Teilnehmer setzten sich auf dem VII. Rechtshistorikertag zum Ziel, die Geschichte des Prozessrechts, der Justiz und ihrer Institutionen in der ganzen Bandbreite des Ostseeraums zu erforschen und zu präsentieren. Die Referate widmeten sich in der Horizontalen den einzelnen Anrainerstaaten der Ostsee: Dänemark, Schweden, Baltikum, Finnland, Russland/Sowjetunion, Polen und Norddeutschland (Schleswig-Holstein, Mecklenburg). In der Vertikalen reichten die Referate von der Höchstgerichtsbarkeit im Ostseeraum bis zur Dorfjustiz des russischen Bauerntums. Ebenso vielfältig waren die Anknüpfungspunkte in der Gerichtsorganisation: Sie reichten von den Obergerichten über die Spruchfakultäten und Laiengerichte bis zur Kirchengerichtsbarkeit. Zu den Referaten von Jukka Kekkonen über „The administration of justice after crisis episodes in Finland; experiences from postwar (1918– and 1945–) situations“ und von Joachim Rückert über „Savigny, Justiz und Justizverfassung – auch am Beispiel zweier Staatsratsgutachten“ liegt keine Schriftfassung vor. Die Referate von Tatiana Borisova über „Russian judiciary and the problem of law interpretation in late imperial Russia“ und von Pia Letto-Vanamo über „Finnische Justiz im 20. Jahrhundert“ werden bei Lindsay Farmer u.a. (Hg.), From the Judge's Arbitrium to the Legality Principle bzw. in der Zeitschrift für Neuere Rechtsgeschichte abgedruckt.

Unser besonderer Dank für die Vorbereitung dieses Tagungsbandes gilt den Mitarbeiterinnen und Mitarbeitern am Lehrstuhl für Bürgerliches Recht, Europäische und Deutsche Rechtsgeschichte sowie Historische Rechtsvergleichung am Juristischen Seminar der Christian-Albrechts-Universität zu Kiel. Ferner sind wir der Deutschen Forschungsgemeinschaft sowie der Prof. Dr. Werner Petersen-Stiftung für die Unterstützung der Tagung verbunden.

Kiel, Juni 2013 *Frank L. Schäfer und Werner Schubert*

Inhaltsverzeichnis

Autorenverzeichnis

Andres Andresen	Dr. phil., Senior Research Fellow, Institut für Geschichte und Archäologie, Universität Tartu, Lossi 3, 50090 Tartu, Estland
Tatyana Doroshenko	Dr. phil., Dozentin, Abteilung für Zivilrecht, Rechtsfakultät, Staatliche Universität Nowgorod, Bul. St. Peterburgskaya 41, 173003 Weliky Nowgorod, Russland
Danuta Janicka	Dr. iur., Professorin, Lehrstuhl für die Geschichte des deutschen Rechts in Polen, Fakultät für Rechtswissenschaften, Nikolaus-Kopernikus-Universität, W. Bojarskiego 3, 87–100 Torun, Polen
Nils Jörn	Dr. phil., Stadtarchivar, Archiv der Hansestadt Wismar, Altwismarstraße 10–17, 23966 Wismar, Deutschland
Rusnė Juozapaitienė	Promotionsstudentin an der Universität Vilnius, Rechtsfakultät, Mitglied des Instituts für Rechtsgeschichte, Saulėtekio ave. 9, Vilnius LT-10222, Litauen
Hans-Georg Knothe	Dr. iur., Professor emeritus für Bürgerliches Recht und Rechtsgeschichte, Wolfgang-Koeppen-Str. 1, 17489 Greifswald, Deutschland
Jānis Lazdiņš	Dr. iur., Professor für Rechtsphilosophie, lettische Rechtsgeschichte und Steuerrecht, Rechtsfakultät, Universität Lettlands, Raiņa blv. 19, Rīga, Lettland
Marju Luts-Sootak	Dr. iur., Professorin für Rechtsgeschichte, Rechtsfakultät, Universität Tartu, Näituse 20, 50409 Tartu, Estland
Elena Makarova	Dr. phil., Dozentin, Abteilung für Staats- und Rechtsgeschichte, Rechtsfakultät, Staatliche Universität Nowgorod, Bul. St. Peterburgskaya 41, 173003 Weliky Nowgorod, Russland
Sanita Osipova	Dr. iur., Professorin für Europäische Rechtsgeschichte und Rechtssoziologie, Rechtsfakultät, Universität Lettlands, Raiņa blv. 19, Rīga, Lettland
Alexander Rogatschewski	Dr. iur., Professor an der Rechtsfakultät der Staatlichen Ingenieurökonomischen Universität St. Petersburg, 191186, Postf. 146, St. Petersburg, Russland
Frank L. Schäfer	Dr. iur., LL.M., Professor für Bürgerliches Recht, Europäische und Deutsche Rechtsgeschichte, Historische Rechtsvergleichung, Juristisches Seminar, Universität Kiel, Leibnizstr. 6, 24118 Kiel, Deutschland
Werner Schubert	Dr. iur., Professor emeritus für Rechtsgeschichte der Neuzeit, Römisches Recht, Bürgerliches Recht und Zivilprozessrecht, Juristisches Seminar, Universität Kiel, Leibnizstr. 6, 24118 Kiel, Deutschland

Ditlev Tamm Dr. iur., Dr. phil., Dr. h.c., Professor für Rechtsgeschichte, Zentrum für rechtskulturelle Studien, Die rechtswissenschaftliche Fakultät, Universität Kopenhagen, Studie-straede 6, 1455 Kopenhagen, Dänemark

Anna Tarnowska Dr. iur., Adjunkt, Lehrstuhl für die Geschichte des deutschen Rechts in Polen, Fakultät für Rechtswissenschaften, Nikolaus-Kopernikus-Universität, W. Bojarskiego 3, 87–100 Torun, Polen

Ecclesiastical Administration of Justice in the Baltic Region of the Russian Empire during the Early State Modernization: The Case of the Province Estland

Andres Andresen

I. Introduction

The previous research has quite unanimously pointed to the Baltic provinces Estland, Livland and Kurland between c. 1800 and 1880 as – at least for nineteenth century Europe – anachronistic examples of comprehensive estate privileges. At times when constitutionalism and liberalism had become the modern catchwords in contemporary European politics, on the Baltic soil and under the supremacy of the Russian tsars, the Baltic German noble estates and town elites still enjoyed rights of corporative self-government which partly dated back to the Middle Ages. According to general knowledge, the Baltic corporative privileges in the fields of administration and judiciary were decimated with the major unification reforms of the late nineteenth century (the infamous Russification).[1] Some recent studies, however, have emphasized that these reforms were preceded by interventions of central state power in provincial privileges several decades earlier which should be considered as elements of the same line of development – the modernization of the state administration, especially regarding reforms targeted at the unification of different regions.[2] This paper follows the same rationale and takes a closer look at the Lutheran ecclesiastical administration of justice in the Baltic provinces in the context of state policies during the early nineteenth century.

The provinces Estland, Livland and Kurland formed a very distinct region of the empire, especially due to their common cultural and historical background of western Christianity and also due to their long-standing institutional traditions. In Estland and Livland the Russian rule had replaced that of the Swedish monarchs during the course of the Great Northern War, in 1710. The capitulations concluded by the local estates and the Russian military leadership guaranteed the domination of the Lutheran confession, the self-government of the noble landlord corporations

---

1 As an introduction see for example *Michael Haltzel*, Der Abbau der deutschen ständischen Selbstverwaltung in den Ostseeprovinzen Rußlands. Ein Beitrag zur Geschichte der russischen Unifizierungspolitik 1855–1905, Marburg/Lahn 1977; *Gert v. Pistohlkors* (Hg.), Baltische Länder, Berlin 1994, esp. pp. 397 sqq.

2 See for example *Lea Leppik*, The provincial reforms of Catherine the Great and the Baltic common identity, Ajalooline Ajakiri [The Estonian Historical Journal] 2012 1/2 (139/140), pp. 55–78; *Andres Andresen*, Unifying the Periphery of a Conglomerate State: Ecclesiastical Legislation in Estland and Livland (1686–1832), in: Marju Luts-Sootak/Sanita Osipova/Frank L. Schäfer (Hg.), Einheit und Vielfalt in der Rechtsgeschichte im Ostseeraum. Sechster Rechtshistorikertag im Ostseeraum, 3.–5. Juni 2010 Tartu (Estland)/Riga (Lettland), Frankfurt a. M. u. a. 2012.

(*Ritterschaften*) of Estland and Livland as well as of the town elites in Tallinn (Reval) and Riga, the local legal tradition and court system, and German as the local official language. These terms were later confirmed by Tsar Peter I, by the provisions of the 1721 Treaty of Nystad as well as by later monarchs.[3] As a result of the third Polish partition in 1795 Russian supremacy extended over Kurland. Also in this province the privileges of the estates were guaranteed by the monarchs.

The Baltic provincial privileges and historical institutional traditions contributed to the relatively strong institutional particularism in both secular and clerical fields of society. In Estland, Livland and Kurland the early modernizing efforts of the central government were mostly directed at overcoming the secular institutional particularism and unifying the structures of society with the core area of the state. First and foremost this pertained to the fields of province administration and the secular judicial system. During the late eighteenth and early nineteenth centuries the Russian monarchs Catherine II and Alexander I initiated several reform attempts which were targeted at updating various spheres of the state according to the contemporary European examples. For a short while, the liberal-minded Alexander I even took up the idea of transforming the autocratic empire into a constitutional monarchy of the enlightened European type. All through this period of early state modernization the domain of state administration enjoyed the most attention.[4]

At this period of time, until the late 1820s, Lutheran church governance and ecclesiastical administration of justice in the Baltic region were spared of any major coordinated intervention. Although Alexander I had worked on some ideas regarding centralized Protestant church governance, eventually these ideas had no direct impact on Estland, Livland and Kurland. Then finally in 1832 the new Act for the Evangelical Lutheran Church of the Russian Empire comprehensively unified the Lutheran ecclesiastical institutions throughout the Empire.

The aim of this article is twofold. The primary objective is to study the Baltic ecclesiastical administration of justice in the early nineteenth century before 1832. To this end, I shall take up the case study on the province Estland. My secondary intention is to briefly examine the most important changes in the system of ecclesiastical judiciary which were prescribed by the 1832 Lutheran Church Law.

---

3 *Eduard Winkelmann* (Hg.), Die Capitulationen der estländischen Ritterschaft und der Stadt Reval vom Jahre 1710 nebst deren Confirmationen. Nach den Originalen mit andern dazu gehörigen Documenten und der Capitulation von Pernau, Reval 1865; *Carl Schirren* (Hg.), Die Capitulationen der livländischen Ritter- und Landschaft und der Stadt Riga vom 4. Juli 1710 nebst deren Confirmationen. Nach den Originaldokumenten mit Vorausstellung des Privilegium Sigismundi Augusti und einigen Beilagen, Dorpat 1865. On religious privileges see *Andres Andresen*, Formal stipulation and practical implementation of religious privileges in Estland, Livland and Courland under Russian supremacy: researching the core of Baltic regional identity, Ajalooline Ajakiri [The Estonian Historical Journal] 2012 1/2 (139/140), pp. 33–54.

4 For a general overview see *v. Pistohlkors*, Baltische Länder (supra fn. 1), pp. 287 sqq.

The history of the Lutheran ecclesiastical judicial system in the provinces Estland, Livland and Kurland has been one of the most neglected areas in the Baltic legal historiography. Several church historians have touched upon the system of church courts, but only rather generally.[5] Legal historians working on the Baltic region have almost entirely abandoned the themes of ecclesiastical courts, ecclesiastical administration of justice and Lutheran church law.[6] A recent study in the field of historical research examines the influence of state power on church governance, church institutions and church law in Estland during the period of 1710–1832.[7]

The most important archival sources for the study of the ecclesiastical administration of justice in the Baltic provinces are, firstly, the protocols of the church consistories, and secondly, the acts of law issued by the provincial governments. In the case of the province Estland all these sources are preserved in the Estonian Historical Archives in Tartu. Among the published sources the Swedish Church Law of 1686 and the Swedish consistorial code of procedure of 1687,[8] numerous

---

5 *Hermann Dalton*, Verfassungsgeschichte der evangelisch-lutherischen Kirche in Rußland, Gotha 1887; *Juhan Kõpp*, Kirikuvalitsemisõpetus, Tartu 1940; *Wilhelm Lenz*, Zur Verfassungs- und Sozialgeschichte der baltischen evangelisch-lutherischen Kirche 1710–1914. Der Aufbau der Landeskirchen und die Stellung des Pastors in Liv-, Est- und Kurland, in: Reinhard Wittram (Hg.), Baltische Kirchengeschichte: Beiträge zur Geschichte der Missionierung und der Reformation, der evangelisch-lutherischen Landeskirchen und des Volkskirchentums in den baltischen Landen, Göttingen 1956, pp. 110–129.

6 In the Baltic German overviews of the Baltic history of law, church law has been studied extremely superficially. For example Friedrich Georg von Bunge has written four pages on canon law, but Lutheran church law in Estland has been summarized only in a few lines (*Friedrich Georg v. Bunge*, Einleitung in die liv-, esth- und curländische Rechtsgeschichte und Geschichte der Rechtsquellen, Reval 1849, pp. 170–174, 205–206); also the part on the system of Lutheran church courts is very laconic (*Friedrich Georg v. Bunge*, Geschichte des Gerichtswesens und Gerichtsverfahrens in Liv-, Est- und Curland, Reval 1874, pp. 170, 175, 177–178, 203). Oswald Schmidt only mentions the church laws of 1686 and 1832 (*Oswald Schmidt*, Rechtsgeschichte Liv-, Est- und Curlands. Aus dem Nachlasse des Verfassers hg. von Dr. Eugen von Nottbeck, Dorpat 1895, pp. 174, 277–278). However, F. G. v. Bunge regarded all the acts of law which were applied in a Baltic province as *provincial law* (*Marju Luts*, Juhuslik ja isamaaline: F. G. v. Bunge provintsiaalõigusteadus, Tartu 2000, pp. 133–135), thus also ecclesiastical law has to be considered an integral part of the provincial law.

7 *Andres Andresen*, Eestimaa kirikukorraldus 1710–1832. Riigivõimu mõju institutsioonidele ja õigusele [Church constitution in Estland, 1710–1832. The influence of state power on institutions and law], Tartu 2008. I have used some parts of my monograph for this article.

8 In the Baltic provinces and in the Lutheran congregations of Russia proper the German translations were used: Kirchen-Gesetz und Ordnung, So der Großmächtigste König und Herr, Herr Carl, der Eilffte, Der Schweden, Gothen und Wenden König, etc. Im Jahr 1686 hat verfassen und Im Jahr 1687 im Druck ausgehen und publiciren lassen. Mit denen dazu gehörigen Verordnungen. Stockholm [*sine anno*]; Ihr: Königl. May.t Verordnung, Wie es mit den Gerichts Processen bey denen Thumb-Capituln soll gehalten werden. Gegeben auf dem Schloß zu Stockholm den 11. Februarij Anno 1687, in: Kirchen-Gesetz und Ordnung, pp. 175–189.

decrees of the imperial government[9] and the Act for the Evangelical Lutheran Church of the Russian Empire of 1832 (together with the instruction for the clergy and with the new liturgy)[10] are to be mentioned as the most prominent ones.

II. Lutheran Territorial Church of Estland

Until about mid-nineteenth century Lutheranism formed the solely dominating confession in the Baltic region. Only since the 1840s did Russian Orthodoxy gain ground to a notable extent, as a result of a wide-scale conversion movement among the Estonian and Latvian peasantry in the province of Livland, caused by social and economic reasons.[11]

Due to the Lutheran Reformation several territorial churches had emerged in the Baltic region, among others the territorial church of the province Estland. The absolutist rule of King Charles XI brought about the unification of the Lutheran ecclesiastical organization throughout the Swedish conglomerate state, mainly as the consequence to the implementation of the 1686 Church Law. This institutional interlude proved to be short-lived, as under the early Russian rule the Lutheran church organization of the Baltic region once again split up into several territorial churches. This resulted from the self-government of the estates in Estland, Livland, Ösel, Tallinn and Riga.

In the early nineteenth century the territorial church of the province Estland was governed by the consistory, situated in Tallinn.[12] The consistory comprised six Lutheran pastors as assessors and a secular president, all of which were life-long posts. The senior pastor of the Cathedral Church on the Tallinn Dome Hill was ex officio a member of the consistory. The vacancies of the other clerical assessors were filled according to the decision of the consistory itself. In case of a presidential vacancy the clerical assessors proposed three candidates from among the *Landräte*, after which the *Landratskollegium* elected the new president.[13] According to the procedure dating back to the Swedish period only the secretary of the consistory

---

[9] Полное Собраніе Законовъ Россійской Имперіи (hereafter ПСЗ) [Собраніе первое], Т. IX–XLV; Собраніе второе, Т. I–VII, Санктпетербургъ 1830–1833.

[10] Устав Евангелическо-Лютеранской Церкви въ Россіи (ПСЗ II. Т. VII. Nr. 5870); Наказъ Духовенству и Начальствамъ Евангелическо-Лютеранской Церкви въ Россіи (ПСЗ II. Т. VII. Nr. 5871); Gesetz für die Evangelisch-Lutherische Kirche in Russland. Instruction für die Geistlichkeit und die Behörden der Evangelisch-Lutherischen Kirche in Russland. Agende für die Evangelisch-Lutherischen Gemeinden im Russischen Reiche [*sine loco sine anno*.]

[11] See *Hans Kruus*, Talurahva käärimine Lõuna-Eestis XIX sajandi 40-ndail aastail [Mit einem Referat: Die Bauernbewegung in Südestland in den 40er Jahren des XIX. Jahrhunderts], Tartu 1930.

[12] The town of Tallinn had its own Lutheran territorial church, completely separate from the Estland church.

[13] Twelve *Landräte* or councillors composed the *Landratskollegium* – the permanent executive body of the *Ritterschaft*.

was salaried by the state, and thus only in his case the provincial government (i.e. the state) had to appoint him to office.[14]

The church of Estland was divided into provost districts, these again into parishes. One of the parish pastors carried out the office of the provost as an additional task. On parish level a number of institutions complemented the office of the pastor. Two *Oberkirchenvorsteher*, elected to the office by the local noble landlords from among themselves for three years, looked after the economic problems of the parish church and fulfilled numerous other tasks related to general administration, communication and police.[15] The pastor and the two *Oberkirchenvorsteher* constituted the *Kirchengericht*, the institution which took care of the ecclesiastical police of the parish. All the landlords of the parish, with the *Oberkirchenvorsteher* presiding, composed the *Kirchenkonvent* (also called *Kirchspielskonvent*). The *Kirchenkonvent* settled various tasks related to the *externa* of the parish church.[16] The *Küster* acted as an assistant to the pastor. At every parish church one or two peasants were appointed to the post of the *Kirchenvormünder*, to carry out the orders of the pastor and the *Oberkirchenvorsteher*.[17]

In the early nineteenth century each of the several Lutheran territorial churches in the Baltic provinces boasted its own particularistic system of ecclesiastical law. The law of the Estland church was founded mainly on the legal sources of Swedish origin. The Swedish Church Law (1686) together with the consistorial code of procedure (1687) has been mentioned above with regard to the main sources already. In addition the special supplement to the Church Law for Estland (1692),[18]

---

[14] Eesti Ajalooarhiiv [Estonian Historical Archives, hereafter EAA] [archive] 1187– [series] 2– [record] 47, pp. 26 o.l. [overleaf] 27; 1187–2–326, p. 82 o.l.; 854–2–2891, p. 45; 1187–2–110, pp. 147–148; 1187–2–121, pp. 73–73 o.l. See also *Hugo Richard Paucker*, Ehstlands Geistlichkeit in geordneter Zeit- und Reihefolge, Reval 1849, p. 21.

[15] See *Andresen*, Eestimaa kirikukorraldus (supra fn. 7), pp. 161–163.

[16] *Andresen*, Eestimaa kirikukorraldus (supra fn. 7), pp. 120–123. On the proposal of the *Landtag* (the diet of the *Ritterschaft*), on March 22, 1809 the provincial government issued a provincial decree which required some improvements concerning the *Kirchenkonvent* (EAA 1187–2–327, pp. 453–453 o.l.).

[17] *Andresen*, Eestimaa kirikukorraldus (supra fn. 7), p. 123. See also the special supplement of the 1686 Church Law for Estland: Declaration der Kirchen-Ordnung. Königliche Majestäten gnädigste Resolution und Erklärung derer von Ritter- und Priesterschaft in Ehstland, durch den Bischof Johann Heinrich Gerthius, unterthänigst vorgetragenen Fragpunkte und Erinnerungen, angehende etliche Fälle, so bey der publicirten und in Druck ausgegangenen Kirchenordnung in ihrer Vorstellung an dem Orte in Bedenken kommen. Gegeben Stockholm, den 30sten November 1692, in: *Gustav Johann von Buddenbrock* (Hg.), Sammlung der Gesetze, welche das heutige livländische Landrecht enthalten, kritisch bearbeitet, Bd. 2: Aeltere hinzugekommene Landesrechte. Zweite Abteilung und Anhang. Kirchenrecht und Richterregeln, Riga 1821, pp. 1641–1656, zum Cap. 19. § 31.

[18] See fn. 17.

the Priest Privilege Act of 1675, regulating the personal rights of the clergy[19] as well as the decree of Estland's governor on the income of rural pastors (1645)[20] should be mentioned in this context.

During the period of Russian rule the provincial government of Estland complemented the local ecclesiastical law with numerous decrees. State authority regulated various aspects of church and religion: issues concerning the whole Russian empire, such as state holidays, general peace and order; issues concerning all Lutherans in the empire, such as relations between different confessions; and issues concerning individual provinces, such as church property, church roads, church discipline, ecclesiastical holidays and ceremonies, the judicial subordination of the clergy, the tasks of the pastors concerning communication, and the tasks of the *Oberkirchenvorsteher*.[21]

The ukase of the empress Anna from February 23, 1734 ordered the Council of Justice of Livland and Estland Matters[22] to act as the highest imperial authority in all affairs related to the confessions other than Russian Orthodoxy, proceeding from the "main regulations" of these confessions.[23] Consequently this Council used the 1686 Swedish Church Law together with the 1687 consistorial code of procedure as its legal basis concerning the Lutheran confession.[24] For the Baltic territorial churches the Council performed mostly the functions of the high court of appeal.

The early period of the reign of Alexander I (1801–1825) was marked with extensive reforms of imperial governance. Since 1810 the newly-founded central institution, the General Administration of the Religious Matters of Foreign Confessions (*главное управление духовных дел иностранных исповеданий*) took

---

[19] Privilegia, zuerst von Ihro Königl. Majest. der Königin Christina; nachgehends aber von dem Großmächtigsten Fürsten und Herrn, Herrn CARL dem Eilften, der Schweden, Gothen, und Wenden König, etc. Im Jahre 1675, auf dem Reichstage zu Upsal übersehen, und auf das neue confirmiret, vor denen Bischofen und sämtlicher Priesterschaft in Schweden, und darunter gehörigen Landschaften, in: *Heinrich Johann Derling* (Hg.), Auswahl derer wichtigsten in denen Landes- und Stadtgerichten des Herzogthums Ehstland, auch noch jetzt geltenden Königl. Schwedischen Verordnungen, Reval 1777, pp. 144–166.

[20] See the later copy of the decree Interims Verordnung angehende der Land-Priesterschaft nothdürftigen Unterhalt, in: EAA 1187–1–1, pp. 5–11 o.l. The decree has been published: Einige in Ehstland ergangene, die Prediger-Einkünfte, wie auch die Bauer-Heirathen, betreffende, ältere Verordnungen, in: *August Wilhelm Hupel* (Hg.), Von den Kosaken. Nebst andern kürzern Aufsätzen. Der nordischen Miscellaneen 24stes und 25stes Stück, Riga 1790, pp. 439–448.

[21] *Andresen*, Eestimaa kirikukorraldus (supra fn. 7), p. 193.

[22] This institution was called the Council of Justice of Livland, Estland and Finland Matters during the period 1763–1812.

[23] ПСЗ I. T. IX. (supra fn. 9) Nr. 6548; *Hermann Dalton* (Hg.), Urkundenbuch der evangelisch-reformirten Kirche in Rußland, Gotha 1889, pp. 28–31.

[24] For matters of the Lutheran congregations in Russia proper, a special institution – the *Consistorial Session* (*Konsistorialsitzung*, *Консисториальная заседания*) was established at the Council of Justice of Livland and Estland Matters.

over the supervision of all confessions except the Russian Orthodoxy.[25] In 1817 this institution was merged with the Ministry of National Education. The new central institution, based on a Prussian model, was called the Ministry of Religious Matters and National Education (*министерство духовных дел и народного просвещения*).[26]

III. The Consistory of Estland as a Judicial Institution in the Early Nineteenth Century

According to the Swedish 1686 Church Law and the 1687 consistorial code of procedure, the bishop or the superintendent together with the consistory formed the ecclesiastical court. All cases related to religious life, doctrine, duties of the clergy and school teachers[27] and social care of the poor and ill belonged to the jurisdiction of the ecclesiastical court. Likewise the ecclesiastical court sentenced on lawsuits concerning marriage.[28]

The Estland consistory was involved in administering justice on two regular sessions a year – the winter and the summer session. Only for these sessions did the consistory convene in a body. In the meantime the senior pastor of the Cathedral Church and the secretary dealt with the routine business, in more important cases the president decided the questions. The regular session lasted for two or three weeks, six days a week, according to the number of the pending cases. During the session the consistory administered justice, but also dealt with the more important problems of church governance, like the revision of several treasuries, inspection of various protocols and reports of the pastors and the provosts, the election of

25 Главное управление духовных дел иностранных исповеданий, in: Государственность России. Государственные и церковные учреждения, сословные органы и органы местного самоуправления, единицы административно-территориального, церковного и ведомственного деления (конец XV века – февраль 1917 года). Словарь-справочник. I. Составители О. Ф. Козлов, В. Ф. Янковая, Москва 1996, pp. 182 sq.

26 Министерство духовных дел и народного просвещения, in: Государственность России. Государственные и церковные учреждения, сословные органы и органы местного самоуправления, единицы административно-территориального, церковного и ведомственного деления (конец XV века – февраль 1917 года). Словарь-справочник. III. Составители О. Ф. Козлов, В. Ф. Янковая, Москва 2001, pp. 75 sq.

27 In the consistorial code of procedure the term *persons of the ecclesiastical and school estate* is used (*Priester- und Schulen-Standes Personen*) (Gerichts Processen bey denen Thumb-Capituln [supra fn. 8], § XV).

28 Kirchen-Gesetz und Ordnung (supra fn. 8), Cap. XV. § I; Cap. XVI. §§ I, III, VI; Cap. XIX. §§ XVIII, XXXII, Cap. XXII. § IV, Cap XXIV. § II; Gerichts Processen bey denen Thumb-Capituln. §§ IV, XV. In like manner, the lawbook of the Estland Knight and Land Law stipulates, that the bishop and the consistory have the jurisdiction over matters related to the ecclesiastical office (Des Herzogthums Ehsten Ritter- und Land-Rechte. Erstes Buch. II. Tit. Art. 5).

provosts or members of the consistory.[29] On request of the nobles to divorce their marriage, the consistory sometimes arranged an extraordinary session.[30]

For the everyday life of the common man, administering justice in the field of marriage – especially the divorce cases – made up the most important part of the activities of the ecclesiastical court. Marriage cases also formed the lion's share of all judgments passed by the ecclesiastical court.

According to the Church Law of 1686 the marriage cases were divided between secular and ecclesiastical jurisdiction. The secular court passed judgments in "secular" cases: if a person was at all (*von Natur wegen*) suited for marriage; questions related to the parents of the married couple and their rights; problems related to the engagement presents and adultery; in case of a divorce, the subsistence of the children and division of the property – all in all everything related to the financial and economic rights and obligations of the married couple and their parents.[31] The consistory and the bishop (in the actual case of Estland in the early nineteenth century only the consistory), i.e. the ecclesiastical court, had jurisdiction over the following cases: the determination of the degree of kinship; if the couple can get engaged or get married in a certain case; the divorce of the engagement and marriage; if the married couple can live separately (*vom Bett und Tisch geschieden*); if the adulterer may marry again – all in all cases related to "the Word of God and conscience".[32] Family law and cases concerned with guardianship are also regulated to some extent in the Second Book of the Estland Knight and Land Law (*Des Herzogthums Ehsten Ritter- und Land-Rechte*).

The main reasons why the Estland consistory divorced an engagement or a marriage can be summed up as following: slovenliness, adultery, lack of love, discordance, excessive drinking, bad treatment, irreconcilable enmity (*odium implacabile*).[33] On one occasion a tavern girl wished to divorce her engagement because she had become afraid of the hard work of a peasant wife.[34]

The investigation process of the consistory is not described separately in the consistorial code of procedure. The procedure of the consistory in civil cases was verbal, if the parties did not demand otherwise, and summary. In some single cases, though, the treatment of a case could last for a longer period of time, also longer than a year.[35] In case of need the clarification of the facts took place by the means

---

[29] EAA 1187–2–107, p. 189 o.l.

[30] See for example EAA 1187–2–110, pp. 63 o.l.–64.

[31] For the marriage, the consent of the parents was needed (Kirchen-Gesetz und Ordnung [supra fn. 8], Cap. XV, § VI).

[32] Kirchen-Gesetz und Ordnung (supra fn. 8), Cap. XV, § I; Cap. XVI, §§ I, VI.

[33] EAA 1187–2–109, pp. 226 o.l., 227 o.l.

[34] EAA 1187–2–109, pp. 28 o.l.–30.

[35] EAA 1187–2–109, p. 227.

of correspondence.[36] According to the consistorial code of procedure the consistory had to try to reconcile the parties in the beginning of the process.[37] In practice the reconciliation attempt took place in front of the consistory after the hearing of both parties. According to the consistorial code of procedure the judgment of the consistory could be appealed to the royal Court of Appeal (*hovrätt*, *Hofgericht*). In especially important cases of religion and church matters, the monarch in person was the highest authority.[38] As mentioned earlier already, during the period of Russian supremacy the Council of Justice of Livland and Estland Matters served as the court of appeal.[39]

It was compulsory for the members of the consistory to take part in the sessions, but in case of a motivated excuse non-attendance was allowed. For example, the president of the consistory in 1787–1802, Otto Friedrich von Stackelberg, used this privilege quite often during his last years at office.[40] In some cases the role of the president was limited to signing the documents compiled in his name.[41] The session workday began with the revision of the judgments which were passed on the day before.

What were the main lines of consistorial procedure? After the complaint had arrived at the consistory, the summons (*Citation*) was sent to the defendant, with the content of the complaint, the date for the court session and the warning that in case the defendant does not show up, upon request of the plaintiff the trial can still take place. The call (*Notification*) to turn up to the court at a given date was also sent to the plaintiff.[42]

If the defendant did not show up on the given date without any excuse, a new summons was sent with a new date and a warning that a fine has to be paid if the summons is ignored.[43] If the location of the defendant was unknown, then the consistory sent an order to all the provosts to be relayed to all the pastors that the summons might be announced at all the churches of the province Estland (*Edictal-Citation*). If the defendant still did not show up at the court, then the judgment could be passed in absentia.[44] The consistory could also request help from secular authorities to bring someone to the court.[45]

---

36 Gerichts Processen bey denen Thumb-Capituln (supra fn. 8), § XIX.

37 Gerichts Processen bey denen Thumb-Capituln (supra fn. 8), § XVIII. See also Kirchen-Gesetz und Ordnung (supra fn. 8), Cap. XVI, § 1.

38 Gerichts Processen bey denen Thumb-Capituln (supra fn. 8), § XXIV.

39 See also *v. Bunge*, Geschichte des Gerichtswesens (supra fn. 6), p. 203.

40 See for example EAA 1187–2–106, p. 205.

41 See for example EAA 1187–2–107, pp. 39 o.l.–41.

42 See for example EAA 1187–2–109, pp. 5 sq.

43 See for example EAA 1187–2–109, pp. 20 o.l., 21.

44 See for example EAA 1187–2–109, pp. 21 o.l.–22 o.l.

45 Gerichts Processen bey denen Thumb-Capituln (supra fn. 8), § XVII.

At the trial first the plaintiff was summoned to listen to the complaint. Then the plaintiff was sent out, the defendant was summoned, the complaint was disclosed to him and he or she gave his or her evidence. Then the plaintiff was summoned again and the court listened to the opinion of both parties. After both parties had left the room, the court discussed the case and passed the judgment. In case of a final judgment (*Bescheid, Urteil*) the court tax was charged from either the defendant or the plaintiff, according to the outcome of the judgment.[46] In the written judgment the main facts from the testimony of the plaintiff and the defendant were given in addition to the final solution.[47]

Since the second quarter of the eighteenth century it was possible to appeal to a special institution – the *Oberappellationsgericht*. The position of the president of the *Oberappellationsgericht* was filled by the governor of Estland or the rank-oldest *Landrat*, the members comprised two *Landräte*, two other members of the *Ritterschaft* and four pastors.[48] The members of this institution were appointed separately for each case.[49] The *Ritterschaft* appointed the secretary of the Harju (*Harrien*) *Manngericht* (a district-level court in Estland) as the secretary of the *Oberappellationsgericht*.[50] Persons of both the noble and of the burgher estates appealed to the *Oberappellationsgericht*, mostly in marriage cases.[51] Unfortunately little source material has been preserved about this institution.

When someone wanted to sue a pastor in a secular court, the consistory had to control the suit in the first place. Only in case the consistory found the sued pastor guilty could he be taken to the secular court.[52]

According to the 1686 Church Law, the widow could not marry earlier than one year after the death of her husband, the widower earlier than half a year after the death of his wife.[53] The peasants quite often submitted petitions asking for permission to marry before the end of the official period of mourning with the explanation

---

[46] See for example EAA 1187–2–109, pp. 10 o.l.–14 o.l.

[47] See for example EAA 1187–2–109, pp. 11, 16 o.l.

[48] See for example EAA 1189–1–2, p. 126. See also *August Wilhelm Hupel* (Hg.), Topographische Nachrichten von Lief- und Ehstland, Bd. 1, Riga 1774, pp. 464 sq.; *Olaf Sild*, Kas Tallinna doomkirik on kirikuloolises arenemiskäigus olnud piiskopi-kirikuks?, in: Usuteadusline Ajakiri. Lisavihk, 1 (1926), p. 22.

[49] *Hellmuth Weiss*, Ein Bericht Philipp Christian Moiers über die kirchlichen und sozialen Verhältnisse in Estland um 1770, in: Rudolf von Thadden/Gert von Pistohlkors/Hellmuth Weiss (Hg.), Das Vergangene und die Geschichte. Festschrift für Reinhard Wittram zum 70. Geburtstag, Göttingen 1973, p. 168; *Hasso von Wedel*, Die Estländische Ritterschaft vornehmlich zwischen 1710 und 1783. Das erste Jahrhundert russischer Herrschaft, Königsberg/Berlin 1935, p. 171 sq.

[50] EAA 1187–2–110, pp. 147–147 o.l.

[51] See for example EAA 1189–1–1, pp. 1–147.

[52] According to the decree of the Swedish government from July 24, 1666 for the province of Estland (EAA 854–1–841, pp. 69 sq.).

[53] Kirchen-Gesetz und Ordnung (supra fn. 8), Cap. XV, § XXIV.

that there were many underage children in the family or a lot of work to do in the farm. In these cases the permission was given with a special decision (*Resolution*) and this could happen also between the sessions.[54]

Marriages of close kinship were strictly forbidden, but this rule could be dispensed as well. The decree of the Swedish king Karl XII from 1698 reserved the right to dispense the marriages of close kinship solely to the monarch.[55] On the orders from the empress Anna, the Senate passed a ukase on October 3, 1733, giving the right to dispense marriages of close kinship to the Council of Justice of Livland and Estland Matters.[56] The ukase from February 23, 1734, ordering the Council of Justice of Livland and Estland Matters to act as the highest authority in all affairs related to the Lutheran confession, confirmed the aforementioned right of dispensation to this institution.[57] After the foundation of the General Administration of the Religious Matters of Foreign Confessions (1810) it acquired the authority to dispense marriages.[58]

After obtaining the permission from the higher authority to dispense a certain marriage, the Estland consistory passed the judgment of its own (*Bescheid*). The respective pastor was let to know that there were no obstacles to wed the person, who had submitted the petition for the dispensation, with his chosen bride.[59] The dispensation cost the applicant a lot of money, a marriage with a cousin cost ten to twenty five rubles.[60] This money was sent to the institution that gave the dispensation to be used "on pious purposes".[61]

The next change in the procedure of dispensing marriages occurred in 1823, as Alexander I, on February 20, confirmed the decision of the minister of the Religious Matters and National Education to temporarily assign the authority to dispense marriages to the consistories. This regulation had to last only until the foun-

---

54 See for example EAA 1187–2–109, pp. 3 o.l., 4.

55 The degrees of kinship, prohibited for marriage, are discussed in detail in the Estland Knight and Land Law (Des Herzogthums Ehsten Ritter- und Land-Rechte. Anderes Buch. II. Tit. Art. 1–11; III. Tit. Art. 1–4). See also *Friedrich Georg v. Bunge*, Geschichte des Liv-, Est- und Curländischen Privatrechts. Geschichtliche Uebersicht der Grundlagen und der Entwickelung des Provincialrechts in den Ostseegouvernements, Besonderer Theil. III. Privatrecht, St. Petersburg 1862, p. 133. According to the 1686 Church Law the pastor who wed the persons, who had no legal right to marry, faced one-month imprisonment on water and bread and after that he was to be exiled (Kirchen-Gesetz und Ordnung [supra fn. 8], Cap. XV, § III).

56 EAA 1187–2–318, pp. 89 sq. o.l.

57 See supra fn. 23.

58 The Council of Justice of Livland and Estland Matters published the respective decree to the Estland consistory on October 7, 1810 (EAA 1187–2–115, p. 215).

59 See for example EAA 1187–2–109, pp. 4 o.l., 5.

60 For comparison: A farm laborer working at the manor of the lord got about five rubles plus clothing as a year's salary.

61 See for example EAA 1187–2–106, p. 223 o.l.; EAA 1187–2–106, pp. 119, 223, 254.

dation of the General Consistory of the empire. The supervision over the issue of dispensations lay in the hands of the minister of the Religious Matters and National Education.[62]

The consistory regularly sent the Council of Justice of Livland and Estland Matters reports on its court cases.[63] During the first five years of the nineteenth century (1801–1805), for instance, the consistory had forty-five cases on the average per year.[64] On a regular basis the consistory also reported to the Council of Justice of Livland and Estland Matters on the petitions, which were mostly related to the dispensation of unlawful marriages or marriage before the end of the official period of mourning.[65] Since 1805 a similar report was presented to the provincial government. That year the consistory reacted to 280 petitions.[66]

Every year the consistory carried out a church visitation in some of the parishes. The president of the consistory usually performed the task of the principal of the visitation commission.[67] Two other members of the consistory belonged to the visitation commission as well.[68] During the winter session of 1803 the consistory decided that on future visitations the visitation commission cannot carry out divorces or other court judgments that belong to the jurisdiction of the consistory – as had been common practice earlier – any more, unless the visitation commission had been given detailed instructions to do so beforehand.[69]

In some single cases the Estland consistory initiated the issue of new laws. For instance, the consistory had a case of a peasant wife who had gone to work as a wet nurse against the will of her husband. Resulting from the proposition of the consistory the provincial government issued a decree on August 4, 1826, prohibiting the landlords to give married women the permit to get employed against the will of their husbands.[70] Next year, the Governor General of Estland, Livland and Courland Filippo Paulucci took up this problem. As there had been several cases of peasant wives leaving their babies, only some weeks old, to get employed as wet nurses – in this way endangering the life and health of their own babies – on the orders of Paulucci the Estland provincial government issued a decree on June 14, 1827, prohibiting the women to get employed as wet nurses before their own babies

---

[62] EAA 1187–2–128, p. 85–86 o.l.; 854–1–841, pp. 78 sq.

[63] See for example EAA 1187–2–106, pp. 255 o.l.–264; EAA 1187–2–110, pp. 77, 103 o.l.

[64] EAA 1187–2–106, pp. 255 o.l.–264; 1187–2–107, pp. 251–260; 1187–2–108, pp. 214–221; 1187–2–109, pp. 226–235.

[65] See for example EAA 1187–2–108, p. 193.

[66] EAA 1187–2–110, p. 251 o.l.

[67] *Olaf Sild*, Kirikuvisitatsioonid eestlaste maal vanemast ajast kuni olevikuni, Tartu 1937, pp. 82–87.

[68] See for example EAA 1187–2–107, pp. 45 sq.

[69] EAA 1187–2–108, pp. 21 o.l.–22 o.l.

[70] EAA 1187–2–333, p. 198.

are at least three months old and under the care of reliable people. The local pastor had to attest in written form that these conditions were fulfilled, before anyone could be employed as a wet nurse.[71] Later, under the rule of the next Governor General, this decree was declared void with the justification that it had caused "inconvenience for mothers of higher estates".[72]

IV. Ecclesiastical Police in the Parishes in the Early Nineteenth Century

In the nineteenth century ecclesiastical police formed a lower-level part of the ecclesiastical administration of justice. In Estland every parish had to have two *Oberkirchenvorsteher*. But as this official had numerous different tasks to fulfill, it was not always easy to find candidates to this post. At times some parishes had no *Oberkirchenvorsteher* at all. On the ground of the respective complaint of the consistory, the provincial government issued a decree on March 14, 1817, which ordered the landlords to appoint the *Oberkirchenvorsteher* as the law insisted.[73]

The *Kirchengericht*, comprising the pastor and two *Oberkirchenvorsteher*, dealt with cases of ecclesiastical police such as quarrels and brawls in the church and its near vicinity, rowing in the church, missing the service in the church, matters of the way of living of the people, especially slovenliness and adultery.[74] In more severe cases the *Kirchengericht* had only to investigate the facts and to report to the relevant institutions – to the consistory or the secular court.[75]

The Peasant Law Act of 1816, best known for abolishing serfdom in Estland, also reformed the police order in the newly-founded peasant communities. Ac-

---

[71] EAA 1187–2–334, p. 47.

[72] According to orders of the Minister of the Interior and State Council and the ukase of the Senate from April 16, 1830. The decree of the provincial government from January 16, 1831 invalidated the decree from June 14, 1827 (EAA 1187–2–336, pp. 1–1 o.l.).

[73] EAA 1187–2–330, p. 109. The governor of Estland issued the instruction on the election of the *Oberkirchenvorsteher* and on their duties in 1650 (*Gustaf Oskar Fredrik Westling*, Kirchengesetz und Kirchengesetzarbeiten in Ehstland zur Zeit der schwedischen Herrschaft, in: Ehstländische Literärische Gesellschaft (Hg.), Beiträge zur Kunde Ehst-, Liv- und Kurlands, Bd. 5, Reval 1900, pp. 55 sq.; *Gustaf Oskar Fredrik Westling*, Mittheilungen über die Kirchenverfassung in Estland zur Zeit der schwedischen Herrschaft, a.a.O., pp. 171–173). According to one later copy of this instruction, it was issued on February 24, 1651 (EAA 854–1–841, p. 29). The institution of the *Oberkirchenvorsteher* is regulated also in the Estland Knight and Land Law (Des Herzogthums Ehsten Ritter- und Land-Rechte, Sechstes Buch, II. Tit. §§ 1, 3).

[74] The provincial government issued special decrees concerning problems of slovenliness and adultery on August 25, 1697 (EAA 1187–2–316, pp. 3 o.l.–4), on July 20, 1765 and on September 13, 1772 (EAA 1187–2–328: pp. 85 o.l.–86 o.l.). The Senate issued relevant ukases on April 6, 1764 (published by the Estland provincial government on April 16 (EAA 1187–2–320, pp. 161 sq.) and on October 20, 1832 (published by the Estland provincial government on December 24 (EAA 1187–2–336, p. 345 o.l.).

[75] EAA 1187–2–27, p. 13 o.l.

cording to the new system the police (*Gemeindepolizey*) was carried out by the peasant officials, the *Gemeinde-Älteste* and the *Kirchen-Untervorsteher*.[76] The peasant community police officials were supervised by the landlords, who also executed the second level or the manorial police (*Gutspolizey*).[77] The manorial police itself was subordinated to the supervision of the parish level police institution, the *Kirchspielspolizeygericht*.[78]

In matters of ecclesiastical police, the jurisdiction was divided between the community police and the manorial police officials on the one hand and the *Kirchengericht* on the other. In case the pastor or some ecclesiastical official made a complaint to the community or manorial police institutions, the respective institution had to solve the case. Otherwise the *Kirchengericht* was in charge.[79]

V. Preparation of the 1832 Church Law

In the Baltic provinces and in the Lutheran congregations of Russia proper the 1686 Church Law formed the basic part of the Lutheran ecclesiastical law, but in addition a great number of other acts of law were in use. This kind of legal diversity hindered the efficiency of imperial institutions which had the task to supervise the Lutheran church institutions.

The ukase of Nicholas I from May 22, 1828 ordered the preparation of the new Lutheran[80] church law act. This was motivated with the need for greater clarity and uniformity in the Lutheran church organization. The emperor gave two starting-points: the new law act had to correspond, firstly, to the present general principles regarding the doctrine as well as the church organization and governance, and, secondly, to the present situation and needs of the state authority concerning the relations to the Lutheran church organization.[81]

The preparatory committee of the new Lutheran church law act comprised clerical and secular representatives of the Estland, Livland and Kurland territorial churches and of the St. Petersburg consistorial district, a professor of theology of the Tartu University, and, on the special request of the emperor and by consent of the Prussian king, the general superintendent of Pommern, Georg Carl Benjamin Ritschl, who had to pass on the experiences of the Prussian church organization.

---

[76] Ehstländisches Bauer-Gesetzbuch, in: ПСЗ I. T. XXXIII. (supra fn. 9) Nr. 26 279. §§ 210–214, 225–227.

[77] Ehstländisches Bauer-Gesetzbuch (supra fn. 76), §§ 230 sq., 238.

[78] Ehstländisches Bauer-Gesetzbuch (supra fn. 76), §§ 245–248.

[79] Ehstländisches Bauer-Gesetzbuch (supra fn. 76), § 360. This procedure is confirmed by the decree of the provincial government from February 27, 1820 (EAA 1187–2–331, p. 122).

[80] The term *protestant-evangelical* is used in the ukase.

[81] ПСЗ II. T. VII. (supra fn. 9) Nr. 5870 (the ukase of the emperor from December 28, 1832, preamble).

Senator and count Paul von Tiesenhausen, the former *Ritterschaftshauptmann*[82] of the Estland *Ritterschaft*, acted as the president of the committee. The General Administration of the Religious Matters of Foreign Confessions supervised the work of the committee.[83]

The committee proceeded, above all, from the 1686 Swedish Church Law and the 1693 liturgy, as well as from the Prussian church law acts.[84] The state authority advocated the idea of subordinating all Lutheran church organizations to one central institution in St. Petersburg. The representatives of the Baltic territorial churches were very much against this idea, but they could not change this point.[85] In the end the State Council controlled and revised the project of the church law act.[86]

VI. Evangelical Lutheran Church of the Russian Empire

Nicholas I sanctioned the Act for the Evangelical Lutheran Church of the Russian Empire[87] together with the instruction for the clergy and ecclesiastical institutions[88] with the ukase for the Senate on December 28, 1832. The new law act was implemented in the whole of the Russian Empire, except the Grand Duchy of Finland.[89] All preceding legal acts on Lutheran church organization were invalidated.[90] The new church law act was compiled in Russian, but in 1833 also the official German translation was published.[91] The new liturgy was published only in Ger-

---

[82] The senior official of the Estland *Ritterschaft*.

[83] In the course of time the personnel of the committee changed, see *Andresen*, Eestimaa kirikukorraldus (supra fn. 7), pp. 160 sq.

[84] Ueber die Organisation des Evangelisch-lutherischen Kirchenwesens in Rußland, St. Petersburgische Zeitung 1832, p. 63.

[85] *Dalton*, Verfassungsgeschichte (supra fn. 5), p. 313.

[86] Ueber das neue Gesetz für die Evangelisch-lutherische Kirche in Rußland. Aus dem Journal des Ministeriums des Innern (aus dem Russischen übersetzt), St. Petersburgische Zeitung 1833, p. 141.

[87] Устав Евангелическо-Лютеранской Церкви въ Россiи (ПСЗ II. Т. VII. [supra fn. 9] Nr. 5870).

[88] Наказъ Духовенству и Начальствамъ Евангелическо-Лютеранской Церкви въ Россiи (ПСЗ II. Т. VII. [supra fn. 9] Nr. 5871).

[89] *Gunnar Prawitz*, Kyrkans rättsliga ställning i Finland och Sverige, in: Svenska Pastoratens Riksförbund (ed.), Stat och kyrka i skilda länder. Del I. Finland, Sverige, Wales, Skottland, Stockholm 1957, pp. 15 sq.

[90] ПСЗ II. Т. VII. (supra fn. 9) Nr. 5870 (preamble).

[91] Ueber das neue Gesetz, 1833 (supra fn. 86), p. 145.

man, as the third part of the German publication, following the church law act and the instruction for the clergy and ecclesiastical institutions.[92]

The new law fundamentally changed the legal and institutional framework of the Lutheran church organizations in the Russian Empire. The new church law act stated the establishment of the *Evangelical Lutheran Church of the Russian Empire*. All territorial churches and separate congregations of the empire were united into one single organization.[93]

The new church organization was divided into eight consistorial districts: Estland, Livland, Ösel, Kurland, St. Petersburg, Moscow, Riga and Tallinn.[94] The last two ones included only the respective town.[95] The consistory under the leadership of a secular president governed each consistorial district. The office of the consistorial vice president – general superintendent – was held by a pastor.[96] Besides, two secular and two clerical assessors belonged to each consistory.[97] In the consistorial districts of Estland, Livland, Ösel and Kurland the respective *Ritterschaft* proposed two candidates to the office of the consistorial president as well as to that of the clerical vice president. The *Landräte* served as candidates for the president. On the recommendation of the Ministry of the Interior and the General Consistory the emperor appointed the candidate to office.[98] The candidates of the secular member were proposed by the *Ritterschaft*, the candidates of the clerical members were nominated by the clergy of the consistorial district. On the recommendation of the Governor General, the Minister of the Interior appointed the new member to office.[99] The office of the consistory's member was held lifelong.

The state financed the consistories.[100] The activities of the consistories were supervised by the General Consistory and the Ministry of the Interior.[101]

The highest institution of governance and justice of the Evangelical Lutheran Church of the Russian Empire was the General Consistory in St. Petersburg.[102] The

---

[92] Gesetz für die Evangelisch-Lutherische Kirche in Russland. Instruction für die Geistlichkeit und die Behörden der Evangelisch-Lutherischen Kirche in Russland. Agende für die Evangelisch-Lutherischen Gemeinden im Russischen Reiche [*sine loco sine anno*].

[93] See also *Reinhard Wittram*, Baltische Geschichte. Die Ostseelande Livland, Estland, Kurland 1180–1918, München 1954, p. 184.

[94] Gesetz für die Evangelisch-Lutherische Kirche (supra fn. 92), § 290.

[95] Gesetz für die Evangelisch-Lutherische Kirche (supra fn. 92), § 291.

[96] Gesetz für die Evangelisch-Lutherische Kirche (supra fn. 92), §§ 275, 292.

[97] Gesetz für die Evangelisch-Lutherische Kirche (supra fn. 92), § 292. The staff of the consistories in Ösel, Tallinn, Riga and Moscow exhibited slight deviations from this general scheme.

[98] Gesetz für die Evangelisch-Lutherische Kirche (supra fn. 92), §§ 276, 293.

[99] Gesetz für die Evangelisch-Lutherische Kirche (supra fn. 92), § 294.

[100] Except the town consistories of Tallinn and Riga (Gesetz für die Evangelisch-Lutherische Kirche [supra fn. 92], § 295).

[101] Gesetz für die Evangelisch-Lutherische Kirche (supra fn. 92), § 302.

members of the General Consistory were elected for three years: the secular president, the clerical vice president, two secular and two clerical members. The emperor appointed the president and the vice president to office.[103] The *Landratskollegien*, the town councils of Tallinn and Riga and the consistories of St. Petersburg and Moscow could nominate candidates for the secular members. All the consistories had the right to propose clerical candidates. The Ministry of the Interior appointed the candidate to office.[104]

The General Consistory convened only for the sessions which took place twice a year.[105] This institution acquired the right to dispense marriages of close kinship.[106] In administrative matters the General Consistory was subordinated to the Ministry of the Interior, in judicial matters to the Senate.[107] As an exception, in matters of marriage divorce the General Consistory itself served as the highest court,[108] as was also the case in matters of suspending and discharging the clerics from the office, as well as unfrocking the clerics.[109] All consistories had to report regularly on their court cases to the General Consistory.[110]

In matters of doctrine, service and clerical office the emperor served as the highest authority.[111] A special secular official, the procurator of the General Consistory, supervised the General Consistory.[112] The Council of Justice of Livland and Estland Matters was dissolved.[113]

The everyday matters of the General Consistory were conducted in German, but reports to the Senate and the Ministry of the Interior had to be submitted in Russian.[114]

The consistories and the General Consistory formed a part of the Russian state machine. The new Lutheran church organization was practically a state church in the sense of an officially acknowledged and controlled church, but certainly not in the sense of the church of the dominating confession. By the side of the Russian

---

102 Gesetz für die Evangelisch-Lutherische Kirche (supra fn. 92), § 317.

103 Gesetz für die Evangelisch-Lutherische Kirche (supra fn. 92), §§ 309 sq., 312.

104 Gesetz für die Evangelisch-Lutherische Kirche (supra fn. 92), § 311.

105 Gesetz für die Evangelisch-Lutherische Kirche (supra fn. 92), § 325.

106 Gesetz für die Evangelisch-Lutherische Kirche (supra fn. 92), § 317, 5).

107 Gesetz für die Evangelisch-Lutherische Kirche (supra fn. 92), §§ 318 sq.

108 Gesetz für die Evangelisch-Lutherische Kirche (supra fn. 92), § 318, 1).

109 Gesetz für die Evangelisch-Lutherische Kirche (supra fn. 92), § 318, 3).

110 Gesetz für die Evangelisch-Lutherische Kirche (supra fn. 92), § 302, 3).

111 Gesetz für die Evangelisch-Lutherische Kirche (supra fn. 92), § 318, 2).

112 Gesetz für die Evangelisch-Lutherische Kirche (supra fn. 92), §§ 313, 323.

113 ПСЗ II. T. VII. (supra fn. 9) Nr. 5866 (the ukase of the emperor from December 28, 1832); *Erik Amburger*, Geschichte der Behördenorganisation Russlands von Peter dem Großen bis 1917, Leiden 1966, p. 175.

114 Gesetz für die Evangelisch-Lutherische Kirche (supra fn. 92), § 324.

Orthodox established church, the Russian Lutheran state church had substantially lesser rights.[115]

The implementation of the new law lasted for more than a year. The ukase of the emperor from February 25, 1833 nominated the former president of the preparatory committee, P. Tiesenhausen, as the president of the General Consistory, and the other former member of the preparatory committee, pastor of St. Petersburg Johann Friedrich August Volborth, as the vice president of the General Consistory. The preparations, led by the Ministry of the Interior, lasted for the whole year of 1833 to establish the new system of church governance.[116] The first session of the General Consistory in St. Petersburg began on August 15, 1833.[117]

The 1832 Lutheran Church Law was the first comprehensive law act in the Russian empire which was implemented state-wide. This was an important step to modernize the legal system of the empire in the sense of implementing state-wide laws and overcoming the legal particularism.[118] This church law act, together with its later supplements, remained valid in the Russian empire until its very end.

VII. The Consistory of Estland as a Judicial Institution after 1832

As described above, the implementation of the new Lutheran church law act in Estland lead to the unification of the local territorial church with the Lutheran Church of the Russian Empire. Hereafter the Estland Lutheran church organization had the status of the consistorial district.

Three members of the earlier staff of the Estland consistory continued to work in the new institution. The *Landrat* Reinhold Gottlieb von Maydell, member of the preparatory commission of the new law, stayed in the office of the secular president of the consistory.[119] The senior pastor of the Cathedral Church Paul Eduard Hörschelmann died on November 3, 1833, and in a couple of weeks the emperor appointed pastor Arnold Friedrich Johann Knüpffer, the former assessor of the Estland consistory, to the office of the Estland general superintendent.[120] The first meeting of the consistory which followed the rules of the new church law act took

115 See also: *Wittram*, Baltische Geschichte (supra fn. 93), p. 184; *Gert Kroeger*, Die evangelisch-lutherische Landeskirche und das griechisch-orthodoxe Staatskirchentum in den Ostseeprovinzen 1840–1918, in: Reinhard Wittram (Hg.), Baltische Kirchengeschichte. Beiträge zur Geschichte der Missionierung und der Reformation, der evangelisch-lutherischen Landeskirchen und des Volkskirchentums in den baltischen Landen, Göttingen 1956, pp. 177–206.

116 Ueber das neue Gesetz, 1833 (supra fn. 86), p. 145.

117 EAA 1187–2–336, p. 419.

118 *Andresen*, Unifying the Periphery (supra fn. 2), pp. 10–14.

119 See for example EAA 1187–2–137, pp. 101 sq.

120 *Paucker*, Ehstlands Geistlichkeit (supra fn. 14), pp. 19, 67.

place on November 30, 1833.[121] The ukase of the Senate from the same date liquidated the institution of the *Oberappellationsgericht*.[122]

Until March 6, 1834 the Estland consistory had only one clerical member, pastor Jacob Johann Anton Hirschhausen, assessor of the consistory since 1819 already. Then Knüpffer gave up the office of the general superintendent and carried on as an ordinary member of the consistory. Pastor Carl Christian Friedrich Rein of the Tallinn St. Nicholas church was appointed to the office of the general superintendent. Representatives of the Estland *Ritterschaft* Friedrich Gustav Theodor von Rehekampff and Gustav von Rosen held the posts of secular members.[123] In the parishes the new Church Law was implemented mostly during the year 1834.[124]

According to the new law act, the main task of the consistory was to provide that the Lutheran clergy adhered to the general imperial laws and the new Church Law, together with the instruction and liturgy, in all church matters.[125] As regards the ecclesiastical jurisdiction of the consistory, the following points are specifically mentioned in the law act:

The consistory was the court of first instance in marriage matters;[126]

It dealt with the conflicts – which belonged to the jurisdiction of the ecclesiastical court – between the pastors and between the pastor and the parish members;[127]

It investigated complaints against provosts, superintendents and general superintendents, and presented the results to the General Consistory;[128]

It dealt with the job-related offences and crimes of the pastors.[129]

Compared to the 1686 Church Law, the new law act regulated in a much more detailed way the penalties for several offences of the pastors.[130]

As before, the Estland consistory had to convene in a body for sessions twice a year. In the meantime three members – two secular and one clerical or two clerical and one secular – had to settle the less important matters.[131] In judicial cases, including divorces, only the plenary session of the consistory could pass judg-

---

121 EAA 1187–2–136, pp. 103–105.

122 ПСЗ II. T. VIII. (supra fn. 9) Nr. 6598.

123 EAA 1187–2–37, pass.; *Paucker*, Ehstlands Geistlichkeit (supra fn. 14), pp. 30 sq., 187, 369.

124 See also *Aadu Must*, Eestlaste perekonnaloo allikad, Tartu 2000, p. 106.

125 Gesetz für die Evangelisch-Lutherische Kirche (supra fn. 92), § 301.

126 Gesetz für die Evangelisch-Lutherische Kirche (supra fn. 92), § 301, 9).

127 Gesetz für die Evangelisch-Lutherische Kirche (supra fn. 92), § 301, 16).

128 Gesetz für die Evangelisch-Lutherische Kirche (supra fn. 92), § 301, 17).

129 Gesetz für die Evangelisch-Lutherische Kirche (supra fn. 92), § 301, 18).

130 Gesetz für die Evangelisch-Lutherische Kirche (supra fn. 92), §§ 228–258.

131 Gesetz für die Evangelisch-Lutherische Kirche (supra fn. 92), § 303.

ment.[132] The judgments of the consistory could be appealed to the General Consistory.[133]

The investigation procedure, concerned mostly with the job-related offences and crimes of the pastors, as well as the civil process (*Verfahrens-Prozess*) between two parties, are described in great detail in the eighth chapter (§§ 330–437) of the law.

The civil procedure could be usual or summary.[134] In the summary procedure all major formalities of the usual process were followed, but the process was shorter due to shorter deadlines and to the condition, that the parties had to present all evidence right away in the beginning of the process.[135]

In case a cleric faced criminal charges in a secular court, the consistory had to ensure that a representative of the clergy was present at the process. Only the consistory had the jurisdiction to suspend and discharge the clerics from the office, as well as to unfrock them.[136]

VIII. Ecclesiastical Police in the Parishes after 1832

The new law act modified only the supervision of the church police of the parishes.[137] On the earlier example of Livland also in other consistorial districts the institution of the *Ober-Kirchenvorsteher-Amt* was established. Its purpose was to supervise the activities of the *Oberkirchenvorsteher* (who were called the *Kirchen-Vorsteher* according to the new law act), including the field of the ecclesiastical police.[138] A *Landrat* as the secular president, a representative of the *Ritterschaft* as the secular member and the rank-oldest provost of the district as the clerical member belonged to the *Ober-Kirchenvorsteher-Amt*. The provincial government commissioned the secular members to the office.[139]

IX. Conclusion

The Lutheran church system in the Baltic provinces did not encounter any coordinated state intervention during the first period of state modernization in the Russian Empire, that is in the late eighteenth century and the early years of the nineteenth century. In this time frame, as we have seen according to the example of

---

[132] Gesetz für die Evangelisch-Lutherische Kirche (supra fn. 92), § 304, 4), 5).

[133] Gesetz für die Evangelisch-Lutherische Kirche (supra fn. 92), § 317, 1).

[134] For an overview of the procedure in Livland see: Sammlung der Gesetze. II. 2 (supra fn. 17), pp. 1888 sqq.

[135] Gesetz für die Evangelisch-Lutherische Kirche (supra fn. 92), §§ 345, 355–407.

[136] Gesetz für die Evangelisch-Lutherische Kirche (supra fn. 92), § 301, 19).

[137] Gesetz für die Evangelisch-Lutherische Kirche (supra fn. 92), §§ 486 sq.

[138] Gesetz für die Evangelisch-Lutherische Kirche (supra fn. 92), §§ 486 sq., 492, 494.

[139] Gesetz für die Evangelisch-Lutherische Kirche (supra fn. 92), § 492.

the province Estland, the Lutheran ecclesiastical administration of justice remained under the jurisdiction of the local estates. Marriage cases formed the largest part of Estland consistory's judicial activities, including divorce and different dispensations. Swedish heritage of ecclesiastical law from the seventeenth century formed the legal basis of the consistory's judicial action.

After 1832, Estland consistory's main activities in administering justice were carried out mostly along previous lines. The new church law act regulated the consistory's judicial matters in a much more detailed way than previous laws. What did change profoundly, however, was the position of Estland's consistory as the ecclesiastical court in the general structure of state-controlled institutions in the Russian Empire. As the new Lutheran Church Law brought an end to the institutional particularism in Lutheranism, unifying all previous territorial churches into one single church organization throughout the Baltic provinces as well as Russia proper, it also subordinated Estland's consistory to much greater state control. The newly-founded Evangelical Lutheran Church of the Russian Empire, comprising all the former separate Lutheran territorial churches and congregations, was a state institution. The General Consistory and the provincial consistories were funded by the state and the staffs of these institutions were appointed to office by the state. The consistories were directly subordinated to the imperial institutions of governance and jurisdiction. All this is to be regarded as a significant act of state modernization in the Russian Empire.

Consequently, the 1832 Church Law institutionally integrated the Lutheran ecclesiastical administration of justice – together with other spheres of the Lutheran church – to the imperial state system. This is to be considered a significant step of state modernization at the expense of estate privileges.

Die Rezeption der preußischen Justizverfassung am Beispiel Thorn in Westpreußen

Danuta Janicka

I. Die Gerichtsbarkeit im alten Thorn im Umriss

Thorn (polnisch: Toruń) entstand an der unteren Weichsel, an der Stelle der sich hier kreuzenden Handelswege. Die Stadt wurde vom Deutschen Orden gegründet. Die Gründungsurkunde, die berühmte Kulmer Handfeste, wurde 1233 ausgestellt.[1] Das mittelalterliche Thorn bestand aus drei separaten Teilen: der Altstadt, der Neustadt sowie der Burg des Deutschen Ordens.[2] Die Einwohnerzahl der Alt- und Neustadt Thorn wird für das 15. Jahrhundert auf 8.500 geschätzt. Mitte des 15. Jahrhunderts sagte sich Thorn, zusammen mit der ganzen Ostseeprovinz, vom Deutschen Orden los und beschloss, sich dem polnischen König zu unterwerfen. Unter der Herrschaft der polnischen Könige besaß die Stadt große Selbstständigkeit und blieb weiterhin ein wichtiges Zentrum des Nah- und Fernhandels sowie ein bedeutender Mittelpunkt der Gewerbeproduktion. Im 16. Jahrhundert zählte sie bereits 12.000 Einwohner. Mit den schwedischen Kriegen brach für Thorn im 17. und vor allem im 18. Jahrhundert eine schwere Zeit an. Durch die zweite Teilung Polens (1793) fiel Thorn, zusammen mit Danzig, an Preußen.[3]

Sowohl im Mittelalter als auch in der Neuzeit verfügte Thorn über ein ausgebautes Gerichtswesen. Im Laufe der Jahrhunderte wandelte sich die städtische Gerichtsbarkeit nur wenig. Das wichtigste Organ der Jurisdiktion in Thorn war das Schöffengericht. Es urteilte nach dem Magdeburger Recht.[4] Die Gerichtsbarkeit lag

---

[1] Vgl. *Guido Kisch*, Die Kulmer Handfeste, Text, rechtshistorische und textkritische Untersuchungen nebst Studien zur Kulmer Handfeste, dem Elbinger Privilegium von 1246 und einem Beitrag zur Geschichte des Begriffs „ius teutonicum", „deutsches Recht" im Deutschordensgebiet, Sigmaringen 1978; *Karola Ciesielska* (Hg., Vorwort), Przywileje lokacyjne Torunia [Gründungsprivilegien Thorns], Toruń 2008 (hier Übersetzungen der Kulmer Handfeste ins Deutsche, Englische, Polnische).

[2] *Danuta Janicka*, Zur Topographie der Städte des Magdeburger Rechts in Polen: das Beispiel Kulm und Thorn, in: Heiner Lück/Matthias Puhle/Andreas Ranft (Hg.), Grundlagen für ein neues Europa. Das Magdeburger und Lübecker Recht in Spätmittelalter und Früher Neuzeit, Köln/Weimar/Wien 2009, S. 67–81.

[3] *Antoni Czacharowski* (Hg.), Historischer Atlas polnischer Städte, Bd. 1. Königliches Preußen und Hochstift Ermland, Thorn, Toruń 1995, S. 13–17. Vgl. die monumentale, sechsbändige, auf Polnisch verfasste Geschichte der Stadt Thorn von *Marian Biskup* (Red.), Historia Torunia pod redakcją Mariana Biskupa, Teil 1–3, Toruń 1992–2006.

[4] Infolge der Verleihung des Privilegs für die Städte Kulm und Thorn entstand das Kulmer Recht. Es basierte grundsätzlich auf dem Magdeburger Recht, modifizierte es aber in erheblichem Umfang. Das Kulmer Recht war eine der wichtigsten Sonderformen des Magdeburger Rechts auf polnischem Boden. Sein Geltungsbereich dehnte sich allmählich über den größten Teil des Ordenslandes und auf viele Städte Zentral- und Südpolens, mit Warschau an der Spitze, aus. Vgl.

auch in den Händen des Stadtrates. Der Stadtrat bildete zusätzlich die Berufungsinstanz für die Urteile aller städtischen, vorstädtischen und dörflichen Gerichte. Im 15. Jahrhundert (1459) übernahm der Thorner Stadtrat zusätzlich die Kompetenzen des Obergerichts für das Kulmer Recht. Als Oberhof war er für zahlreiche Städte im königlich preußischen Gebiet, in Kujawien, im Ermland und in Masowien tätig. Neben dem Stadtrats- und Schöffengericht wirkte in Thorn seit dem 16. Jahrhundert (1528) das Wettgericht, das als Instanz für Handelssachen eingerichtet wurde. Eine besondere Rolle spielten außerdem Zunftgerichte, die für Mitglieder der Innungen zuständig waren.[5]

Die Gerichtsbarkeit war in Thorn im altstädtischen Rathaus – im wichtigsten öffentlichen Stadtgebäude – untergebracht.[6] Im Erdgeschoss des Rathauses wurde eine Gerichtsstube errichtet. Sie diente der Ausübung der Stadtjustiz bis zum 19. Jahrhundert und ist bis heute erhalten geblieben. Das Gerichtsverfahren war öffentlich, weil die Gerichtstube nach drei Seiten hin – nach Süden, Westen und Norden – geöffnet war. Gerichtssitzungen in offenen Gerichtshallen waren in den deutschen Städten üblich.[7]

Die herkömmliche, der alten Tradition entsprechende Organisation der Rechtspflege wurde am Ende des 18. Jahrhunderts unterbrochen.

II. Die Einführung des preußischen Gerichtswesens

Eine entscheidende Änderung der für Thorn bedeutsamen Rechts- bzw. Gerichtsverhältnisse setzte ein, als die Stadt in Folge der zweiten Teilung Polens im Jahre 1793 an Preußen fiel. Bereits Mitte desselben Jahres hat der preußische König

---

Danuta Janicka, Zur Bedeutung des Magdeburger Vorbilds in der städtischen Gerichtsbarkeit Nordpolens: Das Beispiel Kulm und Thorn, in: Hans-Georg Knothe/Marc Liebmann (Hg.), Gerichtskultur im Ostseeraum: Vierter Rechtshistorikertag im Ostseeraum, 18.–20. Mai 2006 in Greifswald, Frankfurt a.M. 2007, S. 29 f.

5 Vgl. eine ausführliche polnische Darstellung mit einer deutschen Zusammenfassung: *Krystyna Kamińska*, Sądownictwo miasta Torunia do połowy XVII wieku na tle ustroju sądów niektórych miast Niemiec i Polski [Die Gerichtsbarkeit der Stadt Thorn bis zur Mitte des 17. Jahrhunderts auf dem Hintergrund einiger Städten Deutschlands und Polens], Warszawa/Poznań/Toruń 1980.

6 Die Neustadt Thorn verfügte über ihr eigenes Rathaus, in dem der neustädtische Rat sowie das neustädtische Schöffengericht ihren Sitz fanden. Die Neustadt Thorn wurde mit der Altstadt 1454 verbunden.

7 *Danuta Janicka*, Die Rezeption des Sachsenspiegels und des Magdeburger Rechts am Beispiel von Thorn im Kulmer Land, in: Ernst Eichler/Heiner Lück (Hg.), Rechts- und Sprachtransfer in Mittel- und Osteuropa, Berlin 2008, S. 61 f. Vgl. *Arthur Semrau*, Das Dinghaus in Thorn, Mitteilungen des Coppernicus-Vereins für Wissenschaft und Kunst, 1919, Hf. 29. Vgl. auch eine polnische Darstellung: *Michał Woźniak*, Ratusz Staromiejski w Toruniu. Dzieje – architektura – adaptacja [Altstädtisches Rathaus in Toruń. Geschichte – Architektur – Adaptation], in: Ratusz w miastach północnej Europy. Materiały z sesji Ratusz w miastach nadbałtyckich [Rathaus in den Städten Nordeuropas. Materialien aus der Konferenz Rathaus in den Ostseestädten], Gdańsk 1997, S. 158 f.

Friedrich Wilhelm II. ein Patent für Danzig und Thorn erlassen, das die bisherige städtische Selbstverwaltung sowie Gerichtsverfassung abschaffte.[8] Verwaltung und Gerichtsbarkeit wurden nach dem organisatorischen Vorbild der Stadt Elbing neu gestaltet. Elbing, gelegen nahe der Ostseeküste, war bereits durch die erste Teilung Polens (1772) an Preußen gefallen, d.h. rund 20 Jahre früher als Thorn und Danzig, und hatte sofort eine neue, preußische Stadtverfassung bekommen.

Als oberste Behörde in Verwaltungs- und Rechtsangelegenheiten wurde in Thorn der sog. Vereinigte Magistrat eingerichtet. Er bestand aus zwei Abteilungen: dem Polizeidepartement und dem Justizdepartement, das auch als Stadtgericht bezeichnet wurde. An der Spitze des Vereinigten Magistrats stand ein Oberbürgermeister, der zugleich der Vorsitzende des Polizeidepartements war. An der Spitze des Stadtgerichts stand ein Justiz-Bürgermeister.[9] Die wichtigsten Thorner Behördenposten wurden mit fremden Beamten besetzt, das heißt mit Personen, die aus anderen Gebieten der preußischen Monarchie stammten.[10]

Das Thorner Stadtgericht übte die rechtsprechende Gewalt über alle Einwohner der Stadt und der Vorstädte mit Ausnahme privilegierter Personen aus. Das Gericht hatte die Gerichtsbarkeit erster Instanz in allen Zivilsachen sowie in kleinen Strafsachen. Es urteilte nach dem alten, überlieferten Kulmer Recht.[11] Als subsidiäres Recht kam das Allgemeine Landrecht für die Preußischen Staaten von 1794 zur Anwendung.[12] Der Sitz des Stadtgerichts war weiterhin das altstädtische Rathaus. Die obere Kriminalgerichtsbarkeit stand dagegen der Westpreußischen Regierung in Marienwerder zu, die gleichzeitig erste Instanz für privilegierte, von der städtischen Gerichtsbarkeit befreite Personen war. Zu den privilegierten Personen, dem sog. eximierten Gerichtsstand, wurden vor allem Adelige, Staatsbeamte und Geist-

---

8 Patent wegen künftiger Einrichtung des Justiz-Wesens in den Städten Danzig und Thorn, De Dato Berlin den 2ten Junius 1793, in: *Christian Carl Leman* (Hg.), Historisch-geographische Einleitung in die Provinzial-Rechte Westpreußens, Marienwerder 1830, S. 197 f., Punkt IV i V.

9 *Carl Gotthelf Prätorius*, Beschreibung der Stadt Thorn und ihres Gebietes, hg. von Julius Emil Wernicke, Culm 1832, S. 377 f.; *Leman*, Einleitung (oben Fn. 8), S. 20 f.

10 Zum Oberbürgermeister wurde Christian Friedrich Ledrich aus Gąbin (etwa 100 km nordwestlich von Warschau) und zum Justiz-Bürgermeister Johann Schmidt aus Angermünde ernannt. Vgl. *Karola Ciesielska*, Ustrój i organizacja władz i kancelarii miasta Torunia w latach 1793–1919 [Verfassung und Organisation der Behörden und der Kanzlei der Stadt Thorn in den Jahren 1793–1919], Warszawa 1972, S. 24.

11 Neben dem Kulmer Recht wurde auch die Thorner Willkür von 1634 angewandt. Vgl. *Danuta Janicka*, Toruńskie sądy pod zaborem pruskim, in: Toruń jako ośrodek wymiaru sprawiedliwości w przeszłości i obecnie. Materiały z konferencji naukowej odbytej w Toruniu 24.5.1999 [Thorner Gerichte unter der preußischen Herrschaft, in: Thorn als Sitz der Justiz in der Vergangenheit und heute. Materialien aus der Wissenschaftskonferenz in Thorn am 24.05.1999], Toruń 2000, S. 17 f.

12 *Danuta Janicka*, Das Allgemeine Landrecht und Polen, in: Barbara Dölemeyer/Heinz Mohnhaupt (Hg.), 200 Jahre Allgemeines Landrecht für die preußischen Staaten. Wirkungsgeschichte und internationaler Kontext, Frankfurt am Main 1995, S. 442 f. Vgl. *Leman*, Einleitung (oben Fn. 8), S. 21 f.; *Prätorius*, Beschreibung (oben Fn. 9), S. 379.

liche gezählt.[13] Die erwähnte Ausnahme von der städtischen Gerichtsbarkeit erhielt in Preußen wie auch in Thorn die Standesgerichtsbarkeit aufrecht.

Abschließend sei gesagt, dass nach der Änderung der staatlichen Zugehörigkeit und der Einführung des preußischen Rechts die Thorner Gerichtsbarkeit neu organisiert wurde. Das Stadtgericht gehörte jedoch noch immer zur traditionellen, ständischen Gerichtsbarkeit in dem Sinne, dass es den Bedürfnissen der Stadtbürger sowie den Einwohnern der Stadtterritorien diente.

III. Unterbrechung der preußischen Entwicklung in der napoleonischen Zeit

Die erste Phase der preußischen Entwicklung wurde unterbrochen, als Thorn mit einem großen Teil der Provinz Westpreußen im Jahre 1807 dem Herzogtum Warschau einverleibt wurde. In dem von Napoleon errichteten Herzogtum wurde das französische Recht eingeführt. Thorn gehörte zum Bromberger Departement, wurde dabei jedoch zur selbstständigen Munizipalstadt erhoben. An ihrer Spitze stand ein Präsident.

Die Gerichtsbarkeit wurde im Herzogtum Warschau überall verstaatlicht. Demgemäß sollte es keine besondere städtische Gerichtsbarkeit mehr geben. Thorn erhielt ein Friedensgericht, ein Untergericht und ein Handelsgericht. Vorübergehend wurde hier auch ein Kriminalgericht geschaffen – später blieb nur ein Kriminalunterrichter des Departements in Bromberg.[14]

Das Thorner Untergericht ersetzte das ehemalige Stadtgericht und war für das ganze städtische Gebiet zuständig. Die Gerichtsbarkeit des Friedensgerichts wurde auf kleine Zivil- und Strafsachen wie auch Einigungen in Streitfällen beschränkt. Dem Friedensgericht unterstanden alle Einwohner des Thorner Kreises, sowohl Bürger als auch Bauern und – in gewissen Sachen – Adlige. Dem Thorner Friedensgericht war das Tribunal in Bromberg als Berufungsinstanz übergeordnet. Die Rolle des Kassationsgerichtshofes übte der Staatsrat in Warschau aus.[15]

Es sei wiederholt, dass die Grundlage der Rechtsprechung das französische Recht war, darunter der Code Napoleon und das französische Handelsgesetzbuch.[16]

IV. Thorner Justiz nach den Reformen von 1815

Im Jahre 1815 fiel Thorn aufgrund der Beschlüsse des Wiener Kongresses wiederum unter die preußische Herrschaft. Die Stadt wurde zur Grenzfestung. Die

---

[13] *Justus Wilhelm Breithaupt*, Justizverfassung und Provinzialrecht in Westpreußen seit 1772, Marienwerder 1872, S. 22 f.

[14] *Karola Ciesielska*, Ustrój i organizacja (oben Fn. 10), S. 32–40.

[15] *Juliusz Bardach/Monika Senkowska-Gluck*, Historia państwa i prawa Polski. Tom 3 [Staats- und Rechtsgeschichte Polens, Bd. 3], Warszawa 1981, S. 122 f.

[16] *Leman*, Einleitung (oben Fn. 8), S. 41.

Staatsgrenze zwischen Preußen und Russland verlief lediglich 10 km östlich von Thorn.

Nach dem Ende der Franzosenzeit wurde das preußische Gerichtswesen wiederhergestellt. Bereits 1816 wurden das Allgemeine Landrecht für die Preußischen Staaten von 1794 sowie die Allgemeine Gerichtsordnung von 1806 eingeführt.[17]

Thorn gehörte zum Regierungsbezirk Marienwerder und wurde eine Kreisstadt. Die Stadt erhielt ein Land- und Stadtgericht, das im Prinzip für alle Einwohner der Stadt und der Umgebung zuständig war. Eine Ausnahme bildeten weiterhin privilegierte Personen, für die ein Obergericht in erster Instanz zuständig war. Das Thorner Land- und Stadtgericht bestand aus einem Direktor und fünf Richtern. Es war im Rathaus untergebracht.[18] Dem Land- und Stadtgericht war das Oberlandesgericht in Marienwerder übergeordnet. Dieses Obergericht war sowohl erste Instanz für den eximierten Gerichtsstand als auch Appellationsinstanz und Aufsichtsbehörde über Untergerichte seines Bezirks. Als letzte Instanz war das Tribunal in Königsberg zuständig, das als Kassationsgerichtshof eingerichtet wurde.

Die preußischen Justizbehörden vergrößerten sich in den nächsten Jahren. 1817 wurde eine besondere offizielle Einrichtung für die Ausübung der Kriminaluntersuchungen ins Leben gerufen. Es war ein Inquisitoriat, bestehend aus einem Direktor, einem Strafrichter und drei Gerichtsangestellten. Das Thorner Inquisitoriat war für das ganze Kulmer Land zuständig. Die von ihm vorbereiteten Untersuchungsakten wurden nach Marienwerder zum Kriminalsenat am hiesigen Oberlandesgericht versandt. Das Inquisitoriat war eine besondere, typisch preußische Justizbehörde, bestand in Thorn jedoch nur kurze Zeit (bis 1839).

Am Ende der zwanziger Jahre des 19. Jahrhunderts nahmen Schiedsrichter ihre Tätigkeit in Thorn auf. Sie wurden in der ganzen Provinz auf Antrag der Stände eingeführt (1827–28).[19] Es sei betont, dass ihre Einrichtung ein gelungenes Experiment war, das wenige Jahre später auf andere Provinzen der preußischen Monarchie

---

[17] Patent wegen der Besitznahme des an Preußen zurückfallenden Theiles des Herzogthums Warschau. Vom 15ten Mai 1815 (GS. S. 45); Patent wegen Wiedereinführung des Allgemeinen Landrechts und der Allgemeinen Gerichtsordnung in die mit der Provinz Westpreußen vereinigten Distrikte, den Culm- und Michelauschen Kreis und die Stadt Thorn mit ihrem Gebiete. Vom 9ten November 1816 (GS. S. 217). Vgl. *Janicka*, Landrecht (oben Fn. 12), S. 444.

[18] Es befand sich im Königssaal im ersten Stock des Rathausgebäudes. Es fehlt zuverlässiges Quellenmaterial zu den Schwerpunkten der Arbeit des Land- und Stadtgerichts. Eine detaillierte Aufstellung der im Thorner Archiv verwahrten Materialien zur Rechtsprechung, bearbeitet von der Autorin, befindet sich im Werk von *Barbara Dölemeyer* (Hg.), Repertorium ungedruckter Quellen zur Rechtsprechung. Deutschland 1800–1945, Erster Halbd., Frankfurt a.M. 1995, S. 276 f.

[19] Es ging damals um die Provinz Preußen. Sie entstand 1824 (formell 1829) aus der Verbindung der Provinzen Ost- und Westpreußen. 1877 wurde sie wieder in die zwei erwähnten Provinzen geteilt.

ausgedehnt wurde. Die Schiedsmänner strebten einen Vergleich bzw. eine Rücknahme durch die Parteien an, erledigten eine große Menge an Streitsachen und entlasteten auf diese Weise die ordentlichen Gerichte.[20]

V. Organisation der Rechtspflege nach der Märzrevolution von 1848/1849

Die Organisation der Gerichtsbarkeit in der preußischen Monarchie wurde wesentlich aufgrund der Märzrevolution von 1848 reformiert. Die Revolution brachte letzten Endes die erste preußische Verfassung[21] und sicherte damit die Gleichheit vor dem Gesetz[22] und die Unabhängigkeit der Judikative.[23]

1849 traten staatliche Kreisgerichte an die Stelle der bisherigen Land- und Stadtgerichte. Es wurde ein einheitlicher Instanzenzug staatlicher Gerichte von den Kreisgerichten über Appellationsgerichte bis hin zum Obersten Gericht geschaffen.[24] Außerdem wurde eine moderne Staatsanwaltschaft aufgebaut. Auf diese Weise wurden auch in Thorn die Reste der städtischen bzw. standesherrlichen Gerichtsbarkeit beseitigt. Ab 1849 unterstand jeder Thorner Stadtbürger den ordentlichen staatlichen Gerichten.[25]

Thorn wurde Sitz eines Kreisgerichts. Es war für Zivil- und Strafsachen zuständig. Das Kreisgericht war teilweise in den Räumen des Rathauses und teilweise in einem gemieteten Raum im Stadtzentrum untergebracht. Sein Personalbestand betrug zehn Richter, einige Assessoren und Referendare wie auch dutzende Büroassistenten. Beim Kreisgericht wurde für Fälle schwerer Kriminalität ein Schwurgericht eingerichtet. Auch ein Staatsanwalt fand hier seinen Amtssitz. Das Appellationsgericht blieb in Marienwerder.[26]

Die geschilderte Gerichtsorganisation bestand bis zum Inkrafttreten der Reichsjustizgesetze im Jahre 1879.

---

[20] Preußens Rechts- und Gerichtsverfassung mit Vorschlägen, Erfurt ca. 1845, S. 142 f.

[21] Verfassungsurkunde für den Preußischen Staat vom 31. Januar 1850 (GS. S. 17). Vgl. die übliche Veröffentlichung: *Ernst Rudolf Huber* (Hg.), Dokumente zur deutschen Verfassungsgeschichte, Bd. 1, Stuttgart 1978, S. 501–514.

[22] Für die Gleichheit vor dem Gesetz sowie für die neue Organisation der Judikative war die Verordnung über die Aufhebung der Privatgerichtsbarkeit und des eximierten Gerichtsstandes sowie über die anderweitige Organisation der Gerichte von 2. Januar 1849 (GS. S. 1) maßgebend.

[23] Die für die Unabhängigkeit des Richters wichtigste Vorschrift war das Gesetz vom 7. Mai 1851 betreffend die Dienstvergehen der Richter und die freiwillige Versetzung derselben auf eine andere Stelle oder in den Ruhestand (GS. S. 218).

[24] Verordnung über die Aufhebung der Privatgerichtsbarkeit und des eximirten Gerichtsstandes sowie über die anderweitige Organisation der Gerichte von 2. Januar 1849 (GS. S. 1). Auch Justizämter und Patrimonialgerichte wurden im ganzen Staat durch Kreisgerichte ersetzt. Die Appellationsgerichte traten an die Stelle der Oberlandesgerichte.

[25] Vgl. Fn. 22.

[26] *Georg Steinmann*, Der Kreis Thorn. Statistische Beschreibung, Thorn 1866, S. 305 f.

VI. Thorner Gerichtsbarkeit nach der großen Justizreform von 1877/1879

Bekanntermaßen vereinheitlichte man die rechtsprechende Gewalt im Deutschen Kaiserreich. Die partikulare Gerichtsverfassung, darunter auch die preußische, wurde überall aufgehoben. Die am Anfang des Jahres 1877 veröffentlichten und am 1. Oktober 1879 in Kraft getretenen Reichsjustizgesetze betrafen die ganze Gerichtsbarkeit, darunter die Gerichtsverfassung,[27] wie auch die Prozessordnung.[28] Die Organisation der Rechtspflege stützte sich auf Amts-, Land- und Oberlandesgerichte. Das oberste Gericht war das Reichsgericht in Leipzig.[29]

Die Stadt Thorn war in der zweiten Hälfte des 19. Jahrhunderts eine typische Provinzstadt, geprägt durch die Grenznähe. Im Deutschen Reich wurde Thorn neben Danzig, Königsberg, Köstrin, Posen und Glogau zur Festung ersten Ranges erhoben. Der Ausbau der Thorner Festung deckte sich zeitlich mit der Entwicklung der Eisenbahnverbindungen. All diese Rahmenbedingungen waren Impulse für die Vergrößerung und neue Raumgestaltung Thorns.[30] Am Anfang des 20. Jahrhunderts zählte die Stadt fast 25.000 Einwohner. Die bisher vorhandenen Gerichte blieben erhalten. Daneben entstanden neue Justizorgane.

Das bisherige Kreisgericht wurde zum Amtsgericht. Bei dem Amtsgericht wurde für Kriminalfälle ein Schöffengericht eingerichtet, an dem Laienrichter mitwirkten. Als weitere Justizbehörde wurde das Landgericht eingerichtet. Zum Bezirk des neu geschaffenen Landgerichts Thorn gehörten fünf Amtsgerichte aus der nächsten Umgebung.[31] Das Thorner Landgericht hatte die Gerichtsbarkeit erster bzw. zweiter Instanz in Zivil-, Handels- wie auch Strafsachen. Für die letzteren war entweder eine Strafkammer oder ein besonderes Schwurgericht zuständig, das beim Landgericht seinen Amtssitz erhielt. Das Schwurgericht war für die schwersten Verbrechen zuständig.[32] Die Berufungsinstanz für Thorn blieb in Marienwerder. Aus dem bisherigen Appellationsgericht in Marienwerder wurde ein Oberlandesgericht, das für die ganze Provinz Westpreußen zuständig war.[33]

---

[27] Gerichtsverfassungsgesetz vom 27. Januar 1877 (RGBl. S. 41); Einführungsgesetz zum Gerichtsverfassungsgesetz vom 27. Januar 1877 (RGBl. S. 77).

[28] Zivilprozessordnung vom 30. Januar 1877 (RGBl. S. 83); Strafprozessordnung vom 1. Februar 1877 (RGBl. S. 253).

[29] *Eduard Kern*, Geschichte des Gerichtsverfassungsrechts, München/Berlin 1954.

[30] *Czacharowski*, Atlas (oben Fn. 3), S. 18.

[31] Thorn, Kulm, Strasburg (an der Drewenz), Löbau und später noch Briesen.

[32] Im Thorner Archiv wird wesentliches Material zur Rechtsprechung des Amts- und Landgerichts aufbewahrt. Vgl. näher *Danuta Janicka,* Polnische Archive, in: Dölemeyer, Repertorium (oben Fn. 18), S. 299 f.

[33] *Josef N. Pawlowski*, Die Provinz Westpreußen in ihrer geschichtlichen, culturhistorischen und sprachlichen Entwickelung, Danzig 1879.

Neben den ordentlichen Gerichten entstanden in Thorn einige moderne Sondergerichte.[34] Sie gehörten zur preußischen außerordentlichen Gerichtsbarkeit. Erstens wurde, und zwar in allen preußischen Provinzen, eine Verwaltungsgerichtsbarkeit eingerichtet.[35] Die Rolle der ersten Instanz übte in Thorn der Kreisausschuss aus – ein Selbstverwaltungsorgan. Zweitens wurden in der Stadt ein Kaufmanns- und ein Gewerbegericht errichtet (1890). Sie dienten als schiedsgerichtliche Institutionen, doch können sie auch als Auftakt zur Arbeitsgerichtsbarkeit betrachtet werden.[36] Drittens waren in Thorn Schiedsgerichte tätig. Ihre Grundlage bildete die neue Schiedsmannordnung von 1879.[37]

Die meisten Thorner Ämter drängten sich weiter im altstädtischen Rathaus. Im Laufe der Zeit erwiesen sich seine Räume als nicht mehr ausreichend. Deswegen wurden im letzten Jahrzehnt des 19. Jahrhunderts mehrere repräsentative öffentliche Amtsgebäude in Thorn errichtet. Sie bildeten eine Kette um das enge Zentrum der Stadt. Die meisten wurden im neugotischen Stil entworfen und passten sehr gut zur mittelalterlichen Landschaft der Stadt.

Das Amtsgericht, das Landgericht, das Kreisamt wie auch die Landespolizei erhielten dort ihr Zuhause. Das Amts- und Landgericht lagen sehr nah nebeneinander. Zwischen den beiden Gerichtsgebäuden befand sich ein Innenhof. Dicht daneben fand ein Gefängnis seinen Platz. Es war ein besonderes Gebäude in der Form einer Rotunde, mit einem riesigen runden Treppenhaus in der Mitte.[38] Der Komplex der Justizbehörden ist bis heute erhalten geblieben und dient weiterhin der rechtsprechenden Gewalt.[39]

Die dargestellte Organisation der Thorner Gerichtsbarkeit überdauerte bis zum Ersten Weltkrieg. Aufgrund des Friedensvertrags von Versailles fiel Thorn an Polen. Die Stadt wurde 1920 zur Hauptstadt der Wojewodschaft Pommerellen und zum Sitz wichtiger Verwaltungsinstitutionen. Die für die Justiz zuständigen Behörden wurden polonisiert. Die deutsche Gerichtsverfassung als solche blieb jedoch bis

---

[34] Zum Unterschied zwischen der alten, traditionellen und der neuen funktionellen Sondergerichtsbarkeit vgl. *Dölemeyer*, Repertorium (oben Fn. 18), S. 8 f.

[35] Kreisordnung vom 13. Dezember 1872 (GS. S. 661); Gesetz über Zuständigkeit der Verwaltungs- und Verwaltungsgerichtsbehörden vom 1. August 1883 (GS. S. 237).

[36] *Eugen Christiani*, Gerichtswesen und gerichtliches Verfahren in Preußen, Hannover 1879, S. 6. Vgl. *Dölemeyer*, Repertorium (oben Fn. 18), S. 8 f.

[37] Schiedsmannordnung vom 29. März 1879, GS. S. 321.

[38] Vgl. eine ausführliche polnische Monographie mit einer deutschen Zusammenfassung: *Joanna Kucharzewska*, Architektura i urbanistyka Torunia w latach 1871–1920 [Architektur und Urbanistik Thorns in den Jahren 1871–1920], Warszawa 2004, S. 130–135 und 428.

[39] Im Gebäude des ehemaligen Amtsgerichts befindet sich heute das Amtsgericht Thorn (Sąd Rejonowy w Toruniu); im Gebäude des ehemaligen Landgerichts – das Bezirksgericht Thorn (Sąd Okręgowy w Toruniu). Das Gefängnis dient als Untersuchungshaft und Gefängnis zugleich.

Ende 1928 erhalten.[40] Neben dem Kreisgericht (dem früheren Amtsgericht) und dem Bezirksgericht (dem früheren Landgericht) entstanden viele neue Verwaltungs- und Rechtsorgane, darunter auch ein Appellationsgericht.

VII. Zusammenfassung

Im 19. Jahrhundert entstand in Thorn ein modernes Justizsystem. Die Modernisierung bedeutete Verstaatlichung der Rechtsprechung, Vereinheitlichung der Justizorganisation und schließlich Ausbildung neuer Sondergerichte in Gestalt von außerordentlichen Rechtsprechungszweigen für Verwaltungsrecht, Handelsrecht, Gewerberecht und ähnliche Rechtsangelegenheiten.

Nachdem Preußen sich 1793 Thorn einverleibt hatte, wurden dort stufenweise preußische Justizbehörden eingerichtet. Die Entwicklung vollzog sich in mehreren Abschnitten: im ersten Abschnitt mit der Einführung des preußischen Rechts an der Wende vom 18. zum 19. Jahrhundert, in einem zweiten Abschnitt in der Zeit nach der napoleonischen Periode bis zur Märzrevolution, in einem dritten Abschnitt in der Zeit nach der Märzrevolution und in einem letzten Abschnitt in der Zeit nach der Rechtsvereinheitlichung durch die Reichsjustizgesetze. Diese zeitliche Gliederung war typisch für die meisten Städte der preußischen Monarchie.

Die erste Phase der preußischen Herrschaft brachte bereits 1793 eine neue Organisation der städtischen Justiz. Nach der endgültigen Besitzergreifung Thorns durch Preußen im Jahre 1815 entstand das Land- und Stadtgericht. Es diente immer noch den Einwohnern der Stadt und des städtischen Territoriums und muss deswegen als traditionelle, ständische rechtsprechende Instanz eingeordnet werden. Die ständische Gerichtsbarkeit stand Thorn bis in die Mitte des 19. Jahrhunderts zu. Nach der Märzrevolution von 1848 wurde in Thorn ein Kreisgericht gegründet. Es gehörte zur ordentlichen staatlichen Gerichtsbarkeit und diente allen Bürgern ohne Rücksicht auf ihren gesellschaftlichen Stand. Nach dem Inkrafttreten der Reichsjustizgesetze wurde das Kreisgericht in ein Amtsgericht umgewandelt. Daneben entstanden ein Landgericht und einige Sondergerichte, die neu ausdifferenzierten Bereichen (besonders in Verwaltungs- und Arbeitsrechtssachen) dienten. Die Entwicklung der Thorner Gerichtsorganisation schloss vorläufig am Ende des 19. Jahrhunderts ab und überdauerte bis zur Zwischenkriegszeit.

---

[40] Die polnische Republik in der Zwischenkriegszeit war ein Mosaik verschiedener, von den Teilungsmächten geerbter Rechtssysteme. Das Gerichtswesen wurde erst im Jahre 1928 aufgrund der Verordnung des Staatspräsidenten über die Verfassung der ordentlichen Gerichte vereinheitlicht: Rozporządzenie Prezydenta Rzeczypospolitej z dnia 6 lutego 1928 r. Prawo o ustroju sądów powszechnych, Gesetzblatt der Republik Polen (Dz.U.R.P.) Nr. 12, Pos. 93.

Gerichtsverfassung in Krisenzeiten. Die letztinstanzliche Rechtsprechung in den schwedischen Reichslehen während des Großen Nordischen Krieges

Nils Jörn

Als der Große Nordische Krieg im Jahre 1716 Wismar erreichte, fand er das Tribunal in seiner absoluten Blüte vor.[1] Ein schwedischer Hochadliger als Präsident,[2] ein pommerscher Adliger als Vizepräsident und Direktor[3] sowie fünf Assessoren, die an führenden Universitäten des Alten Reiches studiert und promoviert hatten,[4] bildeten das Richterkollegium. Das organisatorische Fundament für dieses Kollegium bildete eine Kanzlei mit Protonotar,[5] Sekretär,[6] Registrator,[7] Boten- und Postmeister, zwei Kanzlisten, zwei Kopisten, drei Boten, zwei Trabanten, einem Diener und einem Pedell, die den alltäglichen Gerichtsbetrieb zuverlässig führten. Mithilfe eines Fiskals,[8] der einige Fälle von Amts wegen verfolgte und ansonsten als Prokurator tätig war, sowie eines eigenen Gerichtsarztes sorgten diese Männer dafür, dass die Prozesse aus den Herzogtümern Bremen, Verden und Vorpommern *cum annexis*, dem Hamburger Domkapitel und der Herrschaft Wismar zügig und unstrittig erledigt werden konnten.

Die Finanzierung des Tribunals stand auf sicherem Fundament, das Gehalt des Präsidenten hatte die schwedische Krone übernommen, das Geld für alle anderen Gerichtsbediensteten wurde über eine Tribunalssteuer eingetrieben, die seit der Mitte der 1660er Jahre zuverlässig in den Provinzen erhoben wurde. Dabei waren

---

1 *Nils Jörn*, Die Blütephase des Tribunals, in: ders. (Hg.), Servorum Dei Gaudium. Das ist Treuer Gottes Knechte Freuden=Lohn. Lebensbeschreibungen aus dem Umfeld des Wismarer Tribunals, Greifswald 2003, S. 209–217.

2 Baron Gustav Faltzburg, Landeshauptmann von Växjö und Kronoberg Län wurde nach dem Tod seines Vorgängers Baron Johann Rosenhane, der zwischen 1685 und 1710 dieses Amt innehatte, am 11. November 1710 berufen.

3 Cord Balthasar von Thessin (1655–1726) war zwischen 1694 und 1711 Assessor am Tribunal, wurde dann zum Vizepräsidenten berufen und übte dieses Amt bis zu seinem Tode aus.

4 1716 amtierten Johannes Oldenburg (1655–1726) seit 1696, David Georg von Gerdes (1664–1729) seit 1701, Sebastian von der Lieth (1674–1740) seit 1704, Friedrich Wagner (um 1648–1728) seit 1708 und Albrecht Heinrich Hagemeister (1659–1726) seit 1711. Die Stelle des 1715 verstorbenen Franz von Chemnitz war noch nicht wiederbesetzt worden.

5 Der Wismarer Hermann Christoph Schlaff amtierte von 1695 bis zu seinem Tode 1726.

6 Der Wismarer Henning Joachim Gerdes übte das Amt, das nach dem verlustreichen Nordischen Krieg mit dem Protonotariat zusammengelegt wurde, zwischen 1693 und 1721 aus.

7 Der Wismarer Victor Dahlmann amtierte zwischen 1705 und 1730, übernahm dann das Amt des Fiskals und starb 1732.

8 Der Wismarer Prokurator Dr. David Gerdes amtierte zwischen 1709 und seinem Tode im Jahre 1727.

Bremen, Verden, das Hamburger Domkapitel und die Herrschaft Wismar für eine Hälfte des Gerichtsetats verantwortlich, Pommern für die andere. Stolze 12.234 Rtlr kostete das Gericht die Steuerzahler jedes Jahr und es konnte am Ende der Großmachtzeit von sich behaupten, jeden einzelnen Schilling wert zu sein.[9]

Ein Richteramt am Tribunal stellte für einheimische Juristen die höchste und prestigeträchtigste Karrierestufe dar, die sie erreichen konnten. Das Gericht war aber auch für Männer aus Hamburg, Lübeck, Preußen oder Schweden attraktiv, die sich dementsprechend auf Posten bewarben. Dass die Arbeit des Tribunals genau beobachtet wurde, zeigen die Nachkarrieren einzelner Assessoren am Reichshofrat,[10] am schwedischen Hof[11] oder am Hof des Herzogs von Württemberg.[12] Verstarb einer der Richter oder wurde er auf ein anderes Amt abberufen, so dauerte es in der Regel ein halbes Jahr, bis sein Amt innerhalb einer einfachen, klar geregelten Präsentationsreihenfolge wiederbesetzt wurde. Wie bei der Finanzierung gab es auch bei der Besetzung der Stellen eine Teilung zwischen Pommern und Bremen. Letzterem wurden nicht nur finanzierungs- sondern auch präsentationstechnisch das Herzogtum Verden, das Hamburger Domkapitel und die Herrschaft Wismar zugeschlagen. Innerhalb beider Präsentationsgruppen teilten sich die Präsentationsrechte in die Landesregierungen, Ritterschaften und Städte auf – es gab also sechs Präsentationsberechtigte in festgelegter Reihenfolge. Auch die Besetzungsrechte für die niederen Gerichtsämter waren klar festgelegt und wurden entsprechend durchgesetzt.[13]

Die bedeutende, mehr als 10.000 Bände umfassende Bibliothek, die Gründungsdirektor David Mevius „seinem“ Gericht hinterlassen hatte, war nach seinem Tode gepflegt und mit Hilfe von Strafgeldern und Buchdonationen erweitert worden.[14] Sie bildete nicht nur die zuverlässige Arbeitsgrundlage für die Anwälte,

---

[9] Bisher fehlen Untersuchungen zur Finanzierung des Tribunals. Da das Tribunalsarchiv in den Kriegen seit 1675–1680 mehrfach aufgeteilt und zerstreut wurde, führt der sicherste Weg, um zuverlässige Angaben zu finden, über die landständische Überlieferung in den Stadtarchiven Buxtehude, Greifswald, Stade, Stralsund, Verden und Wismar, den Landesarchiven in Stade und Greifswald, im Wojewodschaftsarchiv Szczecin sowie im Reichsarchiv Stockholm. Für die Probleme bei der zuverlässigen Bereitstellung des Tribunalsetats siehe vorläufig beispielhaft *Nils Jörn*, Von Stade nach Wismar. Juristen aus Bremen-Verden am Wismarer Tribunal, Mitteilungen des Stader Geschichts- und Heimatvereins 80,1/2005.

[10] Friedrich Wilhelm Leopold von Horn (1651–1709).

[11] Wilhelm Julius Coyet (1647–1709), Johann Graf von Lilienstedt (1655–1732).

[12] Joachim Rüdiger von Owstin (1634–1698).

[13] Dazu *Jörn*, Von Stade nach Wismar (oben Fn. 9); *ders.*, Greifswalder, Rostocker, Bützower und Erlangener Professoren am Wismarer Tribunal, in: Dirk Alvermann/Jürgen Regge (Hg.), Justitia in Pommern, Münster 2004, S. 205–234; *ders.*, Wismarer Juristen als Richter am Tribunal, Wismarer Beiträge 16/2006, S. 85–104.

[14] *Kjell Åke Modéer*, David Mevius und die Bibliothek des Tribunals, in: Nils Jörn (Hg.), David Mevius (1609–1670). Leben und Werk eines pommerschen Juristen von europäischem Rang, Hamburg 2007, S. 157–164.

Prokuratoren und Assessoren, sie war auch ein Anziehungspunkt für zahlreiche Jurastudenten, die im Umkreis von mehreren hundert Kilometern auch an den Universitäten keine vergleichbare Sammlung fanden. Auch das Gericht als solches war für viele Norddeutsche zum Ziel der *peregrinatio academica* nach ihrem Studium geworden, um zu erleben, wie Rechtsprechung effektiv organisiert werden konnte. Im prächtigen Fürstenhof traf man sich viermal im Jahr zu öffentlichen Gerichtstagen, ansonsten entfaltete sich hinter den Kulissen ein emsiges Treiben der Juristen, die dafür sorgten, dass die Fälle in beeindruckender Geschwindigkeit erledigt wurden. Einfache Fälle wie Bitten um Mandate *de solvendo* oder *de non turbando* wurden üblicherweise binnen eines Tages beschieden, aber auch bei komplizierteren Sachverhalten setzte das Gericht enge Termine zur Beantwortung und Reaktion für die Parteien und verwarnte diese, wenn sie in den Verdacht gerieten, den Prozess zu verschleppen. Da das Gericht täglich besetzt war, konnte man sogar zu Heiligabend oder Ostersonntag auf dringende Schriftsätze reagieren und entsprechende Mandate erlassen.[15] Man wehrte sich aber auch mit Strafgeldern gegen unberechtigte Appellationen, ungebührliches Benehmen oder Beleidigungen des Gerichts. Diese Strafzahlungen kamen zumeist der Bibliothek zugute.

Wichtig für die Zeitgenossen war, dass die Urteile des Gerichts zuverlässig und umgehend vollstreckt wurden. In den Provinzen gab es an den Hofgerichten sogenannte Exekutoren, die vom Tribunal beauftragt wurden, Geld einzutreiben oder Urteile umzusetzen. Hatten sie nicht auf Anhieb den gewünschten Erfolg, konnte das Gericht auf die schwedische Militärmacht zurückgreifen, die Soldaten entsandte und dafür sorgte, dass die Mandate des Tribunals befolgt wurden. Einen eigenen Exekutor beschäftigte das Tribunal nur in den Jahren zwischen 1691 und 1716, die Besetzung dieses Amtes war eine Anregung der Visitation gewesen, die das Tribunal ab 1688 untersucht hatte. Es ist schwierig, den Erfolg dieser Maßnahme einzuschätzen, da die pommerschen Prozessakten sehr scharf kassiert wurden. So ist zwar davon auszugehen, dass in der Herrschaft Wismar alle Forderungen auf kurzem Wege vollstreckt werden konnten, wie sich dies in Pommern gestaltete, wird sich jedoch nicht mehr belastbar einschätzen lassen. Für die Herzogtümer Bremen und Verden, für die die in Stade erhaltenen Prozesse ebenfalls inventarisiert worden sind, existieren noch keine entsprechenden Forschungen.[16]

Die Zustände am Tribunal erscheinen umso paradiesischer, wenn man sie mit den Verhältnissen am Reichskammergericht in Wetzlar vergleicht. Durch die

[15] In den im Archiv der Hansestadt Wismar erhaltenen Akten, die in den Jahren 2003 bis 2012 inventarisiert worden sind, gibt es zahlreiche Beispiele für Mandate des Tribunals, die Heiligabend oder am Ostersonntag erlassen und zugestellt wurden. Siehe *Nils Jörn* (Bearb.), Inventar der Prozessakten des Wismarer Tribunals, Teil 1: Bestand des Archivs der Hansestadt Wismar, Band 1–8, Wismar 2008–2012.

[16] *Beate-Christine Fiedler* (Bearb.), Akten des Schwedischen Tribunals zu Wismar im Niedersächsischen Landesarchiv – Staatsarchiv Stade – Herzogtümer Bremen und Verden, 1653–1715, Hannover 2012.

sogenannte Ingelheimsche Affäre zu Beginn des 18. Jahrhunderts praktisch lahmgelegt,[17] fristete das oberste Reichsgericht ein vergleichsweise trauriges Schicksal. Nur sieben Richter waren in Wetzlar versammelt, um für das gesamte Alte Reich Recht zu sprechen, die restlichen Präsentationen waren teilweise seit Jahren blockiert, entweder durch die Reichskreise, die sich nicht auf einen Kandidaten einigen konnten oder durch die leere Gerichtskasse, die es nicht zuließ, neue Männer den Dienst antreten zu lassen. Die Kammerzieler, die zum Unterhalt des Gerichts im gesamten Alten Reich erhoben wurden, wurden zwar u.a. aus den schwedischen Reichslehen zuverlässig eingetrieben und nach Wetzlar überwiesen, aus vielen sogenannten reichsnahen Territorien, die näher am RKG lagen und dieses häufig nutzten, gelangte jedoch kein Geld an die Lahn. So hatten sich erschreckende Zahlungsrückstände angetürmt, das Personal erhielt kein Geld und sah sich trotz des hohen Sozialprestiges, das das Gericht nach wie vor hatte, teilweise nach anderen Ämtern um.[18]

Wir haben also auf der einen Seite ein seit gut zwei Jahrhunderten bestehendes, in zehntausenden Prozessen erprobtes und bewährtes, seit 1693 in Wetzlar ansässiges, mittlerweile aber finanziell und personell ausgeblutetes Gericht, in dem sich alle Probleme des Alten Reiches widerspiegelten.[19] Auf der anderen Seite strahlte in Norddeutschland die Alternative mit guter Ausstattung und großen Ambitionen. Wer wusste denn, ob es der schwedischen Krone nicht gelingen würde, im gerade tobenden Nordischen Krieg weitere Gebiete hinzuzuerobern, die dann in den Gerichtssprengel des Tribunals eingegliedert werden könnten? Natürlich hatte es auch für die schwedische Krone verlorene Schlachten gegeben, umso besser konnte man sich in den schwedischen Reichslehen aber an die großen Siege des letzten Wikingers, des jungen Karls XII., vor Kopenhagen, bei Narwa oder Warschau erinnern. Bei seinem Geschick als Feldherr ließen sich solche Siege jederzeit wiederholen, zumindest glaubte man in den schwedischen Provinzen trotz des wechselvollen Verlaufs des Nordischen Krieges fest daran.[20]

---

[17] *Heinz Duchhardt*, Reichskammerrichter Franz Adolf Dietrich von Ingelheim 1659/1732–1742, Nassausche Annalen 81/1970, S. 273 ff.

[18] *Nils Jörn*, Beobachtungen zur Steuerzahlung der Territorien des südlichen Ostseeraumes in der Frühen Neuzeit, in: ders./Michael North (Hg.), Die Integration des südlichen Ostseeraumes in das Alte Reich 1495–1806, Köln/Weimar/Wien 2000, S. 311–391.

[19] Grundlegend dazu: *Sigrid Jahns*, Das Reichskammergericht und seine Richter. Verfassung und Sozialstruktur eines höchsten Gerichts im Alten Reich, Köln/Weimar/Wien 2011.

[20] *Herbert Langer*, Die „Schwedenzeit" in Mecklenburg und Pommern, in: Stadtgeschichtliches Museum Wismar (Hg.), Schwedenzeit, Wismar 1998, S. 9–14; *Ernst Münch/Rolf Rehberg*, Mecklenburg, Pommern und der Kampf um die Ostseeherrschaft (1628–1815), in: a.a.O., S. 15–30; *Karl-Heinz Steinbruch*, Der Nordische Krieg in Mecklenburg, in: a.a.O., S. 38–54. Als wichtige Primärquelle für die Hoffnungen und Wünsche der Wismarer siehe dazu vor allem das Tagebuch des Gabriel Hermann von der Fehr im AHW. Für Stralsund: *Jörg Zapnik*, Ein Leben am Sund. Das Tagebuch des Klosterschreibers Jürgen Dreves (1687–1720), Stralsund 2011. So schreibt Dreves am 18.12.1700: Schiffer Klinckmann von Reval „bringt Gottlob! die feste und

Doch im Jahre 1716 verstärkten sich die Hinweise, dass Wismar, das nicht nur Gerichtsort, sondern auch eine große, strategisch günstig gelegene Festung war, nicht mehr lange zu halten sein würde. Karl XII. hatte am 21. Dezember 1715 Stralsund verlassen und über Rügen nach Schweden fliehen müssen,[21] die Übermacht der nordischen Alliierten hatte sich durch den Kriegseintritt der Preußen verstärkt – im Frühjahr 1716 war nur noch Wismar in schwedischer Hand. Der Krieg hatte sich der Stadt bereits zweimal bedrohlich genähert und beide Male hatte das Tribunal angemessen reagiert. Mit dem Rat von Lübeck hatte man ein Übereinkommen getroffen, wichtige Akten sicher auf neutralem Boden unterstellen zu können. In zwei Wellen waren diese Akten mittlerweile ausgelagert worden, die Richter und ihre Familien sorgten privat ebenso vor. Die meisten von ihnen verließen die Stadt vor bzw. mit den schwedischen Truppen, die die Festung am 23. April 1716 übergeben mussten.[22]

---

sichere Nachricht, daß Narva den 20. November entsetzt, die Muscowiter geschlagen, 25000 auf dem Schlachtfeld geblieben, 70 Stücke erobert und 300 Wagen mit Proviant bekommen. I.K.M. von Schweden sind 2 Stunden in Narva gewesen und danach ohne Verzug dem flüchtigen Feinde nachgesetzt. Gott dem Allmächtigen sei für diese Gnade und herrlichen Sieg ewig Lob und Dank gesagt." (*Zapnik*, S. 72). Am 16.02.1701 berichtet Dreves: „Der gestrige Tag, so von I.K.M. zu einem extraordinairen Dank- und Jubelfest wegen der über die Russen bei Narva erhaltenen unvergleichlichen Victorie benannt, wurde mit den erdenklichsten Solennitäten, sowohl in devoter Verrichtung des Gottesdienstes, mit einem herzbrünstigen te deum laudamus, mit Donnern des Geschützes, mit einträchtigen Salven der Milice, als auch mit Bezeugung der größten Freude von allen Bürgermeistern, Ratsherren und Bürgern in der ganzen Stadt celebrirt. Wozu der Himmel eben ein sehr vergnügliches Gewitter mit schönen Sonnenblicken schenkte, da es doch die vorigen und nachfolgenden Tage böses regnerisches Wetter war. In den Illuminationibus, so die ganze Nacht hindurch standen, war so viel auserlesenes Sinnreiches, daß man mit höchster Verwunderung sah, wie einer mit dem anderen um den Vorzug stritt, so daß man versichern kann, solange Stralsund gestanden, dergleichen nicht gesehen zu haben. Besonders machte das Bildnis I.K.M. mit einem blinkenden Schwert in Lebensgröße zu Pferde saß und ein Haufen erschlagener Russen unter sich liegen hatte und weil es mit lebendigen Farben dargestellt und mit über einhalb Tausend Lichtern erleuchtet war, vor dem Rathaus eine sehr vortreffliche Figur. Die Kaufgesellen schossen die ganze Nacht aus Stücken, wie dann die Schützencompagnie es nicht minder tat und versammelten sich dieselbe auf St. Johannishof, von wo sie mit Trompeten und Heerpaucken und fliegenden Fahnen abmarschierten. Am späten Abend um 9 Uhr wurde ein Feuerwerk vor dem Kniepertor angezündet und glücklich geendiget." (*Zapnik*, S. 74 f.).

[21] Dreves notiert sehr nüchtern: 21.12.1715: „Ging I.K.M. von Schweden in der Nacht von hier weg nach Schweden." 22.12.1715: „Wurde mit den Feinden capitulirt und zogen die Schweden den 23. Dezember aus und den 24. Dezember die Feinde oder Überwinder wieder ein, so daß wir am heiligen Christtag noch friedlich in die Kirche gehen und den Gottesdienst verrichten konnten. Es wäre dieses viel weitläufiger zu notiren. Ich lasse aber solches demjenigen zu verrichten über, der mehr Geld als ich dafür bekommt." (*Zapnik*, S. 110).

[22] Siehe dazu *Nils Jörn*, Das Archiv des Wismarer Tribunals, in: ders./Bernhard Diestelkamp/ Kjell Åke Modéer (Hg.), Integration durch Recht. Das Wismarer Tribunal 1653–1806, Köln/ Weimar/Wien 2003, S. 329–366 sowie *ders.*, „Daß diese elende Stadt von derselben so kostbar anscheinenden justice, als auch denen übrigen Beschwerden liberirt werden möge". Das Wismarer Tribunal während der sogenannten Dänenzeit 1716–1721, in: Martin Krieger/Joachim Krüger

Es stellte sich schnell heraus, dass die nordischen Alliierten Dänemark, Kurhannover und Preußen offenbar nicht daran interessiert waren, das Tribunal als Institution weiterzuführen. Kurhannover hatte Bremen und Verden bereits von Dänemark erworben, das die Schweden aus den Herzogtümern vertrieben hatte. Es wollte die Territorien nun auch in seine bestehende Gerichtsstruktur einbinden.[23] Preußen hatte sich im Westfälischen Frieden nur schweren Herzens entschließen können, den Oderstreifen mit Stettin abzutreten. Bereits im Frieden von St. Germain 1679 waren kleine Teile des Grenzgebietes an Preußen rückübertragen worden. Als die preußische Armee das Gebiet 1713 komplett erobern konnte, war klar, dass sie es wieder in alte Zusammenhänge integrieren würde. Übrig blieb nur Dänemark, das Altvorpommern erobert hatte und Wismar besetzt hielt, damit aber nicht seinen Besitz abrunden konnte, sondern Territorien außerhalb seiner Herrschaftsbereichs erworben hatte, bei denen sehr unsicher war, ob man sie als Reichslehen erhalten könnte. Die sinnvolle Integration in Bestehendes fiel hier also schwer, zudem war nicht klar, ob man den Kaiser dazu bewegen können würde, die dänische Krone mit den besetzten Gebieten zu belehnen.[24]

Um sich eine Übersicht über die bisherige Rechtsprechung, die Privilegien der Landstände, einzelner Adliger und Städte zu verschaffen, teilten zwischen dem 10. März und dem 17. Mai 1717 Beauftragte der Könige von Preußen, Dänemark und Großbritannien in Wismar das Gerichtsarchiv nach der Provenienz der Kläger bzw. Appellanten unter sich auf. Ein Teil der Akten, der nicht zuzuordnen war, verblieb in Wismar ebenso wie die meisten Generalia und wurde im Gerichtsarchiv mit drei Schlössern verschlossen. Die 3 Schlüssel erhielten die Alliierten, so dass sie nur nach gemeinsamer Absprache in das Archiv gelangen konnten.[25] Doch wie wurde die Rechtsprechung nun organisiert?

Organisieren wir unseren kleinen Rundblick nach der Qualität der Nachfolgeeinrichtungen des Tribunals, so müssen wir zwangsläufig im Westen beginnen. Fälle aus Bremen-Verden und dem Hamburger Domkapitel wurden von Kurhannover an das OAG Celle übertragen. Dort fanden die Parteien ein funktionierendes

---

(Hg.), Regna firmat pietas. Staat und Staatlichkeit im Ostseeraum. Festgabe zum 60. Geburtstag von Jens E. Olesen, Greifswald 2010, S. 359–378.

[23] *Volker Friedrich Drecktrah*, Die Gerichtsbarkeit in den Herzogtümern Bremen und Verden und in der preußischen Landdrostei Stade von 1715 bis 1879, Frankfurt a.M. 2002.

[24] *Nils Jörn*, Das Tribunal während des Nordischen Krieges und der dänischen Okkupation Wismars, in: Servorum Dei Gaudium (oben Fn. 1), S. 297–301; jüngst *Martin Meier*, Vorpommern nördlich der Peene unter dänischer Verwaltung 1715 bis 1721. Aufbau einer Verwaltung und Herrschaftssicherung in einem eroberten Gebiet, München 2008; *ders.*, Landesherrliche Einquartierungspolitik in „Dänisch-Vorpommern" 1715–1721 dargestellt am Beispiel der militärischen Exekution, Militärgeschichtliche Zeitschrift 63/2004, S. 300–323; *ders.*, Dänische Kirchenpolitik in Vorpommern nördlich der Peene 1715–1721, Baltische Studien 90/2004, S. 143–160.

[25] Siehe *Jörn*, Das Archiv (oben Fn. 22), S. 347 f.

Gericht vor, das 1711 nach dem Vorbild des Tribunals eingerichtet worden war und seitdem erfolgreich arbeitete. Für die Prozessparteien änderte sich praktisch also nur der Ort der Rechtsprechung, die Rahmenbedingungen blieben dieselben. Die bisher gezahlten Tribunalssteuern wurden seit 1716 für das OAG Celle eingesammelt, für die Präsentation zweier Assessoren für die Herzogtümer Bremen und Verden durften die Landstände Vorschläge unterbreiten, die Summe, ab der Appellationen zulässig waren, blieb bei 200 Rtlr, die Grundlagen, nach denen das Gericht arbeitete, waren dieselben wie am Tribunal: altes Herkommen, Privilegien der Stände und bisher geltende Gesetze in den beiden Herzogtümern. Nach dem kurzen dänischen Intermezzo von 1712–1715, als die Parteien nach der Eroberung im Krieg durch die dänischen Truppen direkt am Hof in Kopenhagen appellieren sollten und die Appellationssumme auf 400 Rtlr verdoppelt worden war, war für die Bremer und Verdener also gerichtsorganisatorisch eine sehr gute Lösung gefunden worden.[26]

Anders sah es hingegen in den anderen Territorien aus. Prozesse aus den schwedisch-vorpommerschen Gebieten von jenseits der Peene wurden an das hinterpommersche Hofgericht in Stargard verwiesen. Das dortige Hofgericht war seit der Belehnung Preußens mit Hinterpommern für alle Fälle aus dem früheren Pommern-Stettin zuständig. Seit Ende 1713 gehörten auch die Parteien aus dem Oderstreifen mit Stettin dazu, waren also praktisch mit ihrem alten Gerichtssprengel wiedervereinigt worden. Sie bemerkten aber sehr rasch die Unterschiede zwischen der Justizorganisation in Schwedisch-Vorpommern und der in Preußisch-Hinterpommern. Da der Kurfürst von Brandenburg für seine nicht kurfürstlichen Territorien 1648 kein *privilegium de non appellando* hatte erwerben können, hatten die Prozessparteien das Recht behalten, sich ab einem Streitwert von 500 fl. an die obersten Reichsgerichte zu wenden. Nach der Königskrönung Friedrichs I. im Jahre 1701 hatte Preußen die Bemühungen um höhere Appellationsprivilegien verstärkt und die Appellationssumme für Hinterpommern am 16. Dezember 1702 immerhin auf 2.500 Rtlr anheben können.[27] Damit war den meisten Prozessparteien aus Hinterpommern der Weg an die obersten Reichsgerichte praktisch versperrt, die Gerichte im Territorium hätten also eigentlich gestärkt werden müssen, um eine letztinstanzliche Rechtsprechung zu ermöglichen.

Während in Schwedisch-Vorpommern in der Schwedenzeit umfangreiche Bemühungen zur Neuorganisation und Effektivierung des Gerichtsbetriebs am Greifswalder Hofgericht unternommen worden waren, bestätigten die branden-

---

[26] Siehe dazu *Drecktrah*, Gerichtsbarkeit (oben Fn. 23) sowie *Stefan Andreas Stodolkowitz*, Das Oberappellationsgericht Celle und seine Rechtsprechung im 18. Jahrhundert, Köln/Weimar/Wien 2011; *ders.*, Das Oberappellationsgericht Celle als Mittler zwischen Reichsjustiz und territorialer Gerichtsbarkeit, in: Anja Amend-Traut (Hg.), Die höchsten Reichsgerichte als mediales Ereignis, München 2012, S. 191–219.

[27] *Tobias Freitag/Nils Jörn*, Zur Inanspruchnahme der obersten Reichsgerichte im südlichen Ostseeraum 1495–1806, in: Integration des südlichen Ostseeraumes (oben Fn. 18), S. 63.

burgischen Kurfürsten dem anerkannt reformbedürftigen Hofgericht in Stargard nur immer wieder die alten Privilegien aus der Herzogszeit und behielten seine Gerichtsorganisation weitgehend bei. Der Kurfürst hatte sich in der Regimentsverfassung von 1654 zudem einen starken Einfluss auf das Hofgericht gesichert, durch unklare Kompetenzenregelung zwischen Hofgericht und Landesregierung nahm er diesen wahr und regierte oftmals in die Arbeit des Gerichts hinein.[28]

Das verstärkte sich noch unter Friedrich Wilhelm I. seit 1713, die Kompetenzen der Gerichte wurden eher verwirrt als klarer. Das kam dadurch, dass der König verstärkt richterliche Kompetenzen an die Landesregierungen verwies, die eigentliche Verwaltung hingegen zunächst den Kriegskommissariaten, dann den Kriegs- und Domänenkammern übertrug. Die Landesregierungen wurden zu Gerichten zweiter und dritter Instanz und übernahmen die Zuständigkeit für Lehnssachen, einen Bereich, der eigentlich den Hofgerichten seit alters zustand.[29] Diesem alles in allem wenig befriedigenden Zustand wurden also die Bewohner des Oderstreifens seit der Eroberung Stettins im Jahre 1713 unterworfen. Die Verhältnisse wurden zusätzlich dadurch verwirrt, dass die seit 1702 auf 2.500 Rtlr erhöhte Appellationssumme nicht für den im Krieg erworbenen Landstrich galt, hier also weiterhin theoretisch ab 500 Gulden an die Reichsgerichte hätte appelliert werden können. Ob von dieser Möglichkeit Gebrauch gemacht wurde, wissen wir nicht. Die nahezu 100%ige Kassation der Prozessakten aus diesem Bereich im 19. Jahrhundert durch Preußen hat die Möglichkeiten der Forschung dazu sehr stark eingeschränkt.[30] Was jedoch klar ist: Die Bewohner des Oderstreifens gelangten aus der hervorragend organisierten schwedischen Gerichtsverwaltung in eine rückständig gebliebene Gerichtsstruktur mit unklaren Kompetenzen.

Noch schlechter sah es in Vorpommern und Rügen aus, wo die Prozesse von der dänischen Regierungskanzlei in Stralsund letztinstanzlich bearbeitet werden sollten. Das Problem war, dass die Regierungskanzlei personell unterbesetzt war und es zudem keine funktionierenden Untergerichte gab, von denen aus Fälle an die Regierungskanzlei hätten gelangen können. Die Richter des Greifswalder Hofgerichts hatten jede Zusammenarbeit mit den Dänen verweigert, sie fühlten sich an ihre Eide gegenüber der schwedischen Krone gebunden und gingen davon aus, dass diese die Dänen zügig wieder aus der Provinz vertreiben würde. Das Greifswalder Konsistorium als oberstes geistliches Gericht folgte diesem Beispiel. Es gab nur einen von den Dänen eingesetzten Theologie-Professor, der mit den Besatzern kollaborierte. Unter diesen Umständen war es für die Dänen schwierig, eine

[28] Die Forschungslage zu den pommerschen Hofgerichten ist unbefriedigend. Siehe zu den Stettiner Hofgerichten vor allem *Pawel Gut*, Die Hofgerichte in Stettin, in: Nils Jörn (Hg.), Die Pommerschen Hofgerichte, Hamburg 2007, S. 275–288 mit einer Zusammenfassung der älteren Literatur sowie *Nils Jörn*, Das Vorpommersche Hofgericht – ein kurzer Abriss seiner Geschichte und Perspektiven der weiteren Forschung, a.a.O., S. 17–82.

[29] *Gut*, Hofgerichte (oben Fn. 28).

[30] Dazu *Jörn*, Das Archiv (oben Fn. 22), S. 353.

befriedigende letztinstanzliche Rechtsprechung zu etablieren, die Verantwortung für die erstinstanzlich tätigen Stadt- und Gutsgerichte in diesem Territorium stieg also.[31] Ob diese in der Lage waren, sie wahrzunehmen und welche Probleme es durch die praktisch fehlende mittlere Ebene, die schlecht ausgestattete und durch fehlende Archive zudem schlecht informierte letzte Instanz gab, ist bisher nicht befriedigend erforscht worden. Es zeigt sich jedoch, dass sich die Dänen offenbar unsicher waren, ob sie das eroberte Territorium auch lehnsrechtlich würden an sich binden können und dementsprechend zögerlich vorgingen.

Für die Herrschaft Wismar wurde ein Oberlanddrost eingesetzt, der nicht nur die Zivilverwaltung übernehmen, sondern auch ein entsprechendes Gericht schaffen sollte. Diese Aufgabe wurde dem selbstbewussten mecklenburgischen Agrarreformer Joachim Friedrich von der Lühe auf Panzow (um 1675–1742)[32] aufgetragen, der sich in die mecklenburgischen Ständekonflikte auf Seiten des Adels eingemischt hatte. Während der Belagerung Wismars sorgte er dafür, dass zwar hannoversche, preußische und dänische Truppen in die Herrschaft einrückten, die Russen und die Truppen Karl Leopolds von Mecklenburg jedoch nicht eingelassen wurden. Diese verwüsteten daraufhin seine Güter und erklärten ihn für vogelfrei, die Dänen wählten von der Lühe jedoch für das Amt eines Landdrosten über die Herrschaft Wismar aus. Erst im Oktober 1718 erhielt er seine Bestallung auch von Kurhannover, von den Preußen liegt kein offizielles Mandat vor. Trotzdem betonte der Mecklenburger immer wieder, sich bei der Verwaltung der Herrschaft allen drei Kronen verpflichtet zu fühlen.[33]

Ihm wurden von den Dänen die Räume des Tribunalspräsidenten im Fürstenhof als Dienstwohnung, die darunter liegenden Räume des Tribunals als Amtsräume angewiesen, sein Gehalt sollte 2.000 Rtlr betragen. Dafür hatte er die *jura ducalia et episcopalia* im Namen der Besatzer zu verwalten und musste sich dementsprechend mit den alliierten Königen und ihren Regierungen sowie dem Stadtkommandanten abstimmen, Probleme zwischen der Stadt und den beiden Ämtern sowie dem mecklenburgischen Umland, den Einwohnern der Herrschaft Wismar und dem einquartierten Militär schlichten, den Wismarer Rat, die Amtsleute auf Poel und Neukloster sowie die Geistlichkeit ebenso kontrollieren wie die Arbeit der städtischen und Amtsgerichte sowie des Wismarer Konsistoriums. Über all das hinaus war durch ihn eine letztinstanzliche Rechtsprechung auf dem Niveau des Tribunals zu organisieren.

---

[31] *Meier*, Vorpommern nördlich der Peene (oben Fn. 24); *Jörn*, Das Vorpommersche Hofgericht (oben Fn. 28).

[32] *Gertrud Schröder-Lembke*, Die mecklenburgische Koppelwirtschaft, in: dies., Studien zur Agrargeschichte, Stuttgart/New York 1978, S. 64–67.

[33] Für das folgende: *Jörn*, Daß diese elende Stadt (oben Fn. 22); *Meier*, Vorpommern nördlich der Peene (oben Fn. 24).

Von der Lühe fehlte für diese Aufgaben jeglicher Apparat. Um sein Gehalt aufzubringen, wurde aus der Herrschaft statt der bisher üblichen 200 Rtlr eine sehr stark erhöhte Tribunalssteuer eingetrieben, für die weitere Zivilverwaltung wurden insgesamt 500 Rtlr veranschlagt, die ebenfalls über Steuern eingetrieben wurden. Seit November 1718 wurde aus diesem Etat immerhin ein Assessor angestellt, außerdem gab es einen Sekretär, der den gesamten Schriftwechsel von der Lühes übernahm. Erfahrungen bei der Gerichtsorganisation hatte von der Lühe nicht, der gut funktionierende Kanzlei-Unterbau des Tribunals stand ihm nicht zur Verfügung, von den Alliierten war nicht einmal geregelt, ob die Tribunalsordnung vollumfänglich oder modifiziert weitergelten oder durch eine andere Gerichtsordnung ersetzt werden sollte. Dementsprechend stellte sich die Tätigkeit des Tribunals dar. Die Parteien aus Wismar und den Ämtern appellierten zunächst wie gewohnt an das Gericht, mussten aber feststellen, dass sie keinerlei Antwort gewürdigt wurden. Das nahm der Wismarer Rat eine Weile hin, beschwerte sich aber am 19. Januar 1719 bei Georg I. von Großbritannien und bat um Abschaffung des Tribunals und Verweisung der Fälle an das Glücksburger Hofgericht, die Ratzeburger Regierungskanzlei oder gar an das Reichskammergericht.[34]

Der König ging in seiner Antwort vom März 1718 mit keiner Silbe auf diese Vorschläge ein, sondern versprach nur allgemein Besserung und wies die Stadt zum Gehorsam gegenüber von der Lühe an. Damit war der Wismarer Rat nicht zufrieden, er ordnete mehrere Bürgermeister und Ratsherren im Juli 1719 nach Hannover ab. Diese Delegation erreichte immerhin, dass der König festlegte, dass die Tribunalsordnung die Grundlage für die Rechtsprechung bilden sollte. Falls gegen ein Urteil Revision eingelegt wurde, versprach Georg I., dass sich die Alliierten „specialiter“ damit beschäftigen würden. Als dieser Fall am 30. Dezember 1719 dann tatsächlich eintrat, als der Bäcker Jacob Detlef Paries sich beim König von England darüber beschwerte, dass sein neuerbauter Backofen abgerissen werden sollte, beschritt von der Lühe jedoch nicht den durch die königliche Resolution vorgezeichneten Weg, sondern wies den Rat zur Urteilsvollstreckung an.[35]

Dieses Beispiel führte zu einer deutlichen Reduzierung des Geschäftsanfalls, vor allem, wenn es um Rechtsmittel gegen Entscheidungen des Tribunals ging. Hatte man sich bisher auf die aufhaltende Wirkung von Rechtsmitteln wie *restitutio in integrum* oder die Möglichkeit, das Problem noch einmal neu vorzutragen, verlassen können, galt diese offenbar während der Besatzungszeit nicht. Also vertagte man seinen Streit überwiegend auf die Zeit, wenn wieder geordnete schwedische Verhältnisse herrschen würden, war aber umso wütender darüber, für eine auf das Zwölffache erhöhte Tribunalssteuer keinerlei Gegenleistung zu erhalten. Der Druck des Rates und der Prozessparteien auf die Besatzer erhöhte sich

---

[34] AHW, Ratsakten, Nr. 2227: Verhandlungen Wismars mit dem vom König von England und dem König von Dänemark berufenen Gouverneur, Oberlanddrost von der Lühe, über die von der Stadt aufzubringenden Salarien und Kontributionen 1718–1719.

[35] AHW, Prozessakten des Tribunals, Nr. 0279.

derart, dass diese reagieren mussten und mit der Berufung des Assessors Landreiter seit Ende November 1718 endlich eine geordnete Rechtsprechung zustandekam. An den überlieferten Prozessakten zeigt sich, dass von der Lühe und Landreiter durchaus dazu in der Lage waren, die Justiz nach den Vorgaben der Tribunalsordnung zu organisieren und auch bereitwillig deren Intention aufgriffen, Prozesse durch einen Vergleich zu beenden.[36] Seit Ende 1718 wurden in mehreren Fällen Termine eingehalten,[37] ergingen Urteile[38] und wurden vollstreckt.[39] Sogar komplizierte Probleme wie ein Grenzstreit mit Mecklenburg konnten mithilfe des Pfandinhabers von Neukloster, des Geheimen Rates von Plessen, dem eine Kommission übertragen worden war, professionell und für alle Beteiligten nachvollziehbar geklärt werden.[40]

Rätselhafterweise überwiegen aber die Prozesse, in denen entweder gar keine Reaktion des Gerichts nachweisbar ist oder wo die Verhandlungen nicht bis zu einem Urteil geführt wurden.[41] Nach welchen Kriterien das höchste Gericht für die Herrschaft Wismar entschied, welchen Fall es bearbeiten und welchen unkommentiert im Archiv verschwinden lassen würde, entzieht sich unserer Kenntnis, klar ist,

---

[36] AHW, Prozessakten des Tribunals, Nr. 0271: Am 22.04.1719 wurde nach kurzen Verhandlungen ein Vergleich zwischen Hans Böckmann und der Witwe Hinrich Edlers um Aufteilung des Erbes Edlers geschlossen.

[37] So bei der Auseinandersetzung des Ratsherrn Anton Scheffel gegen Caspar Töppe im Januar 1719 (AHW, Prozessakten des Tribunals, Nr. 3486) oder beim Streit zwischen dem Wismarer Töpferamt und den Einwohnern der Ämter Poel und Neukloster wegen Verkaufs der Töpfe im Juni 1719 (AHW, Prozessakten des Tribunals, Nr. 3485).

[38] Am 18.11.1720 erreichten Joachim Hinrich Ackermann und Hans Hinrich Bartels die Beschlagnahme von 150 Schafen des Pächters Bolten zu Rohlstorf (AHW, Prozessakten des Tribunals, Nr. 0041). Am 13.10.1719 akzeptierte der Oberstleutnant von Bornefeld auf Flimsdorf Schadensersatz für 272 während der Belagerung Wismars von seinem Gut geraubte Schafe „in Wismarschen Gelde“ (AHW, Prozessakten des Tribunals, Nr. 0272).

[39] So bei der militärischen Vollstreckung des Schadensersatzes von 40 Mk. lüb. gegen den Schneider Walter im Juli 1720 (AHW, Prozessakten des Tribunals, Nr. 3741) oder bei der Akzisezahlung wegen Heringseinfuhr 1719/1720 durch Christian Adam Möller (AHW, Prozessakten des Tribunals, Nr. 2109).

[40] Im Juli und August 1719 stritt sich der Wismarer Scharfrichter Carl Jeltzer mit der Schweriner Justizkanzlei wegen der Grenzen seiner Zuständigkeit. Hintergrund war ein krepiertes Pferd in Zellin im Amt Neukloster, das vom Schweriner Scharfrichter beseitigt worden war. Oberlanddrost von der Lühe setzte sich bei der Justizkanzlei für Jeltzer ein und forderte die Unterstützung des Pfandinhabers des Amtes Neukloster an, der ein Gutachten einreichte (AHW, Prozessakten des Tribunals, Nr. 1521).

[41] Neben zahlreichen anderen so im Fall des Bauern Hinrich Boll, der sich 1719 darüber beschwerte, dass die Kämmerei ehemaliges Festungsland, das er gepachtet und als Viehweide nutzt, erneut verpachtet hatte (AHW, Prozessakten des Tribunals, Nr. 0273) oder im Fall der Witwe des Ratsherrn Johann Schütte, die das Backrecht ihres Hauses in der Lübschen Straße auf das Haus des Losbäckers Jacob Detlef Paries in der Dankwartstraße übertragen wollte, aber keine Antwort auf ihre im Oktober 1719 gestellte Anfrage erhielt (AHW, Prozessakten des Tribunals, Nr. 0277).

dass die Parteien mit dieser Art der Gerichtsausübung hochgradig unzufrieden waren und sich sehr häufig beschwerten. Dementsprechend groß war die Erleichterung, als die Schweden zurückkehrten und das Tribunal im Januar 1721 seine Tätigkeit unter blau-gelber Fahne, mit klarer Zuständigkeit, aber deutlich abgespeckt und seines früheren Glanzes beraubt, endlich wieder aufnahm.[42]

Resümierend ist festzuhalten, dass vor allem den pommerschen und mecklenburgischen Untertanen der schwedischen Krone während der letzten Phase des Nordischen Krieges sehr schnell klargemacht wurde, was sie bisher an ihrem obersten Gericht gehabt hatten. Schnelle, ausgewogene und kompetente Entscheidungen waren angesichts ungeregelter Herrschaftsverhältnisse von den Besatzern nicht zu erwarten. So verwundert es nicht, dass die Bremer und Verdener, die bereits 1715 von den dänischen Eroberern an Kurhannover als neuen Landesherrn übergingen, die Umstellung der Gerichtszuständigkeit am wenigsten bemerkten. Sie trafen auf klare, moderne Gerichtsstrukturen, die erst kurz zuvor nach dem Vorbild des Tribunals eingerichtet worden waren. Die Bewohner des Oderstreifens konnten zwar an ein funktionierendes Hofgericht verwiesen werden, es war aber unklar, welche Appellationsprivilegien für sie galten und ob diese durchgesetzt werden konnten. Zudem hatte der preußische König massiv in die Gerichtskompetenzen eingegriffen und die Verhältnisse zwischen Hofgericht und Landesregierung verwirrt. Wie sich dies auswirkte, wissen wir aufgrund der fehlenden Akten nicht.

Gänzlich unbefriedigend war die Situation für Altvorpommern und Rügen. Mit Hofgericht und Konsistorium verweigerte sich die mittlere Gerichtsebene der neuen Herrschaft, der letztinstanzlichen Rechtsprechung fehlte also die strukturelle Basis, es war auch nicht klar, auf welcher Grundlage diese erfolgen sollte. Von Dänemark war das Territorium zu weit entfernt, um die Parteien dorthin verweisen zu können, man hatte bis zur Rückgabe an die Schweden den Ehrgeiz, das Problem aus eigener Kraft zu beseitigen.

In der Herrschaft Wismar dauerte es hingegen mehrere Jahre, bis die aus zwei Personen bestehende Zivilverwaltung endlich auch als Oberappellationsgericht tätig wurde, fast muss man sagen, tätig werden musste. Seit Ende 1718 bearbeitete sie nach unklaren Auswahlkriterien einzelne Prozesse in durchaus respektabler Qualität, ließ die Bewohner der Herrschaft mit der Masse ihrer als minderwichtig oder für eine schnelle Entscheidung zu kompliziert eingeschätzten Probleme aber weitgehend allein. Insofern war das Aufatmen in Vorpommern und Wismar über die Rückkehr der Schweden und die damit verbundenen geordneten und erprobten Verhältnisse nur zu verständlich.

Dass eine geordnete Rechtsprechung in Kriegszeiten schwer zu organisieren ist, ist mit Sicherheit keine neue Erkenntnis. Hier sollte der interessante Fall vorgestellt werden, dass verschiedene Eroberer auf verschiedene Art mit diesem Problem umgingen. Offenbar ist, dass sich der sehr unterschiedliche Erfolg dadurch erklären

---

[42] *Jörn*, Tribunal (oben Fn. 1), S. 319–328.

lässt, wie sicher sich die Besatzer einer bleibenden Einverleibung des betreffenden Territoriums in ihren Herrschaftsverband sein konnten und wie modern die Gerichtsverfassung in dem Territorium war, an das die Parteien aus den besetzten Gebieten verwiesen wurden.

The Jurisdiction of Secular and Ecclesiastical Courts in the Grand Duchy of Lithuania

Rusnė Juozapaitienė

I. Introduction

The competence of secular and ecclesiastical (spiritual) courts in the Grand Duchy of Lithuania has not yet been in the focus of Lithuanian academic literature. Most often authors just shortly touch upon this issue while examining other aspects of the relationship between the state and the church. Among the latest academic research, articles of Yevgeniy Makhovenko,[1] Professor at the Faculty of Law of the Vilnius University, are worth to be mentioned, but attention to the problem is paid in such articles only in the general sense.

The aim of this contribution to the proceedings is to analyse the jurisdiction of secular and ecclesiastical (spiritual) courts as they are reflected in the legal sources. The primary example is the normative law in the Grand Duchy of Lithuania (further – GDL) in the 16th century concerning marriage and family cases. The legal practice is not in the center of this research. Traditionally it is believed that all marriage and family cases were settled only in ecclesiastical courts. As the jurisdiction of secular and ecclesiastical courts was not clearly delimitated in the Grand Duchy of Lithuania, various rules of law (legal provisions) of the Grand Duchy of Lithuania are analysed, which help to determine the competence of relevant courts. In order to enable better understanding of the jurisdictional questions, especially in marriage and family cases, the context is extended by historical, comparative and synthetic methods.

The object of the article is the body of legal rules (legal provisions) of the Grand Duchy of Lithuania determining the jurisdiction of secular and ecclesiastical courts in marriage and family cases.

The basic sources are the main publications of the texts of the three Statutes of Lithuania, resolutions of the Grand Dukes and the Seimas, the case law and academic literature. Unless specified otherwise, the following editions of the Statutes were used in this paper: FLS[2] – *First Lithuanian Statute (1529)*,[3] SLS – *Статут Вялікага княства Літоўскага 1566 года*[4], TLS – *Statute of Lithuania 1588*.[5]

---

[1] *J. Machovenko*, Pasaulietinių ir bažnytinių teismų kompetencijos atribojimas Lietuvos Didžiojoje kunigaikštystėje [Delimitation of the competence of secular and ecclesiastical courts in the Grand Duchy of Lithuania] // Teisė, No. 43, 2002, pp. 117–127; *J. Machovenko*, Viduramžių Vilniaus universiteto teismas pasaulietinės ir bažnytinės jurisdikcijos atskyrimo kontekstu [The medieval court of the Vilnius University in the context of delimitation of the secular and ecclesiastical jurisdiction] // Teisė, No. 74, 2010, pp. 57–65.

[2] FLS – First Lithuanian Statute, SLS – Second Lithuanian Statute, TLS – Third Lithuanian Statute.

II. The Jurisdiction of Ecclesiastical Courts of the Grand Duchy of Lithuania

1. Jurisdiction of Catholic Ecclesiastical Courts in Western Europe

The jurisdiction of Catholic ecclesiastical courts in Europe was very broad during the 13th and 14th century. Their competence included: cases regarding religious offences (*crimina ecclesiastica*); heresy, apostasy (gr. Apostasis), usury, desecration of church persons or things; incest, adultery, polygamy, violation of ecclesiastical hierarchical interests (violation of the freedom of ecclesiastical elections and provisions on celibacy); besides, cases regarding actions in violation of Christian customs and morality; cases regarding complex crimes: murders, robbery, false oath, insulting the God, abduction of a woman, public insult, arson, duels, etc. In case of the latter crimes, the church used to recognise the case to be in principle finished (*exceptio rei iudicatae*), if the secular court had already passed a relevant verdict, but in practice ecclesiastical courts often examined the case anew if the crime was more relevant to ecclesiastical interests.[6]

According to the tradition in Christian countries, the jurisdiction of ecclesiastical courts is to be divided into three categories: 1) *narrow* jurisdiction for all Christians in a certain territory concerning issues of religion and morality, family and marriage; 2) *full* jurisdiction for all clergymen and *church* people; 3) *broad* jurisdiction for all people residing in the lands owned by the church.[7]

The judicial bodies of the church were the supreme administration – bishops, who had assistants – representatives starting from the 13th century. Cases concerning marriage legitimacy, marriage termination fell within their competence. In the Grand Duchy of Lithuania all property issues in connection with marriage cases were referred to a relevant secular court: to a castle court – cases of all persons, to the land court – cases of noblemen, to magistrates' court – cases of townspeople of towns with Magdeburg rights, also to *pakamaris'* court, commissioners' court and

---

3 *Irena Valikonytė/Stanislovas Lazutka/Edvardas Gudavičius*, Pirmasis Lietuvos Statutas [First Lithuanian Statute], Vilnius 2001.

4 *Доўнар, Таісія Іванаўна*, Статут Вялікага княства Літоўскага 1566 года/Т.І. Доўнар, У.М. Сатолін, Я.А. Юхо. Мінск: ТЭСЕЙ. 2003 [Dounar Taisia Ivanovna, Statute of the Grand Duchy of Lithuania 1566, T. I., Minsk 2003].

5 *Лаппо, Иван Иванович*, 1869–1944. 1588 metų Lietuvos Statutas. Kaunas T. 2. Švietimo m-jos Knygų leid. komisija, 1938 [Ivan Ivanovich Lappo, 1869–1944. Statute of Lithuania, 1588, Kaunas V. 2, 1938].

6 *P. Pakarklis*, Ekonominė ir teisinė katalikų bažnyčios padėtis Lietuvoje (XV–XIX a. vid.) [Economic and legal situation of the Catholic Church in Lithuania (the 15th century – the middle of the 19th century)], Vilnius 1955, p. 33.

7 *Дзербіна Галіна*, Права І Сямя у Беларусі эпохі Рэнесансу. Менск, Тэхналогія. 1997 [Derbina Galina, Law and Family in Belarussia during Renaissance, Minsk 1997], p. 60.

the Supreme Tribunal of Lithuania.[8] Such distribution of jurisdiction was also provided for in the TLS (TLS III, 31–34).[9] According to the TLS, all persons residing on church lands were subordinate to an ecclesiastical court in all cases, both civil and criminal. The ecclesiastical court used to settle civil cases not related to clergymen and real property according to the secular law (TLS III 32–32). But in practice clergymen often took part in secular courts, especially if cases which were related to interests of the church or to people subordinate to the church, also if civil judges invited clergymen for examination of complicated cases, as well-educated jurists could be found among clergymen.[10]

2. Rules of Law regulating the Jurisdiction of Secular and Ecclesiastical Courts in the Grand Duchy of Lithuania

a) Customary Law

Till the middle of the 16th century, the main source of law in the Grand Duchy of Lithuania was local customs.[11] But the customary law was not uniform. It consisted of customs of different territorial units – regions or lands. In the Slavonic lands of the Grand Duchy of Lithuania the customary law which formed itself in the Kievan Rus during the 9th to the 12th century was applicable, later it was replaced with the legislation of the Grand Dukes. Usually it manifested itself as decisions of courts, and later as the legislation issued by dukes (Vladimir Svetoslavich, Yaroslav, etc). The jurisdiction of ecclesiastical courts was separated for the first time in the Statute of Vladimir.[12] Later on, Grand Dukes issued laws not only in the Slavonic lands of the Grand Duchy of Lithuania, starting from the 14th century the rulers of the Grand Duchy of Lithuania regularly issued legal acts which reduced particularism in law. Local courts and dukes' courts referred to territorial customs. In the Lithuanian part of the Grand Duchy of Lithuania there were no sets of customary law. Only in Slavonic lands, the *Russian Truth (Russkaja Pravda)* was applicable. It is a set of customs formed in the Kievan Rus during the 11th and 12th century, which was supplemented with dukes' laws and court decisions.

The Statutes of Lithuania in essence eliminated the use of customs. But the rules of the Statutes could not regulate all the relationships in the society, therefore the rules of the Statutes permitted use of the customs (FLS VI 3, 5, XIII 24), the

---

8 *Дзербіна Галіна*, Права I Сямя (supra fn. 7), p. 61.

9 Here and further in the text Roman numbers are used to mark chapters of the Statute, Arabic numbers – articles of the Statute, without specifying the page of the quoted publication.

10 *Дзербіна Галіна*, Права I Сямя (supra fn. 7), p. 61.

11 *J. Machovenko*, Lietuvos Didžiosios Kunigaikštystės teisės šaltiniai [Sources of law of the Grand Duchy of Lithuania], Vilnius 2000, p. 9.

12 Уставь Святого Великаго князя Владиміра о церковныхь судахь и о десятинахь. Изданіе Императорской Археографической Коммиссіи. Петроградь 1915 [Statute of the Holy Grand Duke Vladimir about the church courts and tithes, edition by the Imperial Archeographic Commission, Petrograd 1915], p. 10.

conscience of judges and examples of other Christian countries (FLS VI 1, 6, 26; SLS IV 30; TLS IV 54). All cases not yet provided for had to be discussed in the nearest Seimas and entered into laws (FLS VI 5).

b) Rules of the Law of Privileges

From the very Catholic christening of Lithuania, the situation (especially the legal one) of the Catholic Church and Catholic feudal lords differed from the situation of laymen. The Grand Duke of Lithuania Jogaila granted its first privilege to Catholic noblemen (20 February 1387), by this privilege he confirmed the title of the feudal lords to their patrimonial estate and land acquired in any other manner, acknowledged their right to transfer it to others or bequeath it to their heirs, released them from duties in kind to the Grand Duke. Besides, Catholic noblemen were granted the right to give their daughters and other women relatives in marriage at their own discretion. So, the prestige and prerogatives of belonging to the Catholic religion were emphasized *de facto* and *de jure*. For example, Jogaila's letter of 22 February 1387 provided for whipping with the rod of those who refused Catholicism in order to marry Orthodox women.

Catholic clergymen as feudal lords were in essence a privileged estate even between feudal lords, their legal status differed from that of laymen. The privilege given by Jogaila on 17 February 1387 gave the absolute ownership of land to the Catholic Church for all times. The land managed by Catholic churches, monasteries and convents, and by clergymen was released from duties to the Grand Duke, to the state and from the court of the Grand Duke. The clergymen were given absolute immunity in their lands.

> "We release, exempt, announce to be free all the areas of ownership, estates with their population and everything else, what is given and entered into books for the honour of God, to those churches […], for now and in the future, from all services to us and to successive Grand Dukes of Lithuania, etc., […], from *our stewards' courts*, from official punishments and fines administered through executors […]."[13]

c) Rules of the Statutes of Lithuania

The secular law of the Grand Duchy of Lithuania specifically emphasized the competence only of secular courts, whereas the competence of ecclesiastical or spiritual courts was mostly determined by the customary law and the canon law. Since the middle of the 16th century, the legal system of the GDL positively belonged to the Western legal tradition as defined by H. Berman.[14] The scholars of the GDL demonstrated perfect knowledge of the Western legal system, often referred to the works of Cicero, Aristotle, Demosthenes, Thomas Aquinas etc.[15] In

---

[13] Lietuvos TSR istorijos šaltiniai [Sources of history of Lithuanian SSR], Vilnius 1955, pp. 67–68.

[14] *Jevgenij Machovenko*, Law Faculty of Vilnius University in 1641–2010, Vilnius 2011, p. 34.

[15] Ibid.

the 16th century, the public attitude towards the Roman law was dominantly positive. Augustinas Rotundus, Petras Roizijus and Mykolas Lietuvis proposed to refer to Roman law in order to develop Lithuanian law.

The First Statute of Lithuania came into power in 1529 and began the epoch of codification of the legal acts. At that time, the normative legal act became the prevailing source of the rules of law in Lithuania. According to Professor Yevgeniy Makhovenko, this process began in Europe only in the 18th century when different normative legal acts in the GDL had already been codified into a hierarchical system surmounted with a constitution.[16] On a plan of subsystems (legislation, jurisdiction and jurisprudence), the legal system of the GDL belonged to the continental branch of the Western law.

FLS III 4 lists all stewards, the courts of which are preserved by the Grand Duke of Lithuania – of Vilnius, Trakai, "[…] we do not in any way diminish […]"[17] other voivode districts and *kashteliones'*, and the chancery, and land Marshals' and estate Marshal's offices, and elders' offices, and our stewards, all they can judge in their administrative districts according to the written law, i.e. this Statute.

The FLS contains few rules intended for deciding cases pertaining to members of the clergy. For example, Article 19 of FLS VI establishes that townspeople of all subordinate towns, both clergymen and laymen, must administer justice in case of injuries and murders according to the land law. FLS VIII 1 regulates uniform rights and duties both of clergymen and of other persons in land cases. Article 9 of FLS I establishes that in the Grand Duchy of Lithuania all persons are to be judged according to the same written law.[18]

The rules of the Statutes of Lithuania often mention courts, but usually it is not indicated specifically what kind of court that is, for example, FLS II 12, 13, 16. Rules on jurisdiction of courts can be found in various chapters of the Statutes, but only some of the rules indicate a specific court in family and marriage cases, e.g.:

if a widow with small children manages property improperly, "[…] uncles, and if there are none, then other relatives must call her *to the presence of us, the ruler, or to the presence of lord councillors* […]" (FLS IV 6);

if a full-aged girl is prevented by uncles or brothers from getting married, she must address other relatives or the *steward*, and the steward or her relatives must allow her to get married. If she marries without a will of her relatives or the steward regarding this, then she will lose her estates (FLS IV 11);

father and mother cannot remove son or daughter from the patrimonial estate by a will (testament), but must "[…] *in the presence of us, the ruler, or in the*

[16] Ibid., p. 36.

[17] *Valikonytė/Lazutka/Gudavičius*, Pirmasis Lietuvos Statutas (supra fn. 3), p. 149.

[18] Ibid., p. 149.

presence of the steward […]" notify about that and specify proper measures of removal (FLS IV 13);

if the guardian of underage children loses some or all of their property, then they, when already adult, can "[…] *in the presence of their steward* […]" seek justice, that the guardian did not find even in court (FLS V 1).

The rule of FLS III 12, though it does not directly define the jurisdiction of courts, regulates that a case of unlawful slander to the effect that a person is an illegitimate child, or in what case a child is to be regarded illegitimate, is to be settled in court. A rule regarding raping of a woman or a girl is also attributable to family cases. The aggrieved woman should institute a case in court against the offender (FLS VII 6) and give an oath in the presence of two to three witnesses.

Chapter VI of the FLS is called "About judges", but it almost does not regulate any issues of family or marriage cases. Chapter VI of the FLS is intended for regulation of courts' work. First of all, it is established that all judges (voivode, elder, land or estate Marshal, etc.) must judge according to written laws, i.e. according to this Statute, and only if the decision is taken not according to these rules, it can be appealed to the court of the ruler or, in his absence, to the court of the council of lords (FLS VI 1). Thus, a court of appellate instance, as it is understood now, was not provided for. Only incorrect application of the rules could be appealed against. Also, it was not allowed to appeal to the King or to the Seimas in the course of the examination of the case (proceedings) (FLS VI 2).

Chapter VIII of the FLS is devoted to land courts. It is determined that persons of any estate, as well as bishops and clergymen, both of the Roman [Catholic] and Greek [Orthodox] religion, are to settle a dispute concerning land in the same court (FLS VIII 1), and only persons of the Roman [Catholic] and Greek [Orthodox] religion can serve as witnesses (FLS VIII 5).

The SLS did not define the exact jurisdiction of ecclesiastical courts. Article 26 of SLS III delimits the competence of ecclesiastical and secular courts, prohibiting the clergymen from inviting laymen to the ecclesiastical court and the laymen from addressing the ecclesiastical court on a secular matter.[19] On the other hand, the very clergymen did not want to be invited to a court of an administrative district concerning land issues, but sought that cases be settled by the court of the Grand Duke. The courts of the Grand Duchy of Lithuania were of an estate character, whereas the court of the Grand Duke acted as an appellate court, which reviewed decisions of the estate courts, and as a court of first instance in certain important cases (crimes to the state). Also, the Grand Duke, as the patron of all the churches, sometimes used to settle internal church disputes. Chapter IV of the SLS is devoted to regulation of court activities and the judicial process, but the ecclesiastical

---

[19] Statut Litewski drugiej redakcyi (1566) [Second Editor's Statute of Lithuania], in: Archiwum Komisyi Prawniczej. T. 7. Krakow 1900, p. 58.

(spiritual) court is not mentioned in this chapter. For example, Article 70 of SLS IV determines the cases falling within the jurisdiction of a *pakamaris'* court.

As for the marriage and family issues, the rules of the SLS are similar:

If a girl marries against her parents' will, she loses a dowry and the right to inherit both her father's and her mother's property (SLS V 7);

if a widow remarries earlier than six months after her husband's death, she loses her *veno*[20], and if she has now dower then she has to pay a fine 20 *rubli* of *groshy* (SLS V 12);

reasons are listed when parents may take away the right of property inheritance from their children, for example, if a son raises his hand against his father or criminally takes estates away from his father; if he does a great wrong; if a son or daughter entrenches upon father or mother not because of a matter of the Republic of Both Nations, but because of their bad will; if a girl wantons or disobeys her parents and does not get married till she is 25; if children do not want to free their captivated parents', though they control their estates; if they do not follow the Christian religion (SLS VIII 7);

if a girl, after her parents died, marries against the will of her brothers and other relatives, she loses her dower and other parental property; and if she is full-aged (15 years) and her brothers and other relatives prevent her from marrying, she must address *a steward*; whereas brothers and other relatives must hold their sisters and unmarried girls in respect, and if they fail to do that, such girls can independently live in their domains, that would belong to them as inheritance, with a guardian appointed by the steward, until they get married (SLS V 8);

if someone married a girl, widow or fiancé by force and this comes to the knowledge of *the ruler or the council of lords* or *the steward*, then the aggrieved woman must be separated (взята до секвестру), whereas the wrongdoer must be hanged, one third of his property going to the ownership of the aggrieved woman as the compensation. But if the girl agreed to marry herself and concealed that from her parents, she loses property as that is established in Chapter V of the SLS (SLS XI 9);

if a free person marries a serf, then both he/she and his/her children becomes serfs. But if a free person did not know that he/she married a serf and, upon becoming aware of this, does not want to live together, then the *spiritual* court must

---

[20] *Veno* was a kind of compensation for the property that a woman brought into the marriage plus some of the husband's property, which she would receive in the case of widowhood if she had a *veno* contract. The *dowry* means the property received by a woman from her native family upon her marriage and the *dower* means the property assigned to a woman by her husband as a security for the *dowry* received (This explanation is taken from the article of *J. Kunsmanaitė*, Widows, property, and law in Lithuania and some other countries, in: Mia Korpiola (ed.), Regional Variation in Matrimonial Law and Custom in Europe, 1150–1600, Boston 2011).

divorce them, and the free person remains free and the serf remains a serf (SLS XII 13).

Divorce cases are settled in the *spiritual* court according to the Christian law. If a husband is guilty according to the *spiritual* (i.e. canon) law, then his property remains to his wife; and if the wife is guilty, she loses her dowry. And if divorce is permissible (слушный розводь), then the *veno* remains with the husband, and the dowry (внесенье) – with the wife (SLS V 18). Divorce was permissible if the marriage was entered into ignoring the effective rules.[21]

Only in 1563 the Trident Church Assembly passed a resolution instructing to register all marriages and christening in church. Most probably, till then marriages were entered into under the secular procedure, and any disputes, violations of the christening and marriage rules, presumably, could be solved on the initiative of one of the spouses or his/her relatives or on the initiative of a church organisation, but in the secular court though.[22] Starting with the SLS, the state of the Grand Duchy of Lithuania admitted marriage to be a matter of the church, and transferred the issues of its implementation to the ecclesiastical court, in this way indirectly acknowledging the validity of the canon law in the Grand Duchy of Lithuania. Meanwhile, the related property issues remained within the competence of secular courts. In Professor V. Andriulis' opinion such delimitation of secular and spiritual courts, threatening clergymen with punishments, allows stating that before the SLS, the divorce cases could be settled in the secular court.[23]

The TLS, differently from the earlier Statutes, pays more attention to the relationship of the state and the church. TLS III 3 announces peace among infidels and the respect for the Christian belief. As the text of the SLS included the privilege of 7 June 1563, equating the rights of Catholic and Orthodox feudal lords, then the text of the TLS includes the 1573 Warsaw Confederation Act on the freedom of the choice of religion, speaking about all Christian religions, i.e. reformationists, too.[24]

On 24 December 1584, in Volkovyskas' General Seimas the noblemen and the clergymen agreed on the competence of secular and ecclesiastical courts and these rules were included into the TLS. But the TLS did not list specific cases falling

---

[21] *Доўнар, Таісія Іванаўна*. Статут Вялікага княства Літоўскага 1566 года/Т.І. Доўнар, У.М. Сатолін, Я.А. Юхо. Мінск: ТЭСЕЙ. [Dounar Taisia Ivanovna, Statute of Grand Duchy of Lithuania 1566, Minsk 2003], p. 295.

[22] *V. Andriulis*, Lietuvos Statutų (1529, 1566, 1588 m.) šeimos teisė. Vilnius: Teisinės informacijos centras [Family law in the Statute of Lithuania (1529, 1566, 1588)], Vilnius 2003, p. 125.

[23] Ibid., p. 128.

[24] *J. Jurginis*, Valstybės ir bažnyčios santykiai trečiajame Lietuvos Statute, in: TLS konferencijos medžiaga [State and church relations in the Third Lithuanian Statute, in: Third Lithuanian Statute, 1588] = Третий Литовский статут 1588 года [material of the republican academic conference intended for commemoration of the 400th anniversary of the Third Statute; Vilnius University, Institute of History of the Academy of Sciences of the Soviet Socialist Republic of Lithuania], Vilnius 1989, p. 11.

within the competence of the ecclesiastical courts, either it only confirmed the right to judge clergymen and laymen according to the rules of the canon law (TLS III 26, 31, 32). It was established when clergymen must address or must be invited to the secular court or when disputes of clergymen and laymen are to be examined in the ecclesiastical court according to the secular law (TLS III 32): a layman subordinate to the church was judged for certain offences in the ecclesiastical court according to the secular law (the Lithuanian Statute). The rules of the TLS regarding the competence of ecclesiastical courts had a halfway character.[25] The TLS expanded the jurisdiction of secular courts. The jurisdiction of ecclesiastical courts became narrower, as the cases of attacking a church, incest, bigamy, abduction of other man's wife, marital infidelity, raping, violation of conditions of entering into marriage, harlotry, witchcraft, persuading a Christian to accept the Jewish or Muslim religion, pimping were assigned to the competence of secular courts:

Jews, Tartars and other Muslims (Massulmans) cannot have Christian slaves, and if they buy such, they have to set them free; and if they buy any other slaves, they cannot force them or their children to accept their religion (SLS XII 5, TLS XII 9);

each master judges his subordinates in his domain for wrongdoings suffered both by laymen and by clergymen, i.e. clergymen are judged by the *spiritual* court, whereas laymen are judged by the court of their lord, and if a clergyman does not want to judge, the bishop's court is to be addressed, which must judge according to the law of the republic and the land Statute (TLS III 32);

article 30 of TLS IV specified in detail what crimes fall within jurisdiction of what court, for example, cases of doing wrong to (raping of) girls and brides or cases of herbalism are attributable to the courts of voivode districts and elders' offices (воеводове и старостовое наши судовие);

everyone must live in marriage according to the godly and Christian law, there must be no incest up to four generations and men must not wish wives of their brothers and other relatives up to three generations, those who enter into an incest marriage, are judged by the land *steward*, one half of their property goes to the needs of the state or the ruler, whereas the other half of their property remain with them only till the end of their life. If a woman knew that she was marrying a close relative according to blood, she was also losing her dowry. Such a marriage must be terminated, and children do not just have any right to property, but also are regarded illegitimate. But if they did not know they were living in incest, they must give an oath in the presence of witnesses and then they do not lose property, but they must still be divorced. And if they want to enter into another marriage, that must be solved according to the *spiritual* law. And if someone marries for the second time while the first wife is still alive, he must be hanged, also his wife, if she married being aware that the first wife was still alive (TLS V 22);

---

[25] *Machovenko*, Pasaulietinių ir bažnytinių teismų kompetencijos atribojimas (supra fn. 1), p. 126.

if a crime is committed in a Christian church, punishment must be the same as for the same crime in the nobleman's house (TLS XI 3);

if someone runs away with another man's wife, he must be punished by the town *steward* and both must be hanged, but if the husband does not want his wife to be hanged – she must remain at his will. If the man who ran away or the chasing man was killed, the punishment must be under Article 30 below (TLS XIV 29);

if a person suspected his/her spouse of infidelity and with witnesses found him/her in adultery, then they must be delivered to the town *steward* and evidence must be given there, and then both the sinners must be hanged; and if the running adulterer was killed, then the decision is to be made as in the analogous situation of attacking a noblemen's estate (TLS XIV 30);

harlots/seductresses are punished by *voivode, eldership and local stewards* by cutting their nose, ear and lips and are driven away from that locality, and if they continue engaging in their business – they must be hanged (TLS XIV 31);

if someone kills an illegitimate child, he is released from punishment by hanging, and if the mother of such an illegitimate child is still alive, she may demand money for his head as for a man of simple estate (TLS XIV 32).

Though the TLS assigned more marriage and family cases to the jurisdiction of secular courts, as indicated in the examples above, but ecclesiastical courts in their domains often used to ignore these restrictions.[26]

d) Resolutions of the Seimas

Noblemen were dissatisfied with the broad jurisdiction of ecclesiastical courts, this dissatisfaction especially gained force in the 16th century, when the very estate of noblemen got stronger. Noblemen sought an estate court for themselves and clear jurisdiction of secular and ecclesiastical courts. There was a constant fight between clergymen and laymen regarding settlement of secular issues, which was also reflected in sources of the secular law. The constitution adopted in the Krakow Seimas in 1543 set strict limits of competence of ecclesiastical courts and big fines for their violation.[27] This resolution lists crimes, which come into the jurisdiction of ecclesiastical courts: for example, heresy (haeresis), schism (schisma), blasphemy (blasphemia), apostasy (apostasia), simony, etc.[28] This resolution also emphasizes that divorce cases fall within the jurisdiction of the ecclesiastical court, but the issue of dowry (dos) – to the Tribunal (*Cognitio tamen seu judicium de dote personae per divortium separatae, remiti debet ad Tribunal S. M. Regiae: secundum veterem*

[26] *J. Machovenko*, Teisingumo vykdymas Lietuvos Didžiojoje kunigaikštystėje. Diskusiniai klausimai [Administration of Justice in the Grand Duchy of Lithuania. Polemic Issues], Vilnius 2007, p. 66.

[27] Volumina legum. 1347–1547. Petersburg, 1859. T. 1. pp. 283–284, point 578.

[28] Ibid.

consuctudinem). A claim was made in the Brest Seimas of 1544 that neither laymen nor clergymen could hold a layman liable before an ecclesiastical court due to secular matters. The Seimas adopted a resolution that laymen could be judged in ecclesiastical courts only concerning spiritual matters.[29] The same resolution was adopted in the Seimas of 1547. In the Vilnius Seimas of 1547 noblemen asked Žygimantas Augustas to remove clergymen from secular courts, and the Grand Duke of the Grand Duchy of Lithuania and King of Poland upheld the validity of the resolutions of the Brest Seimas.[30] The Vilnius Seimas of 1551 adopted a new resolution that no layman could hold another layman liable before an ecclesiastical court due to a secular matter, also that clergymen cannot call another layman to an ecclesiastical court because of a layman's complaint,[31] so laymen cannot be invited to an ecclesiastical court to give an oath.[32]

In the Seimas of 1551 it was also decided that widows cannot themselves, without an approval of their relatives, give their daughters in marriage. If the parties do not agree among themselves, they must address *the ruler's* court, and in his absence, the court of the *administrative district.*[33]

According to the resolution of the Second Vilnius Seimas of 1551, in criminal cases persons subordinate to ecclesiastical feudal lords had to be judged in towns with Magdeburg rights by an ecclesiastical court, but according to secular, not canon law.[34]

e) Decisions of Grand Dukes

The ruler or the secular authority was an arbitrator between secular and ecclesiastical feudal lords, strictly adhering to the rules of laws on the jurisdiction of the church, for example, Žygimantas Augustas confirmed that laymen cannot be invited to an ecclesiastical court according to the canon law.[35] The interesting thing is that Žygimantas Augustas in his letters to the metropolitan of Kiev writes "… according to your Greek law …",[36] i.e. the Orthodox canon law was considered as the successor to the Greek traditions.

---

[29] Zbior praw litewskich od roku 1389– do roku 1529 tudziez rosprawy seimowe o tychze prawach od roku 1544 do roku 1563 (further ZPL) [Lithuanian Laws Collection since 1389 till 1529 and Resolutions of Seimas about these rights since 1544 till 1563], Poznan 1841, pp. 430 sq.

[30] Акты, относящіеся къ исторіи Западной Россіи, собранные и изданные Археографическою Коммиссіею. Т. III. 1544–1587. Санктпетербургъ, 1848 [Acts pertaining to the history of the Western Russia, collected and issued by the Archeographic Commission. V. III. 1544–1587], St. Petersburg 1848, p. 3, 11, appeal/request 16.

[31] Ibid.; ZPL 446.

[32] Ibid.

[33] Ibid.

[34] Ibid., p. 28.

[35] Ibid., p. 12.

[36] Ibid., p. 3.

In 1445 Žygimantas Augustas sent a letter to the metropolitan Makarij of Kiev regarding the complaint of the noblewoman Tomila Gitovtovna (Томила [К]Гитовтовна) to the effect that the Polock archbishop Simeon terminated her marriage with the metropolitan's son Ivan, with whom she had lived in marriage for 18 years. The said Ivan was constantly beating and doing other harm to her and Tomila Gitovtovna complained to the Polock archbishop Simeon and asked him to give her husband a lesson and order him to live with her in unison "according to law". But the archbishop Simeon, not according to the Christian customs and not according to the Greek laws of Holy Fathers, divorced her and Ivan and allowed him to marry his own sister. Tomila Gitovtovna asked archbishop Simeon to give her a letter, on what grounds he divorced her from her husband, but he did not give any. Besides, Ivan drove her out of their home and she had lots of debts. Žygimantas Augustas asked the metropolitan Makarij of Kiev to call the Polock archbishop Simeon and to examine this divorce case and compensation for damages "according to customs and the cannon law" (водле обычаю закону и права вашего духовного) so that in the future archbishops would strictly adhere to the requirements of the canon law, would not unlawfully divorce spouses and would not permit living without marriage.[37]

The Catholic canon law, sanctioned by the rulers of the Grand Duchy of Lithuania, was applicable in spiritual courts to all clergymen and subordinates of the Church, and in cases of religious crimes, marriage and family relations – also in case of persons not subordinate to the Church. A Letter of Žygimantas I of 19 May 1542 announces that all bishops of the Grand Duchy of Lithuania must interrogate and judge all persons suspected of heresy according to the canon law, whereas the local authorities must assist them in this.[38]

On 7 December 1548 Žygimantas Augustas, referring to the letter of the Vilnius bishop Duke Paulius (Павель), saying that Christian women live with Jews, Tartars and Turkish without marrying, and their children are baptised according to their fathers' religion, prohibited doing that.[39] On 15 March 1549 Žygimantas Augustas with his letter to the rulers of Gomel confirmed the right not to judge Church people.[40] In his letter of 23 December 1568 Žygimantas Augustas permitted Orthodox hierarchs to judge offenders according to the canon law of the Greek ceremonial church and obligated the elders to assist them.[41]

---

[37] Ibid., p. 2.

[38] *J. Jurginis*, Lietuvos krikštas. Feodalinės visuomenės socialinės ir kultūrinės raidos studija [Christening of Lithuania. Study of Social and Cultural Development of the Feudal Society], Vilnius 1987, p. 268.

[39] Акты, относящіеся кь исторіи Западной Россіи (supra fn. 30), p. 20.

[40] Ibid., p. 21.

[41] *Machovenko*, Pasaulietinių ir bažnytinių teismų kompetencijos atribojimas (supra fn. 1), p. 119.

f) Case Practice of the Grand Duchy of Lithuania

As the economic influence of the church was getting stronger, it sought to take over more or more secular cases. Ecclesiastical courts in their domains acted as patrimonial courts. In the middle of the 16th century one third of all the land belonged to the Catholic Church. According to the privileges of the Grand Duke of 1387, 1542, the ecclesiastical courts used to settle civil and criminal cases of members of the clergymen estate concerning violations of the state law, all cases of peasants in the estates of the church. From 1576 on only an ecclesiastical court could judge clergymen for all crimes.[42] During the 16th to the 18th century the ecclesiastical Catholic courts exercised influence on the state courts and the Grand Duke, in this way determining their decisions in cases concerning violation of religious dogmas.

Catholic feudal lords had their ecclesiastical courts and did not fall into the jurisdiction of secular courts. Therefore, they often managed to avoid a real punishment for severe crimes. For example, in 1575 the canon Gureckas raped a girl, but as a clergyman he could not be held liable before a secular court. Only following a great indignation in the society, his case was examined by the Chapter of the Vilnius Diocese. Gureckas was given the following punishments: he had to be warned by one of his colleagues, telling him to be more reserved in the future; he was obligated to buy a white chasuble for St. Virgin Magdalene's Church; he was prohibited from entering the church and leaving his home in general for four weeks.[43] For comparison, according to the secular criminal law of those times, a layman was punishable by death for raping, and if there were witnesses and the agrieved was calling for help, a fine was also imposed for disgrace.[44]

Cases of heresy were settled by spiritual courts. Heretics were punishable with property forfeiture according to the privilege of Jogaila of 1433. But noblemen, disagreeing to such a decision, used to refer to the privilege of Jogaila of 1422, which said that the property of noblemen would never be forfeited, stating that they were punished in an ecclesiastical court and, therefore, such a decision had no civil consequences. There was much dispute on this issue in the Seimas of 1519, 1532, 1533.

A case of incest was solved from 1621 to 1623. The Kaunas parson Bartolomėjus Ciešinskis accused Kaunas Lutherans Friderikas Korsakas, Jonas Kalau and

---

[42] *J. Sideravičius*, Katalikų bažnyčios statusas politinėje feodalinės visuomenės organizacijoje. In Krikščionybė ir jos socialinis vaidmuo Lietuvoje [Status of the Catholic Church in the political organisation of the feudal society. In Christianity and its social role in Lithuania], Vilnius 1986, p. 61.

[43] Описание рукописного отделения Виленской публичной библиотеки. Вильна: Типография А. Г. Сыркина, 1895. Выпуск I, С. 60, пункт 78 [Description of the Manuscripts Department of the Vilnius Public Library, Vilnius 1895, first edition].

[44] LTSR valstybės ir teisės istorija [History of the state and law of the Soviet Socialist Republic of Lithuania], Vilnius 1979, p. 79.

Jurgis Šeperis and their wives of incest.[45] The Lutherans reasoned that their religion and the regulations of the Consistory of Sambia permitted such marriages, but the decision of the Vilnius bishop Eustachijus Valavičius was unfavourable to them. The court of assessors of the Grand Duchy of Lithuania considered an appeal in 1623, but the court decided that townspeople of Kaunas were subordinate to the Grand Duchy of Lithuania, besides, the jurisdiction of the Catholic bishop in spiritual and marriage cases is valid for dissenters, too.[46]

g) Supreme Tribunal of Lithuania

After the Supreme Tribunal of Lithuania was established in 1581 a separate panel was formed in it for examination of clergymen's cases. When mixed cases of clergymen and noblemen were examined, six judges – members of the tribunal and representatives of four bishops and chapters had to sit on the panel. But soon the number of laymen and clergymen judges was made even – three on each side. This rule was recorded in Article 32 of the TLS.[47] In 1717 the Catholic Church achieved that tribunal judges should be only Catholics. The constitution of the Seimas of 1733 determined that members of the Seimas and members of the Tribunal may be only Catholics.[48]

For solving the issue of conflict of different jurisdictions, mixed courts were formed, for example the Spiritual Tribunal. The Spiritual Tribunal was a court of appellate instance in cases of clergymen and laymen, which were heard by a secular court as a first instance.[49] But disputes of clergymen with noblemen regarding estates donated by the ruler were settled in the *ruler's* estate (TLS III 23).[50] But such courts did not eliminate the problem; they only enabled settling specific disputes. The Statute of Vladimir already permitted formation of a mixed court for settlement of laymen's and clergymen's disputes. The spiritual court acted as a permanent appellate instance for settlement of laymen's and clergymen's disputes.

In the central courts of the Grand Duchy of Lithuania, in the court of assessors and the relational court of the Grand Duke, cases were settled between communities

---

[45] Extract from Kaunas bench court cases book. MACBRS, fund 43, case 9862. Cited from *Z. Kiaupa*, Kovos tarp liuteronų ir katalikų Kaune iki XVII a. vid. In Religinės kovos ir erezijos Lietuvoje [Fights between Lutherans and Catholics in Kaunas till the middle of the 17th century. In Religious fights and heresies in Lithuania], Vilnius 1977, p. 21.

[46] Decision of assessors' court of GDL, 1623. Lithuanian Metrica (LM) 302, pp. 86 sq. Cited from *Kiaupa*, ibid., p. 21.

[47] *A. Janulaitis*, Vyriausias Lietuvos Tribunolas XVI–XVIII a. Kaunas, 1927. Lietuvos Universiteto Teisių fakulteto darbai [Supreme Tribunal of Lithuania in the 16th–18th centuries], Kaunas 1927, t. 2. p. 84.

[48] *Jozafata Ohryzki* (ed.), Volumina legum. Petersburg [Volumina legum. 1347–1547. Petersburg], 1860. t. 6, p. 286, point 581.

[49] *Janulaitis*, Vyriausias Lietuvos Tribunolas XVI–XVIII (supra fn. 47), t. 2. pp. 70, 84.

[50] Ibid., p. 84.

of different confessions, e.g. Kaunas Catholics and Lutherans. In Kaunas Lutherans had to fight for their right to have their school, church, shelter throughout the 1st half of the 17th century. Lutherans also fought for townspeople's rights (the right to be citizens of the town and be elected to the town's municipality).

Broad jurisdiction of ecclesiastical courts remained till the very middle of the 19th century. For example, when examining cases of harlotry, in 1828 the Consistory of the Samogitian Diocese applied to the police for help, but as the police had doubts, the Consistory applied to the Board of Vilnius Government, which obligated the Telšiai police to fulfil this requirement.[51]

III. Conclusions

Traditionally it is believed that in Christian countries all marriage and family cases fell within the jurisdiction of an ecclesiastical court, but the analysis of legal rules of the Grand Duchy of Lithuania allows to arrive at the conclusion that often these issues were also settled in a secular court. For example, in certain cases the rules of the Statutes instructed to apply to a secular court of the ruler, the council of lords or the steward.

The analysis of the rules of the secular law of the Grand Duchy of Lithuania shows that the competence of ecclesiastical courts of the Grand Duchy of Lithuania was not strictly defined. In marriage and family cases some issues, for example, legitimacy of marriage, were settled in ecclesiastical courts, whereas property issues appeared in secular courts.

---

[51] *A. Janulaitis*, Kunigai ir 1831 m. Revoliucija Lietuvoje [Priests and Revolution of 1831 in Lithuania], Kaunas 1923, p. 49, no. 6.

Gerichtsverfassung und Zivilprozess in Mecklenburg im 19. Jahrhundert bis 1879

Hans-Georg Knothe

I. Einleitung

Die oft anzutreffende Einschätzung, die Zivilgerichtsbarkeit sei ihrer Natur nach unpolitisch und hauptsächlich von rechtstechnischen Gesichtspunkten bestimmt, hält, wie seit Längerem anerkannt ist, einer näheren Betrachtung nicht stand. Insbesondere im 19. Jahrhundert war die Frage nach Zweck und Ausgestaltung des Zivilverfahrens eng verbunden mit den (angesichts des damaligen Übergangs von der traditionellen monarchisch-ständischen Ordnung zum bürgerlichen Rechtsstaat) geführten politisch-ideologischen und verfassungsrechtlichen Auseinandersetzungen. Nicht zuletzt auf dieser Verbindung beruht der von *Knut Wolfgang Nörr* konstatierte Tatbestand, wonach keine rechtsgeschichtliche Periode in Deutschland dem Zivilprozess eine gleich intensive und vielleicht auch geglückte Aufmerksamkeit geschenkt hat wie eben dieses Jahrhundert.[1] Wenn in diesem Vortrag der Werdegang der Ziviljustiz in einem der kleineren deutschen Territorien, in Mecklenburg, behandelt werden soll, so dürfte dieses Thema im Hinblick auf die für dieses Land eigentümlichen ständestaatlichen Verhältnisse, die sich besonders auf das Rechtswesen ausgewirkt haben, nicht ohne Interesse sein. Der zeitliche Umfang der Untersuchung erstreckt sich auf die Periode vom Beginn des 19. Jahrhunderts bis zur völligen Umgestaltung des mecklenburgischen Gerichtswesens 1879 durch die Reichsjustizgesetze.

II. Die mecklenburgische Zivilgerichtsbarkeit zu Beginn des 19. Jahrhunderts

Zunächst soll die überkommene Gestalt der Zivilgerichtsbarkeit in Mecklenburg am Anfang des 19. Jahrhunderts als Ausgangspunkt ihrer weiteren Entwicklung skizziert werden.

1. Staatsrechtliche Grundlagen

Zum Verständnis des mecklenburgischen Justizwesens ist ein kurzer Überblick über die staatsrechtlichen Verhältnisse des Landes erforderlich. Die mecklenburgischen Lande, die seit dem 14. Jahrhundert als Herzogtum Lehensträger des Reiches waren, bestanden seit dem Hamburger Vergleich von 1701[2] aus den beiden Herzogtümern Mecklenburg-Schwerin und Mecklenburg-Strelitz. Kennzeichnend für die

---

1 *Knut Wolfgang Nörr,* Hauptthemen legislatorischer Zivilprozeßreform im 19. Jahrhundert, ZZP 87 (1974), S. 277–283.

2 Abgedruckt bei *Hugo Sachsse*, Mecklenburgische Urkunden und Daten, Rostock 1900, Nr. 152.

staatliche Struktur Mecklenburgs war die außerordentlich starke Stellung, die den beiden privilegierten Ständen, dem grundbesitzenden Adel, der sog. Ritterschaft, und den als Landschaft bezeichneten Städten, gegenüber den Herzögen zukam.[3] Nachdem in der ersten Hälfte des 18. Jahrhunderts unternommene Versuche des Herzogs von Mecklenburg-Schwerin zur Ausweitung der landesherrlichen Macht gescheitert waren, weil die Stände hiergegen den Reichshofrat angerufen und eine Reichsexekution gegen den Herzog bewirkt hatten, musste der Herzog mit den Ständen 1755 den sog. Landesgrundgesetzlichen Erbvergleich – LGGEV –[4] abschließen.[5] Der Erbvergleich bildete fortan die Grundlage der Verfassungsordnung in beiden Mecklenburg. Die ständischen Rechte wurden in dem Vertrag voll bestätigt und festgeschrieben. In Mecklenburg bestand damit, ganz im Gegensatz zum benachbarten Preußen, keine einheitliche Staatsgewalt mit dem Landesherrn als Träger, sondern die öffentliche Gewalt war zwischen Herzog und Ständen aufgrund der jeweiligen Herrschaft über Land und Leute funktional und territorial aufgeteilt.[6] Die Stellung von absoluten Monarchen kam den Herzögen nur in denjenigen Landesteilen zu, über die sie selbst die Grundherrschaft innehatten, dem sog. Domanium. Das übrige flache Land setzte sich durchgängig aus Rittergütern zusammen, deren damals noch durchweg adeligen Inhabern, aus eigenem Recht, nicht als Beauftragten des Herzogs, die Polizeigewalt und die untere Gerichtsbarkeit über die Bewohner ihres Bezirkes zustand. Alle Bauern unterlagen der im LGGEV den Ständen ausdrücklich garantierten[7] Leibeigenschaft. Desgleichen wurden den Städten ihre hergebrachten Rechte gewährleistet, die bei den „Seestädten" Rostock und Wismar[8] besonders umfangreich waren. Entsprechend eingeschränkt

---

[3] Vgl. hierzu *Gerhard Heitz*, Die landständische Verfassung Mecklenburgs, Bad Doberaner Jb. 1995, S. 23 ff.

[4] Bei *Sachsse*, Urkunden (oben Fn. 2), Nr. 169; hierzu *Otto Vitense*, Geschichte von Mecklenburg, Gotha 1920 (ND Würzburg 1985), S. 274 ff.

[5] Zu den jahrzehntelangen Auseinandersetzungen zwischen Herzog und Ständen s. *Peter Wick*, Versuche zur Errichtung des Absolutismus in Mecklenburg, Berlin 1964.

[6] Zur mecklenburgischen Verfassungsstruktur s. *Otto Büsing*, Das Staatsrecht der Großherzogthümer Mecklenburg-Schwerin und Mecklenburg-Strelitz, in: Heinrich Marquard (Hg.), Handbuch des Oeffentlichen Rechts der Gegenwart in Monographien III 2: Kleinere deutsche Staaten, Freiburg i. B./Tübingen 1884, S. 1, 38 ff.; *Erich Schlesinger*, Staats- und Verwaltungsrecht des Großherzogtums Mecklenburg-Schwerin, Berlin 1909, § 14.

[7] LGGEV §§ 325–336, bes. § 325: „Wir und unsere Nachkommen (i. e. die Herzöge) wollen und werden überhaupt Unserer Ritter- und Landschaft … in Ansehung des Zustandes und Wesens der Leibeigenschaft, und der damit behafteten Unterthanen und Bauersleute, nie Zweifel und Hindernis machen, hingegen alle Wege ernstlich darüber halten, und durch Unsere Landes-Gerichte halten lassen …".

[8] Wismar war 1648 im Westfälischen Friedensvertrag an die Krone Schweden abgetreten worden und damit aus dem Herzogtum Mecklenburg(-Schwerin) ausgeschieden. Erst mit der 1803 auf 100 Jahre erfolgten Verpfändung der Stadt durch Schweden an den Herzog von Mecklenburg-Schwerin gelangte Wismar wieder unter mecklenburgische Herrschaft. 1903 verzichtete Schweden auch formell auf den längst obsolet gewordenen Besitz der Stadt.

war die Rechtssetzungsbefugnis der Herzöge durch die Rechte des aus Ritter- und Landschaft bestehenden, für beide Mecklenburg einheitlichen Landtags, der einmal jährlich zusammentrat und zwischen den Tagungen von einem „Engeren Ausschuss“ vertreten wurde. In alleiniger Zuständigkeit konnte der Herzog lediglich die für die Angehörigen des Domaniums geltenden Gesetze erlassen.[9] Von den für das gesamte Land geltenden Gesetzen hatte der Herzog die Gesetzgebungsbefugnis für die das allgemeine Wohl betreffenden inne, jedoch musste er vor ihrer Verkündung den Landtag, bei Gefahr im Verzug den Engeren Ausschuss, anhören und dessen Vorstellungen möglichst berücksichtigen.[10] Gesetze schließlich, die in die wohlerworbenen Rechte und Befugnisse der Ritterschaft oder Landschaft oder einzelner ihrer Mitglieder eingriffen, bedurften hingegen der ausdrücklichen Bewilligung dieser Stände.[11]

1815 wurden die beiden Herzöge durch den Wiener Kongress zu Großherzögen erhoben und beide Länder Mitglieder des Deutschen Bundes.

2. Gerichtsverfassung

Eine umfassende landeseinheitliche Regelung der Gerichtsverfassung hat es zu Beginn des 19. Jahrhunderts auch in Mecklenburg nicht gegeben. Die Gerichtsorganisation stimmte im Wesentlichen mit derjenigen überein, die sich auch in den anderen deutschen Territorien seit dem Spätmittelalter herausgebildet hatte. Die ordentlichen Gerichte gliederten sich in Unter- und Obergerichte.[12]

(1) Untergerichte waren für das Domanium entsprechend der Unterteilung dieses Gebiets in Ämter die Amtsgerichte, für die Rittergüter die Patrimonialgerichte und für die Städte die unteren Stadtgerichte. Hiervon standen nur die Stadtgerichte grundsätzlich in landesherrlicher Trägerschaft, waren also Landes- d.h. staatliche Gerichte, die außer dem vom Landesherrn ernannten Stadtrichter aus von den städtischen Magistraten bestellten Beisitzern bestanden; die Seestadt Rostock hatte allerdings die Gerichtsbarkeit selbst inne und die Untergerichte der sog. Vorderstädte (Parchim, Güstrow, Neubrandenburg, Friedland und Malchow) standen unter gemeinschaftlicher landesherrlicher und städtischer Gerichtsbarkeit. Dagegen waren Träger der Patrimonialgerichtsbarkeit die Inhaber der Rittergüter, denen der Fortbestand dieser Gerichtsbarkeit im LGGEV, dessen Art. 21 (§§ 381–433) vom Justizwesen handelte, ausdrücklich zugesichert worden war.[13] Patrimonialer Natur

[9] LGGEV § 193.

[10] LGGEV §§ 195–197.

[11] LGGEV §§ 198, 199.

[12] Hierzu näher *Karl Christoph Albert Heinrich v. Kamptz*, Handbuch des Mecklenburgischen Civil-Processes, Berlin 1811, §§ 4, 6.

[13] LGGEV § 423 „… erklären Wir Uns nochmals … dahin, daß wir Ritter- und Landschaft, bey der ihnen mit den Lehn- und übrigen Gütern verliehenen, auch denen Magistraten in den Städten zustehenden Jurisdiction und erster Instanz, durch unsere Collegia, Gerichte und Beamte, oder andere beeinträchtigen zu lassen, nicht gemeinet, sondern einem jeden seine Jurisdiction, um die

waren auch die Amtsgerichte, denn dem Herzog stand hier die Gerichtsherrschaft nicht als Landesherr zu, sondern als Grundeigentümer des Domaniums.

(2) Die Obergerichte waren demgegenüber, mit Ausnahme des städtischen Obergerichts Rostock, Landesgerichte in Trägerschaft des Herzogs qua Landesherr. Sie bestanden auf der mittleren Stufe aus den drei Justizkanzleien Schwerin, Rostock (für Mecklenburg-Schwerin) und Neustrelitz (für Mecklenburg-Strelitz). Über den Justizkanzleien und dem Rostocker Obergericht stand schließlich auf der dritten Stufe das für beide Landesteile zuständige Hof- und Landgericht in Güstrow.

Die für das Ancien Régime typische Zweiteilung der Gerichtsbarkeit in Obergerichtsbarkeit für die Eximierten (Adelige, Beamte, Offiziere, Geistliche, Akademiker usw.) und Niedergerichtsbarkeit für die übrige Bevölkerung bestand auch in Mecklenburg.[14] Für die Nichteximierten („Amtssässigen") waren Eingangsgerichte die Amts-, Patrimonial- bzw. unteren Stadtgerichte, Gerichte des zweiten Rechtszuges die Justizkanzleien bzw. das Obergericht Rostock und des dritten Rechtszugs das Hof- und Landgericht. Die Eximierten standen in erster Instanz unter den Justizkanzleien (daher „Kanzleisässige") bzw. dem Obergericht Rostock, in zweiter und dritter Instanz unter dem Hof- und Landgericht. Bis 1806 konnten in Sachen über 1.000 Goldgulden nach dem Mecklenburg zuletzt 1651 eingeräumten beschränkten Appellationsprivileg[15] Rechtsmittelgerichte auch die Reichsgerichte (Reichskammergericht und Reichshofrat) sein.

3. Verfahren

Ebenso wenig wie die Gerichtsorganisation war das gerichtliche Verfahren für alle mecklenburgischen Gerichte in einer Prozessordnung einheitlich geregelt. Nur für einzelne Gerichte existierten besondere Gerichtsordnungen, vornehmlich die Hof- und Landgerichtsordnung von 1622 und die Güstrowsche Kanzleiordnung von 1669. Der LGGEV sah zwar die Schaffung einer gesamtmecklenburgischen Prozessordnung mit dem Ziel einer Beschleunigung der Verfahren vor,[16] dieses

---

Sache seines Hintersassen, zu verhören und entscheiden, überlassen, mithin daß vorhero die Cognition vor die Landes-Gerichte gezogen werde, nicht gestatten wollen".

[14] Vgl. *v. Kamptz*, Handbuch (oben Fn. 12), § 6.

[15] Abdruck des Privilegs bei *Sachsse*, Urkunden (oben Fn. 2), Nr. 136; vgl. auch LGGEV §§ 391, 392.

[16] LGGEV § 403: „Wir wollen … binnen Jahresfrist, die Hof-, Land- und Gerichts-Ordnung, mit Zuziehung unserer Ritter- und Landschaft, und Vernehmung ihrer unterthänigsten Erinnerungen, verbessern, …, mithin dahin sorgen, daß darnach eine uniforme Prozeß-Ordnung, bey Unsern gesammten Landes- und Unter-Gerichten, eingeführet werde"; § 404: „…wollen Wir, bey Nachsicht und Verbesserung der Proceß-Ordnungen, hauptsächlich auf künftige Abkürzung der Processe das Augenmerk richten…"; § 432: „Was im übrigen bey diesem [21.] Articul, vom Justitz-Wesen noch abgehen mögte, das soll bey künftiger Verfassung des versprochenen Land-Rechts, und der ebenfalls verheißenen Verbesserung der Mecklenburgischen Proceß-Ordnungen,

Vorhaben konnten jedoch in der Folgezeit, wie auch der Plan eines mecklenburgischen Land-Rechts, nicht verwirklicht werden, was auf das durch die ständischen Befugnisse äußerst komplizierte und schwerfällige mecklenburgische Gesetzgebungsverfahren zurückzuführen war. Auch insoweit bestand ein deutlicher Gegensatz zur Kodifikation des Verfahrensrechts in Preußen mit der AGO von 1793. Da die mecklenburgischen Gerichtsordnungen, die von den Gerichten zu Einzelfragen erlassenen „Gemeinen Bescheide" und der sonstige Gerichtsgebrauch nur rudimentären Charakter aufwiesen, kam den von der deutschen Rechtswissenschaft und Rechtspraxis aufgrund der RKG-Ordnungen und insbesondere des Jüngsten Reichsabschieds von 1654[17] entwickelten Regeln des sog. gemeinen deutschen Prozesses als subsidiär geltenden Quellen für das mecklenburgische Gerichtsverfahren eine größere Bedeutung zu als für viele andere deutsche Länder.[18] Die bekannten Eigenarten des gemeinen deutschen Prozesses trafen daher auch auf das mecklenburgische Verfahren zu:

(1) Die Prozessparteien bestimmten nicht nur den Gegenstand des Rechtsstreits, sondern allein ihre Sache war grundsätzlich auch die Beschaffung des für dessen Entscheidung relevanten Tatsachenstoffs. Aufgabe des Gerichts war neben der in der Sorge für den vorschriftsmäßigen Ablauf des Verfahrens bestehenden Prozessleitung nur die rechtliche Würdigung des beigebrachten Materials zur Entscheidungsfindung. Es galt also der Dispositions- und der Beibringungsgrundsatz.

(2) Vor allem für das ordentliche Verfahren vor den Landesgerichten galt der Grundsatz der Schriftlichkeit.[19] Allein das schriftliche Parteivorbringen bildete die Grundlage der gerichtlichen Entscheidung (*quod non est in actis, non est in mundo*). Nur im niedergerichtlichen und in den außerordentlichen Verfahren (summarischer, Mandatsprozess) fanden auch mündliche Verhandlungen statt.

(3) Für die Vornahme jeder Prozesshandlung durch Einreichung eines entsprechenden Schriftsatzes war eine Frist vorgeschrieben, bei deren Versäumnis die Partei mit dem betreffenden Vorbringen für die Instanz präkludiert wurde. Der Verfahrensablauf gliederte sich damit in mehrere Abschnitte: Klageerhebung, Klageerwiderung einschließlich vorzuschützender Einreden, Replik des Klägers, Duplik des Beklagten, bei Gestattung durch das Gericht noch Triplik des Klägers und Quadruplik des Beklagten. Für alle Prozesshandlungen galt die sog. Eventual-

---

in Obacht gezogen und von Uns dahin gesorget werden, daß das Justitz-Wesen auf den besten Fuß gesetzet werden möge."

[17] Textausgabe bearbeitet von *Adolf Laufs*, Der jüngste Reichsabschied von 1654, Bern 1975.

[18] Vgl. *v. Kamptz*, Handbuch (oben Fn. 12), Vorrede: „Der Mecklenburgische Proceß hat … weniger Eigenthümlichkeiten, als der der mehresten übrigen deutschen Staaten…"; *Johann Christoph Schwartz*, Vierhundert Jahre deutscher Civilproceß-Gesetzgebung, Berlin 1898, S. 317, 322.

[19] *v. Kamptz*, Handbuch (oben Fn. 12), §§ 30, 33.

maxime.[20] Jede Partei musste sämtliche Angriffs- und Verteidigungsmittel in dem betreffenden Prozessabschnitt bei Strafe der Präklusion kumulativ vorbringen, auch die nur hilfsweise geltend gemachten. Unterließ der Beklagte die die Streitbefestigung (Litiskontestation) vollziehende Klagebeantwortung, so verlor er durch diese Säumnis seine Einreden, das Vorbringen des Klägers wurde aber – anders als nach heutigem deutschem Recht (§ 331 ZPO) – nicht als zugestanden, sondern weiterhin als bestritten angesehen (negative Litiskontestation) und der Kläger blieb beweisfällig.[21] Nach dem Schriftsatzwechsel, regelmäßig nach der Duplik, ggf. nach der Quadruplik, wurden die Akten geschlossen und es fand in einem besonderen Termin in der Registratur oder der Kanzlei des Gerichts die Rotulation der Akten statt, d. h. der Aktenbestand wurde in Anwesenheit der beiderseitigen Anwälte auf seine Vollständigkeit geprüft und zu einem Konvolut geheftet.[22] Dies war notwendig, weil nach dem schriftlichen Verfahren die in den Akten festgehaltenen Tatsachen die alleinige Entscheidungsgrundlage für das erkennende Gericht bildeten.

(4) Das Erkenntnisverfahren war zweigeteilt in das Behauptungsverfahren und das Beweisverfahren. Nach Beendigung des Behauptungsverfahrens mit der Aktenrotulation erließ das Gericht ein als Endurteil mit Rechtsmitteln anfechtbares Beweisinterlokut, das die beweisbedürftigen Tatsachen und die Beweislast festlegte.[23]

(5) Als Folge der Schriftlichkeit des Verfahrens gelangte das erkennende Gericht zu seinem Urteil nicht aufgrund eigenen unmittelbaren Eindrucks von der Verhandlung und der von einem kommissarischen Richter durchgeführten Beweisaufnahme, sondern nur aufgrund des Akteninhalts und deshalb nur mittelbar. Das Verfahren war also nicht öffentlich. Die Kenntnis der Akten wurde dem Kollegialgericht von einem Mitglied als Referenten in einer Relation mit Entscheidungsvorschlag vermittelt. Auf Antrag einer Prozesspartei musste grundsätzlich die Aktenversendung an eine – den Parteien nicht bekannt zu gebende – juristische Fakultät erfolgen, deren Urteil dann als vom Gericht erlassen galt.[24]

(6) Es bestand die für den gemeinen Prozess typische Vielfalt von Rechtsmitteln,[25] deren Kompliziertheit durch die weitgehende Freiheit der Parteien in der Wahl zwischen mehreren zulässigen Rechtsmitteln, die u. U. auch nebeneinander

---

[20] Hierzu allg. *Werner Schubert,* Das Streben nach Prozeßbeschleunigung und Verfahrensgliederung im Zivilprozeßrecht des 19. Jahrhunderts, ZRG GA 85 (1968), S. 127, 128 ff.

[21] *v. Kamptz*, Handbuch (oben Fn. 12), § 51.

[22] *v. Kamptz*, Handbuch (oben Fn. 12), § 61.

[23] *v. Kamptz*, Handbuch (oben Fn. 12), § 74.

[24] Regelung in LGGEV §§ 399, 400; hierzu *v. Kamptz*, Handbuch (oben Fn. 12), § 20.

[25] Überblick bei *v. Kamptz*, Handbuch (oben Fn. 12), § 160; *Friedrich August Mehlen*, Ueber die Appellationen und andere Impugnativ-Mittel gegen richterliche Erkenntnisse besonders in Rücksicht auf Schwedisch-Pommern und Mecklenburg, Berlin/Stralsund 1791, § 6, §§ 174 ff.

eingelegt werden konnten, und sogar in der Wahl des Rechtsmittelgerichts[26] noch gesteigert wurde. Ordentliche d. h. suspensivisch wirkende Rechtsmittel waren in erster Linie die – auch Devolutiveffekt zeitigende – Appellation,[27] hinzu kamen die Restitution (Wiedereinsetzung) wegen Verletzung,[28] ferner die sog. Nullitäts-Deduktion[29] zur Geltendmachung einer Nichtigkeit der Entscheidung oder des Verfahrens aus einem der von der gemeinrechtlichen Lehre und Praxis entwickelten zahlreichen Nichtigkeitsgründe, sowie die Supplikation[30] gegen Entscheidungen in nicht kriminellen fiskalischen Sachen. Als außerordentliche Rechtsmittel ohne Suspensiveffekt standen zur Verfügung die bei offensichtlicher Nichtigkeit der Entscheidung statthafte Nullitäts-Querel,[31] die Avokation[32] gegen untergerichtliche Verfahren wegen Bedenken gegen die Person des Richters oder Verzögerung oder ungebührlicher Verwaltung der Justiz und schließlich bei geringeren Verfahrensverstößen die außerordentliche Restitution.[33]

III. Veränderungen in der Zeit des „Vormärz" (bis 1848)

1. Die mecklenburgischen Reformbestrebungen im Lichte der allgemeinen deutschen Diskussion über die Gestaltung des Zivilverfahrens

Die intensive Grundlagendiskussion, wie sie seit Beginn des 19. Jahrhunderts in der deutschen Prozessrechtswissenschaft und Rechtspolitik unter dem Einfluss des Rechtsdenkens der Aufklärung und dem Eindruck des umwälzenden Ereignisses der Französischen Revolution über die Theorie des Zivilverfahrens geführt wurde, hat in der nunmehr zu behandelnden Periode bis zur Revolution von 1848 auch in Mecklenburg ein deutliches Echo gefunden. Dies gilt etwa für die Frage nach der Bedeutung der hauptsächlich von dem bayerischen Prozessualisten *Gönner* entwickelten Antithese zwischen der dem gemeinen deutschen Prozess und – freilich in völlig anderer Ausführung – dem Verfahren des französischen Code de procédure civile von 1806 zugrunde liegenden Verhandlungsmaxime und der für den Prozess nach der preußischen AGO von 1793 charakteristischen Untersuchungsmaxime.[34] Die Verhandlungsmaxime verstanden *Gönner* und die ihm

[26] Näher hierzu *v. Kamptz*, Handbuch (oben Fn. 12), §§ 161, 165.

[27] Vgl. *v. Kamptz*, Handbuch (oben Fn. 12), §§ 164–175.

[28] *v. Kamptz*, Handbuch (oben Fn. 12), §§ 176–178; *Mehlen*, Appellationen (oben Fn. 25), § 202.

[29] *v. Kamptz*, Handbuch (oben Fn. 12), §§ 179–181; *Mehlen*, Appellationen (oben Fn. 25), § 201.

[30] *v. Kamptz*, Handbuch (oben Fn. 12), §§ 182–184; *Mehlen*, Appellationen (oben Fn. 25), § 203.

[31] *v. Kamptz*, Handbuch (oben Fn. 12), §§ 185 f.

[32] *v. Kamptz*, Handbuch (oben Fn. 12), § 187.

[33] *v. Kamptz*, Handbuch (oben Fn. 12), § 188.

[34] Zur Entstehung und Entwicklung der beiden Maximen umfassend *Falk Bomsdorf*, Prozeßmaximen und Rechtswirklichkeit, Berlin 1971, S. 121 ff., 159 ff.; ferner *Peter Böhm*, Der Streit um die Verhandlungsmaxime, IUS COMMUNE 7 (1978), S. 136–159; *Hernández Marcos*, Die Prozeßrechtsreform und das ALR sowie die Polemik um die Inquisitionsmaxime in der ersten

folgenden „Maximentheoretiker“ dahingehend, dass hier die Beibringung des Tatsachenstoffs für den Rechtsstreit allein den Parteien obliege, das Gericht hieran nach dem Grundsatz „nichts von Amts wegen“ (*iudex ex officio non procedit*) völlig unbeteiligt und nur auf die rechtliche Würdigung des ihm unterbreiteten Faktums beschränkt sei (*iudex secundum allegata et probata partium iudicare debet*), während der Untersuchungsgrundsatz den instruierenden Richter zur Ermittlung der materiellen Wahrheit verpflichte, wozu ihm das Parteivorbringen nur Anhaltspunkte liefere, also der umgekehrte Grundsatz „alles von Amts wegen“ gelte.[35] Die Kritiker wandten ein, dass ein solcher absoluter Gegensatz zwischen den beiden Maximen den positiven Rechten fremd sei, indem einerseits sowohl der gemeine als auch der französische Prozess dem Richter eine Frage- und Aufklärungsbefugnis hinsichtlich des Parteivorbringens und das Recht zu dessen Prüfung auf seine Erheblichkeit zuerkannten und umgekehrt der preußische Prozess die Verfügungsbefugnis der Parteien über den Streitgegenstand unberührt ließ, dem Richter die Verwertung von Wissen ohne Anhaltspunkte im Parteivortrag verbot, das Geständnis für verbindlich und bei Säumnis des Beklagten das Klagevorbringen – anders als im gemeinen Verfahren – für zugestanden erklärte.[36] Auch in dem ganz auf gemeinrechtlicher Grundlage beruhenden mecklenburgischen Prozess bildete die hiernach an sich geltende Verhandlungsmaxime kein unbedingt zu befolgendes Dogma, sondern nur einen von beträchtlichen Ausnahmen durchbrochenen Grundsatz. Zu diesem Befund gelangte ein 1824 veröffentlichter Aufsatz eines ungenannten Mecklenburger Praktikers.[37] Wie der Verfasser in einer eingehenden Analyse der Rechtsprechung nachwies, wirkte der Richter in Mecklenburg in ähnlicher Weise wie im gemeinen deutschen Verfahren auf die Beibringung des streiterheblichen Tatsachenstoffs und die Durchführung der Beweisaufnahme aktiv gestaltend ein, weshalb von einer uneingeschränkten Geltung des Satzes *iudex ex officio non procedit* hier ebenfalls keine Rede sein konnte.[38]

Die in Mecklenburg meist von Praktikern geäußerten Reformüberlegungen entsprachen i. W. den in Deutschland von liberaler Seite allgemein erhobenen Forderungen. Die Trennung der Justiz von der Verwaltung war allerdings weniger

---

Hälfte des 19. Jahrhunderts, in: Barbara Dölemeyer/Heinz Mohnhaupt (Hg.), 200 Jahre Allgemeines Landrecht für die preußischen Staaten, Frankfurt a.M. 1995, S. 327, 342 ff.

[35] *Nikolaus Thaddäus Gönner*, Handbuch des deutschen gemeinen Prozesses, Bd. I, Erlangen 1801, S. 253 ff.

[36] Vgl. *Carl Joseph Anton Mittermaier*, Ueber den Gang der Civilprozeßgebung in den deutschen Staaten im Jahre 1818, AcP 2 (1819), S. 169 f.; *ders.*, Der gemeine deutsche bürgerliche Prozeß, Bonn 1820, S. 20 ff., 36: „Kampf zwischen dem gemeinen, preußischen und französischen“ Prozess, 42; rückblickend *Bomsdorf*, Prozeßmaximen (oben Fn. 34), S. 42 ff., 90 ff.

[37] Ueber die Grenzen des Richteramtes in bürgerlichen Rechtssachen, in: Christian Carl Friedrich Wilhelm v. Nettelbladt (Hg.), Rechtssprüche des Ober-Appellations-Gerichts zu Parchim, Bd. 2, Berlin 1824, S. 1 ff.

[38] So auch *Carl Trotsche*, Der Mecklenburgische Civil-Prozeß, Bd. I, Wismar u.a. 1866, S. 488 f.; *Bomsdorf*, Prozeßmaximen (oben Fn. 34), S. 212 f.

akut, da diese in Mecklenburg schon bisher in stärkerem Umfang verwirklicht war als in zahlreichen anderen deutschen Staaten,[39] was auf die Macht der Stände zurückzuführen war, die damit einer Beeinträchtigung ihrer Rechte durch den Landesherrn vorbeugen wollten. Befürwortet wurde vereinzelt die generelle Einführung des mündlichen Verfahrens,[40] wobei unausgesprochen das Vorbild des überhaupt als Muster einer freiheitlichen Verfahrensordnung gepriesenen Code de procédure civile[41] vor Augen stand. Einen Schwerpunkt bildete das Ziel einer Vereinfachung und Straffung des hoch komplizierten, schwerfälligen und langwierigen gemeinrechtlichen Verfahrens durch Abschaffung veralteter Förmlichkeiten,[42] Verminderung der zahlreichen Gründe einer Nichtigkeit der Urteile,[43] Verkürzung des Instanzenzuges und Beschränkung der Vielfalt der Rechtsmittel,[44] Geständniswirkung der Säumnis[45] u.a. Das Institut der Aktenversendung, das auch in der Deutschen Bundesakte[46] für das Verfahren vor gemeinschaftlichen obersten Gerichten mehrerer Bundesstaaten gewährleistet war, sollte hingegen als Mittel zur

---

[39] Vgl. die detaillierten Regelungen in LGGEV §§ 393–398; *v. Kamptz*, Handbuch (oben Fn. 12), Vorrede u. § 15; eine völlige Beseitigung aller noch bestehenden judikativen Befugnisse der großherzoglichen Verwaltung, der nur noch die Sorge für ein reibungsloses Funktionieren der Justiz obliegen sollte, verlangte im Hinblick auf die geplante Errichtung eines OAG *Christian Carl Friedrich Wilhelm v. Nettelbladt*, Bemerkungen über das Verhältnis der regiminellen Gewalt zur Justizpflege in Mecklenburg in Bezug auf die Errichtung des Ober-Appellations-Gerichts, Güstrow 1817, S. 37 ff. u. pass.

[40] So *Johann Gottfried Berg*, Ueber den Mecklenburgischen Civilprozeß, Rostock 1832, S. 54 ff., 72 f.

[41] Zum frz. Prozess *Mittermaier*, AcP 2 (1819), S. 169, 120 ff.; *Schwartz*, Gesetzgebung (oben Fn. 18), S. 605 ff.; *Bomsdorf*, Prozeßmaximen (oben Fn. 34), S. 330 ff.; zum Einfluss in Deutschland *Gerhard J. Dahlmanns*, Der Strukturwandel des deutschen Zivilprozesses im 19. Jahrhundert, Aalen 1971, S. 28 ff.; *Elisabeth Koch*, Zum Einfluss des Code de procédure civile auf die deutsche Zivilprozeßrechtsreform, in: Reiner Schulze (Hg.), Französisches Zivilrecht in Europa während des 19. Jahrhunderts, Berlin 1994, S. 157–176.

[42] Vgl. *Friedrich Fromm*, Einige processualische Betrachtungen in Bezug auf die Einrichtung eines Oberappellations-Gerichts in Mecklenburg, Hamburg 1817, S. 48 ff.; *Friedrich Wilhelm Sibeth*, Kritik des gemeinen und mecklenburgischen Processes, Güstrow 1818, Abt. 2, § 129 (Appellationseid), § 130 (Interposition der Appellation vor Notar und Zeugen).

[43] *Sibeth*, Kritik (oben Fn. 42), §§ 132–154.

[44] *Fromm*, Betrachtungen (oben Fn. 42), S. 19 f.; *Sibeth*, Kritik (oben Fn. 42), Abt. I, S. 47.

[45] *Berg*, Civilprozeß (oben Fn. 40), S. 22 ff. mit scharfer Kritik an der bisherigen Praxis, nur eine negative Litiskontestation mit fortdauernder Beweisfälligkeit des Klägers für die anspruchsbegründenden Tatsachen anzunehmen. Hierin läge ein Hauptgrund der für Mecklenburg, das deshalb als „Vaterland der Advokaten“ gelte, typischen Prozessverschleppungen.

[46] Art. 12 Abs. 4 der Deutschen Bundesakte v. 8.6.1815, in: *Günter Dürig* (Hg.), Texte zur deutschen Verfassungsgeschichte, 2. Aufl., München 1979, S. 11 ff.

Sicherung einer qualifizierten und unabhängigen Justiz, als „Palladium der deutschen Freiheit“[47] in eingeschränktem Umfang beibehalten werden.[48]

Nachdem Verfassung und Verfahren der Gerichte der oberen und mittleren Ebene im Zusammenhang mit der 1818 erfolgten Errichtung eines mecklenburgischen OAG in einigen Zügen modernisiert worden waren (hierzu sogleich unter 2), konzentrierte sich die Diskussion auf eine durchgreifende Erneuerung der niederen Gerichtsbarkeit, also der großherzoglichen Amtsgerichte für das Domanium, der städtischen Untergerichte und der gutsherrlichen Patrimonialgerichte. Der Reformbedarf erschien hier als besonders dringend, weil bei den für die nicht eximierten Mecklenburger und damit für den weitaus größten Teil der Bevölkerung erstinstanzlich zuständigen Niedergerichten nach allgemeiner Ansicht noch gravierendere Unzulänglichkeiten zu konstatieren waren als bei den höheren Gerichten. Auf eine bloße Verbesserung der Verhältnisse beschränkten sich die in Mecklenburg gemachten Vorschläge, da eine völlige Beseitigung der unterschiedlichen Gerichtsbarkeiten für die privilegierten Stände und das einfache Volk zugunsten einheitlicher Eingangsgerichte unabhängig von der Standeszugehörigkeit der Rechtssuchenden nach dem Vorbild der aus der Revolution hervorgegangenen französischen Justizverfassung, wie dies von liberaler Seite in Deutschland gefordert wurde, unter den ständischen Verhältnissen Mecklenburgs in der Reaktionsperiode vor 1848 politisch noch weniger durchsetzbar war als etwa im Geltungsbereich der preußischen AGO. Nahezu allgemein gefordert wurde die Ausgestaltung aller Niedergerichte als mit drei Richtern zu besetzende Kollegialgerichte zwecks erhöhter Richtigkeitsgewähr der Entscheidungen.[49] Bei den Amtsgerichten wurde der entscheidende Mangel in der Doppelbelastung der Amtsrichter gesehen, denen neben der Rechtspflege auch die landesherrliche Domänen-(Kammer-)Verwaltung oblag, in der sie ihre Hauptaufgabe erblickten mit der Folge einer Vernachlässigung der justiziellen Tätigkeit und der Gefahr von Interessenkollisionen besonders, wenn der Rechtsstreit auch die Interessen der Kammer berührte; als notwendig erschien daher eine strikte Trennung von Rechtsprechung und Verwaltung auch auf der Ebene der Ämter unter Beschränkung der Amtsrichter allein auf die Justiz.[50] Auch an der städtischen Niedergerichtsbarkeit wurde die Vernachlässigung der Amtstätigkeit durch die Unterrichter und die Verschleppung der Prozesse kritisiert, deren Grund

---

[47] So *Heinrich Ernst Bornemann*, Beyträge zur Verbesserung des Appellations-Verfahrens und zur bessern Einrichtung der Nieder-Gerichte, Rostock/Schwerin 1820, S. 31.

[48] *Fromm*, Betrachtungen (oben Fn. 42), S. 85 ff.; *Bornemann*, a.a.O., 28 ff.; *Berg*, Civilprozeß, (oben Fn. 40), S. 66 f.

[49] *Bornemann*, a.a.O., S. 80 ff., 93 ff.; *Anonymus*, Ueber die Gerechtigkeitspflege bei den Niedergerichten, und deren Verbesserung, Freimüthiges Abendblatt 2 (1819), S. 65, 68; *W.*, Bemerkungen über die bessere Einrichtung der Untergerichte in Mecklenburg, Freimüthiges Abendblatt 3 (1821), S. 129, 130; *Berg*, Civilprozeß (oben Fn. 40), S. 56 f.; ablehnend *v. Wackenhausen*, Ueber Zeitgeist, Rechte, Gerichts-Verwaltung, Freimüthiges Abendblatt 3 (1821), S. 732, 737.

[50] *Bornemann*, a.a.O., S. 86 f.; *Anonymus*, Freimüthiges Abendblatt 2 (1819), S. 65; ablehnend insoweit *W.*, Freimüthiges Abendblatt 3 (1821), S. 129; *v. Wackenhausen*, a.a.O., S. 732, 736 f.

darin lag, dass die gering besoldeten Richter gezwungen waren, nebenher die Advokatur zu betreiben und auf diese ihr Hauptaugenmerk zu richten, was wiederum zu Interessenkonflikten führen konnte.[51]

Im Bereich der Patrimonialgerichtsbarkeit, der sämtliche nicht eximierten Bewohner des flachen Landes und damit die überwiegende Mehrheit des nahezu reinen Agrarstaates Mecklenburg unterlagen, galten die Verhältnisse allgemein als untragbar.[52] Die auch von mecklenburgischen Autoren erhobene Forderung nach Beseitigung dieser mit den Prinzipien des bürgerlichen Rechtsstaats völlig unvereinbaren Form der Privatgerichtsbarkeit[53] hatte aber in diesem Lande angesichts der ausschlaggebenden Stellung des Gutsbesitzerstandes in dieser Epoche keine Chance auf Verwirklichung. Grundlegender Missstand war die persönliche und sachliche Abhängigkeit der als Patrimonialrichter fungierenden Justiziare von den die Gerichtsherrschaft innehabenden Rittergutsbesitzern, woraus naturgemäß die Gefahr einer Entscheidung der Prozesse im Sinne der Gutsherrschaft resultierte, besonders wenn diese ein unmittelbares oder mittelbares eigenes Interesse an dem Rechtsstreit hatte, mit der Folge entsprechender Nachteile für die Gegenpartei.[54] Hinzu kam die oft unzureichende juristische Qualifikation der Justiziare, für deren Anstellung das Bestehen einer Prüfung nicht vorgeschrieben war.[55] Das Bestreben der ritterschaftlichen Gerichtsherren, die von ihnen zu bestreitenden Kosten für ihre Gerichte zu minimieren, hatte ferner eine „beharrliche Justizverzögerung der Patrimonialgerichte“ in noch stärkerem Maße als bei den sonstigen Niedergerichten zur Folge.[56] Ganz unzulänglich geregelt war zudem das patrimonialgerichtliche Verfahren, was eine willkürliche Handhabung der Prozesse durch die Patrimonialrichter ermöglichte; so war etwa umstritten, ob den in der Hof- und Landgerichtsordnung und in der Güstrower Kanzleiordnung für das niedergerichtliche Verfahren im Allgemeinen festgelegten Normen auch für die Patrimonialgerichtsbarkeit Geltung zukam.[57] Die Mindesterfordernisse einer Reform der Patrimonialgerichtsbarkeit erblickten die Kritiker der bestehenden Zustände daher in der Besetzung der als Kollegialgerichte auszugestaltenden Gerichte mit Richtern, deren Befähigung durch eine Prüfung nachzuweisen war, sowie in der Sicherung ihrer Unabhängig-

---

[51] *Bornemann*, a.a.O., S. 87 f.; *Anonymus*, Freimüthiges Abendblatt 2 (1819), S. 66.

[52] Vgl. *Bornemann*, a.a.O., S. 74 ff., 88 ff.

[53] Für Aufhebung *Bornemann*, a.a.O., S. 88: „Die Fortdauer der Patrimonial-Gerichte ist mit einem löblichen Zustande der Justizpflege nicht vereinbar.“; auch *Anonymus*, Freimüthiges Abendblatt 2 (1819), S. 65, 67 f.

[54] *Anonymus*, a.a.O., S. 66 f.

[55] *Anonymus*, a.a.O., S. 67.

[56] *Anonymus*, a.a.O., S. 67.

[57] Hierzu *Kaemmer*, Sind die Patrimonial-Gerichte verpflichtet, denjenigen Proceß-Vorschriften, welche in der LuHGOrdnung und der Güstrowschen-Canzley-Ordnung für die Untergerichte normiren, nachzugehen?, in: Beylage zu den wöchentlichen Rostockschen Nachrichten und Anzeigen 1832, Nr. 8, S. 29 ff.

keit gegenüber den Gutsherren.[58] Einzelne Stimmen befürworteten sogar die Übernahme der im ehemaligen Schwedisch-Pommern 1806/10 eingeführten und nach dem 1815 erfolgten Übergang dieses Gebietes als Neu-Vorpommern an Preußen beibehaltenen Gerichtsverfassung mit nur noch aus staatlichen bzw. städtischen Kreis- und Stadtgerichten bestehenden Niedergerichten,[59] was aber wegen der damit verbundenen Beseitigung der Patrimonialgerichtsbarkeit für Mecklenburg unrealistisch war. Als Vorteil der Niedergerichtsbarkeit galt allerdings dessen im Vergleich zu den höheren Gerichten weniger an die Förmlichkeiten des gemeinen Prozesses gebundene und daher schnellerer und einfacherer Verfahrensgang.[60]

2. Reformen durch die Gesetzgebung

Zu einer kodifikatorischen Regelung der Gerichtsverfassung und des gerichtlichen Verfahrens ist es auch bis 1848 nicht gekommen. Es ergingen aber mehrere Einzelgesetze, die einige der angeregten Reformen umgesetzt und dadurch eine gewisse Modernisierung der mecklenburgischen Justiz bewirkt haben. Dies waren die Oberappellationsgerichtsordnung – OAGO – von 1818,[61] die 1840 revidiert wurde,[62] die Patrimonialgerichtsordnung von 1821[63] und die Rechtsmittelverordnung von 1840.[64]

a) Gerichtsverfassung

Auf dem Gebiet der Gerichtsverfassung waren mit dem Untergang des Heiligen Römischen Reiches Deutscher Nation 1806 auch die beiden Reichsgerichte (RKG und RHR) als bisherige Höchstgerichte für das nur mit einem beschränkten Appellationsprivileg ausgestattete Mecklenburg entfallen und die beiden zu souveränen Staaten gewordenen Mecklenburg waren zu Trägern der gesamten Gerichtsbarkeit in ihren Territorien geworden. Sie errichteten daher 1818 ein für beide Staaten gemeinsames OAG mit Sitz zunächst in Parchim – darüber hat Herr Glöckner auf

---

[58] *Bornemann*, Beyträge (oben Fn. 47), S. 89 f., 93 ff.; für Kollegialgerichte auch *Berg*, Civilprozeß (oben Fn. 40), S. 56 f.; für eine obligatorische Prüfung der Patrimonialrichter auch *W.*, Freimüthiges Abendblatt 3 (1821), S. 131.

[59] So *Anonymus*, Freimüthiges Abendblatt 2 (1819), S. 65, 70 f.; dagegen *v. Wackenhausen*, Freimüthiges Abendblatt 3 (1821), S. 732, 736.

[60] Freimüthiges Abendblatt 3 (1821), S. 131 f.

[61] Bei *Raabe* (Hg.), Gesetzessammlung der für die Mecklenburgisch-Schwerinschen Lande, Zweite Folge, Zweiter Band: Justiz- und Militairsachen, 2. Aufl., Wismar und Ludwigslust 1866, S. 217 ff. (Nr. 1396): Oberappellationsordnung v. 1.7.1818.

[62] Revidirte Oberappellationsgerichtsordnung v. 20.7.1840 (bei *Raabe*, a.a.O., S. 251 ff. [Nr. 1400]).

[63] Patrimonialgerichtsordnung v. 21.7.1821 (bei *Raabe*, a.a.O., S. 243 ff. [Nr. 1397]).

[64] Von den Rechtsmitteln in Civil- und nicht criminellen Strafsachen v. 20.7.1840 (bei *Raabe*, a.a.O., S. 353 ff. [Nr. 1590]).

dem Ersten Rechtshistorikertag im Ostseeraum 2000 referiert[65] - und seit 1840 in Rostock. Die Oberappellationsgerichtsordnungen von 1818 und 1840 regelten nicht nur die Einrichtung, die Stellung und das Verfahren des OAG selbst, sondern enthielten auch Vorschriften über die Gerichtsbarkeit insgesamt.

Die Unabhängigkeit der Justiz gegenüber der landesherrlichen Regierung und Verwaltung, die schon der LGGEV grundsätzlich anerkannt hatte,[66] brachte die OAGO zum durchgängigen Abschluss. Die bisher für gewisse Streitigkeiten noch bestehende Gerichtsbarkeit der Regierung wurde aufgehoben.[67] Alle Beschwerden gegen Gerichtsentscheidungen, auch die auf offenkundige Nichtigkeit gestützten, über die der LGGEV noch ein Entscheidungsrecht des Landesherrn vorbehalten hatte, waren jetzt vor den für die Appellation zuständigen Gerichten zu verfolgen. Die Großherzöge sicherten zu, aufgrund ihres Rechts zur Visitation der Gerichte oder auf Beschwerde hin niemals eine Entscheidung des OAG aufzuheben, abzuändern oder die Vollstreckung zu verhindern, sondern die Sachentscheidung oder das Verfahren der Beurteilung des Gerichts zu überlassen.[68] Der bisher wenig klare Aufbau der mecklenburgischen Gerichte wurde eindeutig geregelt und die sachlichen und örtlichen Zuständigkeiten präzise voneinander abgegrenzt. Das OAG bildete die oberste Instanz.[69] Es war, anders als das bisherige Hof- und Landgericht, ausschließlich letztinstanzliches Rechtsmittelgericht.[70] Die noch bei den Reichsgerichten anhängig gewesenen Verfahren waren dabei nach den für diese geltenden Vorschriften abzuwickeln.[71] Unter dem OAG standen die Justizkanzleien, deren Zahl sich durch Aufhebung des Hof- und Landgerichts und Bildung einer Justizkanzlei zu Güstrow auf vier – Schwerin, Rostock und Güstrow für Mecklenburg-Schwerin, Neustrelitz für Mecklenburg-Strelitz – erhöhte; sie waren dem OAG untergeordnet, nicht mehr wie bisher dem Hof- und Landgericht

---

[65] *Hans Glöckner*, „Es tritt ein Zustand der Verdumpfung ein …“ – die Geschichte des Oberappellationsgerichts zu Parchim (1818–1840), in: Jörn Eckert/Kjell Åke Modéer (Hg.), Geschichte und Perspektiven des Rechts im Ostseeraum. Erster Rechtshistorikertag im Ostseeraum 8.–12. März 2000, Frankfurt a.M. 2000, S. 79 ff.; auch *Wilhelm Pöhl*, Zur Erinnerung an das Oberappellationsgericht für die Großherzoglich Mecklenburg-Schwerinschen und Mecklenburg-Strelitzschen Lande, Rostock 1918.

[66] LGGEV §§ 393–398.

[67] Hierzu und zum Folgenden PublicationsVO zur OAGO 1818 §§ 1–12; damit folgte der Gesetzgeber i. w. den Forderungen von *Nettelbladt*, Bemerkungen (oben Fn. 39).

[68] Vgl. OAGO 1818 § 87.

[69] PublicationsVO § 30, OAGO 1818 § 35, OAGO 1840 § 1.

[70] OAGO 1818 § 36, OAGO 1840 § 1.

[71] OAGO 1818 § 36; s. hierzu und überhaupt zur Situation in Mecklenburg nach dem Ende der Reichsgerichte *Hans-Konrad Stein*, Das Schicksal der unerledigten Mecklenburger Reichskammergerichtsprozesse und die Idee einer obersten Berufungs-Instanz nach dem Ende der Reichsgerichte 1806, in: Bernhard Diestelkamp (Hg.), Das Reichskammergericht am Ende des Alten Reiches und sein Fortwirken im 19. Jahrhundert, Köln/Weimar/Wien 2001, S. 217 ff.

gleichgeordnet.[72] Die Jurisdiktion der Justizkanzleien erstreckte sich fortan auf festgelegte territoriale Bezirke;[73] das bisherige Wahlrecht der Parteien zwischen den Justizkanzleien entfiel damit. Alle schriftsässigen Personen und die Kommunen standen jetzt erstinstanzlich unter der Gerichtsbarkeit der Justizkanzlei ihres durch den Wohnort bzw. Sitz bestimmten Bezirks.[74] Jede Justizkanzlei wurde ausschließlich zuständig für Rechtsmittel gegen Entscheidungen der zu ihrem Bezirk gehörenden Untergerichte.[75]

Eine Neuregelung der dringend reformbedürftigen ritterschaftlichen Patrimonialgerichtsbarkeit war nach Aufhebung der bäuerlichen Leibeigenschaft, die in Mecklenburg als einem der letzten deutschen Länder erst 1820 erfolgte,[76] unerlässlich. Sie erfolgte für Mecklenburg-Schwerin in der 1821 ergangenen Patrimonialgerichtsordnung.[77] Die erhobenen Reformforderungen wurden aber in diesem Gesetz nur in beschränktem Maße erfüllt,[78] was angesichts des auf seine Gerechtsame pochenden Gutsbesitzerstandes, zu dem jetzt zunehmend auch Bürgerliche gehörten, nicht verwunderlich ist. So blieb der Gutsherr grundsätzlich Vorsitzender seines Patrimonialgerichts, dem er nur bei eigener Beteiligung an dem Rechtsstreit nicht präsidieren durfte.[79] Ferner war das Gericht zu besetzen mit einem Justitiar, dem die Prozessleitung, die Fassung des Protokolls und der Sachentscheidung ausschließlich oblag, sowie in Zivilsachen mit einem nicht notwendig rechtskundigen, vom Gutsherrn unabhängigen Beisitzer und einem Aktuar für Protokollführung und Registratur.[80] Nicht erreicht werden konnte der Ausbau der Patrimonialgerichte als mit drei Richtern besetzte Kollegialgerichte.[81] Der auf Sicherung der fachlichen Qualifikation des Justiziars und der Stärkung seiner Stellung gegenüber der Gutsherrschaft gerichteten Zielsetzung wurde in gewissem Umfang entsprochen. Der Justitiar musste die Befähigung zum Richteramt durch Bestehen einer vor einer Justizkanzlei abzulegenden Prüfung erworben haben; der Erwerb des Doktorgrades reichte nicht aus.[82] Er wurde zu seinem Amt vom Gutsherrn

---

[72] PublicationsVO § 13.

[73] PublicationsVO § 15.

[74] PublicationsVO § 16.

[75] PublicationsVO § 16.

[76] Patentverordnung wegen Aufhebung der Leibeigenschaft v. 18.1.1820, Großherzoglich Mecklenburg-Schwerinsches officielles Wochenblatt 1820, S. 25 ff.

[77] Patrimonialgerichtsordnung v. 21.7.1821, in: *Raabe*, Gesetzessammlung (oben Fn. 61), S. 243 ff. (Nr. 1397).

[78] Vgl. *Michelsen*, Niedergerichte, Freimüthiges Abendblatt 3 (1821), S. 801: „Für den Augenblick konnte nicht mehr erreicht werden …“.

[79] PatrGO §§ 3, 4, 6.

[80] PatrGO § 3.

[81] Dies bedauerte *Michelsen*, Gerichte erster Instanz, Freimüthiges Abendblatt 3 (1821), S. 745, 746 ff.; *ders.* ebd. S. 802 f.

[82] PatrGO § 16.

bestellt, der ihn aus drei ihm von der Justizkanzlei zu präsentierenden Kandidaten auswählen konnte.[83] Seine Unabhängigkeit sollte dadurch gewahrt werden, dass ihn der Gutsherr für mindestens drei Jahre anzustellen hatte und ihm danach nur mit einjähriger Frist ordentlich kündigen konnte; nach zehnjähriger Dienstzeit war eine ordentliche Kündigung mangels abweichender vertraglicher Vereinbarung nicht mehr möglich.[84]

b) Zivilverfahren

Für das zivilgerichtliche Verfahren galten in diesem Zeitabschnitt weiterhin grundsätzlich die bisherigen Prozessgesetze und damit letztlich das Recht des gemeinen deutschen Prozesses; für das Verfahren des OAG brachte die OAGO einzelne neue Bestimmungen, von denen einige auch für die übrigen Landesgerichte anwendbar waren.[85] Insbesondere blieb es bei dem Grundsatz der Schriftlichkeit des Prozesses.[86]

Umfassend und systematisch geregelt wurde aber 1840 in der RechtsmittelVO für alle Gerichte beider Mecklenburg das Rechtsmittelverfahren in Zivilsachen und nicht kriminellen Strafsachen. Zwecks Abkürzung und Vereinfachung der Verfahren sollte die unübersehbar gewordene Vielfalt der gemeinrechtlichen Rechtsmittel reduziert, ihr oft wenig klares Verhältnis zueinander präzisiert und der Verfahrensgang insbesondere durch Verkürzung der Fristen und Verschärfung der Sanktionen für Säumnis gestrafft werden.

Vorgeschrieben wurde eine Höchstzahl der in einem Rechtsstreit möglichen Entscheidungen von zwei, unter bestimmten Voraussetzungen von drei oder vier.[87] Es gab nur noch zwei Arten von ordentlichen Rechtsmitteln:[88] einerseits die Appellation und die Restitution, andererseits die Querel und die Repräsentation. Appellation und Restitution waren statthaft gegen ein Endurteil oder ein zur Grundlage eines Beweisverfahrens dienendes oder das Ergebnis einer Beweisaufnahme aussprechendes Zwischenurteil und zwar bei einem Streitgegenstand ab 200 Thalern zwecks Anfechtung eines nicht vom OAG erlassenen Urteils die Appellation, ansonsten die Restitution. Querel und Repräsentation waren gegen sonstige gerichtliche Erlasse statthaft, die Repräsentation gegen solche des OAG im zweiten oder dritten Rechtszug. Appellation und Restitution zeitigten im Gegensatz zu Querel und Repräsentation Suspensiveffekt. Die Appellation wirkte, anders als die Restitution, auch devolutiv; über sie entschied, wenn ein niedergerichtliches Urteil ange-

[83] PatrGO § 8.

[84] PatrGO § 12.

[85] Vgl. § 56 OAGO 1818, § 13 OAGO 1840.

[86] § 55 OAGO 1818, § 14 OAGO 1840 für Verfahren des OAG; zu diesem Grundsatz allg. *Carl Trotsche*, Materialien zu einem Handbuche des Mecklenburg-Schwerinschen Particular-Civil-Processes, Güstrow 1837, §§ 60, 61.

[87] RechtsmittelVO § 1.

[88] Hierzu und zum Folgenden RechtsmittelVO § 2.

fochten wurde, die übergeordnete Justizkanzlei; bei Anfechtung eines Urteils der Justizkanzlei oder der Obergerichte von Rostock und Wismar das OAG.[89] Entsprechendes galt für die Querel,[90] während die Repräsentation nicht devolutiv wirkte.[91] Im Übrigen wurden alle Rechtsmittelverfahren wesentlich vereinfacht: Alle Fristen begannen mit Verkündung bzw. Zustellung der angefochtenen Entscheidung,[92] wobei die Nichteinhaltung ohne weiteres die Präklusion der Prozesshandlung zur Folge hatte;[93] in jeweils einer Rechtsmittelinstanz war jeder Partei grundsätzlich nur ein Schriftsatz zugelassen,[94] der Rotulationstermin wurde abgeschafft[95] und die Aktenversendung auf Antrag stark eingeschränkt.[96] Außerordentliche Rechtsmittel waren die Wiedereinsetzung in den vorigen Stand gegen mit ordentlichen Rechtsmitteln nicht mehr anfechtbare Urteile, die mit bestimmten Mängeln behaftet waren, z. B. auf falschen Urkunden beruhten,[97] die Nichtigkeitsbeschwerde, wobei Nichtigkeit einer Entscheidung nur noch bei Vorliegen eines wesentlichen Mangels hinsichtlich Gerichtspersonen, Parteien oder des Verfahrens eintrat,[98] und Rekurs bei ungebührlicher Verzögerung des Verfahrens.[99] Die nach gemeinem Recht 30 Jahre ab Erlass des nichtigen Urteils betragende Frist für die Erhebung der Nichtigkeitsbeschwerde setzte die RechtsmittelVO auf zehn Jahre herab.[100]

IV. Reformbestrebungen im Zuge der Revolution von 1848/49

1. Errichtung einer konstitutionellen Monarchie

Die im März 1848 in Deutschland ausgebrochene Revolution mit dem Ziel einer Einigung Deutschlands unter einer freiheitlichen, auf der Rechtsgleichheit aller Staatsbürger beruhenden Verfassung erfasste auch Mecklenburg und löste dort die Hoffnung auf Überwindung der besonders rückständigen monarchisch-ständischen Ordnung aus.[101] Eine aus allgemeinen Wahlen hervorgegangene Abgeordneten-

---

[89] RechtsmittelVO § 25.
[90] RechtsmittelVO § 38.
[91] RechtsmittelVO § 39.
[92] RechtsmittelVO § 40.
[93] RechtsmittelVO § 42.
[94] RechtsmittelVO § 45.
[95] RechtsmittelVO § 51 Nr. 2.
[96] Vgl. RechtsmittelVO §§ 37, 51 Nr. 3.
[97] RechtsmittelVO § 54.
[98] RechtsmittelVO § 55.
[99] RechtsmittelVO § 56.
[100] RechtsmittelVO § 54 Nr. 1 letzter Satz, § 55 Abs. 5 letzter Satz.
[101] Zum Verlauf der Revolution in Mecklenburg s. *Vitense*, Geschichte (oben Fn. 4), S. 447 ff.; *Hartmut Pogge von Strandmann*, Revolution in Mecklenburg, in: Stiftung Mecklenburg (Hg.), Modernisierung und Freiheit. Beiträge zur Demokratiegeschichte in Mecklenburg-Vorpommern, Schwerin 1995, S. 165–185; über die Zeit bis Mai 1848 auch *Adolf Werner*, Die politischen Be-

Kammer verabschiedete für Mecklenburg-Schwerin ein vom Großherzog am 10.10.1849 sanktioniertes Staatsgrundgesetz.[102] Nach dieser neuen, an die Stelle des LGGEV getretenen Verfassung war Mecklenburg-Schwerin zu einer konstitutionellen Monarchie geworden. Festgelegt waren besonders die Gleichheit aller Mecklenburger vor dem Gesetz unter Abschaffung aller Standesvorrechte und Aufhebung des Adels als Stand sowie eine die aufgehobenen Landstände[103] ersetzende Abgeordnetenkammer, die nach allgemeinem Wahlrecht zu wählen war und deren Zustimmung neben der des Großherzogs zum Zustandekommen eines Gesetzes erforderlich war.

2. Geplante Modernisierung der Ziviljustiz

Das Staatsgrundgesetz enthielt zahlreiche Bestimmungen, die auf die Einrichtung einer den liberalen, rechtsstaatlichen Forderungen entsprechenden Gerichtsbarkeit gerichtet waren. Hierzu gehörten besonders die Abschaffung der privilegierten Gerichtsstände[104] und der Patrimonialgerichtsbarkeit,[105] die Öffentlichkeit und Mündlichkeit der Gerichtsverfahren[106] sowie die lebenszeitliche Anstellung der Richter[107] unter Garantie ihrer Unabsetzbarkeit und Unversetzbarkeit.[108] Zur hiernach erforderlichen Umgestaltung der Justiz wurden schon vor Inkrafttreten der Verfassung im Schrifttum detaillierte Vorschläge diskutiert. Allgemein befürwortet wurde ein dreistufiger Gerichtsaufbau in Unter- und Mittelgerichte sowie ein Höchstgericht.[109] Umstritten war, ob für das Untergericht das Einzelrichter- oder das Kollegialitätsprinzip gelten sollte.[110] Auch nach Abschaffung der privilegierten Gerichtsstände sollte es zwei Eingangsinstanzen geben, deren Zuständigkeit sich statt nach der Standeszugehörigkeit der Parteien nach dem Streitwert und der

---

wegungen in Mecklenburg und der außerordentliche Landtag im Frühjahr 1848, Berlin/Leipzig 1907.

[102] Bei *Raabe*, Gesetzessammlung (oben Fn. 61), Band IV: Kirchensachen, Unterrichts- und Bildungsanstalten, Zweite Folge, 2. Ausgabe, Wismar/Rostock/Ludwigslust 1876, S. 664 ff. (Nr. 3759); hierzu *Hermann Brandt*, Das Staatsgrundgesetz für das Großherzogtum Mecklenburg-Schwerin 10. Oktober 1849 im Lichte der mecklenburgischen Verfassungsbemühungen des 19. Jahrhunderts, in: Stiftung Mecklenburg (Hg.), Modernisierung und Freiheit (oben Fn. 101), S. 497–522, bes. S. 503 ff.

[103] Aufhebung der landständischen Verfassung v. 10.10.1849, bei *Raabe*, Gesetzessammlung (oben Fn. 61), S. 661 f. (Nr. 3757).

[104] StGG § 52.

[105] StGG § 145.

[106] StGG § 53.

[107] StGG § 151.

[108] StGG § 154.

[109] Vgl. *Hermann Buchka*, Gedanken über die Reform des Mecklenburgischen Civil-Processes, Neustrelitz 1848, S. 5; *Gustav Floerke*, Randnotizen zu v. Schröter's Bemerkungen über die beabsichtigte neue Ordnung der Rechtspflege in Mecklenburg, Rostock/Schwerin 1850, S. 35 ff.

[110] Vgl. einerseits *Buchka*, a.a.O., S. 3; andererseits *Floerke*, a.a.O., S. 2.

Eilbedürftigkeit der Sache zu richten habe.[111] Ebenso wurde für das künftige mündliche Verfahren unter Ablehnung des französischen Systems der reinen Mündlichkeit eine Unterstützung durch Schriftsätze für notwendig erachtet.[112] Anzustreben war eine weitere Straffung und Beschleunigung der Verfahren besonders durch Stärkung des richterlichen Direktionsrechts.[113]

V. Entwicklung von 1850–1879

1. Restauration der ständischen Verfassung

Das sich im Laufe des Jahres 1849 vollziehende Scheitern der deutschen Revolution hatte in Mecklenburg einen vollständigen Sieg der Kräfte der alten Ordnung zur Folge. Wegen des Widerstands der Ritterschaft gegen das Staatsgrundgesetz wurde das in einer Verordnung von 1817[114] zur Schlichtung von Streitigkeiten zwischen Großherzog und Ständen vorgesehene Schiedsverfahren durch eine von den Königen von Hannover und von Preußen bestellte Kommission durchgeführt. In dem Freienwalder Schiedsspruch vom 12.9.1850[115] erklärte die Kommission das Staatsgrundgesetz und die Aufhebung der landständischen Verfassung für nichtig und verpflichtete den Großherzog von Mecklenburg-Schwerin zur Ausschreibung eines nach dem LGGEV zu konstituierenden Landtags. Daraufhin hob der Großherzog das Staatsgrundgesetz und die Abgeordnetenkammer auf und stellte die landständische Verfassung nach dem LGGEV wieder her.[116] Mecklenburg war damit als einziges deutsches Land bei einer ständischen Ordnung geblieben, während alle übrigen deutschen Monarchien nach 1848 zum konstitutionellen System übergegangen waren. Da in diesem auf patrimonialer Grundlage beruhenden Herrschaftssystem eine einheitliche Staatsgewalt weiterhin fehlte, wurden die beiden Mecklenburg von einem Teil der Staatsrechtler gar nicht als wirkliche Staaten i. S. der im 19. Jahrhundert herrschend gewordenen Staatslehre angesehen.[117] Insbesondere bestand in Mecklenburg keine gewählte Volksvertretung; denn die nach dem LGGEV zusammengesetzten Landtage repräsentierten gerade nicht das Gesamtvolk, sondern sie waren Versammlungen lediglich der (privilegierten) Stände zur Wahrnehmung ihrer eigenen Interessen gegenüber dem Großherzog; die überwiegende Mehrheit der Bevölkerung blieb daher von jeder politischen Mitwirkung

---

[111] So *Buchka*, a.a.O., S. 3 f.

[112] *Buchka*, a.a.O., S. 5 ff.; *Heinrich Tschierpe*, Entwurf eines Gesetzes betreffend das Verfahren der Mecklenburger Gerichte erster Instanz im ordentlichen Prozeß, Güstrow 1848, bes. S. 4 f.

[113] Diese Tendenzen bestimmten durchgängig den Entwurf von *Tschierpe*, a.a.O.: vorgeschaltete obligatorische Güteverhandlung (§ 2), richterliches Fragerecht zwecks vollständiger Sachverhaltsaufklärung (§ 5), affirmative Litiskontestation bei Säumnis (§ 16).

[114] Ordnung der Compromißinstanz v. 28.11.1817, in: *Sachsse*, Urkunden (oben Fn. 2), Nr. 213.

[115] Bei *Raabe*, Gesetzessammlung (oben Fn. 61), S. 764 f. (Nr. 3776).

[116] Verordnung v. 14.9.1850, in: *Raabe*, Gesetzessammlung (oben Fn. 61), S. 766 (Nr. 3777).

[117] Vgl. *Büsing*, Staatsrecht (oben Fn. 6), S. 38 f.

ausgeschlossen. Mit dieser Fortdauer der patrimonial-ständischen Ordnung nahmen die beiden Mecklenburg seit 1850 unter den deutschen Staaten eine Sonderstellung ein.

2. Veränderungen auf dem Gebiet des Zivilverfahrens

Mit der Aufhebung des Staatsgrundgesetzes war auch den Plänen einer durchgreifenden Umgestaltung des mecklenburgischen Justizwesens die verfassungsrechtliche Grundlage entzogen. Nicht zuletzt wurde auch das auf der vorrevolutionären Ständeordnung beruhende überkommene System der Gerichtsverfassung in Mecklenburg grundsätzlich beibehalten; erhalten blieb insbesondere die Verschiedenheit von Ober- und Niedergerichtsbarkeit einschließlich der Patrimonialgerichtsbarkeit. Da die in der Revolution von 1848 erfolgte Abschaffung dieser dem Prinzip der staatsbürgerlichen Gleichheit widersprechenden Justizstruktur in den anderen deutschen Staaten[118] auch nach dem Scheitern dieser Revolution nicht rückgängig gemacht wurde, nahm Mecklenburg für die folgenden knapp 30 Jahre bis zum Inkrafttreten der Reichsjustizgesetze auch insofern eine Sonderstellung ein. Gleichwohl herrschte auch in dieser letzten Phase einer partikulären mecklenburgischen Justizpolitik kein völliger Stillstand, sondern es kam, wie schon vor 1848, in Teilbereichen weiterhin zu nicht unerheblichen Reformen.

a) Neuordnung des Verfahrens der Niedergerichte und Justizkanzleien

Mit zwei 1855 ergangenen Verordnungen wurde das Zivilverfahren vor den Niedergerichten[119] und den Justizkanzleien[120] neu geregelt. Erklärtes Ziel beider Verordnungen war die Vereinfachung und Abkürzung des Prozessganges. Hierzu wurde das bestehen bleibende gemeinrechtliche Verfahren durch Stärkung der richterlichen Leitungsmacht und Erweiterung der Möglichkeit mündlichen Verhandelns beträchtlich modifiziert, wobei der erwähnte Entwurf von *Tschierpe*[121] offenbar als Vorbild gedient hat.

Dies galt besonders für den niedergerichtlichen Prozess, der wegen seiner geringeren Formalisierung von jeher der amtswegigen Gestaltung durch den Richter und der Mündlichkeit größeren Spielraum gelassen hatte als der obergerichtliche. Die NiedergerichtsVO machte dem Richter die Sorge für eine klare und

---

[118] So in Preußen durch die VO über die Aufhebung der Privatgerichtsbarkeit und des eximirten Gerichtsstandes usw. v. 2.1.1849 (prGS S. 1).

[119] Verordnung, betreffend das Verfahren bei den Niedergerichten in Civilsachen v. 6.2.1855, in: *Raabe*, Gesetzessammlung (oben Fn. 61), S. 387 ff. (Nr. 4387); hierzu *Trotsche*, Civil-Prozeß (oben Fn. 38), S. 624 ff.; *Schwartz*, Gesetzgebung (oben Fn. 18), S. 550; *Bomsdorf*, Prozeßmaximen (oben Fn. 34), S. 213.

[120] Verordnung, betreffend das Verfahren bei den Justizkanzleien, in: *Raabe*, Gesetzessammlung (oben Fn. 61), S. 394 ff.; hierzu *Schwartz*, Gesetzgebung (oben Fn. 18), S. 550 f.; *Bomsdorf*, Prozeßmaximen (oben Fn. 34), S. 213.

[121] S.o. Fn. 112.

erschöpfende Darstellung des Sachverhalts durch die Parteivorträge im Behauptungs- wie im Beweisverfahren mit zur wichtigsten Pflicht. Hierfür konnte er dem Kläger schon vor dem Termin die Vervollständigung der schriftlich eingereichten oder mündlich zur Registratur erklärten Klage aufgeben (§ 2 a. E.). Es musste in jedem Fall mündlich verhandelt werden; nur in schwierigen und verwickelten Fällen konnte das Gericht nach erfolgter Erklärung des Beklagten über die Klage eine weitere schriftliche Verhandlung gestatten (§ 9). In dem Termin zur mündlichen Verhandlung, der nur zur Darlegung des Sachverhalts, nicht für Rechtsausführungen bestimmt war, mussten die Parteien grundsätzlich persönlich und ohne Rechtsbeistand erscheinen (§ 5).[122] In dem Termin musste zunächst eine gütliche Beilegung des Rechtsstreits versucht und bei Misslingen des Versuchs die Verhandlung möglichst in diesem Termin abgeschlossen werden. Bei Säumnis des Beklagten war das – ggf. zu vervollständigende und zu verbessernde – Vorbringen des Klägers ohne Berücksichtigung einer etwaigen schriftlichen Klageerwiderung als zugestanden anzusehen, es galt also – anders als im gemeinen Prozess – affirmative Litiskontestation (vgl. § 6). Die Parteivorträge mussten nicht notwendig bis zur Duplik gelangen, sondern die Verhandlung konnte nach genügender Sachverhaltsaufklärung geschlossen werden (§ 8 Abs. 2) und eine Akteninrotulation fand nicht statt (§ 13). Einen notwendigen Augenschein hatte der Richter von Amts wegen vorzunehmen (§ 12). Im Beweisverfahren war der Richter bei der Zeugenvernehmung nicht auf die von den Parteien bezeichneten Tatsachen beschränkt, sondern er musste die Vernehmung bis zu dem von ihm zur Erforschung der Wahrheit für dienlich gehaltenen Umfang ausdehnen (§ 19). Der mecklenburgische Richter erlangte damit eine ähnliche Befugnis wie sie dem preußischen bei der Instruktion nach der AGO vor der Reformgesetzgebung der 40er Jahre zugestanden hatte.[123]

Die VO über das Verfahren vor den Justizkanzleien war von der gleichen Tendenz geprägt, wenn auch in schwächerer Intensität. Das Verhältnis von Mündlichkeit und Schriftlichkeit war hier umgekehrt: Grundsätzlich blieb das Verfahren schriftlich, aber in nicht schwierigen oder nicht verwickelten Fällen konnte das Gericht einen Termin zur mündlichen Verhandlung anberaumen, in dem die Parteien ohne Sachwalt auftreten konnten (nicht mussten) und in dem zunächst eine gütliche Beilegung zu versuchen war (§§ 1, 3). Im Übrigen war bei Säumnis des Beklagten die Litiskontestation ebenfalls affirmativ (§ 2), musste die Verhandlung nicht notwendig bis zur Duplik fortgeführt werden (§ 6), war kein Rotulationstermin anzuberaumen (§ 8 Abs. 2), und galten für das Beweisverfahren die für die Niedergerichte normierten Vorschriften (§ 9).

---

122 Kritisch hierzu *Trotsche*, Civil-Prozeß (oben Fn. 38), S. 625 ff.

123 Insoweit zust. *Trotsche*, Civil-Prozeß (oben Fn. 38), S. 624: „Dem Gesetze kann man nur dank wissen, daß es die krankhaften Auswüchse des Verhandlungsprincips weggeschnitten hat".

b) Neuregelung des Rechtsmittelverfahrens

1861 erging eine neue Rechtsmittelverordnung,[124] die die Verordnung von 1840 ablöste. Die neue Verordnung wollte die mit den Verordnungen von 1855 für das erstinstanzliche Verfahren verfolgte Zielsetzung der Straffung und Vereinfachung auch auf das Rechtsmittelverfahren ausdehnen. Die zulässigen Rechtsmittel waren die gleichen wie in der VorgängerVO (§ 5); es konnten in einem Rechtsstreit jetzt höchstens noch drei Entscheidungen ergehen (§ 3). Die VO 1861 führte zwei wichtige Neuerungen ein: Über das Rechtsmittel konnte nicht mehr nur schriftlich, sondern nach Ermessen des Rechtsmittelgerichts mündlich oder schriftlich verhandelt werden (§ 14); die mündlichen Termine mussten immer vor versammeltem Kollegium stattfinden (§ 14), wodurch das gemeinrechtliche Mittelbarkeitsprinzip beseitigt war. Die zweite noch einschneidendere Neuerung bestand in der Leitung des Verfahrens durch das Gericht von Amts wegen (§ 18); der Verhandlungsgrundsatz war damit im Kern eingeschränkt. Insbesondere hatte sich das Gericht durch Ausübung des Fragerechts um die Aufklärung von Unklarheiten in den Parteivorbringen mit der Sanktion zu bemühen, dass bei verweigerter Antwort die gegnerische Behauptung als zugestanden galt (§ 18 IV). Gegen die meisten Ermessensentscheidungen des Gerichts war kein Rechtsmittel mehr statthaft. Der für den gemeinen Prozess typischen Langwierigkeit der Rechtsmittelverfahren war mit diesen Regelungen vorgebeugt.

3. Einführung des reichseinheitlichen Justizsystems

Nach der Auflösung des Deutschen Bundes als Folge des preußischen Sieges über Österreich im Krieg von 1866 traten die beiden mecklenburgischen Großherzogtümer dem 1867 gegründeten Norddeutschen Bund bei[125] und wurden dadurch auch Gliedstaaten des 1871 nach dem Sieg über Frankreich durch den Beitritt der süddeutschen Staaten zum Norddeutschen Bund gegründeten Deutschen Reiches. Die Verfassungsstruktur der beiden Mecklenburg wurde jedoch durch den nunmehrigen Status der Länder als Bundesstaaten des Reiches nicht wesentlich geändert. Wiederholt unternommene Versuche von liberaler und demokratischer Seite, den aus den beiden Ständen der Ritterschaft und der Städte bestehenden Landtag durch eine gewählte Volksvertretung zu ersetzen, wie dies in den übrigen Bundesstaaten der Fall war, scheiterten an dem heftigen Widerstand vor allem des mächtigen Gutsbesitzerstandes. Es gelang daher auch jetzt kein Übergang zur konstitutionellen Monarchie, vielmehr blieb das auf dem LGGEV beruhende monarchisch-ständische Herrschaftssystem als Relikt feudaler Verhältnisse und damit die mecklenburgische

---

[124] VO, betr. die Rechtsmittel in Civilsachen und dem fiskalischen Processe v. 15.1.1861, in: Regierungs-Blatt für das Großherzogtum Mecklenburg-Schwerin 1861, Beilage zu Nr. 5; hierzu *Schwartz*, Gesetzgebung (oben Fn. 18), S. 551; *Bomsdorf*, Prozeßmaximen (oben Fn. 34), S. 213.

[125] Vgl. für Mecklenburg-Schwerin die Publications-Verordnung v. 25.6.1867, betreffend die Verfassung des Norddeutschen Bundes (Regierungs-Blatt für das Großherzogthum Mecklenburg-Schwerin, Nr. 27, S. 185).

Sonderstellung auch im Gefüge des Kaiserreichs bis zum Ende der Monarchie 1918 erhalten.

Trotz des prinzipiellen Fortbestands der alten Ordnung wirkte sich die Einbindung Mecklenburgs in das Reich auf wichtigen Rechtsgebieten durchaus im Sinne einer beträchtlichen Modernisierung des Landes aus.[126] Motor dieser Entwicklung war vornehmlich die Gesetzgebung des Reiches, die gemäß Art. 2 der Reichsverfassung dem (mecklenburgischen) Landesrecht vorging. Mit dem allgemeinen und gleichen Wahlrecht zum Reichstag, dessen Zustimmung zum Zustandekommen der Reichsgesetze erforderlich war, erhielt die Masse der Mecklenburger erstmals die – ihr auf Landesebene versagte – Möglichkeit, auf die Zusammensetzung einer parlamentarischen Körperschaft Einfluss zu nehmen, weshalb die Beteiligung an den Reichstagswahlen in Mecklenburg höher lag als im Reichsdurchschnitt.[127] Die reformfreudigen Kräfte in Mecklenburg suchten daher die Gesetzgebungszuständigkeit des Reiches gegenüber den Bundesstaaten möglichst zu erweitern, gegen den heftigen Widerstand der mecklenburgischen Konservativen und damit der Regierung; so stimmten 1873 im Bundesrat allein die beiden Mecklenburg sowie das kleine Fürstentum Reuß Ältere Linie gegen die für die Schaffung des BGB erforderliche Ausweitung der Gesetzgebungskompetenz des Reiches auf das gesamte bürgerliche Recht durch die verfassungsändernde „Lex Lasker".[128] Die Reichsgesetzgebung verdrängte einige freiheitsfeindliche mecklenburgische Gesetze aus der Reaktionszeit der 50er Jahre, wie sie etwa auf dem Gebiet des Presserechts ergangen waren, die durch das auf dem Grundsatz der Pressefreiheit beruhende Reichspressgesetz von 1874 hinfällig wurden.

Besonders tiefgreifende Folgen zeitigte die Rechtssetzung des Reiches aber in dem hier behandelten Bereich des Justizwesens. Die erste gewichtige Veränderung der mecklenburgischen Justizverfassung erfolgte noch zur Zeit des Norddeutschen Bundes mit der Errichtung des Bundesoberhandelsgerichts (BOHG) durch Bundesgesetz v. 12.6.1869[129] mit Sitz in Leipzig, das am 5.8.1870 seine Tätigkeit aufnahm und nach der Reichsgründung in Reichsoberhandelsgericht (ROHG) umbenannt wurde. Dieses Gericht des Bundes bzw. des Reiches erhielt an Stelle der obersten Gerichtshöfe der Bundesstaaten die letztinstanzliche Zuständigkeit für Streitigkeiten auf den Gebieten des Handels- und Wechselrechts, die noch unter dem

[126] Hierzu näher *Anke John*, „Unterthan" und Staatsbürger – Die deutsche Reichsgründung und der mecklenburgische Ständestaat 1866/67–1890, in: Modernisierung und Freiheit (oben Fn. 101), S. 686–707.

[127] *John*, a.a.O., S. 694.

[128] Vgl. *Schwartz*, Die Geschichte der Kodifikationsbestrebungen in Deutschland und die Entstehungsgeschichte eines bürgerlichen Gesetzbuchs für das Deutsche Reich, ArchBürgR 1 (1889), S. 1, 150.

[129] BGBl. 201; zur Gründung und Tätigkeit des Gerichts s. *Adolf Laufs*, Die Anfänge höchster Gerichtsbarkeit in Deutschland, JuS 1969, S. 256, 258 ff.; *Sabine Winkler*, Das Bundes- und spätere Reichsoberhandelsgericht, Paderborn u.a. 2001.

Deutschen Bund in den als übereinstimmende Landesgesetze aller deutschen Länder in Kraft gesetzten Kodifikationen des Allgemeinen Deutschen Handelsgesetzbuches (ADHGB) und der Allgemeinen Deutschen Wechselordnung (ADWO) vereinheitlicht worden waren. Das mecklenburgische OAG verlor damit seine Zuständigkeit in Handels- und Wechselsachen; über die nach mecklenburgischem Verfahrensrecht statthaften Rechtsmittel gegen Entscheidungen der Justizkanzleien und der Rostockischen und Wismarschen Obergerichte (vgl. o. 2 b) entschied insoweit nunmehr das BOHG bzw. das ROHG. Nach der Reichsgründung wurde die Zuständigkeit des ROHG auch auf Streitigkeiten aus jetzt durch Reichsgesetze geregelten Bereichen erweitert, wie das Urheber-, Markenschutz- und Patentrecht sowie das Haftpflichtrecht nach dem Reichshaftpflichtgesetz von 1871.[130]

Die auf bestimmte Teile des Sonderprivatrechts beschränkte Übertragung der Höchstgerichtsbarkeit auf ein Gericht in Trägerschaft des Reiches ließ das mecklenburgische Gerichtswesen im Übrigen zunächst unberührt. Vollständig umgestaltet wurde die Justiz beider Mecklenburg dann zehn Jahre später mit der Inkraftsetzung der Reichsjustizgesetze[131] zum 1. Oktober 1879. Diesen Vorgang hat Herr *Schubert* auf unserer dritten Tagung 2004 eingehend dargestellt.[132] Meine folgenden die mecklenburgische Entwicklung abschließenden Ausführungen können sich daher auf eine Herausarbeitung der Grundzüge beschränken.

Mit den aus dem Gerichtsverfassungsgesetz, der Civilprozeßordnung, der Strafprozeßordnung, der Konkursordnung und der Rechtsanwaltsordnung bestehenden Reichsjustizgesetzen wurden die Verfassung der Zivil- und Strafgerichte sowie das Verfahren der streitigen Zivil- und der Strafgerichtsbarkeit sowie des Konkurses erstmals in der deutschen Geschichte für das gesamte Reich einheitlich geregelt. Für das Thema dieses Vortrags sind das Gerichtsverfassungsgesetz – GVG – v. 27.1.1877[133] und die Civilprozeßordnung – CPO – v. 30.1.1877[134] entscheidend.

Das GVG brachte für beide Mecklenburg eine völlig neue Gerichtsorganisation mit sich.[135] Alle bisherigen Gerichte, also die Niedergerichte, Justizkanzleien, städtischen Obergerichte und das Oberappellationsgericht wurden mit Ablauf des 30.9.1879 aufgehoben.[136] Das GVG schrieb reichseinheitlich den im Prinzip bis

---

130 *Laufs*, JuS 1969, S. 256, 259.

131 Zu den Reichsjustizgesetzen s. *Wolfgang Sellert*, Die Reichsjustizgesetze von 1877 – ein gedenkwürdiges Ereignis?, JuS 1977, S. 781 ff.

132 *Werner Schubert*, Das Ende des Ancien régime in der Justizverfassung Mecklenburgs. Die neue Stellung der Juristen nach den Ausführungsverordnungen von 1879 zu den Reichsjustizgesetzen, in: Jörn Eckert/Pia Letto-Vanamo/Kjell Åke Modéer (Hg.), Juristen im Ostseeraum. Dritter Rechtshistorikertag im Ostseeraum 20.–22. Mai 2004, Frankfurt a.M. u.a., S. 205–238.

133 RGBl. S. 41.

134 RGBl. S. 83.

135 Darstellung der Veränderungen i. E. bei *Schubert*, Ende (oben Fn. 132), S. 208 ff.

136 Ausführungs-VO zum GVG – AVO – GVG v. 17.5.1879 (Reg.-Bl. f. Mecklenburg-Schwerin 1878, S. 131) § 81.

heute existierenden vierstufigen Gerichtsaufbau vor, bestehend aus Amts-, Land- und Oberlandesgerichten sowie (damals) dem an die Stelle des aufgehobenen ROHG getretenen Reichsgericht mit Sitz in Leipzig.[137] In Mecklenburg wurden dementsprechend 43 Amtsgerichte, die drei Landgerichte in Schwerin, Rostock und Güstrow sowie das beiden Ländern gemeinschaftliche Oberlandesgericht in Rostock errichtet, die am 1.10.1879 ihre Tätigkeit aufnahmen.[138] Alle diese neuen Gerichte befanden sich in der Trägerschaft des Großherzogs als Landesherren, nicht als Grundherren, wie das bei den bisherigen Amtsgerichten im Domanium der Fall gewesen war, und damit in der Trägerschaft des Staates gemäß der Vorschrift des § 15 GVG, die die Gerichte zu Staatsgerichten und die Privatgerichtsbarkeit für aufgehoben erklärte. Diese „Verstaatlichung" des Gerichtswesens bedeutete einmal das Ende der besonders in den Seestädten Rostock und Wismar noch vorhanden gewesenen Gerichtsbarkeit der Städte. Vor allem aber verschwand jetzt endlich auch in Mecklenburg als dem letzten deutschen Land die Patrimonialgerichtsbarkeit der Großherzöge im Domanium und der Rittergutsbesitzer in ihren Gutsbezirken. Mit der Beseitigung dieses typisch feudalen Instituts durch das Reichsrecht war eine der wichtigsten Hoffnungen erfüllt worden, die die liberalen Kräfte in Mecklenburg seit dem Beitritt des Landes zum Norddeutschen Bund gehegt hatten.[139] Dies galt freilich nur für die streitige Zivilgerichtsbarkeit; die freiwillige Gerichtsbarkeit blieb weiterhin städtisch bzw. bei den Ritterschaften patrimonial, während sie im Domanium den neuen Amtsgerichten übertragen wurde.[140] Als weiteres Relikt aus ständischer Zeit entfiel unter der neuen Gerichtsverfassung der Unterschied zwischen niederer und oberer Gerichtsbarkeit. Zwar gab es mit den Amts- und den Landgerichten weiterhin zwei unterschiedliche Eingangsgerichte, deren Zuständigkeit bestimmte sich aber nicht mehr nach der Standeszugehörigkeit der Rechtssuchenden, sondern nach der Art der Streitsachen, insbesondere nach dem Streitwert. Somit erhielt Mecklenburg bei Fortbestand der monarchisch-ständischen Ordnung im Übrigen erst mit der reichsrechtlich gebotenen Einführung des GVG eine den Anforderungen des bürgerlichen Rechtsstaats genügende Gerichtsverfassung.

Auf neue Grundlagen gestellt wurde auch das (streitige) Zivilverfahren mit der Einführung der CPO.[141] Erstmals erhielt Mecklenburg hierdurch ein für alle Gerichte geltendes einheitliches Prozessrecht. Die CPO in ihrer ursprünglichen Fassung verwirklichte weitgehend die liberalen Vorstellungen von Wesen und

---

[137] Zum GVG *Sellert*, JuS 1977, S. 781, 782 ff.

[138] Näher *Schubert*, Ende (oben Fn. 132), S. 211 ff.

[139] Vgl. den mit – b – gezeichneten Aufsatz „Die mecklenburgischen Patrimonialgerichte und der Entwurf einer Norddeutschen Civilprozeßordnung", Die Grenzboten 28.4 (Leipzig 1869), S. 45 ff.

[140] Vgl. *Schlesinger*, Staats- und Verwaltungsrecht (oben Fn. 6), § 121; *Schubert*, Ende (oben Fn. 132), S. 215 f.

[141] Hierzu näher *Schubert*, Ende (oben Fn. 132), S. 227 ff.

Zweck des Zivilverfahrens,[142] als dessen nahezu ideale Positivierung der Code de procédure civile angesehen wurde. Dieser Konzeption stand der gemeinrechtlich geprägte bisherige mecklenburgische Prozess in vielen Punkten entgegen. Da die CPO ganz auf den Maximen der Öffentlichkeit und der Mündlichkeit des Verfahrens beruhte, wurde das bei den Obergerichten bis dahin grundsätzlich schriftliche Verfahren (s. o. 2 a) durch die im Mittelpunkt des Prozesses stehende mündliche Verhandlung ersetzt. Aus dem Grundsatz der Einheit der mündlichen Verhandlung einschließlich der Beweisaufnahme folgte der Wegfall der Unterteilung des Erkenntnisverfahrens in Behauptungs- und Beweisverfahren mit dem Beweisinterlokut als Zäsur, stattdessen konnten Tatsachenbehauptungen, Angriffs- und Verteidigungsmittel bis zum Schluss der mündlichen Verhandlung vorgebracht werden. Damit war auch die auf Prozessbeschleunigung gerichtete Eventualmaxime entfallen.[143] Das Verfahren nach der CPO war von der Herrschaft der Parteien geprägt, die nicht nur über den Streitgegenstand verfügen, sondern auch weitgehend die dem Gericht vorzutragenden Tatsachen bestimmen konnten; der Einfluss des Gerichts auf die Gestaltung des Verfahrens war demgegenüber relativ gering, da sich die Rolle des Richters nach dem – vermeintlichen – französischen Vorbild nur auf die Entscheidung über den ihm von den Streitteilen unterbreiteten Tatsachenstoff beschränken sollte. Für Mecklenburg bedeutete dies eine gewisse Reduzierung der von den Prozessreformen des 19. Jahrhunderts in Einschränkung der gemeinrechtlichen Verhandlungsmaxime geschaffenen richterlichen Einwirkungsmöglichkeiten auf die Tatsachenfeststellung (s. o. 2 a). Weiter vereinfacht wurde mit der Einführung der CPO das System der Rechtsmittel, die jetzt nur noch in Berufung, Revision und Beschwerde bestanden. Gegen amtsgerichtliche Urteile war nur die Berufung zum Landgericht statthaft, gegen erstinstanzliche Urteile der Landgerichte die Berufung zum Oberlandesgericht, gegen Berufungsurteile des Oberlandesgerichts die Revision zum Reichsgericht gegeben. Das OLG Rostock war damit zum Gericht des zweiten statt wie bisher das OAG des dritten Rechtszuges geworden.

VI. Schlussbetrachtung

Das Ergebnis der vorstehenden Untersuchung lässt sich in folgenden Punkten zusammenfassen:

1. Die mecklenburgische Justiz wurde bis 1879 bestimmt durch die auf dem ständischen Prinzip beruhende patrimoniale Verfassungsordnung des Landes.

2. Die Ausübung der hoheitlichen Rechte war in Mecklenburg zwischen Landesherrn und Ständen funktional aufgeteilt. Die hieraus resultierenden Befugnisse hatten die beiden Stände der Ritterschaft und der Landschaft und deren einzelne Mitglieder nicht als landesherrliche Amtsträger inne, sondern kraft eigenen Rechts. Diese ständische Rechtsstellung gegenüber dem Landesherrn beruhte auf

---

[142] Zur CPO 1877 *Sellert*, JuS 1977, S. 781, 786 ff.

[143] Kritisch hierzu *Schubert*, ZRG GA 85 (1968), S. 127, 182 ff.

vertraglicher Grundlage, in erster Linie auf dem LGGEV. Bei den sich auf die Abgrenzung von landesherrlichen und ständischen Rechten beziehenden Fragen handelte es sich folglich nicht um bloße Verwaltungsangelegenheiten, sondern um Rechtsfragen, für deren Entscheidung die Gerichte zuständig waren. Der Gerichtsbarkeit kam infolgedessen in Mecklenburg schon unter dem ancien régime eine stärkere Unabhängigkeit gegenüber dem Landesherrn zu als in den absolutistisch regierten Staaten.

3. Diese relativ starke Position der Justiz kam aber der nicht privilegierten Bevölkerung gerade nicht zugute. Denn diese die große Mehrheit der Einwohner ausmachenden Personen standen, was insbesondere für die bäuerlichen Hintersassen der Rittergutsbesitzer auch nach dem Ende der Leibeigenschaft galt, in einem unmittelbaren Untertanenverhältnis nicht zum Landesherrn, sondern zu ihrer jeweiligen ständischen Obrigkeit und waren daher vor allem an einem wirksamen Rechtsschutz gegenüber diesen Obrigkeiten interessiert. Ein solcher Rechtsschutz war aber deshalb nicht gewährleistet, weil sich die für diese Bevölkerungskreise erstinstanzlich zuständigen Niedergerichte in der Trägerschaft gerade ihrer ständischen Obrigkeiten befanden, die Patrimonialgerichte also in derjenigen der Gutsherren, wobei das Patrimonialgericht selbst für einen Rechtsstreit zwischen einem Gutsuntertanen und dessen Patrimonialherrn zuständig blieb.

4. Im 19. Jahrhundert, genauer, vor 1879, führten die vor allem im Zusammenhang mit der Errichtung des Oberappellationsgerichts betriebenen Reformen zu einer gewissen Modernisierung der Gerichtsverfassung i. S. einer Straffung des Gerichtsaufbaus und eindeutiger Abgrenzung der Zuständigkeiten.

5. Die Unterteilung in niedere und obere Gerichtsbarkeit, deren Zuständigkeit von der Standeszugehörigkeit der Prozessparteien abhing, blieb – anders als in den meisten anderen deutschen Ländern – auch nach 1848 bestehen. Dies schloss den Fortbestand auch der Patrimonialgerichtsbarkeit ein. Die Patrimonialgerichtsordnung von 1821 versuchte nur, den ärgsten Missständen entgegen zu steuern.

6. Das zivilgerichtliche Verfahren, dem die Regeln des gemeinen deutschen Prozesses zugrunde lagen, wurde durch mehrere gesetzgeberische Maßnahmen spürbar modernisiert. Die beiden Verordnungen von 1855 über das Verfahren vor den Niedergerichten und vor den Justizkanzleien bezweckten eine Beschleunigung der Prozesse durch Beseitigung veralteter Förmlichkeiten, Erweiterung der Möglichkeit mündlichen Verhandelns und Stärkung der richterlichen Leitungsmacht. Die Rechtsmittelverordnungen von 1840 und 1861 vereinfachten das Rechtsmittelverfahren.

7. Die Rechtssetzung des Norddeutschen Bundes seit 1867 und sodann des Deutschen Reiches seit 1871 ließ zwar die ständische Verfassung Mecklenburgs im Grundsatz bestehen, bewirkte aber auf einzelnen Gebieten (z.B. Pressewesen) Veränderungen im bürgerlich-liberalen Sinne. Das Justizwesen gestalteten die 1879 auch in den beiden Mecklenburg eingeführten Reichsjustizgesetze durchgreifend

um. Die bedeutsamsten Neuerungen brachte das Gerichtsverfassungsgesetz mit dem Wegfall des der neuen reichseinheitlichen Gerichtsverfassung unbekannten Unterschieds zwischen niederer und oberer Gerichtsbarkeit und vor allem der Patrimonialgerichtsbarkeit als Folge der Erklärung der Gerichtsbarkeit zur Angelegenheit allein des Staates und des Verbots der Privatgerichtsbarkeit. Auf eine neue Grundlage gestellt wurde auch das streitige Zivilverfahren. Hier trat an die Stelle des bisher gemeinrechtlich geprägten Prozesses die in ihrer ursprünglichen Fassung dem Ideal eines liberalen bürgerlichen Rechtsstreits ziemlich weitgehend folgende CPO, deren starke Beschränkung der richterlichen Leitungsmacht sich allerdings in der Folgezeit nicht nur in Mecklenburg als problematisch erweisen und zu entsprechenden Gesetzesänderungen führen sollte. Die Reichsjustizgesetze beendeten mithin die Eigenheiten der mecklenburgischen Gerichtsbarkeit, deren Strukturen fortan mit den auch in den übrigen deutschen Ländern eingeführten übereinstimmte. Die während der Zugehörigkeit des Landes zur DDR unterbrochene Einheit des deutschen Justizwesens wurde als Folge der Wiedervereinigung nach einer kurzen Übergangsphase wiederhergestellt.

Die Justizreform vom Jahr 1889 und ihre Bedeutung für die Baltischen Provinzen Russlands und (später) Lettland

Jānis Lazdiņš

Motto: „*Идея правосудія въ сознаніи народовъ всегда была окружена ореоломъ особаго величія*“[1]
[Die Idee der Rechtsprechung war im Bewusstsein der Völker immer schon mit besonderem Glorienschein umgeben]

I. Einleitung

Das Gesetz des Zaren Alexander III.[2] vom 9. Juli 1889 über die Gerichtsreform in den Baltischen Provinzen[3] legte fest, dass die Anordnungen des Russischen Imperiums vom 20. November 1864 über die Organisation des Justizwesens[4] (sog. *Tiesu uztavi* – in lettischer Sprache[5]) und das Prozessrecht in den Baltischen Provinzen gelten sollten.[6] Dies bedeutete, dass folgende Gesetzbücher in Kraft traten:

---

[1] Судебная реформа [Том 2]. Подъ редакціей [Justizreform (Bd. 2)], hg. von *Н.В. Давыдова и Н.Н. Полянскаго. При ближайшемъ участіи* [unter Beteiligung von]: *М.Н. Гернета*, А.Э. Вормса, Н.К. Муравьева и А.Н. Паренаго. Москва [Moskau] 1915, S. 1.

[2] Александр III Александрович Романов [Alexander III. Alexsandrovic Romanow], 1845–1894, Zar von 1881 bis 1894.

[3] I. О преобразованіи судебной части въ Прибалтійскихъ губерніяхъ [Über die Reorganisation des Justizwesens in den Baltischen Gouvernements] и [und] II. О преобразованіи крестьянскихъ присутсвенныхъ местъ Прибалтійскихъ губерній [Über die Reorganisation der Bauerbehörden in den Baltischen Gouvernements], in: Полное собраніе законовъ Россійской имперіи. [Vollständige Sammlung der Gesetze des Russischen Kaiserreichs] Царствованіе государя императора Александра Третьяго [Die Herrschaft des Zaren Alexander III.]. Том 9 [Bd. 9], Nr. 6188, zugänglich unter: http://www.nlr.ru/eres/law_r/search.php?regim=4&page=411&part=1540 [Stand 30.11.2012].

[4] „Судебные Уставы Императора Александра II и изданныя въ дополненіе къ симъ Уставамъ узаконенія применяются къ губерніямъ Лифляндской, Эстляндской и Курляндской [...]“ [Die Gerichtsordnung des Zaren Alexander II. und die Ausgaben zur Ergänzung der Gerichtsordnung werden in den Livländischen, Estnischen und Kurländischen Gouvernements angewendet], siehe: I. Über die Reorganisation des Justizwesens in den Baltischen Gouvernements, статья 1 [Art. 1] (im Folgenden: Art.).

[5] Siehe: Ķeizara Aleksandra II. [Zar Alexander II.] Teesu uztavi izdoti uz ķeizara Aleksandra Aleksandrowitscha pawehli. Teeslietu Minizterijas uzdewumā pahrtulkojis Kurzemes Guberņas Prokurora Beedrs A. Sterste [Die Gerichtsordnung, ausgegeben auf Befehl des Zaren Alexander Alexandrowitsch. Im Auftrag des Justizministeriums übersetzt von *A. Sterste*, Genosse/Gehilfe des Staatsanwalts des Kurländischen Gouvernements], Jelgava 1889.

[6] Siehe: *Voldemārs Kalniņš*, Latvijas PSR Valsts un tiesību vēsture, I [Geschichte des Staates und des Rechts der Lettischen SSR, I], Rīga 1972, S. 347 f., 350 f.

1) die Gerichtsordnung als Gerichtsverfassungsgesetz (*Учрежденія судебныхъ установленій*, im Folgenden: GO);[7]

2) die Zivilprozessordnung (*Уставъ гражданскаго судопроизводства*, im Folgenden: ZPO);[8]

3) Die Strafprozessordnung (*Уставъ уголовнаго судопроизводства*, im Folgenden: StPO).[9]

Die GO erhielt auch Bestimmungen über die Rechte und Pflichten der Staatsanwälte,[10] vereidigten Rechtsanwälte[11] und privaten Rechtsanwälte.[12] Die Prozessordnungen konkretisierten die Rechte und Pflichten dieser Juristenberufe.

Das Inkrafttreten der Prozessordnungen war in den Baltischen Gouvernements ein essentieller Bestandteil der Gerichtsreform. Der vorliegende Beitrag soll sich innerhalb dieses thematischen Rahmens bei der Analyse des Prozessrechts im Schwerpunkt mit den Prinzipien beschäftigen, welche für die Neuzeit die von den

---

7 Учрежденія судебныхъ установленій [Die Gerichtsordnung] (im Folgenden: GO), in: Полный сводъ законовъ Россійской Имперіи [Vollständige Sammlung der Gesetze des Russischen Kaiserreichs]. Все 16 томовъ со всеми относящимися къ нимъ Продолженіями и съ дополнительными узаконеніями по 1 Ноября 1910 года. Въ 2-хъ книгахъ. Подъ редакціей А.А. Добровольскаго, Оберъ-Прокурора Судебнаго Департамента Правительствующаго Сената. Составиль А.Л. Саатчіанъ. [Alle 16 Bände samt dazu gehörenden Fortsetzungen und zusätzlichen Gesetzgebungen zum 1. November 1910 in 2 Büchern. Hg. von *A.A. Dobrovolsky*, Oberstaatsanwalt der Gerichtsabteilung des Herrschenden Senats. Zusammengesetzt von *A. Saatchian*]. Книга 2 [Buch 2]. Томы IX–XVI [Bd. IX–XVI], St. Petersburg 1911 (im Folgenden: ПСЗ II). – Том XVI [Bd. XVI] (im Folgenden: Bd.), – часть 1 [Teil 1] (im Folgenden: Teil), S. 3869–3967.

8 Уставъ гражданскаго судопроизводства [Die Zivilprozessordnung] (im Folgenden: ZPO), in: ПСЗ II, Bd. XVI, Teil 1, S. 3967–4166.

9 Уставъ уголовнаго судопроизводства [Die Strafprozessordnung] (im Folgenden: StPO), in: ПСЗ II, Bd. XVI, Teil 1, S. 4211–4366.

10 О лицахъ прокурорскаго надзора [Über die Personen der staatsanwaltlichen Aufsicht], in: ПСЗ II, Bd. XVI, GO, Teil 1, Art. 8, 9, 124–136 und Учрежденіе Министерства Юстиціи [Institutionen des Justizministeriums], in: Полный сводъ законовъ Россійкой Имперіи [Vollständige Sammlung der Gesetze des Russischen Kaiserreichs]. Все 16 томовъ со всеми относящимися къ нимъ Продолженіями и съ дополнительными узаконеніями по 1 Сентября 1910 года. Въ 2-хъ книгахъ. Подъ редакціей А.А. Добровольскаго, Оберъ-Прокурора Судебнаго Департамента Правительствующаго Сената. Составилъ А.Л. Саатчіанъ [Alle 16 Bände samt dazu gehörenden Fortsetzungen und zusätzlichen Gesetzgebungen zum 1. September 1910 in 2 Büchern. Hg. von *A.A. Dobrovolsky*, Oberstaatsanwalt der Gerichtsabteilung des Herrschenden Senats. Zusammengesetzt von *A. Saatchian*]. Книга 1 [Buch 1], Bd. I–VIII, St. Petersburg 1911 (im Folgenden: ПСЗ I), Bd. I, Teil 2, Art. 771.

11 О присяжныхъ поверенныхъ [Über vereidigte Rechtsanwälte], in: ПСЗ II, Bd. XVI, GO, Teil 1, Art. 353–406.

12 О частныхъ поверенныхъ [Über private Rechtsanwälte], in: ПСЗ II, Bd. XVI, GO, Teil 1, Art. 406^1–406^{19}.

Gerichten ausgeübte Macht und die damit verbundene Tätigkeit der Juristenberufe erklären.

Am 9. Juli 1889 wurde „Das Gesetz über die Gemeindegerichte in den Baltischen Provinzen“ (*Волостной судебный уставъ Прибалтійскихъ губерній*)[13] verabschiedet. Das Gesetz hat ein zweistufiges System von Gemeindegerichten aufgebaut. Faktisch waren die Gemeindegerichte Gerichte für die Bauernschicht.[14] Mit dem allmählichen Verzicht auf die mittelalterliche Hierarchisierung der Gesellschaft nach sozialen Schichten verloren auch die Gemeindegerichte an Bedeutung. Heutzutage gibt es in Lettland keine Gemeindegerichte mehr.

In Verbindung mit der Implementierung der Gerichtsreform wurde auch eine Reihe anderer Gesetze verabschiedet, beispielsweise:

1) am 20. November 1864 wurde das Gesetz über die von Friedensrichtern aufzuerlegenden Strafen (*Устав о наказаниях, налагаемых мировыми судьями*) verabschiedet;[15]

2) am 14. April 1866 wurde das Notariatsgesetz (*Положения о нотариальной части*)[16] verabschiedet.

Das Gesetz verankerte das sog. lateinische Notariat im Notariatssystem des Russischen Kaiserreichs. Das Inkrafttreten des neuen Notariatsgesetzes war mit der Implementierung der Gerichtsreform verbunden. Die Notare waren Personen, die zur rechtsprechenden Gewalt gehören und über ein den gerichtlichen Amtsträgern angeglichenes Recht verfügen. Sie beglaubigten Dokumente und verliehen ihnen dadurch öffentliche Glaubwürdigkeit. Aus dem Grund war die rechtliche Tätigkeit der Notare mit der rechtsprechenden Gewalt aber nicht vollkommen deckungsgleich. Das zeigt sich besonders in dem Umstand, dass das Notariatsrecht nicht in die GO aufgenommen wurde.[17]

---

[13] Волостной судебный уставъ Прибалтійскихъ губерній [Das Gesetz (die Ordnung) über die Gemeindegerichte in den Baltischen Provinzen]. Учрежденіе Волостныхъ и Верхнихъ Крестьянскихъ Судовъ [Institutionen von Gemeinde- und Obersten Bauerngerichten], in: ПСЗ, Bd. XVI, Teil 1, Книга 1 [Buch 1], S. 4403–4412.

[14] Siehe mehr über die Gemeindegerichte in den Baltischen Gouvernements des Russischen Kaiserreichs bei *Lazdiņš*, Baltijas zemnieku privāttiesības (oben Fn. 6).

[15] Уставъ о наказаніяхъ, налагаемыхъ Мировыми Судьями [Das Gesetz über die von Friedensrichtern aufzuerlegenden Strafen], in: ПСЗ II, Bd. XV, S. 3797–3836.

[16] Положеніе о нотаріальной части [Das Notariatsgesetz], in: ПСЗ II, Bd. XVI, Teil 1, S. 4165–4210.

[17] Mehr zum Notariat im Russischen Kaiserreich bei *Sanita Osipova*, Die allgemeine Bedeutung des österreichischen Rechtssystems für Lettland, in: Michael Geistlinger u.a. (Hg.), 200 Jahre ABGB – Ausstrahlungen, Die Bedeutung der Kodifikation für andere Staaten und andere Rechtskulturen, Wien 2011, S. 225–238.

II. Die formale und die faktische Seite der Gerichtsreform, deren Ziele und Motive in den Baltischen Provinzen

1. Die formale Seite

Das Ziel der Gerichtsreform des Russischen Kaiserreichs war die Abgrenzung der Verwaltungs-, Polizei- und Gerichtskompetenz.[18] Von Bedeutung war auch die Gewährung der Öffentlichkeit bei Verfahrenshandlungen.

Der Herrschende Senat wies bei der Verabschiedung der GO auf folgende Notwendigkeit hin:

> „[...] дать народу правый и равный для всехъ судъ, и какъ средства для этого – „возвышенiе судебной власти и утвержденiе уваженiя къ закону [...]“ [ein für das ganze Volk gerechtes und gleiches Gericht schaffen und als Mittel dafür – Erhöhung der gerichtlichen Macht und Festigung des Respekts vor dem Gesetz.][19]

Respekt vor dem Gesetz ist etwas mehr als nur blinder Gehorsam gegenüber der staatlichen Macht. Die Einhaltung des Gesetzes muss zum Leitmotiv einer jeden Tätigkeit eines jeden Staatsangehörigen werden:

> „[...] уваженiе къ закону, безъ коего невозможно общественное благосостоянiе и которое должно быть постояннымъ руководителемъ действiй всехъ и каждаго, отъ вышаго до низшаго“ [(...) ohne Respekt vor dem Gesetz ist der Wohlstand der Gesellschaft nicht möglich. Respekt vor dem Gesetz muss die Tätigkeiten aller und eines jeden stets begleiten, vom Höheren bis zum Niedrigeren.][20]

Darüber hinaus garantierte die Gerichtsreform, dass die Organisation des Justizwesens und die damit verbundenen Institutionen – die Staatsanwaltschaft, die Rechtsanwaltschaft und das Notariat – künftig sowohl im Russischen Kaiserreich als auch in den Baltischen Provinzen nach [nahezu] einheitlichen Prinzipien und Gesetzen wirkten. Auch der Zivilprozess und der Strafprozess waren gleichförmig ausgestaltet.

---

[18] Das Gericht hatte nicht nur die Streitigkeiten der Staatsangehörigen zu verhandeln, sondern auch zwischen den Staatsangehörigen und dem Staat zu entscheiden. Daraus folgte die Forderung nach Unabhängigkeit der Justiz von der Exekutive. Dies wurde zu einem der Leitmotive für die Reform der Justiz. Siehe: *Головачев, А.А.* Десять летъ реформъ, 1861–1871. Изданiе „Вестника Европы“ [Zehn Jahre der Reform, 1861–1871. Ausgabe „Europäischer Anzeiger”], St. Petersburg 1872, S. 304 f.

[19] *Джаншiев, Г.* Основы судебной реформы (къ 25-ти летiю новаго суда). Историко-юридическiе этюды [Grundlagen der Gerichtsreform (zum 25. Jubiläum des neuen Gerichts). Historisch-juristische Studien], Moskau 1891, S. 3.

[20] *Гессенъ, I.B.* Судебная реформа. Великiя реформы 60-хъ гг. въ ихъ прошломъ и настоящемъ [Gerichtsreform. Die Geschichte und Gegenwart der großen Reform der 60er Jahre], St. Petersburg 1905, S. 180.

2. Die faktische Seite

Gewisse Unterschiede verblieben. Der sichtbarste davon war der Verzicht auf die Einführung der Geschworenenbank in den Baltischen Provinzen.[21] Die Geschworenen waren berechtigt, nach ihrem Gewissen zu entscheiden. Es gab Fälle, in denen das Gewissen dem Gesetz widersprach. Die Motive dafür – emotionelle Überzeugung, ungenügende Bildung, Korruption[22] oder etwas anderes – sind heute nicht mehr bestimmbar.[23] Trotzdem wurden die Vertreter der baltischen Aristokratie, die vor der Gerichtsreform meistens die Posten der Richter und beisitzenden Richter verschiedenen Niveaus bekleidet hatten, als ehrenhafte Treuhänder dieser Justizaufgaben angesehen. Natürlich lässt sich kaum behaupten, kein Vertreter des baltischen Adels habe Bestechungsgelder entgegengenommen oder gegeben oder ein seltsames Urteil gefällt. Die Institution der beisitzenden Richter erschien jedoch attraktiver als die Geschworenenbank. Vor dem Hintergrund dieser historischen Tradition führte man deshalb die Geschworenenbank in Lettland nicht ein und hält an dieser Grundsatzentscheidung bis heute fest.[24]

Die Gerichtsreform „verlieh" der juristischen Ausbildung eine bisher nicht vorhandene Bedeutung. Damit soll nicht auf den Ausbau des Rechtsstaates angespielt werden. Das Leben hat bewiesen, dass das Rechtsstudium einzelner Personen keine Garantie für ein gesteigertes rechtliches Bewusstsein der ganzen Gesellschaft ist. Eher im Gegenteil – die jungen Juristen passten sich nach dem Abgang von der Universität mit Antritt des staatlichen oder eines anderen Dienstes eher der öffentlichen Rechtswelt an als Änderungen anzustreben.

> „Громадное большинство молодыхъ людей бросаетъ, по выходе изъ университета, всякія научныя занятія и, растерявъ мало-по-малу скромный свой научный багажъ, обращается въ обыкновеннаго провинціальнаго чиновника, не получившаго никакого образованія" [Eine hohe Anzahl der jungen Leute geht nach

---

[21] *Kalniņš*, Latvijas PSR (oben Fn. 6), S. 293.

[22] Forschungen von Professor Arved Schwabe belegen, dass sich um die Mitte des 19. Jahrhunderts im russischen Kaiserreich wegen der Korruption, mangelnden Fachkompetenz und anderer negativer Umstände in der Justiz ca. drei Millionen nicht verhandelte Verfahren ansammelten. Die baltischen Richter waren dagegen nach Meinung des Professors besser ausgebildet und ließen sich nicht bestechen. Siehe: *Arveds Švābe*, Latvijas vēsture (1800–1914) [Lettische Geschichte (1800–1914)]. 2. izdevums [2. Aufl.], Uppsala 1962, S. 494.

[23] Gegen die Einführung der Geschworenenbank gab es auch in den Binnen-Gouvernements des russischen Kaiserreichs während der Ausarbeitung der GO beträchtliche Einwände. Es wurde darauf hingewiesen, dass das Volk noch nicht genug rechtlich ausgebildet (reif) sei, um die rechtlichen Nuancen zu verstehen und logisch zu denken. Siehe: Судебная реформа [Том 1]. Подъ редакцiей [Gerichtsreform [Bd. 1]. Herausgegeben von] Н.В. Давыдова и Н.Н. Полянскаго при ближайшемъ участии [unter Beteiligung von]: М.Н. Гернета, А.Э. Вормса, Н.К. Муравъева и А.Н. Паренаго. Moskau 1915, S. 316.

[24] Siehe: Das Gesetz Saeima der Republik Lettland vom 15.12.1992. „Par tiesu varu" [Über die Judikative/Gerichtsbarkeit], zugänglich unter: http://www.likumi.lv/doc.php?id=62847 [Stand: 02.12.2012].

dem Abgang von der Universität keiner wissenschaftlichen Tätigkeit nach. Allmählich verlieren sie ihr bescheidenes wissenschaftliches Kapital und werden zu einfachen provinziellen Beamten, die keine Ausbildung genossen haben].[25]

3. Ziele und Motive

Die Einführungsziele und Motive der Gerichtsordnung des russischen Kaiserreichs in den Baltischen Provinzen waren klar:

1) ein Schritt in die Richtung der Zentralisierung des Staates;

2) die Festigung der Russifizierungspolitik in den Baltischen Provinzen.

Eine vom Staat organisierte, planmäßige Russifizierungspolitik begann in den Baltischen Gouvernements in den 80er Jahren des 19. Jahrhunderts nach der sogenannten Revision des Senators Manasein. Beispielsweise wurde der Universität Dorpat Russisch als Vorlesungssprache aufgezwungen und die Stadt wurde in Jurjew umbenannt. Zu derselben Zeit wurden Lehrer, die kein Russisch beherrschten, allmählich entlassen. Laut Professor Arved Schwabe (1888–1959) funktionierte das russische Kaiserreich nach dem Prinzip:

> „*Kaut vai veselām paaudzēm būtu jāiet bojā, valdība neatkāpsies no sava nodoma*" [Wenn auch ganze Generationen zugrunde gehen sollten, die Regierung wird von ihrer Absicht nicht abweichen].[26]

Am offensichtlichsten kam die Russifizierungspolitik in den Gerichtsorganen als Übergang zum Russischen als der einzigen Sprache des Gerichtsverfahrens im Friedensgericht und den sogenannten allgemeinen Gerichten[27] zum Ausdruck:

> „Въ судебныхъ установленіяхъ губерній Лифляндской, Эстляндской и Курляндской, какъ письменное, такъ и словесное производство происходитъ на Русскомъ языке. Прошенія, жалобы и отзывы, представляемые частными лицами по уголовнымъ и гражданскимъ деламъ, должны быть изложены также на Русскомъ языке" [Sowohl die mündlichen als auch die schriftlichen gerichtlichen Verhandlungen erfolgen in den Livländischen, Estnischen und Kurländischen Gouvernements in russischer Sprache. Ersuchen, Beschwerden und Beurteilungen von Privatpersonen in Straf- und Zivilverfahren müssen in russischer Sprache eingereicht werden].[28]

Andere Quellen, Ziele und Motive des Gerichtssystems sind in den mit dem russischen Kaiserreich verbundenen politischen Geschehnissen der 50er Jahre des 19. Jahrhunderts und in den Reformen der 60er Jahre zu finden.

---

[25] *Гессенъ,* Судебная реформа (oben Fn. 20), S. 183.

[26] *Arveds Švābe,* Latvijas vēsture (1800–1914) [Lettische Geschichte (1800–1914)]. 1. izdevums [1. Aufl.], Uppsala 1958, S. 464 f.

[27] Zu den allgemeinen Gerichten gehörten also das Landgericht, der Gerichtshof und der Herrschende Senat als Oberstes Gericht.

[28] I. Über die Reorganisation des Justizwesens in den Baltischen Gouvernements, Art 2.

III. Die politische Situation in den 50er Jahren des 19. Jahrhunderts

Die Rückständigkeit des russischen Kaiserreichs gegenüber den entwickelten westeuropäischen Ländern manifestierte sich in der Niederlage im Krimkrieg (1853–1856) gegen die von Großbritannien und Frankreich geleitete Staatenkoalition. Diese deckte nicht nur die schwachen Seiten des zaristischen Staatsverwaltungsmodells auf, sondern auch andere Mängel,[29] unter denen zwei hervorzuheben sind:

1) die wirtschaftliche Rückständigkeit. Ihr offensichtlicher Grund war die Nutzung einer unfreien Arbeitskraft, das heißt, der Arbeit von Leibeigenen in der Wirtschaft. Dies betraf weder Polen[30] noch die Baltischen Provinzen, denn dort hatte man die Leibeigenschaft schon anfangs des 19. Jahrhunderts abgeschafft;[31]

2) die den neuzeitlichen Anforderungen nicht entsprechende Organisation des Justizwesens. Beispielsweise war die Judikative von der Exekutive nicht streng getrennt, die Unabhängigkeit der Gerichte und Richter war nicht normativ festgelegt; es bestand keine formelle Gleichheit vor dem Gericht; die Verhandlung in den Verfahren dauerte lange oder fand gar nicht statt; unter den gerichtlichen Amtsträgern herrschte ein hohes Maß an Korruption und es gab noch andere Probleme.

Eine gewisse Ausnahme war das Livländische Gouvernement in der sogenannten Schwedenzeit (17. und 18. Jahrhundert). Damals war die Rechtsprechung in gewisser Weise von der Verwaltung getrennt. Die Bauern waren ebenso wie andere x-beliebige Staatsangehörige berechtigt, sich bei den vom Staat eingerichteten Gerichten zu beschweren. Jedoch hat auch das Gerichtssystem der Schwedenzeit Merkmale eines gesellschaftlich segmentierten Gerichtssystems beibehalten. Beispielsweise waren Bauern berechtigt, gegen übermäßige Unterdrückung beim Obersten Gericht der Provinz – dem Hof-Gericht – nur kollektive Klagen zu erheben.[32]

---

[29] Latvijas PSR vēsture. No vissenākiem laikiem līdz mūsu dienām. Trešais pārstrādāts un papildināts izdevums Latvijas PSR ZA akadēmiķa *A. Drīzuļa* redakcijā [Geschichte der Lettischen SSR. Von den ältesten Zeiten bis heute. Die dritte, überarbeitete und ergänzte Ausgabe in der Fassung von *A. Drizulis*, Akademiker der Akademie der Wissenschaften der Lettischen SSR], 1. sējums [Bd. 1], Riga 1986, S. 140–142.

[30] Siehe: *Benno Ābers*, Vidzemes zemnieku stāvoklis 19.g.s. pirmā pusē [Die Lage der Bauern von Vidzeme/Livland in der ersten Hälfte des 19. Jahrhunderts], Riga 1936, S. 52 f.

[31] Siehe: Полное собрание законов [Vollständige Sammlung der Gesetze]. – Bd. XXXIII – Nr. 26278; Полное собрание законов [Vollständige Sammlung der Gesetze]. – Bd. XXXIV – Nr. 27024; Полное собрание законов [Vollständige Sammlung der Gesetze]. – Bd. XXXVI – Nr. 27735.

[32] *Kalniņš*, Latvijas PSR (oben Fn. 6), S. 166–169; *Lazdiņš*, Baltijas zemnieku (oben Fn. 6), S. 45.

IV. Reformen in den 60er Jahren des 19. Jahrhunderts. Mit der Tätigkeit der gerichtlichen Macht verbundene Prinzipien und das Gerichtssystem

1. Die Reformen

Am 19. Februar 1861 wurde im russischen Kaiserreich die Leibeigenschaft abgeschafft.[33] Mit der Aufhebung der Leibeigenschaft wurden freie Arbeitskräfte freigesetzt. Einen freien Kapitalverkehr gab es teilweise schon zuvor, doch bildete sich erst jetzt ein für alle zugängliches System von Kreditinstituten (Banken) heraus. Die Schaffung eines freien Arbeitsmarktes und eines bedingt freien Kapitalverkehrs waren aber zu wenig, um den Übergang zum Kapitalismus zu bewirken. Der Kapitalismus forderte eine formelle Gleichheit, besonders vor dem Gericht und insbesondere in der sog. streitigen Gerichtsbarkeit, die mit Verfahren zivilrechtlichen Charakters verbunden ist.[34] Um diese zu garantieren, sollten auch ein von der staatlichen Verwaltung unabhängiges Gericht und das Amt des Richters geschaffen werden.

Als Vorlage für die Gerichtsreform diente die Erfahrung der europäischen Länder und des russischen Kaiserreichs. Im Prozessrecht dominierten offenbar die Erfahrungen Frankreichs.[35]

2. Die Prinzipien der Gerichtsbarkeit

Die GO, ZPO und StPO wurden nach Rechtsprinzipien formuliert, die neuzeitlichen Anforderungen standhielten. Dazu gehörten beispielsweise:

1) die formelle Gleichheit vor dem Gericht;[36]

---

[33] Манифест 19 февраля 1861 года [Das Manifest vom 19. Februar 1861]. Siehe z.B.: Хрестоматия по истории отечественного государства и права. X век – 1917 год. Московский Государственный Университет имени М.В. Ломоносова. Составитель: доктор юридических наук, профессор В.А. Томсинов. [Chrestomathie zur vaterländischen Geschichte und zum vaterländischem Recht. X. Jahrhundert – 1917. Die Moskauer Staatliche Lomonossow-Universität. Zusammengesetzt von Prof. *V.A. Tomsinov*, Doktor der juristischen Wissenschaften], Moskau 2004, S. 241–247.

[34] Die Aufhebung der Leibeigenschaft ohne Justizreform würde die ehemals Leibeigenen nicht vollständig befreien, die Freiheit aller Staatsangehörige im Staat wäre ein formeller, jedoch kein reeller Wert. *Головачев*, Десять летъ реформъ (oben Fn. 18), S. 287 f.

[35] Siehe z.B.: *Аннерс*, Э. История Европейского права [Geschichte des europäischen Rechts]. Moskau 1996, S. 363. Vergleich: Es wird die Meinung vertreten, dass das russische Kaiserreich bei der Ausarbeitung von Gerichtsreformen und Prozessrechtsgesetzen kein konkretes europäisches Land kopiert (plagiiert) habe. Es wird jedoch nicht geleugnet, dass für die Vorbereitung der Gerichtsreform und die Ausarbeitung von damit verbundenen Gesetzen die Erfahrung anderer europäischen Länder ausgewertet wurde. Siehe z.B: *Щегловитовъ, И.Г.* Влiянie иностранныхъ законодательствъ на составленie Судебныхъ Уставовъ 20 ноября 1864 года [Der Einfluss ausländischer Gesetzgebungen auf die Ausarbeitung von Gerichtsordnungen vom 20. November 1864], Petrograd 1915.

2) die Konzentration der Rechtsprechung nur beim Gericht;[37]

3) die Unabhängigkeit des Gerichts und der Richter;[38]

4) die Unabsetzbarkeit der Richter;[39]

5) das kontradiktorische Verfahren;[40]

6) die Unantastbarkeit der Person;[41]

---

[36] „Судебная власть [...] распространяется на лица всехъ сословій и на все дела, какъ гражданскія, такъ и уголовныя“ [Die gerichtliche Macht [...] bezieht sich auf Personen aller Schichten und auf alle Verfahren, sowohl Zivil- als auch Strafverfahren] (GO, Art. 2).

Zusätzlich zu der ordentlichen (allgemeinen) Zuständigkeit gab es auch Sondergerichte. Beispielsweise Bauerngerichte (der Gemeinde/des Dorfes), Kriegsgerichte, Kirchengerichte u.a. Die Existenz von Gemeindegerichten wurde kritisiert, denn ohne ausreichende Aufsicht handelten diese oft eigenmächtig. Die Existenz von Gemeindegerichten als Gerichte (faktisch) einer Schicht widersprach auch dem Prinzip der Gleichheit. Siehe: *Товстолесъ, Н.Н.* Учрежденіе судебныхъ установленій [Institutionen gerichtlicher Ermittlungen] (Св. Зак. Т. XVI ч.1, изд. 1914 года [Vollständige Sammlung der Gesetze, Bd. XVI Teil. 1, 1914]), Petrograd 1916, S. 6–8.

[37] GO, Art. 1.

[38] Nach dem Gesetz hatte die Justiz ihre Aufsicht selbst vollständig zu organisieren. (GO, Art. 249, 249[1]). Dieses Ziel ließ sich nicht vollständig verwirklichen, denn der Justizminister war als Generalstaatsanwalt berechtigt, sich in die Tätigkeit der Justiz einzumischen:

„Онъ имеетъ право требовать отъ чиновъ судебнаго ведомства доставленія нужныхъ ему сведеній и объясненій письменно, а въ необходимыхъ случаяхъ также и личнаго представленія оныхъ“ [Er ist berechtigt, von den Beamten der gerichtlichen Institutionen schriftliche Informationen und Erklärungen zu verlangen und, falls erforderlich, auch deren persönliche Vorstellung] (GO, Art. 254).

[39] Die Richter konnten nur mit dem Einverständnis der Richter oder in gesetzlich streng vorgeschriebenen Fällen des Amtes enthoben oder in ein anderes Gericht entsandt werden, beispielsweise wegen Versäumnis der Arbeit, andauernder Krankheit, falls ein entsprechendes Urteil rechtskräftig geworden war usw. Siehe: GO, Art. 228–230, 243, 295 u.a.

[40] Während der Ausarbeitung der ZPO wurde festgestellt, dass zivilprozessuale Gerichtsverfahren auf kontradiktorische Verfahren gestützt werden müssen. Es wurde auch die öffentliche Verhandlung verlangt. Siehe: Судебная реформа [Том 1], S. 312.

[41] *Щегловитов, С.Г.* Судебные уставы императора Александра II съ законодательными мотивами и разъясненіями. Уставъ уголовнаго судопроизводства. Девятое изданіе, исправленное и дополненное по 15-ое февраля 1907 года [Die Gerichtsordnungen des Kaisers Alexander II. mit gerichtlichen Motiven und Erklärungen. Die Strafprozessordnung. Ausgabe 9, korrigiert und ergänzt bis zum 15. Februar 1907], St. Petersburg 1907, S. 1, 13. Siehe auch: StPO, Art. 8:

„Никто не можетъ быть ни задержанъ подъ стражею иначе, какъ въ случаяхъ, законами определенныхъ, ни содержимъ въ помещеніяхъ, не установленныхъ на то закономъ“ [Niemand darf inhaftiert oder anderweitig in seiner Freiheit beschränkt werden als in den gesetzlich vorgesehenen Fällen].

StPO, Art. 1:

„Никто не можетъ подлежать судебному преследованію за преступленіе или проступокъ, не бывъ привлеченъ къ ответственности въ порядке, определенномъ правилами сего

7) die Unschuldsvermutung;[42]

8) die Gleichheit der Beweise[43] und andere Prinzipien.

3. Die Struktur des Gerichtssystems

Gemäß Art. 1 der GO lag die Rechtsprechungskompetenz im russischen Kaiserreich bei:[44]

1) dem Friedensgericht;

2) der Versammlung der Friedensrichter (als Berufungsinstanz der Friedensgerichte);

3) dem Landgericht (*in der lettischen Sprache – apgabaltiesa, in der russichen Sprache – окружной суд, direkte Übersetzung wäre Gebietsgericht*);

4) dem Gerichtshof (*in der lettischen Sprache – Tiesu palāta, in der russichen Sprache – Судебная палата*) (als Berufungsinstanz der Landgerichte);

5) dem Herrschenden Senat als Oberstem Kassationsgericht (*Правительствующему Сенату, въ качестве верховнаго кассацiоннаго суда*).[45]

In erster Instanz wurden Verfahren gemäß der gesetzlich festgelegten Zuständigkeit in den Friedens- und Landgerichten verhandelt. Die Verfahren von Bauern wurden in der ersten Instanz auch vor den Gemeindegerichten verhandelt.[46]

Vor dem Friedensgericht als Gericht erster Instanz wurden Verfahren über Vergehen verhandelt, für die als höchste Strafe Freiheitsstrafe bis zu einem Jahr und sechs Monaten, Geldstrafe bis 300 Rubel und Arrest bis zu 3 Monaten verhängt oder Verwarnung, Tadel oder Belehrung (Ermahnung) ausgesprochen werden

---

Устава“ [Niemand darf wegen Verbrechen oder Vergehen ohne Beachtung der in diesem Gesetz festgelegten Ordnung einer gerichtlichen Ermittlung unterworfen werden].

42 *Щегловитов, С.Г.* Судебные уставы, S. 16. Siehe auch: StPO, Art. 14:

„Никто не можетъ быть наказанъ за преступленiе или проступокъ, подлежащiе судебному ведомству, иначе, какъ по приговору надлежащаго Суда, вошедшему въ законную силу“ [Niemand darf wegen Verbrechen oder Vergehen, die in die Kompetenz der Justiz fallen, anderweitig verurteilt werden als durch Urteil des zuständigen Gerichts].

43 *Kalniņš*, Latvijas PSR (oben Fn. 6), S. 76.

44 Über die im Gesetz festgelegten Gerichte hinaus konnten aufgrund eines besonderen Gesetzes auch Kirchengerichte, Kriegsgerichte, Bauerngerichte, Dorf-(Siedlungs-)gerichte, Handelsgerichte und Gerichte für Ausländer (Vertreter von Fremdvölkern) bestehen (Anmerkung zum Art. 2 der GO).

45 GO, Art. 1.

46 Vor dem Gemeindegericht wurden entschieden: 1) Zivilsachen mit Forderungssummen in Höhe von maximal 100 Rubel, Verfahren über den Besitz von Immobilien oder über die Abwendung der Störungen der Dienstbarkeit; 2) In Verfahren über Vergehen durfte eine Geldstrafe bis 12 Rubel oder sieben Tage Arrest verhängt werden. Von einem Gemeindegericht konnten Arbeiten zum Nutzen der Öffentlichkeit oder Schadenersatz, jedoch bis 1904 auch Leibesstrafen angeordnet werden. Siehe: *Kalniņš*, Latvijas PSR (oben Fn. 6), S. 46.

konnten.[47] In zivilrechtlichen Streitigkeiten bestand die Zuständigkeit bis zu 500 Rubel. Ausgenommen waren Streitigkeiten über Immobilien, Entdeckungen und Erfindungen (diese Sachen waren dem sog. Allgemeinen Gericht zugewiesen). Die Friedensgerichte waren auch für Ansprüche wegen persönlicher Beleidigungen, Störung des Besitzes und ähnliches zuständig.[48]

Vor dem „Allgemeinen Gericht" – dem Landgericht, dem Gerichtshof und dem Herrschenden Senat – wurden Verfahren verhandelt, für welche die Friedensgerichte, Gemeindegerichte und andere besondere Gerichte nicht zuständig waren.

Eine Neuigkeit der GO war die Einführung eines dreistufigen Gerichtssystems – der ersten Instanz, der Appellationsinstanz und der Kassationsinstanz. Ein solches Instanzsystem besteht immer noch in der Republik Lettland. Auch die Namen der allgemeinen Gerichte – das Landgericht oder apgabala tiesa, der Gerichtshof oder tiesu palāta und der Senat – sind seit den Zeiten des russischen Kaiserreichs erhalten geblieben. In diesem Jahr begann freilich eine Diskussion über den Verzicht auf die traditionellen Namen des Gerichtshofs und des Senats.[49]

Die Forderung nach juristischer Bildung für den Richter ist eine neuzeitliche Forderung. Im russischen Kaiserreich mangelte es um die Mitte des 19. Jahrhunderts sogar an gebildeten Juristen, welche die Ämter der Richter der allgemeinen Gerichte bekleiden konnten. Aus dem Grund wurde in der GO noch nicht festgelegt, dass das Amt des Richters am Landgericht nur von einer Person mit juristischer Hochschulbildung bekleidet werden konnte. Die juristische Ausbildung konnte durch eine gewisse Diensterfahrung in den Angelegenheiten des Gerichtsverfahrens ersetzt werden (*или же доказавшихъ на службе свои познанія по судебной части*).[50] Wichtig war jedoch, dass durch das Inkrafttreten der GO die Herkunft oder die Zugehörigkeit zu einer bestimmten Schicht zumindest formell an Bedeutung verlor.

Nach der Gründung der Republik Lettland wurden das Friedensgericht und die Versammlung der Friedensrichter in Amtsgerichte (Gericht der ersten Instanz) mit dem Namen Friedensgericht umgewandelt.[51] Zu Sowjetzeiten wurde auf der Basis

---

[47] StPO, Art. 33. Siehe auch: Das Gesetz über die von Friedensrichtern aufzuerlegenden Strafen, in dem die von Friedensrichtern angeordneten Strafarten und -umfänge konkretisiert wurden.

[48] ZPO, Art. 29, 31. Siehe im Detail: Судебные уставы 20 ноября 1864 года. Съ изложеніемъ разсужденій, на коихъ они основаны. Изданіе Государственной Канцелярiи [Gerichtsordnungen vom 20. November 1864. Mit Erläuterung der Motive, auf die diese gestützt werden. Ausgegeben von der Staatskanzlei]. Часть первая [der erste Teil], St. Petersburg 1866, S. 43–46.

[49] Siehe z.B.: Tieslietu padomes aktuālie lēmumi [Die aktuellen Entscheidungen des Justizrates], in: Jurista Vārds 2012, Nr. 46, S. 30.

[50] GO, Art. 202.

[51] *Valdis Blūzma*, Latvijas Republikas tiesību sistēmas veidošanas sākums [Der Beginn der Formierung des Rechtssystems der Republik Lettland], in: Latvijas tiesību vēsture [Lettische Rechtsgeschichte] (1914–2000), Riga 2000, S. 210.

des Friedensgerichts das Rayon-Volksgericht als Amtsgericht gegründet.[52] Nach der erneuten Unabhängigkeit Lettlands wurden die Rayon-Volksgerichte in Rayongerichte umbenannt.

Das sowjetische Gerichtssystem kannte keine Gerichte in der Berufungsinstanz.[53] Aus diesem Grund ging die Kompetenz der Rayonsgerichte nach der erneuten Einführung der Landgerichte in der Republik Lettland im Vergleich zu den Sowjetzeiten beträchtlich zurück.

Das Landgericht der Republik Lettland verhandelt Verfahren nicht nur in der Berufungs-, sondern auch in erster Instanz. Obwohl nach der erneuten Unabhängigkeit des lettischen Staates *de facto* 1990–1991 formell die Organisation des Justizwesens der Zwischenkriegszeit wiederhergestellt wurde, blieb faktisch der alte, in der GO eingearbeitete Gedanke in Kraft, dass bestimmte Kategorien von Verfahren nur ab der Ebene des Landgerichts in erster Instanz verhandelt werden konnten. Im russischen Kaiserreich war eine solche Beschränkung verständlich, da die Friedensrichter keine konkrete Ausbildung vorweisen mussten, von der juristischen Hochschulbildung gar zu schweigen. Jetzt können in Lettland als Richter – selbst in erster Instanz – nur Personen mit juristischer Hochschulbildung tätig sein.[54] Aus diesem Grund ist der Status des Landgerichts als Gericht erster Instanz für bestimmte Fälle keiner staatlichen Notwendigkeit, sondern nur der historischen Tradition geschuldet.

V. Die Staatsanwaltschaft

Die Herkunft der Staatsanwaltschaft nach heutigem Verständnis ist im Baltikum direkt mit der GO zu verbinden. Damals gehörte die Staatsanwaltschaft zum Justizministerium, mit dem Justizminister als Generalstaatsanwalt an der Spitze:

> „Прокурорскій надзоръ вверяется Оберъ-Прокурорамъ, Прокурорамъ и ихъ Товарищамъ, подъ высшимъ наблюденіемъ Министра Юстиціи какъ Генералъ-Прокурора“ [Die Aufsicht der Staatsanwaltschaft wurde durch Oberstaatsanwälte, Staatsanwälte und deren Genossen/Gehilfen, unter der Oberaufsicht des Justizministers als Generalstaatsanwalt durchgeführt].[55]

---

[52] *Valdi Blūzma,* Latvijas inkorporācija PSRS sastāvā un padomju tiesību uzspiešana Latvijai [Inkorporation Lettlands in die UdSSR und das Aufzwingen des sowjetischen Rechts Lettland] (1940 – 1941), in: Latvijas tiesību vēsture [Lettische Rechtsgeschichte] (1914–2000), Riga 2000, S. 341.

[53] *Jānis Lazdiņš*, Padomju tiesību periods Latvijā [Die Epoche des sowjetischen Rechts in Lettland] (1944/45–1985), in: Latvijas tiesību vēsture [Lettische Rechtsgeschichte] (1914–2000), Riga 2000, S. 404–408.

[54] Siehe: Latvijas Republikas Augstākās Padomes likums [Das Gesetz des Obersten Rates der Republik Lettland vom] 15.12.1992. „Par tiesu varu“ [Über die Judikative/Gerichtsbarkeit], http://www.likumi.lv/doc.php?id=62847 [Stand: 10.01.2013].

[55] Siehe: GO, Art. 124.

Beim Herrschenden Senat waren Oberstaatsanwälte und deren Genossen/ Gehilfen tätig, am Gerichtshof und am Landgericht Staatsanwälte und deren Genossen/Gehilfen.[56] In den Friedensgerichten wurden die Funktionen des Staatsanwalts von der Polizei erfüllt.

Im Unterschied zum russischen Kaiserreich bekleidete in der Republik Lettland der Generalstaatsanwalt nicht gleichzeitig das Amt des Justizministers, und die Staatsanwaltschaft stand nicht unter dem Justizminister:

> „Prokuratūra ir tiesu varas institūcija, kas patstāvīgi veic uzraudzību pār likumības ievērošanu šajā likumā noteiktās kompetences ietvaros." [Die Staatsanwaltschaft ist eine Institution der Justiz, die im Kompetenzrahmen dieses Gesetzes die Einhaltung der Gesetze ständig beaufsichtigt].[57]

Ansonsten waren die Pflichten und Rechte der Staatsanwälte ähnlich. Im russischen Kaiserreich waren die Staatsanwälte hierarchisch organisiert. Dies bedeutete, dass die Staatsanwälte der niedrigeren Gerichtsinstanzen den höheren Gerichtsinstanzen und die Gehilfen des Staatsanwalts dem entsprechenden Staatsanwalt untergeordnet waren. Alle Staatsanwälte waren dem Generalstaatsanwalt gegenüber verantwortlich.[58]

Die Staatsanwaltschaft passte darauf auf, dass die Gesetze eingehalten wurden. Daraus ergab sich die Aufgabe der Staatsanwaltschaft: zu beaufsichtigen (in der sog. allgemeinen Beaufsichtigungs-Ordnung), dass von allen Staatsangehörigen, Behörden und Gerichten die staatlichen Normen eingehalten wurden. Aus diesem Grund wurden die Strafverfolgung und die Anklage vor Gericht zur wichtigsten Aufgabe der Staatsanwaltschaft.[59] Die Staatsanwälte waren auch berechtigt, Einsprüche gegen Gerichtsurteile und -entscheidungen zu erheben. In den gesetzlich festgelegten Fällen nahmen die Staatsanwälte auch an den Verhandlungen in Zivilsachen teil, beispielsweise in auf Initiative der Staatsanwaltschaft eingeleiteten Verfahren über die Verschollenheitserklärung für eine Person,[60] über die Legitimation von Kindern (узаконение),[61] Adoption (усыновление)[62] und in anderen gesetzlich festgelegten Fällen.

---

[56] Siehe: GO, Art. 8, 9, 124–136.

[57] Latvijas Republikas Saeimas likums [Das Gesetz Saeima der Republik Lettland vom] 19.05.1994. „Prokuratūras likums" [Das Gesetz der Staatsanwaltschaft], zugänglich unter: http://www.likumi.lv/doc.php?id=57276 [Stand: 10.01.2013] – Art. 1, Abs. 1.

[58] GO, Art. 129. Siehe auch: *Муравьев, Н.В.* Прокурорскій надзоръ, S. 494 f.

[59] Siehe: StPO, insbesondere ab Art. 510.

[60] ZPO, Art. 1451, 1457.

[61] ZPO, Art. 1460^{5}, 1460^{6}.

[62] ZPO, Art. 1460^{10}, 1460^{11}.

VI. Die Rechtsanwaltschaft

Am vollständigsten übernahm der Lettische Staat aus der GO den Status des vereidigten Rechtsanwalts.[63]

Nach der GO wird [auch jetzt] ein vereidigter Rechtsanwalt aufgrund einer Vollmacht tätig; er verteidigt und vertritt seine Klienten. Die Rechtsanwälte erfüllen auch eine soziale Funktion und verteidigen und vertreten Personen im Auftrag des Rechtsanwälterates oder des Gerichtsvorsitzenden.[64]

Die vereidigten Rechtsanwälte – ein freier Juristenberuf – wurden von einem (von den vereidigten Rechtsanwälten gewählten) Rat der vereidigten Rechtsanwälte, der am Gerichtshof angesiedelt war, beaufsichtigt und koordiniert.[65] Der Gedanke, dass vereidigte Rechtsanwälte vom Gericht beaufsichtigt und koordiniert werden könnten, wurde abgewiesen, denn:

> „[...] присяжные поверенные, какъ представители тяжущихся, по естественной справедливости, [...] не должны состоять подъ надзоромъ судебныхъ местъ и не должны состоять ни въ какой зависимости отъ нихъ“ [...] [vereidigte Rechtsanwälte dürfen als Vertreter von streitenden Parteien aus Gründen der natürlichen Gerechtigkeit [...] durch Gerichte nicht beaufsichtigt werden und von diesen in keiner Weise abhängig sein].[66]

Der Rat hat nicht nur die Aufnahme neuer Mitglieder organisiert, sondern war auch berechtigt, Disziplinarstrafen zu verhängen. Die höchste Strafe war der Ausschluss aus der Rechtsanwaltschaft oder die Einschaltung der Strafverfolgung.[67]

Die innere Organisation der Körperschaft vereidigter Rechtsanwälte erfolgte auf demokratischer Grundlage. Deshalb sollte der Rat vereidigter Rechtsanwälte jährlich neu gewählt werden; auch sollten Mehrheitsentscheidungen getroffen werden. Dies wurde jedoch nicht immer und nicht überall eingehalten. Die Fluktuation von Ratsmitgliedern war meistens nicht hoch. Beispielsweise war von 1866 bis 1913 im Rat von Sankt Petersburg ein Mitglied des Rates durchschnittlich sieben Jahre, im Moskauer Rat acht Jahre und im Rat von Charkow neun Jahre tätig.[68]

---

[63] Siehe: GO, Art. 353–406 und Latvijas Republikas Augstākās Padomes likums [Das Gesetz des Obersten Rates der Republik Lettland vom] 27.04.1993. „Latvijas Republikas Advokatūras likums“ [Das Gesetz der Rechtsanwaltschaft der Republik Lettland], zugänglich unter: http://www.likumi. lv/doc.php?id=59283 [Stand: 10.01.2013].

[64] GO, Art. 353.

[65] Siehe: GO, Art. 357–365.

[66] Исторія русской адвокатуры [Geschichte der russischen Rechtsanwaltschaft]. Томъ третій [Bd. 3]. Подъ редакціей [Herausgegeben von] М.Н. Гернетъ. Сословная организація адвокатуры [Ständische Organisation der Rechtsanwaltschaft] (1964.20.IX.–1914), Moskau 1916, S. 1.

[67] GO, Art. 368. Siehe auch: Das Gesetz der Rechtsanwaltschaft der Republik Lettland, Art. 73 f.

[68] Исторія русской адвокатуры [Geschichte der russischen Rechtsanwaltschaft]. Томъ второй [Bd. 2]. Подъ редакціей [hg. von] М.Н. Гернетъ. Сословная организація адвокатуры

Als vereidigter Rechtsanwalt durfte auftreten, wer nach einem juristischen Hochschulstudium eine mindestens fünfjährige Praxiserfahrung vorweisen konnte. Andere Bedingungen waren: ein Mindestalter von 25 Jahren, Unbescholtenheit und die Einhaltung bestimmter ethischer Normen. Als vereidigte Rechtsanwälte konnten nicht tätig werden: Ausländer, insolvente Personen, im staatlichen Dienst oder im gewählten Amt befindliche Personen, Personen, deren Standeszugehörigkeit (darunter Geistliche) aufgrund eines Gerichtsurteils beschränkt oder aberkannt worden war oder bei denen darüber ein Ermittlungsverfahren nach StPO eingeleitet worden war, Personen, die aus dem Gerichtsdienst verbannt oder von der Liste der vereidigten Rechtsanwälte gestrichen worden waren. Darüber hinaus konnten als vereidigte Rechtsanwälte keine Personen tätig werden, die wegen Unsittlichkeit von der Körperschaft der Adligen oder eines anderen Standes ausgeschlossen worden waren oder denen ein Gericht verboten hatte, andere Personen zu vertreten.[69]

Bei der Ausarbeitung des GO-Projekts war ein Teil der Kommissionsmitglieder der Meinung, dass es im Interesse der Entwicklung der Wissenschaft nicht zulässig sei, dass Professoren der Rechtswissenschaften gleichzeitig auch berechtigt sind, als vereidigte Rechtsanwälte tätig zu sein. Die Praxistätigkeit würde der Forschung zu viel Zeit „wegnehmen". Jedoch war der größte Teil der am Gesetzesprojekt beteiligten Personen anderer Meinung. Man vertrat die Ansicht, dass die praktische Tätigkeit die professoralen Vorlesungen bereichere, wovon sowohl die Wissenschaft als auch die Zuhörer profitierten.[70]

Die heutigen Anforderungen an einen vereidigten Rechtsanwalt sind ähnlich.[71] Man ergänzte sie durch eine Qualifikationsprüfung, von der nur Doktoren der Rechtswissenschaften befreit sind.[72] Vor der Eröffnung der Praxis eines vereidigten Rechtsanwalts ist vor dem Vorsitzenden des Obersten Gerichts ein Eid abzulegen.

Außer vereidigten Rechtsanwälten waren im russischen Kaiserreich für die Führung von Zivilverfahren bei den Gerichten mit der Genehmigung des betroffenen Gerichts auch private Rechtsanwälte tätig. Die privaten Rechtsanwälte unterlagen keinen konkreten Anforderungen bei der Ausbildung. Alles wurde auf die Fähigkeit des privaten Rechtsanwalts, andere Personen zu vertreten, reduziert. Darüber hinaus wurde die Würde und Achtung, die dem privaten Rechtsanwalt in der Gesellschaft geschenkt wurde, als ausreichend angesehen.[73]

[Ständische Organisation der Rechtsanwaltschaft] (1964.20.IX.–1914), Moskau 1916, S. 129–131.

[69] GO, Art. 354, 355.

[70] *Гессенъ, I.B.* Исторія русской адвокатуры [Geschichte der russischen Rechtsanwaltschaft]. Томъ первый [Bd. 1]. Адвокатура, Общество и Государство [Rechtsanwaltschaft, Gesellschaft und Staat] (1964.20.IX.–1914), Moskau 1914, S. 88 f.

[71] Das Gesetz der Rechtsanwaltschaft der Republik Lettland, Art. 14, Abs. 1.

[72] Das Gesetz der Rechtsanwaltschaft der Republik Lettland, Art. 14, Abs. 2.

[73] GO, Art. 406^1–406^{19}.

VII. Zusammenfassung

1. Die Gerichtsordnungen des russischen Kaiserreichs von 1864 schufen die Grundlagen für das neuzeitliche Verständnis der rechtsprechenden Gewalt auf dem Gebiet des ehemaligen russischen Kaiserreichs.

2. Die Gerichtsordnungen hatten eine große Bedeutung für die künftige Entwicklung der rechtsprechenden Gewalt der Republik Lettland und für die damit verbundenen Behörden, Ämter und Berufe.

Über die Dynamik in der Justizverfassung im schwedisch beherrschten Estland im 16. und 17. Jahrhundert[1]

Marju Luts-Sootak

I. Ein wenig allgemeine Geschichte zur Einführung

Das Siedlungsgebiet des estnischen Volkes umfasst das Territorium der Republik Estland seit ihrer Gründung im Jahr 1918 auf den Trümmern des zaristischen Russlands. Um 1200 veranstaltete man Kreuzzüge in diese Territorien zur zwangsweisen Christianisierung der estnischen, livischen, lettischen und kurischen Stämme.[2] Diese Stämme hatten noch nicht den Status der Staatlichkeit erreicht, konnten sich trotz des zähen Widerstandes gegen die Überlegenheit eines Ritterordens und der dänischen Königsmacht nicht wehren und wurden daher im Laufe der folgenden Jahrhunderte von verschiedenen Herrschaften und Oberherrschaften regiert. Da die Kreuzritter und Handelsleute meistens aus den deutschen Territorien kamen (nicht nur, wenn sie Mitglieder oder Gefolgsleute des Deutschen Ordens waren, sondern auch, wenn sie im Dienst der lokalen Bischöfe oder des dänischen Königs standen), etablierte sich eine deutschsprachige lokale Oberschicht. Auch die indigene Oberschicht der sog. Ältesten (in der Chroniksprache ‚*seniores*', auch ‚*meliores*' genannt) assimilierte und germanisierte sich, dic Masse der indigenen Bevölkerung geriet im Laufe der Zeit in die Leibeigenschaft. Politisch entwickelte sich ein Konglomerat der verschiedenen geistlichen Territorien, die dem Heiligen Römischen Reich untergeordnet waren. In den ersten Jahrzehnten des 15. Jahrhunderts bildeten diese feudalen Territorien und die örtlichen Hansestädte eine Föderation mit einem gemeinsamen Landtag, die in der späteren Literatur den Namen ‚Alt-Livland' bekam. Damit soll der Unterschied zu der späteren Provinz ‚Livland' ausgedrückt werden.

---

1 Die Untersuchungen für diesen Beitrag sind mit Hilfe des Grants ETF9209 der Estnischen Wissenschaftsstiftung durchgeführt worden.

2 Diese „nordischen" Kreuzzüge sind in den letzten Jahrzehnten in den Fokus der internationalen Historikergemeinschaft gerückt. S. *Eric Christiansen*, The Nordic Crusades: The Baltic and the Catholic Frontier 1100–1525, London 1997; *Alan V. Murray* (ed.), Crusade and Conversion on the Baltic Frontier 1150–1500, Aldershot/Burlington/Singapore/Sydney 2001; *Nils Blomkvist*, The Discovery of the Baltics. The Reception of a Catholic World-System in the European North (AD 1075–1225), Leiden/Boston 2005, S. 505 ff. und zuletzt: *Marek Tamm/Linda Kaljundi/Carsten Selch Jensen* (Hg.), Crusading and Chronicle Writing on the Medieval Baltic Frontier: A Companion to the Chronicle of Henry of Livonia, Farnham 2011; es sind auch weitere Aufsätze des estnischen Historikers *Marek Tamm* im „Journal of Medieval History", in den „Acta et commentationes Archivi Historici Estoniae" und in verschiedenen Sammelbänden im Erscheinen.

Das spätere Livland und die weiteren zwei baltischen Schwesterländer Estland und Kurland[3] waren ein Ergebnis des sog. Livischen Krieges, der 1558 von Russland kommend ausbrach, zunächst aber noch nicht zur russischen Herrschaft in diesen Territorien führte.[4] Immerhin brach 1561 Alt-Livland zusammen; es wurde zwischen zwei zeitgenössischen aufstrebenden, aber auch miteinander rivalisierenden Großmächten des Ostseeraums aufgeteilt. Das heutige Nordestland als Herzogtum Estland samt der Städte mit Reval an der Spitze unterwarf sich im Juni 1561 freiwillig König Erich dem XIV. von Schweden. Im November 1561 erkannte der Ordensmeister Gotthard Kettler gegenüber dem polnischen König Sigismund II. August zunächst dessen Oberhoheit über alle (übrig gebliebenen) Ordensgebiete an. Letztendlich fielen jedoch nur Kurland und Semgallen als autonomes Erblehen dem polnisch-litauischen Reich (*Rzeczpospolita*) zu. Es sind die Landesteile übriggeblieben, die im Norden indigen estnisch, im Süden lettisch und dazwischen durch das heute fast ganz verschwundene Volk der Liven besiedelt waren. Diese Ländereien gingen 1561 als ‚Livland' in den direkten Besitz des Polenkönigs als Großfürsten von Litauen über – zunächst ohne die Hauptstadt Riga, die für einige Jahrzehnte noch ihre Selbstständigkeit behaupten konnte.

Kurland konnte seine Selbstständigkeit bis zur dritten polnischen Teilung im Jahr 1795 bewahren und ist dann „direkt" vom Russischen Reich unterworfen worden.[5] Nach erneuten kriegerischen Auseinandersetzungen sollte Polen gemäß dem Frieden von Altmark 1629 den größeren Teil seiner livländischen Besitztümer den

---

[3] Die Bezeichnung ‚baltische Länder' für diese Territorien während der deutsch(baltisch)en intermediären Herrschaft wurde von der deutschbaltischen Geschichtsschreibung geprägt. Damit soll einerseits der Unterschied zu den nach dem I. Weltkrieg etablierten ‚baltischen Staaten' Estland, Lettland und Litauen ausgedrückt werden. Andererseits soll der Ausdruck die (deutsch) baltische Identität auch nach dem Verlust der Führungsposition in der Gesellschaft in diesen baltischen Staaten und erst recht nach der deutschen Umsiedlung und Emigration vor und während des II. Weltkriegs symbolisieren. Dazu informativ und lehrreich, engagiert und dabei doch gelassen *Gert v. Pistohlkors*, Die Deutschen in der Geschichte der baltischen Länder Estland und Livland, in: ders. (Hg.), Deutsche Geschichte im Osten Europas. Baltische Länder, Berlin 1994 (ND 2002), S. 13–22.

[4] Zusammenfassend zu dieser kriegerisch äußerst aktiven Zeit im Ostseeraum: *Robert I. Frost*, The Northern Wars: War, State and Society in Northeastern Europa, 1558–1721, Harlow 2000.

[5] Die Gesamtdarstellung: *Alexander V. Berkis*, The History of the Duchy of Courland (1561–1795), Towson 1969; die neuere Forschung in Sammelbandform: *Erwin Oberländer/Ilgvars Misans* (Hg.), Das Herzogtum Kurland 1561–1795: Verfassung, Wirtschaft, Gesellschaft, 2 Bde., Lüneburg 1993, 2001; eine neuere Quellenedition, die auch Rechtsquellen beinhaltet: *Erwin Oberländer/Volker Keller* (Hg.), Kurland: vom polnisch-litauischen Lehnsherzogtum zur russischen Provinz: Dokumente zur Verfassungsgeschichte 1561–1795, Paderborn u.a. 2008; zur Grundlegung der Verfassung und der Prinzipien der Außenpolitik Kurlands vor der Blüte des Landes unter Großherzog Jakob (1642–1682): *Volker Keller*, Herzog Friedrich von Kurland (1569–1642): Verfassungs-, Nachfolge- und Neutralitätspolitik, Marburg 2005.

Schweden abtreten.[6] Damit waren nicht nur alle größeren Häfen an der östlichen Ostseeküste – Riga, Reval und die von der schwedischen Krone besonders geförderte Stadt Narva[7] an der russischen Grenze – an die Schweden gefallen, sondern das ganze estnisch besiedelte Territorium. Bis zur Unterwerfung Liv- und Estlands durch den russischen Zar Peter I. im Großen Nordischen Krieg im Jahr 1710 – bestätigt durch den Nystädter Frieden 1721 – herrschte Schweden nun über das ganze Estenland. In der estnischen Volksüberlieferung ist diese Geschichtsperiode als „die goldene schwedische Zeit" tradiert worden – vor allem wegen der angeblich bauernfreundlichen Politik der Schwedenkönige, die bis zur Aufhebung der Leibeigenschaft oder zumindest bis zu diesbezüglichen Plänen gereicht haben soll. Hier soll es aber um das Justizwesen gehen, wo die Entwicklungen gar nicht so bauernfreundlich waren.[8]

II. Die Unterwerfungskapitulationen als Versteck der Veränderungen im estländischen Justizwesen

Obwohl Livland erst mit dem Frieden von Altmark 1629 an Schweden gefallen war und damit fast siebzig Jahre weniger unter der schwedischen Krone stand als Estland, ist gerade die livländische Rechts- und Justizgeschichte zum Archetyp der Schwedenherrschaft im Baltikum geworden.[9] Das ist auch leicht verständlich, weil man da in dieser Zeit recht viele wichtige Ereignisse finden kann: Gleich im Jahr 1630 führte man eine Gerichtsreform durch, auch wurde ein königliches Hofgericht in Dorpat gegründet, 1632 folgte die Universität zu Dorpat als die zweite Universität des schwedischen Reichs. Vor dem Hintergrund dieser tiefgreifenden Interventionen in das überlieferte Justizsystem Livlands erscheint die Provinzialpolitik

---

6 Genauer gesagt hat man in Altmark einen Waffenstillstand für sechs Jahre vereinbart. Für Livland erwiesen sich die Vereinbarungen aber als dauerhaft. Zu den Einzelheiten näher *Reinhard Wittram*, Baltische Geschichte. Die Ostseelande Livland, Estland, Kurland 1180–1918, München 1954, S. 84 ff.

7 Narva genoss neben der wirtschaftlichen Begünstigung auch eine rechtliche Sonderstellung im Vergleich zu den anderen baltischen Städten. Dazu näher: *Enn Küng*, Die rechtliche Lage der Stadt Narva in schwedischer Zeit (16.–17. Jahrhundert), in: Ilgvars Misāns/Horst Wernicke (Hg.), Riga und der Ostseeraum: Von der Gründung 1201 bis in die Frühe Neuzeit, Marburg 2005, S. 346–357.

8 Einen allgemeinen Überblick bietet auch *Enn Küng*, Das Gerichtswesen in Estland und Livland im 16. und 17. Jahrhundert, in: Nils Jörn (Hg.), Rechtsprechung zur Bewältigung von Kriegsfolgen. Festgabe zum 85. Geburtstag von Herbert Langer, Hamburg 2012, wo es allerdings keine nachvollziehbaren Quellen- und Literaturhinweise gibt und die beigefügte Liste der benutzten Literatur Defizite vor allem auf der spezifisch rechtshistorischen Seite aufzeigt.

9 Exemplarisch etwa R. Tuchtenhagen in seinem monumentalen, aber nicht unbedingt fundamentalen Werk, wo im Kapitel III. über Recht und Justiz von den baltischen Gerichten nur das Hofgericht zu Dorpat näher behandelt wird: *Ralph Tuchtenhagen*, Zentralstaat und Provinz im frühneuzeitlichen Nordosteuropa, Wiesbaden 2008, S. 88 ff.; zum Dorpater Hofgericht speziell S. 101 ff.

der schwedischen Zentralmacht in Estland recht bescheiden zu sein: Es gab keine umfassende Gerichtsreform, die in einem Schritt durchgeführt worden wäre, es ist kein königliches Hofgericht und keine Universität gegründet worden. So hat die Justizgeschichtsschreibung behauptet, dass Estland „seine alten öffentlichen Institutionen meist unverändert" gesichert und erhalten habe, nachdem es „vom Orden gegen die Angriffe der Russen nicht mehr geschützt werden konnte" und die estländische Ritterschaft nebst der Stadt Reval sich freiwillig dem Schwedenkönig unterworfen habe.[10]

Die freieren Hände der Zentralregierung in Livland hat man also damit erklärt, dass Livland militärisch von Polen bezwungen worden war, Estland sich dagegen selbst unterworfen hatte. Gemäß der gemeineuropäischen Praxis geschah dies durch Unterwerfungsvertrag oder Kapitulation: der König erteilte ein Privileg nach den Bedingungen, die die Stände aufgestellt hatten, und die Stände ihrerseits huldigten dem König. Unter anderem gehörte in einen solchen Akt, der Punkt um Punkt oder lateinisch nach ‚*capitula*' niedergeschrieben war, traditionell die Zusicherung, dass alte Privilegien und die vorhandene Rechtsordnung im Ganzen in Kraft bleiben sollten, ebenso wie die ‚jurisdiction' – also die Gerichtsverfassung und Gerichtsordnung. In der Kapitulation der estländischen Ritterschaft hieß es wie folgt:

> „Und dieweil dan obgeschriebene unsere comissarien, procuratoren und vulmächtige gesandten der bemelten ritterschafft und den vom adel ihre wohlhergebrachte alte priuilegien, jurisdiction und gewohnheit auf fernere unser ratification vermüge unsern habenden vulmacht haben confirmiret und bestätiget: So bekennen wir und thun kund für jedermänniglich, den dieser unsere brieff zu sehen, hören oder lesen vorkumpt, was standes, condition oder würden die seyn, für uns, unsere leibeserben und nachkommen, dasz wir alle verstörungen, zusagen, verbriefften und versiegelten confirmationen der alten priuilegien, auch alten löblichen und wohlhergebrachten gebrauch und gewohnheiten der bemelten ritterschafft und den von adel, so wohl zu Jeruen als zu Harrien und Wierlandt, in nahmen und unsertwegen geschehen und versprochen, nachfolgender gestalt ratificiren, dieselben stet, fest und unverbrüchlich halten wollen …".[11]

Die entsprechende Formel in Privileg für die Stadt Reval vom selben Tag war dem Wortlaut nach etwas anders formuliert, aber dem Sinn nach ganz gleich.[12] Kurz gesagt hat der Schwedenkönig Erich der XIV. für sich und seine Nachkommen bestätigt, dass das in Estland von der Ritterschaft und in Reval vom Stadtmagistrat verwaltete Justizwesen intakt wie auch überhaupt die Rechtsordnung und Verfas-

---

[10] *Oswald Schmidt*, Rechtsgeschichte Liv-, Est- und Curlands, in: Johann Engelmann/Carl Erdmann/Woldemar von Rohland (Hg.), Dorpater Juristische Studien, Bd. 3, Jurjew (Dorpat) 1894, S. 238.

[11] Des Königs Erich XIV. Privilegium für die Ritterschaft vom 2. August 1561, in: *Eduard Winkelmann* (Hg.), Die Capitulationen der estländischen Ritterschaft und der Stadt Reval vom Jahre 1710 nebst deren Confirmationen. Nach den Originalen mit andern dazu gehörigen Documenten und der Capitulation von Pernau, Reval 1865, S. 11 f.

[12] S. Des Königs Erich XIV. Privilegium für die Stadt Reval vom 2. August 1561, in: *Winkelmann*, (oben Fn. 11), S. 16. Dazu noch hier unten in Punkt V.

sung des Landes beim Alten bleiben sollte. U.a. bedeutete dies, wie auch anderswo im frühneuzeitlicher Europa, dass die Rechtskreise des Land- und Stadtrechts nach wie vor streng auseinander gehalten wurden. Es sei hier zunächst ein Blick auf die Landesjustiz geworfen.

III. Die Veränderungen in der Landesjustiz

Im Unterschied zu Oswald Schmidt behauptet ein anderer deutschbaltischer Rechtshistoriker namens Friedrich Georg von Bunge, „die Gerichtsverfassung des Landes erfuhr, theils schon zu Anfang, theils im Laufe dieses Zeitraums [d.h. in der Schwedenzeit], manche wesentliche Veränderungen. Zwar blieben dieselben Richterstellen bestehen: der Landesrath, nunmehr *königliches Landgericht* genannt, die Manngerichte, die Hakenrichter; allein es veränderte sich theils ihre Competenz, theils ihre innere Einrichtung."[13]

Bunge nannte Landgericht, Manngerichte und die Hakenrichter. Die allerniedrigste Stufe in der Landesjustiz war aber das Gutsgericht. Bunge erwähnt nur kurz, dass „der Adel" „die peinliche Gerichtsbarkeit über seine Bauern in Sachen, welche an Leib und Leben gehen", verlor und „diese Jurisdiction den königlichen Gerichten – den Manngerichten und dem Landgericht – übertragen" wurde.[14] Der estnische Historiker Arnold Soom beschreibt in seinem Standardwerk über das Gutswesen in Estland im 17. Jahrhundert eingehender, wie vom Gutsgericht über die Bauern die früheren bäuerlichen Rechtsfinder in dieser Zeit verschwanden.[15] Dasselbe passierte auch im schwedisch beherrschten Livland. In Livland ist diese institutionelle Veränderung vor allem auf die Gerichtsreform der Jahre 1630–32 zurückzuführen. In Estland verloren die bäuerlichen Rechtsfinder oder Schöffen ihre Funktion aber durch die Steuerreform: durch den Zerfall der früheren Wacke als Besteuerungsgebiet sind auch die Wackenzusammenkünfte ausgeblieben. Diese hatten früher u.a. als Gerichtsversammlungen fungiert. Als die adeligen Gutsherren in der Schwedenzeit die Halsgerichtsbarkeit über ihre Bauern an die sog. ordentlichen Gerichte übergeben sollten, bekamen sie die zivilrechtliche Kompetenz für die Verhandlung der bäuerlichen Streitigkeiten nun voll in die Hände. Dazu kamen noch das Hauszuchtrecht und auch die allgemeine polizeiliche Gewalt auf dem Gebiet des eigenen Gutes.

Die polizeilichen Funktionen wurden auch von sog. Hakenrichtern ausgeübt. Diese wurden von der Ritterschaft aus der Reihe der eigenen Mitglieder gewählt und eingesetzt. Die Hakenrichter waren seit der Mitte des 15. Jahrhunderts im

---

[13] *Friedrich Georg v. Bunge*, Geschichte des Gerichtswesens und Gerichtsverfahrens in Liv-, Est- und Curland, Reval 1874 (ND Charleston 2010), S. 169.

[14] *Bunge*, Gerichtswesen (oben Fn. 13), S. 169 mit Verweis auf die Gnadenbriefe des Schwedenkönigs Gustav Adolf vom 24.11.1617 und vom Jahr 1630, auf die königliche Resolution vom 20.8.1623, § 20, und auf die Kompilation Estländisches Ritter- und Landrecht I, 2, 4; IV, 18, 4.

[15] *Arnold Soom*, Der Herrenhof in Estland im 17. Jahrhundert, Lund 1945, S. 8–10.

Laufe der vollen Entfaltung der Leibeigenschaft eingesetzt worden und zwar für die Entscheidung der Streitigkeiten, die aus dem Entlaufen der Bauern entstanden. In der Schwedenzeit entwickelte sich die Hakenrichterinstitution immer mehr in die Richtung einer polizeilichen Behörde, der auch die Vollstreckung der Urteile der höheren Gerichtsinstanzen zukam.[16]

Die eigentliche Gerichtsinstanz im heutigen Sinn waren die sog. Manngerichte, von denen es in der schwedischen Zeit in Estland drei gab: eines gemeinsam für die Landkreise Wierland und Jerwland, eines für Harrien und eines für die Wieck. Die Manngerichte entstanden schon im 13. Jahrhundert, nach der Eroberung und Christianisierung des Landes durch die deutschen Kreuzritter und Vasallen des Dänenkönigs. Manngerichte waren ursprünglich Lehn- oder Vasallengerichte, hatten sich dann aber zu „gemeinen Gerichten auf dem Lande" entwickelt, neben denen noch verschiedene Spezialgerichte fungierten.[17] In Livland wurden sie unter der polnischen Herrschaft durch die Landgerichte ersetzt, in Estland blieb aber der Name ‚Manngericht' erhalten – auch nach der schwedischen Herrschaft bis zur russischen Justizreform im Jahr 1889. In der Schwedenzeit wurden die Zivil- und Kriminalsachen des Adels dem Manngericht entzogen und es blieben die Grenzstreitigkeiten, Immissionen, Aufträge und Vollstreckung der Urteile des Landgerichts in der Kompetenz der Manngerichte, ebenso die Untersuchung in Kriminalsachen der Personen aus den niederen Ständen. Aus den ehemaligen Adelsgerichten wurden damit Gerichte für die Nichtadligen.

Bei der höchsten Gerichtsinstanz gab es ebenfalls ganz umwälzende Veränderungen. Der Namenswechsel vom Landesrat zum ‚königlichen Landgericht' war keine große Änderung. Um 1617 wurde aber ein Niederlandgericht für die Schuldforderungssachen abgesondert, und die Höchstgerichtsbarkeit des Landes blieb nunmehr bei dem Oberlandgericht.[18]

Es kommt noch die völlige Umwandlung der geistlichen Gerichtsbarkeit dazu. Die Mitglieder der alt-livländischen Konföderation waren fast ausschließlich geistliche Herrschaften gewesen: Bischofstümer und Deutschordensgebiete. Es ist klar, dass der Untergang Alt-Livlands diese Strukturen zerstörte. Dazu kam noch die Reformation. Vor allem die größeren Städte wie Riga und Reval hatten sich angeblich schon in der ersten Hälfte des 16. Jahrhunderts, d.h. vor der Schwedenzeit, von der geistlichen Gerichtsbarkeit der Bischöfe befreit. Diese wurde durch eine Mischung der weltlichen und geistlichen Instanzen, von Konsistorien ersetzt.[19] Die

---

[16] *Bunge*, Gerichtswesen (oben Fn. 13), S. 169 mit Quellenverweis.

[17] *Oswald Schmidt*, Das Verfahren vor dem Manngerichte in bürgerlichen Rechtsstreitigkeiten zur Zeit der bishöflichen und Ordensherrschaft in Livland, Dorpat 1865, S. 2.

[18] *Bunge*, Gerichtswesen (oben Fn. 13), S. 168 f. mit Quellenverweis; eingehend *Adolf Perandi*, Das ordentliche Verfahren in bürgerlichen Streitsachen vor dem estländischen Oberlandgericht zur schwedischen Zeit, Tartu 1938.

[19] *Bunge*, Gerichtswesen (oben Fn. 13), S. 26 mit Hinweis auf den Vergleich der Stadt Riga mit dem Erzbischof Wilhelm vom 21.8.1542.

Schwedenherrschaft stärkte die Stellung der evangelischen Konfession noch mehr, indem sie nun auch dem flachen Land als Staatskirche aufgezwungen wurde.[20] Wenn die kirchliche Gerichtsbarkeit im schwedischen Mutterland dank des Prinzips der lutherischen Staatskirche mehr als je mit dem Staat verbunden wurde, haben in den baltischen Überseeprovinzen die Träger der lokalen weltlichen obrigkeitlichen Gewalt, d.h. die Ritterschaften und Stadtmagistrate, die Oberhand über die Kirche gewonnen.

Das waren alles Justizinstitutionen, die schon früher vorhanden waren, unter der schwedischen Herrschaft aber erhebliche Kompetenzverschiebungen erleben sollten. So ist es ‚meistens' doch nicht beim Alten geblieben, entgegen der Behauptung Oswald Schmidts. Darüber hinaus wurden in der Schwedenzeit noch ganz neue Behörden errichtet. Bunge nennt in diesem Zusammenhang an erster Stelle den *advocatus* oder *commissarius fisci*, dann das Konsistorium und zuletzt das Burggericht zu Reval.[21] Schon am Ende des 16. Jahrhunderts hatte sich eine Institution herausgebildet, die recht viele Namen trug: Burggericht, königliches Gericht, Schlossgericht, peinliches Halsgericht, Kriegsgericht.[22] Auch die Anzahl der Gerichtsmitglieder war schwankend – nach Adolf Perandi sollte sie von 4 bis 16 reichen. Anfangs wurde das Gericht vom Statthalter oder Gouverneur für die Verhandlung einzelner Fälle eingesetzt und erst um ca. 1650 kam es zu einer festen Institutionalisierung mit festen Sitzungsperioden und Gerichtstag. O. Schmidt lässt in seiner Gesamtdarstellung der baltischen Rechtsgeschichte das Burggericht in Reval nahezu wie ein unwichtiges Provisorium erscheinen:

> „Gegen Ende des 16. Jahrh. errichtete die schwedische Regierung ein Burggericht in Reval, dessen Jurisdiction alle Bewohner des revalschen Schlosses und Domes sowie der königlichen Güter in Estland untergeben waren. Dasselbe wurde nach vielfachen Competenzconflikten mit den Landesbehörden in Folge der von ihm beanspruchten Erweiterung seiner Competenz am Ende dieser Periode auf Bitte des Adels aufgehoben".[23]

So provisorisch und unbedeutend blieb die Episode mit dem Burggericht zu Reval m.E. jedoch nicht. Erstens hatte das Gericht mehr als hundert Jahre getagt. Es ist wahr, dass seine Tätigkeit ständig von Kompetenzkonflikten begleitet war. Diese waren auch von Anfang an voraussehbar. Auf dem Domberg zu Reval gab es nicht

[20] Zu den Reformen in der baltischen Kirchenverwaltung während der Schwedenherrschaft und der darauf folgenden Zarenzeit näher und vergleichend *Andres Andresen*, Unifying the Periphery of a Conglomerate State: Ecclesiastical Legislation in Estlnad and Livland (1686–1832), in: Marju Luts-Sootak/Sanita Osipova/Frank L. Schäfer (Hg.), Einheit und Vielfalt in der Rechtsgeschichte im Ostseeraum. Sechster Rechtshistorikertag im Ostseeraum, 3.–5. Juni 2010 Tartu (Estland)/Riga (Lettland), Frankfurt a.M. u.a. 2012, S. 7–14.

[21] *Bunge*, Gerichtswesen (oben Fn. 13), S. 169 f.

[22] *Adolf Perandi*, Die Aufgaben und Funktionen der estländischen Generalgouvernementsregierung während der schwedischen Zeit, in: Katalog des estländischen Generalgouverneursarchivs aus der schwedischen Zeit, Bd. 1, Tartu 1935, S. 104 (12–110) mit Quellenverweisen.

[23] *Schmidt*, Rechtsgeschichte (oben Fn. 10), S. 266.

nur das Schloss mit königlichen Beamten und sonstigen Schlossleuten, sondern auch die ritterschaftlichen Behörden befanden sich auf dem Domberg. Auch waren die Bewohner des Dombergs meistens adelig, indem sie ihre Winterhäuser auf dem Dom und nicht etwa in der sog. Unterstadt, d.h. rechtlich in der eigentlichen Stadt hatten. Die Lage wurde noch mehr kompliziert durch die ab 1685 vollzogene Güterreduktion, als die Ländereien der Privatgüter von der Krone eingezogen worden waren und dann als Domänegüter denselben Gutsherren zur Pacht zurückgegeben wurden. Dass sie außer ihrer Ländereien auch ihren privilegierten Gerichtsstand verlieren sollten, war für die baltischen Adeligen schon zu viel. Dieser Kompetenzstreit wurde von der Zentralregierung letztendlich zugunsten der ritterschaftlichen Landesbehörden entschieden, und ab 1699 durfte das Burggericht keine neuen Sachen annehmen. Die schon laufenden Sachen verhandelte es aber bis zum Ende. So sind die Protokolle bis 1710 geführt, d.h. bis zum Ende der schwedischen Herrschaft über Estland. Erhalten und im Estnischen Historischen Archiv aufbewahrt sind über zweitausend Gerichtsakten.[24] Es sollte noch mehr Prozesse vor dem Burggericht geben – alle Akten sind nicht erhalten. Wenn man die Bevölkerungsdichte oder vielmehr die Bevölkerungsdünne Estlands mitberücksichtigt, dann soll man eher sagen, dass das Burggericht zu Reval ein sehr aktiver Gerichtshof war. Inwieweit das Gericht als Schnittstelle für den Einfluss des schwedischen Reichsrechts in Estland fungierte, lässt sich ohne nähere Praxisstudien nicht sagen. Solche gibt es aber nicht, obwohl das Quellenmaterial reichlich und gut erhalten ist.[25] Die erwähnte und als Dauerproblem bekannte Bevölkerungsdünne wirkt sich auch auf die estnische Geschichtswissenschaft aus.

Das Burggericht tagte zunächst bei und dann neben dem schwedischen Provinzialoberhaupt, das am Anfang der Periode als Statthalter, dann als Gouverneur und am Ende als Generalgouverneur firmierte. Noch mehr, das Gericht wuchs aus den justiziellen Funktionen und Befugnissen dieses schwedischen Statthalters heraus.

---

[24] Genauer gesagt sind im Archivkatalog 2.212 Akten angegeben. S. Tallinna linnusekohtu arhiiv – Archiv des Tallinner Burggerichts, in: Katalog des estländischen Generalgouverneursarchivs aus der schwedischen Zeit, Bd. I, Tartu 1936, S. 273–417.

[25] Adolf Perandi bietet unter dem Kapitel „Das Tallinner Burggericht“ nur eine allgemeine Übersicht der Funktionen und äußeren Geschichte des Burggerichts, ist aber trotzdem das umfangsreichste Stück der bisherigen Burggerichtsforschung. S. *Perandi*, Aufgaben (oben Fn. 22), S. 103–109 mit Einbeziehung der früheren deutschbaltischen Literatur. Im Kontext der schwedischen Burggerichte in den Ostseeprovinzen, darunter auch in Wismar, hat in der jüngeren Forschung Kjell Åke Modéer das Burggericht zu Reval mitbehandelt. S. *Kjell Åke Modéer*, Svenska borgrätter i Östersjöprovinserna. Ett bidrag till den tidigmoderna processrättsutvecklingen [Die schwedischen Burggerichte in den Ostseeprovinzen. Ein Beitrag zur frühmodernen Prozessrechtsentwicklung], in: Ivo Asmus/Heiko Droste/Jens E. Olesen (Hg.), Gemeinsame Bekannte. Schweden und Deutschland in der Frühen Neuzeit, Berlin u.a. 2003, S. 284 ff., mit Hinweisen auf die frühere schwedische Literatur. Es sei hier nur vermerkt, dass der estnische Parallelname für die Stadt Reval nicht ‚Tartu‘ ist, wie Modéer angibt, sondern ‚Tallinn‘. Tartu hieß auf Deutsch ‚Dorpat‘.

So zählte zu den in Estland neu eingeführten Justizbehörden auch der Gouverneur selbst – die Gewaltenteilung als konstitutives Prinzip der Staatsmacht gehört in die spätere Zeit, und damals hatte die Spitze der königlichen Provinzialverwaltung auch justizielle Funktionen zu erfüllen. Ursprünglich waren der Jurisdiktion des Statthalters die örtlichen schwedischen Beamten, das Militär und die auf den Kronsgütern lebenden Personen unterstellt. Allerding hing es von der Initiative der Parteien ab, ob der Gouverneur zur Verhandlung der Sache schreiten konnte. So bürgerte es sich ein, dass die standesübergreifenden Gerichtssachen vom Gouverneur entschieden wurden, ebenso die Prozesse, wo es um die Standesprivilegien ging.[26] Meistens setzte der Gouverneur für die Entscheidung der Rechtsstreitigkeiten spezielle Kommissare ein. Die Urteile dieser sog. Kommissarialgerichte gelangten immer in die Revision zum Gouverneur, aber auch alle Urteile und Entscheidungen des Burggerichts wurden ihm zur Bestätigung vorgelegt, wobei er durchaus das Abänderungsrecht hatte. Im Oberlandgericht, das eine ritterschaftliche Landesbehörde war, führte er den Vorsitz, mischte sich aber sonst nicht ein. Gegenüber den Manngerichten hatte er ein gewisses Beaufsichtigungsrecht – er konnte einzelne Prozesse verhandeln, aber auch im Allgemeinen die Manngerichte zum Erscheinen und Verhandeln verpflichten. Es gab also einen recht weiten Bereich justizieller Befugnisse und Kompetenzen, der dem schwedischen Statthalter oder Gouverneur bzw. Generalgouverneur in Estland zukam. Auch das war eigentlich ein Novum in der Justizverfassung des Landes.

Dies waren die Gerichte und die anderen justiziellen Behörden, deren Kompetenzen verschoben und abgeändert oder die überhaupt erst in der Schwedenzeit errichtet wurden. Von einem Stillstand und oder von einem Ausharren beim Alten kann man bei den gerade geschilderten Vorgänge doch nicht sprechen. Die grundlegenden Umwälzungen betrafen aber nicht nur das Landesjustizsystem, sondern auch den Instanzenzug, in den die estländischen Rechtssachen nach der Behandlung in den Landesbehörden gelangen konnten.

IV. Appellation und Revision außerhalb des Landes

Schon zu Beginn des 15. Jahrhunderts, am 19. August 1403, hatte der römisch-deutsche König Ruprecht das *privilegium de non appellando* für die Ordensgebiete in Alt-Livland erteilt; spätere Könige wiederholten es.[27] Es gibt aber trotzdem Prozesse baltischen Ursprungs in königlichen bzw. kaiserlichen Gerichten. In den Reichskammergerichtsakten soll es 27 Prozesse von 1530 bis 1564 geben, die aus

---

[26] Z.B. über das Recht der Küstengüter auf das Strandgut. Dazu näher *Otto Liiv*, Ühest suurprotsessist 17. sajandi lõpul [Über einen Großprozess am Ende des 17. Jahrhunderts, in: Ajalooline Ajakiri 3 (1932), S. 129–140; es gibt von der Schrift auch eine schwedische Parallelversion: *Otto Liiv*, Den hävdvunna strandrätten i ljuset av en stor process från 1600–talets slut, in: Svio-Estonica: årsbok utgiven av Svensk-Estniska Samfundet, Tartu 1938, S. 181–198.

[27] Näher m.N. auf die Quellen, teilweise mit Quellenauszügen, *Bunge*, Gerichtswesen (oben Fn. 13), S. 22.

Alt-Livland in das Reichskammergericht gelangten.[28] Wie viele altlivländische Rechtssachen im Reichshofrat verhandelt wurden, ist derzeit noch nicht ermittelt. Es kann hier auch dahingestellt bleiben. Es ist klar, dass die schwedischen Könige in puncto Rechtsmittel bestimmt viel aktiver als die deutsch-römischen Kaiser waren. Man sollte ja auch berücksichtigen, dass etwa die Appellation als Rechtsmittel sich erst in der Frühen Neuzeit richtig etablierte[29] – nachdem die baltischen Gebiete nicht mehr zum römisch-deutschen Reich gehörten.

Dass vom königlichen Burggericht die Appellationen an das königliche Hof- und später an das Svea Hofgericht zu Stockholm gingen, erscheint nur normal. Das ritterschaftlich verwaltete Oberlandgericht und die estländische Ritterschaft selbst versuchten mehrfach, die Inappellabilität der Landgerichtsentscheidungen in Stockholm geltend zu machen – ohne Erfolg. 1614 wurde das Oberlandgericht dem königlichen Hofgericht untergeordnet. Im Jahr 1616 wurde die Appellation aus dem Anlass eines besonderen Falles gestattet, später war sie aber zur Regel geworden.[30]

Gegen die Revision der Oberlandgerichtsurteile hatte die Ritterschaft sich ebenfalls mehrfach gewehrt, aber letztendlich auch hier erfolglos. Durch einen königlichen Brief vom 17. Januar 1651 wurde angeordnet, dass die Revision in allen Sachen zuzulassen sei, wenn folgende Bedingungen erfüllt sind:

> „1) dass der Streitgegenstand sich zum mindesten bis auf tausend Reichsthaler an Werth belaufe; 2) dass die Revision nach Eröffnung des Urtheils beim Landgerichte vor Ablauf von zehn Tagen gesucht werde. 3) Wer die Revision nachsucht, soll sogleich beim Landgericht zweihundert Reichsthaler bis zur Ausführung der Sache deponiren, so dass, wenn er später in der Revisionsinstanz verliert, er zugleich des erlegten Geldes verlustig geht, und dasselbe dem Landgericht zu gute kommt. Gewinnt er dagegen die Sache, so erhält er das Geld zurück. Doch sollen die *personae miserabiles*, welche sich *per querelam* an Uns wenden, dadurch nicht beschränkt werden. 4) Der um die Revision Nachsuchende soll dieselbe binnen Jahr und Tag prosequiren etc. 5) In Gränz-

[28] *Leo Leesment*, Über die livländischen Gerichtssachen im Reichskammergericht und im Reichshofrat, Tartu 1929, S. 14 ff. Es sei allerdings hervorgehoben, dass alle diese Gerichtssachen aus dem späteren Livland und Riga, auch Kurland, aber nicht aus Estland kamen. Aus der Perspektive der Reichsjustiz und für hiesige Fragestellungen unergiebig, sonst doch einschlägig *Bernhard Diestelkamp*, Die Reichsgerichtsbarkeit in den Ostseeländern, in: Nils Jörn/Michael North (Hg.), Die Integration des südlichen Ostseeraumes in das Alte Reich, Köln/Weimar/Wien 2000, S. 13 (17–20 zu Livland).

[29] Dazu sehr informativ m.w.N. auf die frühere Forschungsliteratur *Peter Oestmann*, Ludolf Hugo und die gemeinrechtliche Appellation, in: Ludolf Hugo, Vom Missbrauch der Appellation, Wien u.a. 2012, S. 3 ff.

[30] Dazu näher *Bunge*, Gerichtswesen (oben Fn. 13), S. 193 ff. Im Kontext der schwedischen Uniformierungsbemühungen *Kjell Åke Modéer*, Uniformität und Zentralisation. Rechtsprechung im Ostseeraum durch die schwedische Krone im 17. Jahrhundert, in: Heinz Mohnhaupt/Dieter Simon (Hg.) Vorträge zur Justizforschung: Geschichte und Theorie, Bd. 1, Frankfurt a.M. 1992, S. 217 (230 ff.), zur Uniformierung durch die Rechtsprechung, für Est- und Livland insbes. S. 234 ff.

streitigkeiten aber, wobei es auf Augenschein ankommt, soll keine Revision zugelassen, vielmehr die darin gefällten Urtheile soglich vollstreckt werden."[31]

Gegen Ende des 17. Jahrhunderts hatte sich die Lage dahin geändert, dass die Revision in allen Sachen ohne Ausnahme und ohne Rücksicht auf den Wert des Streitgegenstandes zugelassen wurde. Die Beantwortung der Frage, inwieweit dadurch etwa der Einfluss des schwedischen Reichsrechts gestärkt wurde, bedarf einer genaueren Forschung über die Gerichtsmaterialien. Ein erster Schritt wäre es, die Appellations- und Revisionsakten im Bestand des Svea Hofgerichts im schwedischen Reichsarchiv zu Stockholm überhaupt erst zu ermitteln. Dies gilt auch für die Appellationen und Revisionen aus Reval, so paradox es auch in Anbetracht der Autonomie der Städte und der Stadtrechtsfamilien, ebenso der Unterwerfungskapitulation der Stadt Reval klingt. Es sei hier deshalb noch kurz ein Blick auf die Entwicklungen des Justizwesens in estländischen Städten unter der Schwedenherrschaft geworfen.

V. Die Entwicklungen in der städtischen Justiz

In der Hansestadt Reval (heute estnische Hauptstadt Tallinn) galt das lübische Recht.[32] In der Unterwerfungskapitulation des Jahres 1561 wurde lübisches Recht nicht ausdrücklich als in Reval geltendes Recht erwähnt. Da sprach man nur ganz allgemein von der Weitergeltung des bereits geltenden Rechts oder genauer gesagt, von der Unantastbarkeit der früher gegebenen Rechtsquellen und ausgebildeten Rechtsgewohnheiten:

„3. Sie sollen auch bei ihren priuilegien, jurisdictionen, freiheitenn, begnadigungen, gerichte vnd rechten sowol in peinlichen alse burgerlichen sachen, alten guten billichen rechtmessigen vnd loblichen gewonheiten, gebreuchenn, possession, habender wehre, auffrichtigenn vertregen, siegel vnd brieffen, so ihnen vnd der stadt Reuell von hern zu hern gegebenn, souiel sie der beweisenn, darthun vund beschreiuenn mugenn, vngeturbieret geschutzt vnd gehandhabet werden …".[33]

Später, „z.B. in den Privilegien Johannes III. v[om] 11. Februar 1570 Art. 2, und Sigismunds vom 10. April 1594" sollte sogar „von der Rechtspflege *nach kaiserlichem Rechte*", d.h. nach dem römischrechtlich geprägten gemeinen Recht die

---

31 *Bunge*, Gerichtswesen (oben Fn. 13), S. 194 f., Anm. 123.

32 Der revalsche Kodex vom 1257 ist überhaupt die älteste erhalten gebliebene Aufzeichnung des lübischen Rechts und wird im Stadtarchiv zu Tallinn aufbewahrt. Es kommt noch dazu, dass der Bestand der verschiedenen Handschriften des lübischen Rechts in Tallinn – insgesamt vier, darunter ein richtiges Prachtstück vom 1282 – die weltgrößte Sammlung der Handschriften des lübischen Rechts ist. S. auch *Tiina Kala*, Das mittelalterliche Reval und sein Recht, in: Lübecki õiguse Tallinna koodeks 1282 / transkribeerinud ja tõlkinud Tiina Kala [Der Revaler Kodex des lübischen Rechts 1282, Transkription und Übersetzung ins Estnische von Tiina Kala], Tallinn 1998, S. 19–27.

33 Privilegium Reval (o. Fn. 12), S. 16.

Rede sein.[34] Es ist trotzdem anzunehmen und durchaus glaubwürdig, dass das lübische Recht in Reval in der Schwedenzeit ohne Unterbrechung angewendet wurde. Z.B. hieß es in den sog. Concordaten zwischen dem Rat und der Großen Gilde vom 27. Januar 1672 im Art. 44:

> „Auch sollen sich die litigirenden Parteien in allen und jeden Artikeln, sowohl in Criminal- als Civilsachen, auf die *lübischen Statuta* zu berufen haben, es wäre denn, daß eine unverrückt observirte Gewohnheit denenselben conträr wäre, als welche billig den Vorgang von den beschriebenen Rechte hat etc."[35]

Immerhin, genau in der hier zu betrachtenden Schwedenzeit ist ein erheblicher Bruch in dieser althergebrachten Verbindung mit der lübischen Stadtrechtsfamilie für Reval eingetreten. Nach Bunge blieb es „bei der Appellation vom Revaler Rath an den lübischen, bis im J[ahr]. 1584 die Stadt sich dazu verstand, statt dessen *an den königlichen Hof in Stockholm* zu appelliren".[36] Bunge weist dabei allerdings nicht auf irgendeine städtische Satzung oder Rechtsakte, sondern auf zwei schwedisch-königliche Privilegien hin: auf den königlichen Abschied vom 25. August 1584 Art. 1 und auf das *privilegium* Sigismunds vom 10. April 1594 Art. 2.[37] Ich habe noch keine Gelegenheit gehabt, diese von Bunge angegebenen Quellentexte nachzuschlagen.[38] Das wäre aber bei Bunges Schriften ratsam, wie unsere Erfahrung der letzten Forschungsjahrzehnte mehrfach bestätigt hat. In diesem Kontext hat Bunge auch auf die Unterwerfungsurkunden Revals aus dem Jahr 1561 hingewiesen. Und es ist ja auch wahr, dass im Reversal der schwedischen Bevollmächtigten die Erhaltung des Appellationszuges nach Lübeck ausdrücklich zugesichert wurde:

> „Vund nachdeme die stadt Reuell der deutzschen Anze vorwandt vnd eingeleibett, soll es ihnen, ob sye darynne bleiben willen vnd derselben freyheit ferner geniessen oder nicht, frey vnd offen stehenn, wie dann viellgenantte burgermeistere, [rath]manne,

---

[34] So *Friedrich Georg v. Bunge*, Einleitung in die liv, esth- und curländische Rechtsgeschichte und Geschichte der Rechtsquellen, Reval 1849, S. 225 Anm. b); Hervorhebung wie bei Bunge.

[35] Hier nach *Bunge*, Einleitung (oben Fn. 34), S. 225, Anm. b); Hervorhebung wie bei Bunge.

[36] *Bunge*, Einleitung (oben Fn. 34), S. 225; Hervorhebung wie bei Bunge.

[37] *Bunge*, Einleitung (oben Fn. 34), S. 225 Anm. d). Die jüngere Forschung dagegen geht davon aus, dass „die Stadt Reval … mit ihren Appellationen nach Stockholm verwiesen" wurde, bzw. dass die Änderung des Rechtszuges von Lübeck nach Stockholm der Stadt „vorgeschrieben" wurde. Vgl. *Wilhelm Ebel*, Lübisches Recht, Bd. 1, Lübeck 1971, S. 37, und *Ulrich Simon*, Appellationen von Reval nach Lübeck – aus zurückgekehrten Akten des Archivs der Hansestadt Lübeck, in: Robert Schweitzer/Waltraud Bastman-Bühner (Hg.), Die Stadt im europäischen Nordosten. Kulturbeziehungen von der Ausbreitung des Lübischen Rechts bis zur Aufklärung, Helsinki/Lübeck 2001, S. 56.

[38] In der gedruckten Auswahl sind sie nicht erhalten, da die Sammlung mit der Prozeßordnung des Jahres 1615 beginnt. Vgl. Auswahl derer wichtigsten in edenen Landes- und Stadtgerichten des Herzogthums Ehstland, auch noch jetzt geltenden Königl. schwedischen Verordnungen, Reval 1777, S. 1 ff.

burgerschafft vnd gemeine *die gewontliche appellation[....]z jrem gerichte nach Lubeck sych auch nach dem alten [....b]ehaltenn.*"[39]

Das am Ende zwischen König und Stadt ausgehandelte Privileg bzw. die Unterwerfungskapitulation lautet allerdings schon ganz anders. Auch hier wird im Punkt 13 der Verbleib in der Hanse der Stadt zur freien Wahl überlassen, die gerichtliche Oberhoheit nimmt aber die hohe Krone selbst in Anspruch:

> „13. Vnd nachdem die stadt Reuel der teutschen Antze verwandtt vnd eingeliebt ist, sol es ihnen, ab sie darin bleiben vnd derselben freiheit ferner geniessen wollen oder nicht, frei vnd offen stehen; doch also, dasz sie dadurch keiner andern obrigkeit, wie die mag genent werden, jurisdiction vnd gepiete sich vnderwerffen oder gehorsamen sollen, sondern allein vnsz fur ihren gepietendenn herrn erkennenn."[40]

Ich bin in der frühneuzeitlichen Quellensprache nicht besonders gewandt, weil mein gewöhnlicher Forschungszeitraum eher im 19. Jahrhundert liegt. Immerhin, ich lese die Stelle so, dass Reval zwar in der Hanse bleiben durfte, die Appellation auf die Ratsurteile jedoch nach Stockholm gehen sollte. Oder, wenn man den nächsten Punkt 14 noch dazu nimmt, dann vielleicht mit der Ausnahme der vertraglichen bzw. überhaupt handelsrechtlichen Streitigkeiten, die auch weiterhin im Zug der *gewohnlichen appellation* vor den lübeckischen Rat gelangen konnten:

> „14. Also vnd mit solchem vorbehaldt mugen sich vielgemelte burgermeister, rathman, burgerschaft vnd gemeine der stadt Reuel der gewohnli[che]n appellation jn sachen, die contracte vel quasi handel vnd wandel antreffen, vnd sonst keiner ander furbehalten vnd gebrauchen."[41]

Wie gesagt, sollte auch diese Ausnahme der Lübecker Appellation für bestimmte Zivilsachen im Jahr 1584 abgeschafft worden sein. Es kann auch sein, dass die Appellationen von Reval nach Lübeck schon etwas früher aufgehört hatten. Nach Paul Johansen soll es im Archiv von Lübeck insgesamt 144 Prozessakten aus Reval geben.[42] Dabei nennt er den Zeitraum vom 1421 bis 1580.[43] Das letzte Datum liegt also vier Jahre früher als das von Bunge genannte Jahr 1584 und deutet darauf hin, dass die Appellationen aus Reval schon vor der förmlichen Abschaffung dieses

---

[39] Reversale der schwedischen Bevollmächtigten, ausgestellt für die Stadt Reval, vom 6. Juni 1561, in: Capitulationen (oben Fn. 11), S. 9; die eckigen Klammer deuten auf die Textverluste, die im Druck durch die Tonflecken entstanden sind. Die Hervorhebung von mir.

[40] Privilegium Reval (oben Fn. 12), S. 18.

[41] Privilegium Reval (oben Fn. 12), S. 18. Diese Interpretation entspricht auch dem Forschungsstand der schwedischen Autoren. Vgl. *Modéer*, Uniformität (oben Fn. 30), S. 231.

[42] Nach Wilhelm Ebel sollen aus Reval über 300 schriftlichen Appellationen erhalten sein und Reval damit neben Rostock überhaupt über allen Tochterstädten Lübecks stehen. Vgl. *Wilhelm Ebel*, Der Rechtszug nach Lübeck, in: Hansische Geschichtsblätter 85 (1967), S. 29 und 33. Neben Reval war auch den Bürgern der Stadt Elbing die schriftliche Appellation erlaubt, weil beide Städte von Lübeck weit entfernt waren. Dazu a.a.O., S. 28 ff.

[43] *Paul Johansen*, Lüübeki ja ta arhiivi tähtsusest Tallinna ajaloole [Über die Wichtigkeit Lübecks und seines Archivs für die Geschichte Tallinns], in: Linnad ja Alevid. Eesti Linnadeliidu häälekandja [Städte und Flecken. Das Presseorgan des Städteverbands], Tallinn 1937, S. 71.

Rechtsweges aufhören konnten. Andererseits berichtet Ulrich Simon, der ebenfalls insgesamt 144 Fälle in Lübecker Senatsakten zählt,[44] von einem viel späteren Appellationsfall aus dem Jahr 1610.[45] Ohne weitere Untersuchungen lassen sich diese Widersprüche nicht lösen.

Wie auch früher bei der Appellation nach Lübeck mehrere Formalien erfüllt sein sollten,[46] bestanden vor der Appellation an den schwedischen Königshof ebenfalls mehrere Hürden, wenn auch von den früheren abweichend: der Wert des Streitgegenstandes sollte mindestens 500 Taler sein, die Bau-, Arrest- und Executionssachen wurden inappellabel erklärt, ebenso die Injuriensachen und die Sachen, die aufgrund eines Vergleichs abgeurteilt waren. Unter dieses letzte Genre sollten die Gilde- und Zunftsachen fallen, in denen „von Alters her“ „alle Berufung gegen Erkenntnisse des Rathes ausgeschlossen war“.[47] Eine Appellation sollte im Rat zu Reval binnen zehn Tagen angemeldet und innerhalb von fünf Monaten beim Hofgericht zu Stockholm eingeleitet werden.[48] Wie viele Appellationen von Reval an das königliche Hofgericht zu Stockholm überhaupt gingen, ist noch zu ermitteln. Die Geschichte über die Veränderung des Rechtsweges zeigt jedenfalls klar, dass die revalsche Justizverfassung unter der Schwedenherrschaft doch erheblich umgewälzt wurde.

Es ist allerdings erwähnenswert, dass man in Reval materiellrechtlich ganz entschieden beim lübischen Recht geblieben war. Die Abschaffung des Instanzenzugs nach Lübeck hielt Reval nämlich nicht davon ab, zwei Jahre später die neue revidierte Fassung des lübischen Rechts vom Jahr 1586 anzuwenden. Dies betrifft auch spätere lübische Satzungen und sogar kaiserliche Rechtsakte, die ja in Anbetracht von Revals Zugehörigkeit zum schwedischen Reich gar nicht mehr zur Anwendung kommen sollten. Bunge zählt aber noch mehrere solcher Akte während der Schwedenzeit auf: das Appellationsprivileg Kaiser Rudolphs II. vom 23. Mai 1588, die beiden hansischen Schiffsordnungen vom 1591 und 1614, die lübische Seegerichtsordnung von 1655 und die lübische Wechselordnung vom 22. April 1662.[49]

---

[44] *Simon*, Appellationen (oben Fn. 37) S. 49.

[45] *Simon*, Appellationen (oben Fn. 37), S. 57 f.

[46] Dazu zusammenfassend *Ebel*, Rechtszug (oben Fn. 42), S. 16 ff.

[47] *Bunge*, Einleitung (oben Fn. 34), S. 224.

[48] *Bunge*, Einleitung (oben Fn. 34), S. 223 f., zu allen Appellationsbedingungen mit Quellenverweisen.

[49] *Bunge*, Einleitung (oben Fn. 34), S. 228. Es soll auch der Kommentar von David Mevius in Reval in regem Gebrauch gewesen sein – nicht nur seit dem 24. April 1664, als „beim Revaler Rath ein Schreiben von Mevius nebst einem Exemplar seines neu aufgelegten Commentars“ eingegangen war (ebd. S. 229 Anm. v), sondern bis zur zweiten Hälfte der 1860er Jahre. Im 19. Jahrhunder hat man anscheinend die von W. A. Schoepf besorgte Frankfurter Auflage aus dem Jahr 1744 benutzt. Diese wird nämlich von Bunge in seiner Gesamtdarstellung des est- und livländischen Privatrechts als jüngste Ausgabe angegeben. Vgl. *Friedrich Georg v. Bunge*, Das liv- und esthländische Privatrecht, wissenschaftlich dargestellt, 2. Aufl., Bd. 1, Reval 1847, S. 68

Inwieweit die innerstädtische Justizverfassung Revals in der Schwedenzeit verändert oder nicht verändert wurde, kann ich beim jetzigen Forschungsstand noch nicht berichten. Es ist aber anzunehmen, dass die Zahl der städtischen Untergerichte anwuchs. Ein anachronistischer Rückschritt über das Jahr 1845, als die lokale Behördenverfassung durch ein öffentlich-rechtliches Provinzialgesetzbuch[50] nochmals zusammengefasst und vom russischen Zaren bestätigt wurde, kann hier dem Bild etwas kräftigere Konturen verleihen. Es sollen in der Mitte des 19. Jahrhunderts zwölf Untergerichte in Reval tätig gewesen sein:

das Stadt- oder Niedergericht (§§ 1125 ff.) – für Untersuchungen in Strafsachen, Grenz- und Baustreitigkeiten, Injurien- und Pfandsachen, nichtstreitigen Schuldforderungen, Wechselsachen, Streitigkeiten aus Verträgen und Verschreibungen; ebenso Vereidigung der Stadtbeamten u.a.;

das Waisengericht (§§ 1128 ff.) – für Vormundschaft und Kuratorium;[51]

das Kommerzgericht (§§ 1133 ff.) – für die Aufsicht über ordnungsgemäßen Handel;

das Amtsgericht (§§ 1142 f.) – für die Streitigkeiten innerhalb der Handwerksinnungen und Zünfte;

das See- und Frachtgericht (§§ 1144 ff.) – für die Streitsachen zwischen Befrachtern, Schiffern und Schiffsvolk und Seeunfallsachen;

das Wettgericht (§§ 1148 ff.) – für die Aufsicht über das Gewerbe der Fremden, Viktualientaxen, Stadtabgaben der durchreisenden Künstler;

das Baugericht (§§ 1151 f.) – für die Baustreitigkeiten;

die Stadtkämmerei (§§ 1153 ff.) – für die Leitung des Stadtbauwesens, Untersuchung der Grenzstreitigkeiten außerhalb der Stadt, Aufsicht über die gemeinen Arbeiter und Masse;

das Stadtkriegsgericht (§§ 1156 ff.) – für Urteile über die Amtsvergehen der Mitglieder der Stadtkompagnie;

das Mündliche Gericht (§§ 1159 ff.) – für die Schuldsachen aus mündlichen Angaben der Beteiligten;

die Amtspatronen (§§ 1164 ff.) – für die Aufsicht über die Handwerksämter und Zünfte;

---

viide b). Bunge sollte sich auskennen – er war zu dieser Zeit schon fünf Jahre als Syndikus und Bürgermeister im Rat Revals tätig gewesen. Als Erscheinungsort gibt Bunge allerdings irrtümlich Ulm an.

[50] Provinzialrecht der Ostseegouvernements. Erster Theil: Behördenverfassung. St. Petersburg 1845.

[51] Beim Waisengericht ist es sehr wahrscheinlich, dass es in der Schwedenzeit eingerichtet wurde. Der sich entwickelnde Obrigkeitsstaat kümmerte sich sehr um das Vormundschaftswesen, auch wenn er die eigentliche Sorge den lokalen intermediären Gewalten wie dem Stadtmagistrat auferlegen sollte. Die schwedische Vormundschaftsordnung von 1697 war noch im 19. Jahrhundert, unter der russischen Zarenherrschaft in Est- und Livland in Geltung. S. dazu *Christoph Christian Dabelow*, Geist der Schwedischen Vormünder-Ordnung vom 17ten März 1669 und Verhältniss dieses Gesetzes zu dem übrigen Livländischen Vormundschafts-Recht, Dorpat 1820.

das Subhastations- und Auktionsdirektorium (§§ 1173 ff.) – für die Veranstaltung und Aufsicht über die Versteigerungen.

Wie gesagt, ist es ohne weitere Recherchen, die sich möglicherweise auch auf die archivalischen Materialien erstrecken sollten, schwer zu sagen, welche dieser Instanzen in der Schwedenzeit entstanden sind. Darüber hinaus ist anzunehmen, dass sich in der Stadt ebenso wie auf dem Land die Kompetenzen der einzelnen Instanzen veränderten.

Dies alles betraf nur die größte Stadt Reval. Das Justizwesen der kleineren Städte Estlands erlebte noch gravierendere Umwälzungen. Die Stadt Wesenberg (est. Rakvere), die im Jahr 1302 vom dänischen König Erich VI. Menved die Stadtrechte samt des lübischen Rechts als Rechtsgrundlage verliehen bekommen hatte, wurde vom Schwedenkönig Gustav II. Adolf im Jahr 1618 dem niederländischen Gesandten Reinhold von Brederode belehnt. Im Jahr 1669 kam die Stadt in den Besitz des Adelsgeschlechts Tiesenhausen und erlangte erst 1783 die Stadtrechte zurück, als sie von der Zarenregierung zur Kreisstadt erhoben wurde.[52] Die im Jahr 1345 vom dänischen König Waldemar IV. Atterdag ebenfalls mit dem lübischen Recht beliehene Stadt Narwa (est. Narva) an der russischen Grenze sollte nach der Absicht der schwedischen Krone zur wichtigsten Handels- und Hafenstadt an der Ostsee werden. Man führte dementsprechend im Jahr 1585 in Narwa das allgemeine schwedische Stadrecht ein.[53] Der Rechtszug von diesen beiden Städten nach Reval[54] war durch die benannten Veränderungen nun auch abgeschnitten.

Außer diesen beiden Städten der lübeckischen Stadtrechtsfamilie[55] sind auch zwei weitere Kleinstädte in der schwedischen Zeit dem Herzogtum Estland untergeordnet und in private Hände beliehen worden: Hapsal (est. Haapsalu), aus dem die älteste Fassung des rigischen Stadtrechts aus dem Jahr 1279 bekannt ist,[56] fiel

---

[52] Belletristisch hat der estnische Schriftsteller Jaan Kross – von seiner Ausbildung her ein Jurist – den Kampf der Stadt um ihre Rechte gegen das Herrenhaus Tiesenhausen dargestellt: *Jaan Kross*, Die Frauen von Wesenberg, oder, der Aufstand der Bürger, München 1997.

[53] Narwa ist auch später eine Stadt des wechselhaftesten Schicksals geblieben. Dazu etwas näher und m.w.N., aber keinesfalls erschöpfend: *Marju Luts-Sootak*, Die baltischen Privatrechte in den Händen der russischen Reichsjustiz, in: Zoran Pokrovac (Hg.) Rechtsprechung in Osteuropa. Studien zum 19. und frühen 20. Jahrhundert, Frankfurt a.M. 2012, S. 314 ff.

[54] Dazu sehr kurz und ohne Anspruch auf Vollständigkeit, auch sonst eher anspruchslos *Tobias Kämpf*, Das Revaler Ratsurteilsbuch: Grundsätze und Regeln des Prozessverfahrens in der frühneuzeitlichen Hansestadt, Köln u.a. 2013, S. 228 nur für Narwa, ohne Erwähnung Wesenbergs.

[55] Beide fehlen in der Liste von *Ebel*, Rechtszug (o. Fn. 42), S. 2 f., Fn. 6. Narwa wird allerdings in Haupttext erwähnt als die östlichste Stadt mit lübischem Stadtrecht, Wesenberg aber überhaupt nicht.

[56] Der Text ist abgedruckt in *Jakob Gottlieb Leonhard Napiersky*, Die Quellen des rigischen Stadtrechts bis zum Jahr 1673, Riga 1876 (ND Hannover/Dören 1976), S. 15–49; dazu auch *Friedrich Georg v. Bunge*, Die Stadt Riga im dreizehnten und vierzehnten Jahrhundert. Geschichte, Verfassung und Rechtszustand, Leipzig 1878 (ND Amsterdam 1968) m.w.N., u.a. auf eigene frühere Publikationen.

nach einem vierzehnjährigen Interregnum unter dem dänischen Herzog Magnus (1559–73) und dem Dänenkönig im Jahr 1581 ebenfalls den Schweden anheim. Man bildete aus der Stadt mitsamt der Ländereien rundum – später der Kreis Wieck – ein Reichslehen mit einem Schlossvogt an der Spitze. Im Jahr 1628 kaufte Jakob De La Gardie, ein Graf französischer Herkunft, die Stadt mitsamt Burg und umliegenden Lehensländereien von der schwedische Krone. Er übte dort trotz der Beibehaltung der Ratsverfassung[57] u.a. auch die Obergerichtsbarkeit aus. Eine weitere Kleinstadt, mittelhochdeutsch Wittensten und später hochdeutsch Weißenstein (est. Paide) genannt, war im Jahr 1293 von Ordensmeister Halt mit dem rigischen Stadtrecht, ebenfalls in der Fassung des Jahres 1279, beliehen worden. In der Schwedenzeit, von 1636 bis 1699, d.h. 63 Jahre lang, musste die Stadt aber einen zähen Rechtsstreit gegen die Gutsherren von Mexhof führen, weil die Vormundsregierung der Königin Christina 1635 versehentlich oder auch absichtlich samt dem Landgut auch die Stadt dem Grafen Lennart Torstenson beliehen hatte. An die Beibehaltung des rigischen Stadtrechts oder an ein selbstständiges städtisches Justizsystem war hier nicht zu denken.

Es gab also keine einzige Stadt in Estland, wo es nicht zu Veränderungen im Gerichtswesen und Justizverfassung kam. Teilweise waren die Umwälzungen enorm, wie etwa bei den Kleinstädten, die überhaupt ihre städtische Autonomie verloren hatten. Aber auch in den größeren Städten war es nicht beim Alten geblieben. Es bestätigt sich der Befund einer unübersehbaren Dynamik in der Justizverfassung also auch im Bereich der Stadtjustiz.

VI. Fazit und Ausblick

Ein Fazit lässt sich kurz und knapp formulieren: Es ist in der Justizverfassung Estlands unter der Schwedenherrschaft kein Stein auf dem anderen geblieben. Stück für Stück durchdrangen die Kompetenzverschiebungen, die neuen Instanzen sowie die Abschaffung der alten Rechtswege und der ganzen Rechtsprechungsorgane diesen Bereich.[58] Nur die Zusicherungen der Unterwerfungskapitulationen über die Beibehaltung des althergebrachten Rechts- und Gerichtssystems, ebenso die evolutionäre, nicht revolutionäre Durchführung der Veränderungen durch eine einmalige

---

[57] Zu der etwas komplizierten Geschichte der Einführung des lübischen Rechts und Unterordnung des Hofgerichts zu Dorpat durch die Befehle der Schwedenkönige einerseits, denen andererseits die Zulassung der Anwendbarkeit des früheren rigischen Rechts durch den Grafen De La Gardie gegenüberstand: *Bunge*, Einleitung (oben Fn. 34), S. 231; s. auch *Bunge*, Privatrecht (oben Fn. 49), S. 42 Anm. r).

[58] Mit einem ganz ähnlichen Befund für die Kirchenverwaltung in Estland und die von der früheren, vor allem deutschbaltischen Geschichtsschreibung vertretene These über die Statik des Verwaltungs- und Rechtssystems dieser Provinz grundsätzlich kritisch: *Andres Andresen*, „Kõige selgem õiguslik järjepidevus valitses Eestimaa kubermangus." Ühe baltisaksa ajalookirjutuse paradigma kriitika [Abstract: „The strongest legal continuity was in the province of Estland."A critique of a paradigm in Baltic German historiography], Ajalooline Ajakiri. The Estonian Historical Journal 1 (2013), S. 29–54.

umgreifende Gerichtsreform verstellen den Blick auf die oben geschilderte Dynamik.

Es fragt sich allerdings, inwieweit ein von der Dynamik geprägtes Geschichtsbild zu Estlands Justizverfassung in der Schwedenzeit einem rein statisch gezeichneten Bild überlegen ist. Die behauptete Statik, Narrativ „des Bleibens beim Alten", führt zu einem gewissen Desinteresse und wächst sich zu einer Blockade gegenüber berechtigten Forschungsinteressen aus. Und es gibt durchaus reichlich Material zum Forschen. Die über zweitausend Akten des Burggerichts zu Reval wurden schon erwähnt, ebenso die womöglich vorhandenen Appellationsakten im schwedischen Reichsarchiv. Vom gut erhaltenen Stadtarchiv Revals ist nur ein Bruchteil in der Forschung ausgewertet. Der Rest wartet in der heutigen estnischen Hauptstadt Tallinn in einem wunderschönen Altstadtgebäude auf Auswertung. Das Archivmaterial der Behörden der Landesjustiz wird im Estnischen Historischen Archiv in der freundlichen Universitätsstadt Tartu aufbewahrt. Zumeist sind all diese Quellen auf Deutsch bzw. Mittelhochdeutsch, teilweise auch auf Latein, selten auf Schwedisch, manchmal in einer komischen deutsch-schwedischen Mischsprache verfasst und deshalb für die estnischen Forscher ziemlich schwer zu erschließen. Die Kollegen in Tartu und Tallinn sind aber nicht nur bereit, die deutschkundigen Forscher auf allerlei Weise zu unterstützen, sondern haben ihrerseits ebenfalls die Augen für die regen Entwicklungen in Estlands Justizverfassung während der Schwedenzeit geöffnet, wie der vorliegende Beitrag bezeugen kann.

Legal Educational Activities of the Judiciary in the Novgorod Region during the 1970s

Elena Makarova and Tatyana Doroshenko

I. Introduction

During the 1960s and 1970s, legal education of the Soviet citizens was one of the strategic directions of the government and the ideology of the USSR. At the time, legal propaganda was seen by the Soviet leaders as a kind of mechanism driving the formation of the political and legal culture of the Soviet society: it was an intrinsic part of the ideological and political education and a powerful way of the individual development to the higher standards of the socialist community and the communist ideals.

Legal acts of both the state and the party had largely determined the formation of the socialist legal system of a culture that included such elements of the socialist legal behavior as mastery of the necessary legal knowledge, development of skills of an independent legal assessment of reality, high respect for the socialist law in the mind of every citizen, based on the intransigence of any offenses, and protection of the socialist rule of law. Implementation of these objectives could only be achieved through deep involvement into the process of legal education of all of the enforcement agencies, especially the judiciary, the activities of which are being considered in great detail in this paper.

This paper is based on the archival funds of the Novgorod Region Prosecutor's Office, the Bureau of the Regional Court, the Novgorod Regional Committee of the Communist Party of the USSR stored in the State Historical Archive of the Novgorod Region[1] and in the State Archive of the Modern History of the Novgorod Region.[2]

II. Political and Ideological Background

During the aforementioned period, there were very important changes in the economic and political development that took place on the way to liberalization after the Historic XX Congress of the Communist Party in 1956. The denouncement of Stalin's regime had led to a certain rate of democratization, simultaneously converting the economic and political views toward humanization. Free of dogmatic fetters of the past, the social and cultural life of the Soviet people had been

---

[1] The official site of the State Historical Archive of the Novgorod Region (ГИАНО): http://www.novarchiv.org/index.php/gano.html [21.11.2012].

[2] The official site of the State Archive of the Modern History of the Novgorod Region (ГАНИНО): http://www.novarchiv.org/index.php/ganino.html [21.11.2012].

suddenly revived causing the rise of creative and innovative forces. The state policy had become more socially oriented.

By the early 1970s, however, these positive movements were accompanied by the increase in crime and strengthening of the legal nihilism due to collapse of the old ideals and principles in the minds of the public. This conflicting situation in the Soviet society required a radically different work of the courts and law enforcement organs. Understanding of tasks entrusted to the specialists in law and their duties had to change. Thus the primary task of a person in any legal capacity had become trifold with a focus on active prevention efforts aimed at reducing the crime; developing a sense of public intolerance to any fact of violation of the law; and creating a positive image of the police officers, prosecutors, lawyers, and judges. The legal education of the Soviet people was proclaimed to be the top priority of the law enforcement agencies' activities.[3]

There was a big circle of subjects, both federal and regional, that were involved in the process of improvement of the Soviet citizens' legal consciousness and education: the governmental bodies, the social organizations, the cultural and scientific institutions, the mass media, the labor and academic groups, etc. In the Novgorod region alone as in many other regions of the USSR, a new detailed system of legal education was created and implemented. It was tailored specifically to various subgroups of the general population and based on such categories, for example, as age as well as educational and professional backgrounds.

A special role in this process was played by the judiciary system. Since the time of the Great October Revolution, Court was perceived as a factor in the cultural and political education, and especially in the creation of the socialist identity. Mikhail Kalinin,[4] one of the most well-known politicians and heroes of the Revolution, had said:

---

3 On the concept of the nature and goals of legal propaganda in the 1970s see: *В.Б. Никитин/В.В. Орехов* [V.B. Nikitin/V.V. Orekhov], Вопросы теории и практики правовой пропаганды [Problems of Theory and Practice of Legal Propaganda], Leningrad 1973, C. 17–30; *Н.Я. Соколов* [N.Y. Sokolov], Организация правовой пропаганды [Organization of Legal Propaganda], Moscow 1974, C. 11; *В.В. Оксамытный* [V.V. Oksamytniy], Правовое воспитание – важный фактор формирования социально активной личности [Legal Education – the Important Factor of the Formation of Social-Active Person], Kiev 1979; *В.С. Основин/А.П. Глебов* [V.C. Osnovin/A.P. Glebov], Курс „Теория и методика правового воспитания“: из опыта преподавания [Course "Theory and Practice of Legal Education": on the Experience of Teaching], Правоведение [Jurisprudence], 1979, 6, C. 13–15, http://law.edu.ru/article/article.asp?articleID=187708 [21.11.2012].

4 Mikhail Ivanovich Kalinin (1875–1946) was one of the founders and outstanding leaders of the Communist Party and of the Soviet state, and a loyal disciple and colleague of Lenin and Stalin. He became the first chairman of the central executive committee of the USSR, or titular head of state (1919–46). For a biography of Mikhail Kalinin see: *A. Dementyev/A. Pyanov*, Michael Kalinin, Moscow 1975.

> "A good trial is no less important than a report on the international and domestic situation ... During these reports, often 50, and perhaps 75% of people fall asleep. In the analysis of the complaints, even if it is an ordinary judge ..., but would solve the problems with the soul, and want to make the right decision, then I guarantee that no one of the attended people would fall asleep".[5]

The words of a person called the "All-Union headman"[6] served as a slogan for the courts in the 1970s too.

III. Legislative Framework

Any legal educational activity in that time was based on the special Resolutions of the Communist Party of the Soviet Union (CPSU). The Resolution "On the Way of Increasing the Legal Education of Workers"[7] noted that the enhancement of legal education and strengthening of the socialist legality constituted one of the important tasks of the state. This act had opened the way for a broad study of the legal framework in the curricula and programs, in the ideological and political work among the public.

Special attention was paid to the role of the judiciary, prosecutors and militia (Russian police force) being the experts in law. In the Resolution of the Central Committee of the CPSU and the Council of Ministers "On Measures to Improve the Work of Judicial and Prosecutorial Authorities"[8] it was indicated that the prosecuting authorities and the courts were weakly related to the state and other public organizations; they did not provide much assistance to the militias and comrades' courts in the process of the promotion of the Soviet law and its legal education, especially among the young generation. Responsibility for changing the existing situation and the organizational management of the courts was entrusted into the hands of the Ministry of Justice.[9] The most important function of the Ministry was

---

[5] *М.И. Калинин* [M.I. Kalinin]. Вопросы советского строительства [Problems of Soviet Affairs], Moscow 1958, С. 513.

[6] In Russian „Всесоюзный староста".

[7] Постановление ЦК КПСС от 15.09.1970 „О мерах по улучшению правового воспитания трудящихся" [Resolution of the Central Committee of the CPSU "On the Way of Increasing the Legal Education of Workers"], in: Вопросы идеологической работы КПСС. Сборник документов (1965–1973) [Problems of Ideological Policy of the CPSU. Collection of Papers], Moscow 1973, С. 295–300.

[8] Постановление ЦК КПСС и Совета Министров СССР от 30.07.1970 „О мерах по улучшению работы судебных и прокурорских органов" [Resolution of the Central Committee of the CPSU and the Council of Ministers "On Measures to Improve the Work of Judicial and Prosecutorial Authorities"], in: КПСС в резолюциях и решениях съездов, конференций и пленумов ЦК [CPSU in Resolutions and Decisions of the Congress, Conferences and Plenums of the Central Committee], Moscow 1986/87, т.11, С. 549–554.

[9] Ministry of Justice was dissolved both on the Union and the All-Union level in May, 1956 on the grounds of stopping "unnecessary" centralization. One of the reason was the desire during the "Khrushchev's thaw" to relieve courts from the control of the administration, established by the

to systematize and to prepare the proposals for the codification of the law. The methodical management and coordination of the work of state institutions and public organizations to promote legal knowledge and interpretation of legislation also fell into the realm of the Ministry's duties. The main principles of the work were determined in the Decree (15 April, 1971) "The Tasks of the Judiciary to Improve the Legal Awareness and Legal Education of the Citizens".[10]

After the adoption of these acts, the Novgorod regional authorities had significantly increased their educational activities in the legal area. Courts and law enforcement agencies were obliged to create plans of the specific activities in the sphere of the promotion of the legal propaganda under the Resolution of the Novgorod Regional Committee of CPSU "On Measures to Improve the Legal Education of Workers".[11]

Implementation of the central and regional directive act in the Novgorod region had been coordinated by the special methodological Council, which consisted of the representatives from various organizations, including the judiciary. According to the recommendation of the Council, the Bureau of the Novgorod Regional Court had developed special plans with many different forms of legal educational activities of the judiciary: public lectures, organized meetings and discussions on any legal topics, special question and answer townhall meetings, publications in the regional newspapers and magazines, radio speeches and others.

Regulation of the People's Commissariat of Justice (December 8, 1936), according to which the Commissariat and its local authorities could provide the guidance on the correct using the legal norms by the courts, supervise the elections of judges and check their work. For the legal framework see: Указ Президиума Верховного Совета СССР от 31.05.1956 „Об упразднении Министерства юстиции СССР" [Decree of the Supreme Soviet of the CPSU "On the Abolition of the Minister of Justice"] in: http://base.consultant.ru/cons/cgi/online.cgi?req=doc;base =ESU;n=19997 [21.11.2012]. The Ministry Of Justice was reestablished in 1970 by Указ Президиума Верховного Совета СССР от 31.8.1970 „Об Образовании союзно-республиканского Министерства Юстиции СССР" [Decree of the Presidium of the Supreme Soviet of the USSR „On the Formation of the Union-Republican Ministry of Justice of the USSR"], in: Ведомости Верховного Совета СССР [Bulletin of the Supreme Soviet of the USSR], 1970, 36, С. 36.

[10] *Т.Н. Наумова* [T.N. Naumova], Работа правоохранительных органов по правовому воспитанию населения во второй половине 1950–х – конце1970 годах (на примере Новгородской области) [Law Enforcement Activities on the Legal Education During the Second Half of 1950s–1970s (on the example of Novgorod Region], дисс.канд.истор.наук [Dissertation of candidate of historical sciences], 07.00.02. Moscow, Russian State Library (Department of Dissertation), (61 07–7/486) 2007, С. 61.

[11] State Archive of the Modern History of the Novgorod Region (ГАНИНО). Ф. 260. Оп. 42. Д. 69. Л. 1–15.

IV. Different Forms of Educational Activity

1. Lectures

Lecture was undoubtedly the most popular format. Each of the Regional and City Court judges spoke publicly at least 1–2 times per month at institutions such as factories, colleges, universities, collective and state farms, with a sole purpose of explaining a legislation. The topics varied,[12] and the following are the examples of the chosen few, "The Causes of Juvenile Delinquency", "Family Legislation", "Alcoholism and Crime", "Criminal Law Protection of the Socialist Property", "Administrative and Criminal Liability for the Hooliganism", etc.

Thus in 1971, the judges and the other Novgorod City Court staff alone arranged for and gave 183 such public lectures. The average number of the lectures read by the regional court judges per year was around 150 as could be counted in Graph 1:

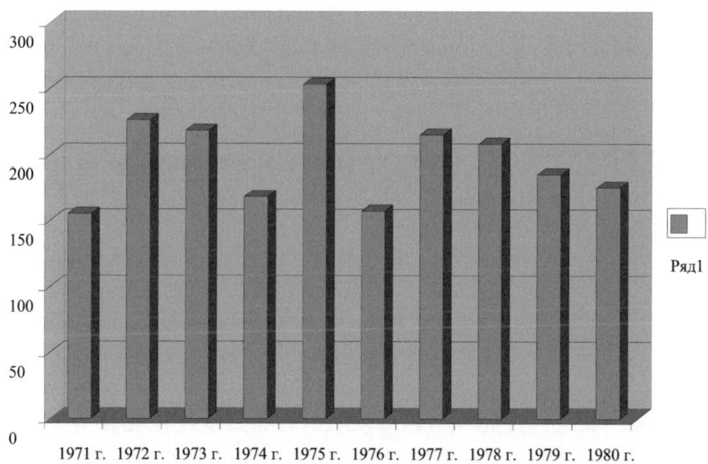

Graph1. Public lectures by Regional court staff[13]

However, during some years, the number of lectures increased. There were objective reasons for it: in 1972–1973, the Soviet people celebrated the 50th anniversary of the USSR;[14] in 1975 – the 30th anniversary of the victory in the Great Patriotic War. The high rise in 1977–1978 can be explained by the preparation and the first

---

[12] State Historical Archive of the Novgorod Region (ГИАНО). Ф. 3701. Оп. 11. Д. 1050. Л. 15–25.

[13] Sources: State Historical Archive of the Novgorod Region (ГИАНО). Ф. 3701. Оп. 11. Д. 1050. Л. 17; Д. 1164. Л. 34; Д. 1439. Л. 27; Д. 1440. Л. 20; Оп. 16. Д. 7. Л. 10; Д. 18. Л. 78; Д. 42. Л. 51.

[14] The previous anniversaries of the foundation of the USSR weren't celebrated practically.

steps of the implementation of the new Constitutions of both the Soviet Union and the RSFSR. Under the leadership of the state and party leaders of the country and its various regions, there were many events to commemorate the Soviet state and its heroes: the Court could not stay out of that process, so the additional lectures were being read on the themes of various such celebrations. In other years, the judges and court employees gave only the required minimum of speeches.

Certainly, the majority of all lectures were read in the cities. For example, in 1972, only 17 out of total 226 were read outside of the cities. Qualified experts did not want to leave the regional cities and travel far away to small villages. Steadfast attention was paid to those enterprises where there was incompliance with the law. Also, the judges and other legal experts regularly visited the detention centers and prisons with lectures[15] for the declared purpose of future crime prevention through overcoming the legal nihilism of the community of the convicted felons.

Texts of any lecture were discussed and evaluated by the party and the courts' leaders. Those lectures, deemed best from the ideological and legal point of view, became exemplary for all the judges, and all the judges were required to follow the established formats. The Bureau of the Novgorod Regional Court developed methodological model lectures and sent them to the courts and other legal organizations. The topics of the lectures included "The New Anti-Hooligan's Legislation" and "Soviet Labor Law to Protect the Rights and Interests of Citizens and the Compliance of the Working Discipline."[16] These model lectures possessed an accurate structure and provided a detailed analysis of the reasons for the anti-social behavior of the Soviet citizens. In addition, they offered an explanation of the state policy directed at fighting the criminals. The factual details were supported by statistics and local cases. For out-of-the-city lectures, a special methodological review was created and named "The Civil Cases in the Collective Farms".

Such serious attention to the methodological control by the court's leaders was not accidental. The state and the party leaders considered these lectures as a basic form of the effective legal propaganda and required to consistently improve their quality due to the belief that "the increased level of education and awareness of the Soviet people needs to replenish and update their knowledge".[17] However, first, it was necessary to increase the overall professional level of the court staff itself.

---

[15] The topics of these lectures were drafted and adopted by the Novgorod Regional Department of the Ministry of Internal Affairs. On the legal background of the structure and enforcement power of regional law enforcement agencies see in the collection of documents: *А.К. Богданов/М.Н. Петров* [A.K. Bogdanov/M.N. Petrov] (eds.), Новгородская полиция, милиция и органы внутренних дел (1733–2000) [Novgorodian police, militia and internal affairs agencies, 1733–2000], Novgorod the Great 2001.

[16] State Historical Archive of the Novgorod Region (ГИАНО). Ф. 3701. Оп. 11. Д. 761. Л. 1.

[17] Постановление ЦК КПСС от 27.2.1978 „О состоянии и мерах улучшения лекционной пропаганды" [Resolution of the Central Committee of the CPSU "On Conditions and Measures for Improvement the Propaganda by Lectures"], in: КПСС в резолюциях и решениях съездов,

In the Soviet era, the educational qualification for the judges had not been determined by the law for a long time. In the early 1970s, only around 30% of the total number of all judges in the Novgorod Region acquired higher legal education,[18] the rest had secondary legal education (completing 2-year college programs) or just secondary education in various other disciplines. Starting in 1989, only the individual with a high legal diploma could become a judge.[19] That is why the high judicial authorities had to offer special classes to the court staff and the judges in order to explain any legislative novelties and amendments to the law.

2. Circuit Court

Apart from the lectures, there existed other forms of legal education. In order to attract public attention to the trials, to strengthen their educational impact on citizens, to create an atmosphere of intolerance for all violations of the law, and, finally, to prevent the occurance of any new offenses in the USSR, the practice of adjudication of the criminal and civil cases at the places where crime took place, i.e. at the place of residence, work or study of the plaintiff and/or of the defendant, was implemented.

When deciding on the off-site sessions, court would take into account not only the nature of the act and the prevalence of this type of crime at the local level, but also the objective and subjective aspects of the case and the presence of circumstances requiring a broader public condemnation. The decision to hold a circuit court would be stated in the decree of the judge or pronounced by the decision of the court to try both criminal and civil cases. In the 1960–1970s, 25% of all criminal cases (with indictment) and about 7–9% of all civil cases (action proceedings)[20] were reviewed in the circuit courts. In some districts of the Novgorod region, up to one of third of the cases were tried in such off-site sessions.

конференций и пленумов ЦК [CPSU in Resolutions and Decisions of the Congress, Conferences and Plenums of the Central Committee], Moscow 1986/87, т.13, С. 231–234.

[18] The highest number of legally educated among all law enforcement agencies have been lawyers (93% of them have got a higher legal education).

[19] Закон СССР от 4.8.1989 „О статусе судей в СССР“ [Law of the USSR "On the Status of Judges in the USSR"] in: Ведомости Съезда народных депутатов СССР и Верховного Совета СССР [Bulletin of the Congress of People's Deputies and the Supreme Soviet of the USSR], 1989, 9, Art. 223.

[20] Большая советская энциклопедия [Great Soviet Encyclopedia], Moscow 1969–1978, http://bse-soviet-encyclopedia.info/Большая_Советская_энциклопедия/6267/Выездная_ сессия _суда [21.11.2012].

According to the resolutions of the Plenum of the Supreme Court[21] and the Novgorod Regional court's plan, the most significant criminal and civil cases were to be considered in the off-site court sessions at the factories, collective farms and within the communities of the offenders. The judgments of these cases needed to be discussed among the offender's former colleagues.

3. Assistance to the Comrade Courts

Another important task of the judiciary was the legal assistance to the special *comrade courts*. The Soviet ideology and law provide various forms of public participation in the legal system. An important place was taken up by the public militia and a so called comrade court – *a semi-official committee set up by a local community – to consider complaints by residents against one another.* These public organizations consisted of several elected officials and were created to strengthen and to deepen the communist attitude toward labor in the mind of the Soviet people. In accordance with Art. 22 of the Regulation on the Comrades' Courts, approved by the Decree of the Presidium of the Supreme Soviet of the RSFSR of 11.03.1977,[22] management of all of the comrade courts was pursued by the local councils of people's deputies, as well as factories, factory committees and trade unions, but the

---

[21] Постановление Пленума Верховного Суда СССР от 25.2.1967 N 2 „О практике применения судами ст.31 Основ уголовного законодательства Союза ССР и союзных республик" (с изменениями и дополнениями) [Resolution of the Plenum of the Supreme Court of the USSR "On Practice of Applying the Article 31 of the Foundations of Criminal Legislation of the Union of the SSR and Union Republics" (with amendments)], http://base.garant.ru/1305207/ [21.11.2012].

[22] Ведомости Верховного Совета РСФСР [Bulletin of the Supreme Soviet of the RSFSR], 1977, 12, С. 14.

legal assistance to the comrade courts had to have been provided by the justice agencies, prosecutors, state and local courts.

The legal basis for proper communication between the judiciary agencies and the comrade courts was the Decree of the Bureau of the Novgorod Regional Court "On the Work of the Regional Court to Provide the Legal assistance to the Comrades' Courts and Volunteer Militia's Teams".[23]

The court staff had organized lectures and special classes for the purposes of legal training of the comrade courts' chairmen and their members as well as the people's militia.[24] (i.e. Legal assistance was provided to 36 comrades' courts and 29 public militia's units in 1979.) The Bureau of the Novgorod Regional Court heard quarterly reports on the work of the judiciary to provide legal advice to the comrade courts and the voluntary militia teams. The positive experience of such work was always illustrated by the local press.

V. Legal Education of the Juvenile Population

The legal propaganda had been organized for many categories of the Soviet citizens. One of the important tasks of the legal policy in the Novgorod region during that period was to prevent juvenile delinquency. In the early 1970s, the population of Novgorod was growing rapidly due to increase in migration from other areas of the region. It was the time of the robust industrial development of the regional capital. The migrants had to work hard to make a living and did not have enough time to take care of their children. Consequently, it had led to a dramatic rise in the juvenile delinquency cases. For example, the number of juvenile crimes in 1973 had grown by more than 10% in comparison to 1972.[25] That explains why the issue of the juvenile delinquency and its prevention among the children and teenagers had become very urgent indeed.

According to the plan of the Novgorod Regional Court in 1975, the judges of the regional, city and district courts were required to give a series of lectures on the fundamental aspects of the Soviet law in the secondary and vocational schools. In September of 1974, a special meeting of the judges and young workers (under 18

---

[23] State Historical Archive of the Novgorod Region (ГИАНО). Ф. 3701. Оп. 11. 1357. Л. 27.

[24] Also, many of comrade court's participants and militia's members were the students of the People's University of Legal Knowledge. In Novgorod region in 1970s there were 16 People's Universities with more than 5125 students at 38 faculties. For the goals of such educational organizations see: Постановление ЦК КПСС от 8.9.1968 „Об улучшении работы народных университетов" [Resolution of the Central Committee of the CPSU "On Improvement of the Work of People's Universities"], in: КПСС в резолюциях и решениях съездов, конференций и пленумов ЦК [CPSU in Resolutions and Decisions of the Congress, Conferences and Plenums of the Central Committee], Moscow 1986/87, т. 11, С. 374–378.

[25] State Historical Archive of the Novgorod Region (ГИАНО). Ф. 3701Оп. 11. Д. 1165. Л. 177.

years old) was called at the plant named after the 50th Anniversary of the Great October Revolution, which was at time the largest factory in the region.[26]

The judicial officers paid utmost attention to identifying the underlying causes of juvenile delinquency.[27] In order to prevent juvenile delinquency, the courts cooperated with various state and public institutions to correct undesirable behaviors of the teenagers who had already been sentenced and received punishment in non-custodial cases.

VI. Use of Mass Media

It was a common belief among the government officials and the court staff, that the aforementioned educational activities could bring positive results only when mass media resources were widely used. The judges gave regular radio addresses and published their articles in local magazines and newspapers. Periodically (1–2 times per quarter) the regional newspaper "Novgorodskaya Pravda" published materials of the judicial practice.

Particular attention in such publications was paid to the role of "the collective voice of the workers" in the fight against crime. In the article by one of the regional judges called "The Trial of the Comrades",[28] there was an explanation of a comrade court's decision to let the group of workers to take their colleague and the defendant in this case out on bail[29] and their responsibility helped this man to transform from a former drunk into a good citizen. In another article, called "The Community is Your Teacher and Friend",[30] the author told about the opportunity given to an offender to escape the punishment and even a court trial due to the colleagues' readiness to control the future life for him in case of a small damage he caused to the society. It should be noted that in that period, the use of this kind of preventive measures had been widely spread.

The legal propaganda was carried on systematically. All regional newspapers published weekly the materials under the common name "From the Court Room" with the explanation of sentences in the cases tried. For example, "Punishment for

---

[26] Ibid., Л. 190.

[27] For the role of legal education in the prevention of juvenile delinquency see: *А.И. Долгова* [A.I. Dolgova] Правовое воспитание несовершеннолетних [Legal Education of the Juveniles], Moscow 1977; *А.Г. Маркушин* [A.G. Markushin] Правовое воспитание несовершеннолетних – важное средство предупреждения преступности [Legal Education of the Juveniles – the Important Means of Preventing Crime], in: Сборник статей адъюнктов и соискателей [Collection of Articles of Adjuncts and Candidates for a Degree], Moscow 1972, Вып.1, С. 69–74.

[28] Заря коммунизма [Zarya Kommunizma], 28.3.1970.

[29] It meant that co-workers would be responsible for the lawful behavior in future.

[30] Звезда [Zvezda], 10 January1970.

the Illegal Mowing", "Prison for Robbery", "Hooligans are Punished." Special programs were televised locally in order to introduce the adopted legislation.

In the early 1970s, a particular attention in the Soviet mass media was given to the anti-alcohol issues. Judges had to take those issues into account in their speeches, publications and all other public educational activities. The articles were appropriately named the following: "The Drunk Driver," "Drunk Beyond Limits," "In the Drunken Trance".[31]

To create a positive image of the people in the legal circles, a lot of publications about the best lawyers and judges in the region were made readily available. One article, as an example, was about the chief of the Novgorod City court and was named "Themis' Sword is in the Savior's Good Hands."[32]

Frequently, the articles were of satirical nature, and the judges tried to uncover the ugliest phenomena of the daily life that could lead to crime. In 1977 alone, one famous local judge V. Nedvedskiy published more than 10 newspaper articles.[33] Here are the titles of some: "After Party on Sunday," "Adventures of the Brave Shopkeeper," "When the Air Smells of Beer", "No Smoke without Fire," "So Politeness!" Through the newspaper, the author had received a lot of letters and responses from the citizens, which prompted to continue these writings even further.

It should be noted here that judges wrote articles about the non-legal issues too. The Soviet ideology had created the communism-minded person and without a doubt, the judiciary had to be deeply entrenched in this process. In regional newspaper material named "What Could We Leave to Our Offsprings"[34] the judge addressed the current ecological problems rather than legal issues.

VII. Shortfalls of the Educational System

But, in spite of all the positive educational work done by the judiciary and all its contributions to the process of raising the legal awareness of the Soviet citizens, there were some gaps left. Firstly, many planned activities were carried out formally without regard to the local conditions. Mostly, the higher authorities were interested in the quantitative rather than the qualitative measures of their work. Secondly, any additional educational activity was carried out on a voluntary basis, i.e. without proper compensation. Lastly, the qualified experts did not want to leave the regional cities and travel far away to small villages to "spread the word."

---

[31] Красная искра [Krasnaya iskra], 1972.

[32] Новгородская правда [Novgorodskaya pravda], 11 February 1978.

[33] In 1977 only in the newspaper "Novgorodskaya pravda" 26 articles and notes by the judges of the Novgorod Regional Court and 7 by the City courts judges were published.

[34] Новгородская правда [Novgorodskaya pravda], 18 October 1978.

Perhaps some of them were not ready to deal with these new kinds of professional responsibilities.

However, the legal educational activities were not only provided by the judiciary agencies. There were a lot of organized activities promoted by lawyers, prosecutors[35] and others altogether. It could be the round table discussions or the town hall format meetings, etc. Officials and experts were required to talk at the theaters and cinemas before the movies and performances took place.

The Soviet citizens were obliged to attend all lectures read generally in the lunch hour or after work, and the greatest desire of the audience were to finish this activity as soon as possible or to find ways to escape it. While the population of the Novgorod region consisted of only 800 thousand people in 1973, the legal professionals gave a whopping amount of lectures, 8367 to be exact. Representatives of the law enforcement organs read 5539 public lectures, prosecutors – 1303, lawyers (advocates) – 1282, and judges – 243.[36] If a good conscious citizen tried to be present at all the lectures by jurists, politicians, economists, etc., he would have to be in attendance on a daily basis. Therefore, the desired result of the legal propaganda could not have been reached fully. All in all, however, the educational activity to improve the legal culture of the Soviet citizens, and especially its younger generation, had been quite effective during the time frame discussed in this paper.

VIII. Conclusions

The level of legal awareness and legal activities of the citizens are generally expressed through understanding of the law while the value of public relations is based on the ability of the individuals to interpret the legal norms, to realize them in the practical sphere and to use these norms to protect human rights. In a democracy, the legal education plays a significant role in the process of effective formation of an individual as both an object of the state's influence and the subject in the implementation of its policies and educational programs.

USSR in the 1970s was neither democratic nor did it posess a well developed legal system. The mechanism of improving the legal culture of the Soviet people was formed under the strict ideological control by the CPSU and was seen largely as political, since the main parties involved were the various state authorities and the so-called non-governmental organizations. The latter included the Communist Party, the Komsomol Organization, the Young Pioneer Organization, all of which,

---

[35] For an analysis of the legal educational activities of prosecutors see, for example: *Т.Н. Дорошенко* [T.N. Doroshenko], Правовоспитательная деятельность органов прокуратуры во второй половине 1950–х – 1960–х гг. (на материалах Новгородской области) [Legal Educational Activities of Prosecutors During 1950–1960s (on the materials of Novgorod Region], История государства и права [History of State and Law], 2010, 5, http://base.consultant.ru/cons/cgi/online.cgi?req=doc;base=CJI;n=42803 [21.11.2012].

[36] Наумова (supra fn.10), pp. 86, 98, 110, 123.

in fact, had been fully integrated into the State's system of power, as well as the educational system and the mass media. The judiciary, along with the other state agencies (the police, the KGB, the Ministry of Justice, etc.) was an active participant in the process of legal socialization of the Soviet people and the formation of the socialist society. The goals of the judges' activities encompassed the training of lawful behavior, crime prevention, and, to a much lesser extent, the real legal education.

However, the Soviet experience of the system of legal education is rather valuable and can be partly (without the ideological and political background) used in the modern day Russian reality. 1960s and 1970s have produced the institutional design of the process of legal education: a rather unique legal system had formed; people's universities of legal knowledge had opened and worked effectively, comrade courts had actually served as functional legal units; voluntary peoples' guards helping the law enforcement agencies to control the public order had been set up. Some positive results had been achieved through the regularity and consistency of the educational activities. Any important sociopolitical event in the country, as well as the adoption of new laws, wasn't left unattended by the propagandists of the Soviet legislation.

Summing up the research, it should be strongly emphasized that despite being an additional burden on their professional lives, both the educational activities performed by the judges and the overall function of the judiciary system at the time were highly instrumental in the process of de-criminalization of the Soviet society. We may safely conclude that yet again, history serves valuable lessons for many generations to come.

Die Entstehung und Entwicklung des Notariats auf dem Territorium Lettlands vom Ende des 19. bis zur Mitte des 20. Jahrhunderts

Sanita Osipova

I. Einleitung

Die europäischen Rechtshistoriker erforschen seit dem 19. Jahrhundert die Geschichte des öffentlichen Notariats (*notarius publicus*); dabei werden einerseits regionale Besonderheiten beschrieben, andererseits wird nach gemeinsamen Grundlagen sowie nach wechselseitigen Einflussen und nach allgemein geltenden Funktionen und Entwicklungsgrundlagen des öffentlichen Notariats im gesamten kontinentalen Europa gefragt. Bisher gibt es nur wenige Veröffentlichungen zur Geschichte des Notariats in Lettland. Dieser Aufsatz behandelt die Entstehung und die Entwicklung des Notariats auf dem Territorium des heutigen Lettland im Zeitraum zwischen der Gerichtsreform des Russischen Kaiserreichs, die sich Ende des 19. Jahrhunderts vollzog, bis zum Zweiten Weltkrieg. Für diesen Zeitraum sind zwei Gesetze relevant, welche die Notariatstätigkeit auf dem Territorium des heutigen Lettland regelten: das Notariatsgesetz „*Временное положение о нотаральной части*" des Russischen Kaiserreichs vom 14. April 1866 sowie das am 14. Dezember 1937 durch das Ministerkabinett der Republik Lettlands verabschiedete „Notargesetz". Dieser Aufsatz untersucht, ob zwischen den beiden genannten Rechtsakten eine Rechtskontinuität besteht oder ob Olga Jurkovska, Mitverfasserin des Gesetzentwurfs, nach der Verabschiedung des lettischen Notargesetzes mit ihrer folgenden These Recht hat:

> „Am 1. Januar 1938, dem hellsten Tage unserer Rechtsgeschichte, traten das Bürgerliche Gesetzbuch des Präsidenten Ulmanis und damit auch das *neue lettische* Notargesetz in Kraft."[1]

Sollte die Behauptung von Olga Jurkovska, nämlich dass das Notargesetz völlig *neuartig* und *national geprägt* sei, nicht nur dem 1936 geäußerten politischen Konzept des lettischen Diktators Kārlis Ulmanis entsprechen:

> „... Unsere Erlebnisse in der Vergangenheit haben uns gelehrt, uns alter Formeln und Begriffe zu entledigen, die nicht nur für uns fremd sind, sondern sich auch anderswo bereits überlebt haben. Vielmehr wollen wir bewusst alles meiden, was für uns einem sklavenhaften Nachahmen fremder Lehren der Neuzeit ähnlich und nach unserer

---

1 *Olga Jurkovska*, Redetext „Notāru tiesiskais stāvoklis" [„Zur rechtlichen Lage der Notare"]. Aus dem Archiv von Vilis Lūkins, im Besitz der Familie von Imants Žodžiks. Die Autorin hat die Materialien am 2.2.2012 eingesehen.

> tiefsten Überzeugung für das eigenständige Leben unseres Staates und für das gesellschaftliche Leben nicht geeignet wäre“,[2]

sondern auch tatsächlich wahr sein, so könnte für Lettland nicht die Rede sein von einem Notariat lateinischer Prägung, wie es in Russland als Folge der Gerichtsreform Ende des 19. Jahrhunderts aufgrund der Erfahrungen Österreichs und Bayerns bei der Einrichtung des lateinischen Notariats eingeführt worden war.[3]

II. Das Notariat auf dem Territorium des heutigen Lettlands im 19. Jahrhundert

In Russland wurde das Notariat endgültig erst durch das Notariatsgesetz vom 14. April 1866 festgelegt, das im Rahmen der Verwaltungs- und Gerichtsreform unter Alexander II. erarbeitet und erlassen wurde.[4] Bereits im Jahre 1860 gründete man die Zentralbank des Russischen Kaiserreichs, darauf folgte 1862 die Reform der Finanzkontrolle. Erst danach, im Jahre 1864, wurde in Russland ein grundlegend neues Gerichtssystem geschaffen, das unabhängig von der Macht der Exekutive war.[5] Die Gerichtsordnung des Russischen Kaiserreichs, die ab dem 9. Juli 1889 auch im Baltikum angewendet wurde, hat das bis dahin geltende traditionelle Gerichtssystem wesentlich verändert und im gesamten Baltikum ein heutigen Vorstellungen entsprechendes Gerichtssystem mit unabhängigen Gerichten geschaffen.[6]

Im Jahre 1835 wurde im Russischen Kaiserreich eine Kommission (*Комиссия прошений* – Antragsprüfungskommission) eingesetzt, die mit der Aufgabe befasst war, Gesetzesvorlagen auszuarbeiten und zu beschließen. Im Jahre 1884 wurde diese Kommission in eine Kanzlei umgewandelt. Bei der Ausarbeitung der Gesetzentwürfe hat sich die Kommission nicht nur auf die Erfahrungen und die bestehende Rechtspraxis in Russland gestützt, sondern auch Gesetze anderer euro-

---

2 *Kārlis Ulmanis*, Die Rede im Rahmen des Festakts zur Feier der nationalen Einheit in der Nationaloper am 15. Mai 1936, in: Latvju radošā gara atdzimšana [Das Erwachen des lettischen schöpferischen Geistes], Rīga 1936, S. 7.

3 *Sanita Osipova*, Die allgemeine Bedeutung des österreichischen Rechtssystems für Lettland, in: Michael Geistlinger u.a. (Hg.), 200 Jahre ABGB – Ausstrahlungen. Die Bedeutung der Kodifikation für andere Staaten und andere Rechtskulturen, Wien 2011, S. 3.

4 *Черемных Г.Г./Черемных И.Г*, Возникновение нотариата в России в период до 1917 г. [Die Entstehung des Notariats in Russland bis 1917] http://konp.org/history/pre1917 (eingesehen am 06.12.2008).

5 *Пашенцев Д.А.*, К вопросу о генезисе правовой системы России [Über die Frage nach der Entstehung des russischen Rechtssystems], http://www.law-n-life.ru/arch/121/121_Pashentsev.doc (eingesehen am 06.12.2008).

6 *Jānis Lazdiņš*, Baltijas zemnieku privāttiesības (XIX gs.) [Das Privatrecht der baltischen Bauern (XIX. Jh.)], Rīga 2000, S. 270.

päischer Länder in dem jeweiligen Bereich analysiert.[7] Es war bewusste Staatspolitik des Russischen Kaiserreichs, das Gerichts- und Rechtssystem entsprechend den Tendenzen im kontinentalen Europa zu gestalten. Deshalb war das im Russischen Kaiserreich geschaffene Gerichtssystem mit den in den europäischen Ländern angewendeten Modellen verwandt. Das Ergebnis der Gerichtsreform im Russischen Kaiserreich war die Einführung französischer Konzepte der Justizinstitutionen sowie des Verfahrensrechts im ganzen Kaiserreich, damit auch auf dem Territorium des heutigen Lettlands. In der zweiten Hälfte des 19. Jahrhunderts, als in Russland die Gerichtsreform umgesetzt wurde, hatten viele französische Neuerungen aus dem Anfang des 19. Jahrhunderts ihre Stärken und Schwächen in der Praxis gezeigt und waren, wie die russischen Juristen behaupteten, auf eine gewisse Weise sogar schon veraltet.[8] Daher wurde bei der Abwicklung der russischen Gerichtsreform ausgiebig auch auf Gesetze zurückgegriffen, die erst Mitte des 19. Jahrhunderts im kontinentalen Europa auf der Grundlage französischer Vorbilder entstanden waren. Die französischen Konzepte wurden im Russischen Kaiserreich umgesetzt, nachdem man ihr Funktionieren in Frankreich beobachtet hatte, sowie aufgrund einer Analyse ihrer aktuellen Modifikationen in anderen Ländern, welche die französischen Institutionen eingeführt hatten; vor allem stützte man sich auf österreichische und deutsche Erfahrungen. Das ausgesprochen liberale französische Recht war auf der Basis der Idee eines Naturrechts entstanden; diejenigen Gesetze, die aus der Mitte des 19. Jahrhunderts stammten, vor allem die deutschen Gesetze, waren wesentlich konservativer, denn sie waren von der historischen Rechtsschule beeinflusst. Man passte in Kontinentaleuropa die liberalen Ideen Frankreichs den Bedürfnissen sowohl konstitutioneller als auch absoluter Monarchien wie Russland an; dabei wurde die Rolle des Staates bei der Rechtsprechung sowie bei der Bildung gerichtlicher Institutionen und bei deren Kontrolle gestärkt.

Der Einfluss der Gerichtsordnungsreform des Russischen Kaiserreichs lässt sich auch heute noch am Justizsystem der Lettischen Republik ablesen. Das markanteste Beispiel dafür sind die Institutionen des vereidigten Notars und des vereidigten Gerichtsvollziehers.[9]

Das Notariatsgesetz des Russischen Kaiserreichs vom 14. April 1866 wurde auf der Grundlage der französisch-deutschen Erfahrung bei der Organisation des

---

[7] *Комаров Н. И./Пашенцев Д. А./Пашенцева С. В.*, Очерки истории права Российской империи вторая половина 19 – начало 20 века. [Aufsätze über die Rechtsgeschichte des russischen Reiches, von der zweiten Hälfte des 19. bis zum Anfang des 20. Jahrhunderts], Moskau 2006, S. 11.

[8] *Мандельштам Л.Б.*, Учреждение нотариата и его организация. [Gründung des Notariats und seine Organisation], Журнал Министерства Юстиции [Zeitschrift des Ministeriums für Justiz], 1899, Heft 4 (April), S. 8.

[9] Siehe *Sanita Osipova*, „Latvijas notariāta funkcijas un tā sniegtās palīdzības pieejamība, to izvērtējums“ [Lettisches Notariat: Funktion und die Verfügbarkeit von Hilfe, die Auswertung], www.tm.gov.lv/lv/.../Osipova_petijums_07022009-final.doc (eingesehen am 1.4.2011).

Notariats und bei der Regelung seiner Tätigkeit ausgearbeitet.[10] Als Vorbild diente dabei das Notariat ‚französischer Art', wie es gegen Mitte des 19. Jahrhunderts in Österreich und Bayern eingerichtet worden war. In Österreich hatte man das nach französischem Vorbild entwickelte Notariat im Jahre 1850 eingeführt, aber bereits fünf Jahre später, 1855, wurde die Notariatsordnung überarbeitet.[11] Dieser überarbeiteten Fassung von 1855 sowie des bayrischen Gesetzes von 1861 und anderer Quellen haben sich die Juristen des Russischen Kaiserreichs bedient, als sie die Regelungen für das eigene Notariat erarbeiteten.[12]

Die Notwendigkeit zur Einführung des Notariats ergab sich im Russischen Kaiserreich aus den Bestrebungen, das Hypothekensystem und das Grundbuchsystem neu zu ordnen.[13] Die Notwendigkeit der Entwicklung des Notariats zu einer professionellen, staatlich eingerichteten Institution ergab sich bereits aus dem Gesetz des Russischen Kaiserreichs vom 29. September 1862, in dem die Grundprinzipien der Umgestaltung des Gerichtssystems festgelegt worden waren. Dieser Rechtsakt verpflichtete die 2. Kanzleiabteilung der Kaiserlichen Majestät, einen Entwurf der Notariatsordnung für das Kaiserreich auszuarbeiten. Im Jahre 1863 wurde der erste Entwurf des Notariatsgesetzes vorgelegt, und am 14. April 1866 wurde eine weitere Fassung des Gesetzesentwurfs als „Vorläufige Ordnung des Notariats" („*Временное положение о нотаральной части*") beschlossen. Schon die Benennung signalisiert, dass dieses Gesetz als ein Provisorium konzipiert und für weitere Verbesserungen offen war. Man ging davon aus, dass man im Reich, sobald das Notariat zu arbeiten begonnen hatte, Unzulänglichkeiten feststellen werde, die sich erst in der praktischen Tätigkeit zeigen. Daher war vorgesehen, das Gesetz zu einem späteren Zeitpunkt zu überarbeiten, um die festgestellten Mängel zu beseitigen.[14]

Man kann behaupten, dass das österreichische Notariatsmodell in Russland zweimal seinen Siegeszug angetreten hat: Bei der Notariatsverfassung von 1866 diente das Gesetz Österreichs von 1855 als ein Vorbild von mehreren, und als am Ende des 19. Jahrhunderts die russischen Juristen die Unzulänglichkeiten des in Russland eingerichteten Notariats analysierten, bewerteten sie das österreichische Gesetz von 1871 als das beste Gesetz in ganz Europa. Der russische Jurist und

---

[10] *Черемных/Черемных*, Возникновение нотариата (oben Fn. 4) (eingesehen am 06.01.2013).

[11] *Christian Neschwara*, Österreich-Ungarn: Geschichte und Historiografie des Notariats, in: Mathias Schmoeckel/Werner Schubert (Hg.), Handbuch zur Geschichte des Notariats der europäischen Traditionen, Baden-Baden 2009, S. 242 f.

[12] *Мандельштам*, Учреждение нотариата и его организация (oben Fn. 8), S. 35.

[13] *Рогачев В.В.*, Развитие ипотечного законодательства в Российской империи второй половины XIX – начала XX века (историко-правовое исследование) [Entwicklung der Hypothek: Rechtsvorschriften im Russischen Reich der zweiten Hälfte des XIX. – Anfang XX. Jahrhunderts (historisch-juristische Untersuchung)], http://www.rgsu.net/netcat_files/107.doc (eingesehen am 06.01.2013).

[14] *Комаров/Пашенцев/Пашенцева*, Очерки истории права (oben Fn. 7), S. 212 f.

Sachverständige in Fragen des Notariats L. B. Mandelstam schrieb in der Zeitschrift des Russischen Justizministeriums:

> „Auf ein großes Interesse stößt die Gründung und die Organisation des österreichischen Notariats, die durch das Gesetz vom 25. Juli 1871 erfolgt ist. Der Gesetzesgeber hat die Notariatsinstitution offensichtlich mit viel Herzblut eingerichtet, ihm eine angemessene Bedeutung verliehen, die Details sorgfältig ausgearbeitet und ihm einen entsprechenden Status gegeben. Das erwähnte Gesetz kann mit einigen wenigen Ausnahmen, die ausgesprochen lokalen Charakter haben, für einen beliebigen Kulturstaat als Vorbild dienen.“[15]

Im Gesetz „*Временное положение о нотаральной части*“ ist der österreichische Einfluss an folgenden Punkten erkennbar:

1. Das Amt des Notars ist vom Beruf des Rechtsanwalts getrennt. Bis zur Einführung des französischen Notariats in den deutschen Ländern war das Notariat nur eine Nebentätigkeit gewesen, die vorwiegend von den Rechtsanwälten ausgeübt wurde.[16] Das französische Notariatsmodell sieht eine Trennung des Notarberufs vom Beruf des Rechtsanwaltes vor. Eine gleichzeitige Ausübung beider Berufe wurde in Frankreich sogar als eine Verletzung der Berufsethik angesehen. Österreich hat das traditionelle Modell des Advokaten-Notariats modifiziert und den Beruf des Notars zu einem eigenständigen Beruf im Rahmen des Gerichtssystems gemacht.[17] In den deutschen Ländern wurde es traditionell als zulässig gesehen, die Berufe des Notars und des Rechtsanwalts gleichzeitig auszuüben, und dieses Prinzip gilt noch heute, denn neben der Notariatsinstitution besteht in Deutschland auch die Institution des Anwaltsnotariats.[18]

2. Das Notariat wurde nach dem territorialen Prinzip an Gerichten gebildet, wobei der Notar eine gewisse dienstliche Autonomie genoss. Dienststellen von Notaren wurden für Hauptstädte, Gouvernementsstädte und Kreisstädte sowie an den Oberlandesgerichten vorgesehen. Mit Inkrafttreten des Gesetzes wurde der Notar *de iure* zur einzigen Amtsperson, die notarielle Akten abfasste. Allerdings bewirkte dies weder in Österreich noch in Russland, dass der Notar sogleich auch *de facto* zur einzigen Amtsperson wurde, die öffentlich beglaubigte Akte abfasste.

3. Eine enge Verbindung zwischen dem Notariat und dem Gerichtssystem wurde auch dadurch geschaffen, dass die Gerichte dazu verpflichtet wurden, die Tätigkeit der Notare zu kontrollieren.[19] Die Kontrolle des Oberlandesgerichts über die Arbeit der Notare war eher formell. In der Realität haben sich die Oberlan-

---

[15] *Мандельштам*, Учреждение нотариата и его организация (oben Fn. 8), S. 11 f.

[16] *Christian Neschwara*, Österreichs Notariatsrecht in Mittel- und Osteuropa. Zur Geltung und Ausstrahlung des österreichischen Notariats, Wien 2000, S. 3.

[17] *Neschwara*, a.a.O., S. 11.

[18] *Werner Schubert*, Geschichte des Notariats und Notariatsrechts in Deutschland, in: Schmoeckel/ders., Handbuch (oben Fn. 11), S. 234.

[19] *Neschwara*, Notariatsrecht (oben Fn. 16), S. 5.

desgerichte nur mit Beschwerden über die Tätigkeit der Notare befasst. Bei der Durchführung der Kontrolle gemäß Artikel 58 des Gesetzes[20] hatten die Richter keine Zeit, sich in den Inhalt der notariellen Akte zu vertiefen. Der Grund dafür waren die enorme Belastung der Oberlandesgerichte und unzureichende Ressourcen, die es den Richtern nicht ermöglichten, Besuche in den Kontoren der Notare vor Ort zu leisten.[21]

4. Die Anzahl und territoriale Verteilung der Notare festzulegen, war nach dem österreichischen Modell (im Unterschied zum französischen Modell) ausschließlich dem Staat vorbehalten, die Notare selbst befanden sich im Staatsdienst.[22] Nach dem russischen Gesetz vom 1866 hatte der Notar einen Doppelstatus: Einerseits gehörten die Notare dem Staatsdienst an (in der Tabelle der Dienstkategorien gehörten die Notare zur Kategorie 8), auch wenn sie keinen Anspruch auf eine gesetzliche Rente hatten (Artikel 17); andererseits war der Notarberuf im Russischen Kaiserreich als freier Beruf anerkannt. Seine Tätigkeit hat der Notar als Freiberufler ausgeübt (Artikel 208). Die zeitgenössischen Notare haben diesen Doppelstatus kritisiert, indem sie darauf hinwiesen, dass die Notare „Stiefkinder der Themis" seien, da sie nicht alle vom Staat vorgesehenen Rechte genießen konnten, die den Angehörigen des Justizsystems zugesprochen wurden.[23]

5. Im russischen Modell verzichtete man auf die Anforderung vorheriger Berufserfahrung, die das französische Modell vorsieht.[24] Der Kandidat musste seine Eignung im Rahmen einer Prüfung nachweisen, so wie es in Bayern und Österreich der Fall war. Gleichzeitig wurden an die russischen Notare, anders als in Österreich, keine Anforderungen an ihre Ausbildung gestellt.[25] Schon im 19. Jahrhundert waren die Juristen der Ansicht, dass das Reichsgesetz die juristische Fachkompetenz der Notariatsinstitution abgewertet habe, da es keine Bildungsanforderungen vorsah. Der Verzicht auf die Forderung nach juristischer Ausbildung lässt sich durch die mangelnde Zahl ausgebildeter Juristen in Russland erklären. Die Kompetenz der Bewerber wurde jedoch als wichtig angesehen und im Rahmen von Eignungsprüfungen festgestellt.

Gemäß dem Notariatsgesetz vom 14. April 1866 konnte Notar werden, wer die russische Staatsbürgerschaft besaß, das 21. Lebensjahr überschritten hatte (Voll-

---

[20] „Die Bücher und die Sachen der Notare und ihren Stellvertreter sowie die Bücher der Leiter der Grundbuchabteilungen dürfen jederzeit von einer durch das zuständige Oberlandesgericht beauftragten Person eingesehen werden, wenn dieses Gericht das für notwendig hält. Das Oberlandesgericht kann die Friedensrichter beauftragen, die Prüfung der Notarbücher und -sachen in den jeweiligen Kreisgrenzen durchzuführen." Art. 58, Notargesetz, Rīga 1933, S. 18.

[21] *Комаров/Пашенцев/Пашенцева*, Очерки истории права (oben Fn. 7), S. 223 f.

[22] A.a.O., S. 204.

[23] *Черемных/Черемных*, Возникновение нотариата (oben Fn. 4) (eingesehen am 06.01.2013).

[24] *Мандельштам*, Учреждение нотариата и его организация (oben Fn. 8), S. 6.

[25] *Neschwara*, Notariatsrecht (oben Fn. 16), S. 5.

jährigkeit), nicht im Staats- oder im öffentlichen Dienst (auch bei lokalen Behörden) stand (mithin erlaubt das Gesetz nicht die gleichzeitige Ausübung mehrerer Ämter), nicht vorbestraft war und eine Eignungsprüfung erfolgreich abgelegt hatte. Gemäß dem Rundschreiben des Justizministers vom 6. Juni 1887 durften jüdische Bürger den Beruf des Notars nicht ausüben.[26] Die Ernennung zum Notar erfolgte durch den Ersten Vorsitzenden des Gerichtskollegiums auf der Grundlage der Empfehlung des Oberlandesgerichtsvorsitzenden; einen Notar aus dem Amt entlassen durfte nur ein Gericht (Art. 16).[27] Bei Amtsantritt musste der Notar eine Kaution entrichten, deren Höhe vom Einsatzort des Notars abhängig war. Dieser Betrag bildete eine Garantie für Schadensersatzforderungen, die womöglich durch die Tätigkeit des Notars entstehen konnten. Der anfängliche Beitrag wurde allmählich aufgestockt, bis folgende Summen erreicht wurden: in Hauptstädten 25.000 Rubel, in Gouvernementsstadten 15.000 Rubel und in Kreisen und Kreisstädten 10.000 Rubel. Nach Beendigung der Tätigkeit wurde die Kaution an den Notar oder im Falle seines Todes an die Erben zurückgezahlt.[28]

Ein wesentliches Problem war die Vergütung der Notare. In anderen Ländern (beispielsweise Frankreich, Deutschland, Belgien, den Niederlanden) existierten für die Notare feste Tarife. Das Honorar einvernehmlich bestimmen durften der Notar und sein Kunde nur in den Fällen, für die keine vom Staat festgelegten Tarife existierten. In Österreich war eine solche Einigung sogar in Ausnahmefällen gesetzlich verboten.[29] Im russischen Gesetz „*Временное положение о нотаральной части*" Art. 208 wird die Frage der Honorare wie folgt geregelt: „Der Notar erhebt die Gebühr auf der Grundlage einer einvernehmlichen Einigung mit den Personen, die sich an ihn gewandt haben." Für die russischen Juristen war diese Lösung nicht zufriedenstellend. So schrieb Mandelstam: „Es ist eine schwere Herabsetzung für eine öffentlich tätige Person, die nicht irgendwelche private Angelegenheiten, sondern öffentlich-rechtliche Funktionen ausübt, seine Tätigkeit mit dem Feilschen statt mit der Sache selbst zu beginnen."[30] Auch das Prinzip der territorialen Verteilung funktionierte nicht problemlos: ein Drittel der Notarstellen im Kaiserreich war nicht besetzt.[31]

Das Justizministerium reagierte auf die Kritik seitens des Berufsstandes und der Wissenschaftler und erließ – entsprechend dem ursprünglichen Plan, der vorsah, dass der ursprünglichen vorläufigen Notariatsverfassung aufgrund der erworbenen Erfahrung ein neues, qualitativ besseres Gesetz folgen werde, – am 19. April 1871

---

[26] *Черемных/Черемных*, Возникновение нотариата (oben Fn. 4) (eingesehen am 06.01.2013).

[27] *Комаров/Пашенцев/Пашенцева*, Очерки истории права (oben Fn. 7), S. 214.

[28] *Черемных/Черемных*, Возникновение нотариата (oben Fn. 4) (eingesehen am 06.01.2013).

[29] A.a.O.

[30] *Мандельштам Л. Б.* Программа для приготовления к должности нотариуса [Programm für die Vorbereitung auf das Amt des Notars] Odessa 1882, http://dic.academic.ru/dic.nsf/ (eingesehen am 06.12.2008).

[31] *Комаров/Пашенцев/Пашенцева*, Очерки истории права (oben Fn. 7), S. 227.

ein Rundschreiben, in dem die Vorsitzenden der Oberlandesgerichte aufgefordert wurden, von den örtlichen Notaren Kommentare zur bestehenden Praxis sowie Vorschläge zur besseren Organisation des Systems einzuholen, um auf dieser Grundlage ein neues Notariatsgesetz auszuarbeiten. Doch erst zwanzig Jahre später wurde am Ministerium ein Ausschuss gebildet, der sich mit der Ausarbeitung einer neuen Gesetzesfassung befasste. Im Jahre 1904 begann man tatsächlich mit der Besprechung der geleisteten Vorarbeiten zu dem Entwurf. Die Autoren des Entwurfs hatten erklärt: „Als Referenzpunkt für die Revision der Notariatsverfassung galt der Wunsch, in dieses so wichtige Gesetz möglichst viele den gegenwärtigen Umständen gerecht werdende Vervollständigungen einzuarbeiten, ohne das Gesetz vom 14. April 1866 aufzuheben [...].“[32] Auch diesmal stützte man sich bei der Erarbeitung des Entwurfs auf das deutsche und österreichische Vorbild.

Im Entwurf war vorgesehen, dass sich um das Amt des Notars Personen bewerben dürfen, die mindestens 25 Jahre alt sind und keine anderen Ämter innehaben, ähnlich wie im österreichischen Notariatsgesetz.[33] In Österreich lag die Altersgrenze allerdings bei 24 Jahren.[34] Eine große Rolle spielte für die Arbeit des Notariats – ähnlich wie in Österreich – der Justizminister. Der Entwurf räumte dem Justizminister das Recht ein, Vorschriften zur Regelung der Tätigkeit der Notare zu erlassen, auf Empfehlung des Oberlandesgerichts die Vereinbarkeit mit einer anderen Berufstätigkeit zu bestätigen, das Programm der Notariatsprüfung zu genehmigen und den Notar in sein Amt zu berufen. Der Justizminister war ebenfalls berechtigt, den Notar aus seinem Amt zu entbinden, wie es auch die österreichische Notariatsordnung vom 1871 vorsieht (§ 10).[35] Vorgesehen war ebenfalls die Institution des Notariatsgehilfen, mit bestimmten Ausbildungsanforderungen sowie dem Erfordernis vorheriger Arbeitserfahrung im Notariatskontor von mindestens sechs Monaten bei absolvierter juristischer Ausbildung bzw. einem Jahr bei absolvierter Mittelschulausbildung. Für den Fall, dass es nicht gelingen sollte, alle freien Dienststellen mit Notaren zu besetzen, war vorgesehen, die Aufgaben des Notars vorläufig den Kreisrichtern anzuvertrauen.[36]

Folgende Leitprinzipien wurden für die Neuordnung des Notariats festgelegt:

1. Die Aufgaben des Notars werden ausschließlich von Notaren wahrgenommen; zum Notar kann nur ein Jurist werden, der über gute theoretische Kenntnisse

---

[32] *Скрипилев Е.* Слово „нотариус“ — латинского происхождения [Das Wort „Notar“ – lateinischen Ursprungs], in: „Российская Юстиция“ [Russische Gerechtigkeit], Nr. 5, Mai 2003, S. 12–14.

[33] *Мандельштам*, Учреждение нотариата и его организация (oben Fn. 8), S. 13.

[34] Notariatsordnung v. 25. Juli 1871, Reichsgesetzblatt für die im Reichsrathe vertretenen Königreiche und Länder. XXXII. St.– 1. August 1871, S. 164.

[35] A.a.O., S. 165.

[36] *Черемных/Черемных*, Возникновение нотариата (oben Fn. 4) (eingesehen am 06.01.2013).

verfügt; diese Kenntnisse werden nach den Anforderungen der juristischen Ausbildung im Rahmen einer Eignungsprüfung festgestellt.

2. Im Gesetzestext werden alle Kompetenzen des Notars festgelegt; unter anderem wird festgelegt, dass der Notar bei der Abfassung eines notariellen Aktes immer selbst anwesend sein muss.

3. Die Oberlandesgerichte werden verpflichtet, eine wirksame Kontrolle und Aufsicht über die Tätigkeit der Notare auszuüben.

4. Es werden Notariatskammern und Notariatsvollversammlungen eingeführt.[37]

Darüber hinaus wurde in der Debatte über die Gesetzesmängel, an der sich die bedeutendsten Juristen des Kaiserreichs (*А. Иваницкий, Л.Б. Мандельштам, С.К. Кузнецов* u.a.) beteiligten, auf folgende unabdingbaren Voraussetzungen für das Notariat hingewiesen: formale Ausbildungsanforderungen, der Nachweis einschlägiger Arbeitserfahrung, die Institution des Notariatsgehilfen, die Einrichtung von Notariatskammern, denen die Aufgabe der internen Kontrolle über die Arbeit der einzelnen Notare zu übertragen wäre. In der ursprünglichen Ordnung des russischen Notariats fehlte das Prinzip der berufsständischen Organisation.[38]

Die Beratungen über den Entwurf erwiesen, dass die vorgesehenen Änderungen nicht ausreichend sein würden, um die bestehenden Probleme zu beseitigen. Es ist nicht gelungen, eine Lösung zu finden, mit der sowohl die Notare als auch die Regierung zufrieden gewesen wären, und eine Neustrukturierung des Notariats noch in der Epoche des Kaiserreiches durchzusetzen. Dieser Prozess wurde zunächst durch die Revolution von 1905 und dann durch den Ersten Weltkrieg blockiert. So wurde bis 1917 das Gesetz von 1866 nicht novelliert.[39]

Auch in den darauffolgenden sowjetischen Jahrzehnten wurde das russische Notariat zu einem großen Teil auf den Grundlagen entwickelt, die aus dem Notariatsgesetz von 1866 hervorgingen. Sowohl die Notariatsordnung von 1922 als auch das 1974 verabschiedete Gesetz über das staatliche Notariat der UdSSR übernahmen nach der Ansicht des russischen Professors Skripilew in vielerlei Hinsicht die Bestimmungen des Gesetzes von 1866.[40]

III. Das Notariat in der Lettischen Republik in den 20er und 30er Jahren des 20. Jahrhunderts

Die am 18. November 1918 gegründete Lettische Republik hat gemäß dem durch den Nationalrat der Lettischen Republik erlassenen Gesetz „Über die Fortgeltung

---

[37] *Скрипилев*, „нотариус" (oben Fn. 32), S. 12–14.

[38] *Комаров/Пашенцев/Пашенцева*, Очерки истории права (oben Fn. 7), S. 216 f.

[39] Вехи советского нотариата (1917–1991) [Stufenentwicklung des sowjetischen Notariats (1917–1991)] http://mirnot.narod.ru/sovetsk-hro.html (eingesehen am 06.12.2008).

[40] *Скрипилев*, „нотариус" (oben Fn. 32), S. 12–14.

der ehemaligen russischen Gesetze in Lettland" vom 5. Dezember 1919 das bis dahin geltende russische Recht beibehalten, wie es zuvor auf dem Gebiet Lettlands angewendet wurde. Das entsprach dem Prinzip der Rechtskontinuität.[41]

Für das Notariat bedeutete das die Fortgeltung des russischen Notariatsgesetzes vom 14. April 1866 „*Временное положение о нотаральной части*". In der Lettischen Republik blieben sowohl das russische Notariatsgesetz des Kaiserreichs als auch die die Notariatstätigkeit betreffende Rechtsprechung weiterhin in Geltung. Dies belegen die lettischsprachigen Fassungen der Notariatsordnung, in denen zusätzlich zu den Artikeln selbst auch die Rechtsprechung des Senats des Russischen Kaiserreiches enthalten ist.[42] Darüber hinaus wurde der Gesetzestext entsprechend den Umwandlungen des lettischen Rechtssystems geändert und vervollständigt. Ein Beispiel hierfür liefert z. B. Artikel 59:

> „Bei Fahrlässigkeiten und Amtsmissbrauch sind die Notare, die Leiter der Grundbuchabteilungen sowie ihre Gehilfen gemäß Artikel 187 bis 217 des Justizverfassungsgesetzes (Fassung von 1924) sowie Artikel 1021 bis 1046 des Strafrechtsprozessgesetzes (Fassung von 1926) zur Verantwortung zu ziehen."[43]

Gleichzeitig darf man nicht vergessen, dass das Justizsystem des neugegründeten lettischen Staates gemäß der durch den Lettischen Nationalrat am 6. Dezember 1918 verabschiedeten vorläufigen Ordnung „Über Gerichte und Gerichtsverfahren in Lettland" aufgebaut wurde, wobei man das zuvor bestehende Gerichts- und Rechtssystem Schritt für Schritt umstrukturierte.[44] Gleichzeitig bedeutete das allerdings, dass ebenfalls all jene Unzulänglichkeiten beibehalten wurden, welche die russischen Juristen in ihren Beiträgen als Mängel des Gesetzes „*Временное положение о нотаральной части*" kritisiert hatten. Das Gesetz, das im Kaiserreich mit dem Status eines Pilotprojekts erlassen worden war und als vorläufige Lösung dienen sollte, um einerseits ein einheitliches staatliches Notariatssystem im ganzen Kaiserreich zu begründen, andererseits Fehler und Unzulänglichkeiten in der Strukturierung und der Regelung der notariellen Arbeit zu bezeichnen, war auf dem Territorium Lettlands vom Jahre 1889 bis zum 14. Dezember 1937 in Kraft, als vom Lettischen Ministerkabinett das „Notargesetz" verabschiedet wurde.[45] Für die Ausarbeitung des Notargesetzes setzte der damalige Justizminister H. Apsītis eine Kommission ein, zu deren Mitgliedern folgende Personen zählten: das Senatsmitglied Professor V. Bukovskis, der Leiter des Gerichtsdepartements A. Meņģelsons, der Rechtsberater am Justizministerium I. Grūbaums, der Notar der Stadt

---

[41] *A. Lēbers* (Hg.), Latvijas tiesību vēsture (1914–2000) [Lettische Rechtsgeschichte (1914–2000)], Rīga 2000, S. 218.

[42] Notariatsordnung. Übersetzung mit Änderungen, Ergänzungen, Erläuterungen und Anlagen. Übersetzt und zusammengestellt von cand. jur. *Olga Jurkovska*, redigiert von Prof. Dr. jur. *Vladimirs Bukovskis*, hg. durch die Autoren, Rīga 1933, S. 19.

[43] A.a.O., S. 18.

[44] Latvijas tiesību vēsture (oben Fn. 41), S. 209.

[45] Notargesetz. Valdības Vēstnesis [Regierungsamtsblatt], Nr. 287 (1937).

Tukums V. Lūkins und die Notarin von Rīga/Jūrmala O. Jurkovska, welche die 1933 erschienene Ausgabe der russischen Notariatsordnung ins Lettische übersetzt hatte.[46] Die Autorin dieses Aufsatzes hatte die Möglichkeit, Einsicht in das Archiv der Familie Žodžiks zu nehmen, das auch die Hinterlassenschaft von Vilis Lūkins umfasst.

Die Arbeitsgruppe, die sich mit der Ausarbeitung des Entwurfs des Notargesetzes befasste, wurde mit dem politischen Auftrag versehen, eine vollständig neue und nationalrechtliche Regelung zu entwickeln.[47] Dieses Konzept entsprach vollständig der auf die Stärkung der nationalen Werte ausgerichteten Politik, die der autoritäre lettische Staat verfolgte. Auch das später verabschiedete Gesetz wurde als ein neues, nationales Gesetz präsentiert.[48] Doch kann man bei der Analyse des angenommenen Gesetzestextes feststellen, dass das Gesetz von 1937 auf der zuvor geltenden Notariatsverfassung unter Berücksichtigung der am Ende des 19. Jahrhunderts im Russischen Kaiserreich geäußerten Kritik an *„Временное положение о нотарьной части*“ und des bereits erwähnten im Jahre 1904 ausgearbeiteten Gesetzesentwurfs beruht. Außerdem ist zu berücksichtigen, dass das neue Notariatsgesetz in einem autoritären Staat entstand, der auf die Dominanz der Exekutive sowie der Staatszentralisierung ausgerichtet war und sich somit dem Vorbild der zentralisierten Staatsgewalt im Russischen Kaiserreich annäherte.

Einen großen Beitrag zur Ausarbeitung des Gesetzesentwurfes leisteten die Notare Olga Jurkovska und Vilis Lūkins (1903–1995). Dessen Tochter Maija Žodžika (geb. 1931) erinnert sich, dass ihr Vater speziell zu dem Zweck die französische Sprache erlernte, um Fachliteratur zum französischen Notariat in der Originalsprache lesen zu können. Bei der Ausarbeitung des Gesetzesentwurfs wurde auf russischsprachige, deutschsprachige, französischsprachige und lateinische Fachliteratur zurückgegriffen. Auf Latein wurde vor allem zurückgegriffen, um Begriffe aus den Fachlexika zu präzisieren.[49]

Im Notargesetz wird der Doppelstatus der Notarinstitution mit der folgenden Bestimmung beibehalten: „Bei der Ausübung ihrer amtlichen Tätigkeiten sind die Notare dem staatlichen Dienstpersonal gleichgestellt.“[50] In das Notargesetz sind die Konzepte eingearbeitet worden, die den Gesetzesentwurf von 1904 kennzeichneten:

Eine engere Verbindung zwischen den Notaren und dem Justizminister (Art. 2, 3, 4, 139 u.a.).

---

[46] *Lettischer Rat der vereidigten Notare* (Hg.), Einblick in die Entwicklung des Notariats in Lettland, Rīga 1998, S. 8.

[47] *Ulmanis*, Die Rede (oben Fn. 2), S. 7.

[48] *Jurkovska*, Redetext (oben Fn. 1), am 2.2.2012 eingesehen.

[49] Von der Autorin geführtes Interview mit Maija Žodžika, der Tochter von Vilis Lūkins, am 2.2.2012. Persönliches Archiv von Sanita Osipova.

[50] Notargesetz. Art. 1. Valdības Vēstnesis (Regierungsamtsblatt), Nr. 287 (1937).

Die Beibehaltung der territorialen Bindung an die Oberlandesgerichte (Art. 22 „Das ordnungsgemäße Entrichten der weiteren Kautionsbeträge durch die Notare wird durch den Vorsitzenden des Oberlandesgerichts beaufsichtigt"; Art. 31 „Mit Einvernehmen des Justizministers kann das Oberlandesgericht dem Notar gestatten bzw. ihn beauftragen, sich an bestimmten Tagen wöchentlich oder monatlich für die Wahrnehmung seiner Aufgaben in die benachbarten Städte bzw. Ortschaften zu begeben, in denen kein Notar vorhanden ist" usw.).

Die Festlegung von neuen Voraussetzungen und Anforderungen: Der Kandidat musste mindestens 25 Jahre alt sein, eine juristische Ausbildung absolviert haben, Arbeitserfahrung haben (zwei Jahre in einem Notarsbüro oder fünf Jahre in Justizeinrichtungen, in denen man mit Aufgaben betraut war, die den Erwerb der für die Ausübung des Notarberufs notwendigen Kenntnisse möglich machten) sowie die notarielle Eignungsprüfung ablegen (diese Anforderungen gelten bis zum heutigen Tag).

Das Prinzip der Verhandelbarkeit des Honorars, mit dem die russischen Juristen im 19. Jahrhundert so unzufrieden waren, wird im Artikel 139 durch die Festlegung eines Tarifs ersetzt: „Die Notare werden für ihre Tätigkeit (Art. 57) entsprechend der vom Justizminister festgelegten Tarife durch ihre Kunden vergütet. Soweit sie nicht durch Gesetz vorgeschrieben bzw. vom Justizminister festgelegt sind, werden die Honorare der Notare von der Notarenkammer geregelt, wobei die Zustimmung des Justizministers einzuholen ist."

Die Einführung der Notariatsgehilfeninstitution: Art. 133 „Der Notar kann Notariatsgehilfen beschäftigen." Art. 134 „Notariatsgehilfen können lettische Staatsbürger werden, die die gesetzliche Volljährigkeit (damals 21 Jahre) erreicht, eine Mittelschulbildung absolviert und vorher mindestens zwei Jahre in einem Notariatskontor gearbeitet haben." Die Altersvoraussetzung von 21 Jahren korreliert mit der Anforderung der Mittelschulbildung, die in den 30er Jahren des 20. Jahrhunderts üblicherweise im Alter von 19 Jahren abgeschlossen wurde, und mit den darauf folgenden zwei Jahren Arbeitserfahrung bei einem Notar. Die Altersvoraussetzung für Notariatsgehilfen ist nicht geändert worden, obwohl nach der aktuell geltenden Regelung für die Ausübung der Tätigkeit des Notariatsgehilfen eine Juristenausbildung verlangt wird.[51] Qualifizierter Jurist kann man allerdings nicht früher als im Alter von 23 bis 24 Jahren werden.

Die Einführung der Notarversammlung und der Notarkammer, durch welche die Tätigkeit der Notare einen berufsständischen Zug erhielt. Diese Aspekte werden in den Artikeln 178 bis 212 geregelt.

---

[51] Gesetz vom 01.06.1993 „Über das erneute Inkraftsetzen des Notargesetzes der Lettischen Republik von 1937 sowie dessen Änderungen und Vervollständigungen (Das Notariatsgesetz). Siehe: http://www.likumi.lv/doc.php?id=59982 (eingesehen am 29.03.2012).

Das neue Gesetz, mit dem in Lettland der im Russischen Kaiserreich erarbeitete Entwurf der Notariatsordnung in Kraft gesetzt wurde, zeichnet sich durch eine weitere Tendenz aus, nämlich die prägende Rolle des Justizministers für die Tätigkeit des Notariats. Überraschend ist die Anmerkung in Artikel 5 Absatz 2 des Gesetzes: „In Ausnahmefällen kann der Justizminister eine Person zum Notar ernennen, die eine Mittelschulausbildung hat, vorausgesetzt, dass diese Person alle sonstigen im Artikel 5 festgelegten Anforderungen erfüllt."[52] Diese Abweichung von den Bildungsanforderungen ist vermutlich auf die Schwierigkeiten zurückzuführen, die Notarstellen in ganz Lettland durch Personen zu besetzen, die eine abgeschlossene juristische Ausbildung hatten; es war jedoch sicher nicht angemessen, dieses Ausnahmerecht dem Justizminister einzuräumen, von dem selbst keine höhere juristische Ausbildung verlangt wurde. Tatsächlich wurde mit dieser Bestimmung die oft kritisierte Praxis des alten Gesetzes legalisiert, nach der zum Notar eine Person ernannt werden konnte, die keine juristische Ausbildung hatte.

Eine solche Notariatsordnung, die vorsah, dass der Justizminister die Notare bestellt, entlässt bzw. von den Amtsverpflichtungen entbindet, war Teil eines autoritären Staatsmodells, in dem es keine Gewaltenteilung gab. Doch in dem demokratischen Rechtsstaat, der Lettland heute ist und in dem „vereidigte Notare dem Gerichtssystem angehören, an Oberlandesgerichte gebunden sind und ihre im Gesetz vorgeschriebenen Aufgaben wahrnehmen" sowie „bei der Ausübung ihrer Tätigkeit [...] den Staatsbeamten gleichgestellt"[53] sind, ist es nicht angemessen, dem Justizminister nach wie vor das Recht einzuräumen, Notare zu ernennen und zu entlassen (Notariatsgesetz vom 1.6.1993, Art. 210 und 211). Dieser Aspekt wird noch eingehender in weiteren Abschnitten dieses Aufsatzes behandelt, die sich mit der Analyse der zurzeit geltenden Rechtsakte beschäftigen.

Außerdem fehlte im Notariatsgesetz von 1937 die Regelung der Grundbuchordnung, wie sie das Gesetz des Russischen Kaiserreichs inkorporiert hatte, wo die Grundbuchführung und das Notariat in einem einheitlichen System zusammengefasst waren und die beiden Bereiche mit einem gemeinsamen Rechtsakt geregelt wurden. Auf diese Weise wurden eine Überschneidung der Funktionen der Notare und der Leiter der Grundbuchabteilungen sowie Unstimmigkeiten in der Regulierung der Immobiliengeschäfte ausgeschlossen. Sowohl das Notariat als auch die Grundbuchabteilungen waren nach dem territorialen Prinzip an das Justizsystem gebunden und unterlagen der Aufsicht und der Kontrolle seitens des Oberlandesgerichts.[54] Darüber hinaus gab es einheitliche Bestimmungen, denn die Ordnung sah vor, dass „die Register der Auszüge und Abschriften [...] gemäß der für die

---

[52] Notargesetz. Art. 1. Valdības Vēstnesis [Regierungsamtsblatt], Nr. 287 (1937).

[53] Gesetz zur Änderungen des Gesetzes „Über die Justizordnung" vom 29.01.1997, verabschiedet von der Lettischen Saeima. Offizielles Amtsblatt der Regierung „Latvijas Vēstnesis", 13.02.1997. – Nr.46/47 (761/762).

[54] Notariatsordnung, Rīga 1933, S. 14.

Notarregister geltenden Bestimmungen geführt" werden.[55] Ebenfalls war eine einheitliche Verantwortung und Aufsicht über die Notare, die Leiter der Grundbuchabteilungen und ihre Gehilfen festgelegt (Artikel 57 bis 64).

Daraus ergibt sich, dass das Notargesetz von 1937 auf der Tradition der im Russischen Kaiserreich entwickelten Kompetenz und Organisation der Notariatstätigkeit aufbaute, wobei man zum großen Teil die für die Neufassung des russischen Gesetzes „*Временное положение о нотариальной части*" von 1904 geplanten Änderungen und Ergänzungen eingearbeitet hatte. Doch muss berücksichtigt werden, dass die russischen Juristen mit dem neuen Gesetzentwurf von 1904 kein innovatives, nationales Gesetz geschaffen hatten. Der Entwurf war vielmehr ein Ergebnis der Untersuchung des Notariats lateinischer Prägung, wie es in derselben Epoche in anderen Ländern existierte.[56] Auch die Kommission, die sich mit der Entwicklung des lettischen Notargesetzes befasste, hat mit Blick auf die Erfahrung anderer Länder im gleichen Zeitraum, d.h. in den 30er Jahren des 20. Jahrhunderts, gearbeitet. Sie bestätigte, dass im russischen Gesetzentwurf von 1904 viele Probleme der ursprünglichen Regelung gelöst worden waren. Darüber hinaus hat die lettische Kommission den russischen Gesetzentwurf von 1904 nicht wörtlich übernommen, sondern sich auf dessen Text und auf viele andere Quellen gestützt, um in Lettland ein besser organisiertes, juristisch ausgebildetes und aus sozialer Sicht „reiferes" Notariat zu schaffen. Dies betont in seinem Aufsatz auch einer der Verfasser des lettischen Gesetzesentwurfes, Vilis Lūkins:

> „Selbst wenn unser Notargesetz es nicht beansprucht, im Bereich des Notariatsrechts das letzte Wort zu sprechen, so stützt sich unser Gesetz doch auf alle rationalen Grundlagen des modernen Notariats. Das Notargesetz ist, ähnlich wie im Falle des Bürgerlichen Gesetzbuchs von Präsident Ulmanis, aus der formellen Sicht ein absolut neues Gesetz, doch sind darin, ebenfalls wie im Ulmanis' Bürgerlichem Gesetzbuch, parallel zu neueingeführten Prinzipien auch bestehende Prinzipien beibehalten, derer sich verschiedene europäische Länder bedient hatten und die unserer Situation völlig angemessen sind."

1990/1991 wurde die Republik Lettland nicht als neuer Staat gegründet, sondern es wurde die im Jahre 1918 gegründete Republik wiederhergestellt. Dies bedeutete auch das erneute Inkrafttreten der Gesetze, die bis zur Okkupation durch die Sowjetunion im Jahre 1940 in Kraft waren. Nicht immer wurde bei dem erneuten Inkraftsetzen der alten Gesetze berücksichtigt, dass Lettland ab 1934 ein autoritärer Staat war, in dem es keine tatsächliche Gewaltenteilung gab. Die Verfassung war demokratisch, da sie während der Periode des Autoritarismus nicht geändert worden war. Die lettische Verfassung (lettisch: Satversme) war nach 1934 nicht außer Kraft gesetzt worden.

Als man im Jahre 1993 das Notargesetz von 1937 erneut in Kraft setzte und dann 1996 ein überarbeitetes neues Notariatsgesetz verabschiedete, hat man nicht

---

[55] A.a.O., S. 15.

[56] Вехи советского нотариата (1917–1991) (eingesehen am 06.01.2013.).

berücksichtigt, dass das Gesetz von 1937 im Widerspruch zur Gewaltenteilung und dem Prinzip der Unabhängigkeit des Justizsystems und der dem Justizsystem angehörigen Personen stand. Als dieses Gesetz Ende des 20. Jahrhunderts erneut in Kraft trat, wurden damit auch die dem autoritären Staat eigene verstärkte Bindung des Notariats an die Exekutive sowie die formelle Bindung an das Justizsystem wieder eingeführt. Das Prinzip der formellen Aufsicht seitens des Oberlandesgerichts haben bereits Ende des 19. Jahrhunderts die russischen Juristen in ihren Aufsätzen kritisiert, doch ist dieses Problem bis heute nicht gelöst worden. Die ursprüngliche Fassung des russischen Gesetzes „*Временное положение о нотаральной части*“ vom 14. April 1866 sah eine stärkere Bindung zwischen dem Notariat und dem Justizsystem vor, als dies in den Entwurf von 1904 eingearbeitet wurde. Der Grund dafür war die enorme Belastung der Gerichte, die es praktisch unmöglich machte, die Tätigkeit der Notare *de facto* zu kontrollieren, doch wurde der Entwurf zum großen Teil gerade aus diesem Grund nicht angenommen. Anstatt nach einem alternativen Verfahren zur Kontrolle des Notariats durch das Gerichtssystem zu suchen, haben die Verfasser des Gesetzes von 1937 dem Justizminister die umstrittene führende Rolle bei der Organisation und Aufsicht der Notarstätigkeit zugewiesen, was dem für autoritäre Staaten charakteristischen Modell einer ungeteilten, in den Händen der Exekutive konzentrierten Macht entsprach.

IV. Schlussfolgerungen

1. Die ersten Notare auf dem Territorium des heutigen Lettlands waren im 13. Jahrhundert deutsche Missionare. Zu jener Zeit wurden die ersten notariell beglaubigten Dokumente auf dem Territorium des heutigen Lettlands erstellt. Das Amt des Notars wurde in Livland nach dem Vorbild des Heiligen Römischen Reiches eingeführt, was die Geschichte des Notariats in Lettland mit der Geschichte des Notariats in Deutschland und im kontinentalen Europa insgesamt verbindet, welche wiederum auf der Rezeption des römischen Rechts beruht.

2. Bis zum Ende des 19. Jahrhunderts richteten sich die Notare auf dem Territorium des heutigen Lettlands bei ihrer Tätigkeit nach den Grundprinzipien des Notariatsgesetzes für das Heilige Römische Reich von 1512. Erst am Ende des 19. Jahrhunderts, als am 9. Juli 1889 im Baltikum das Gesetz des Russischen Kaiserreichs „*Временное положение о нотаральной части*“ vom 14. April 1866 in Kraft trat, wurde im Territorium des heutigen Lettlands ein Notariat lateinischer Prägung eingeführt.

3. Das Notariat lateinischer Prägung wurde im Russischen Kaiserreich auf der Grundlage deutscher (d.h. österreichischer und bayrischer) Erfahrungen eingeführt. Mit dem Inkrafttreten des Gesetzes wurde der Notar zur einzigen Amtsperson, die notarielle Akte tätigte.

4. Die am 18. November 1918 gegründete Lettische Republik hat nach dem vom Nationalrat der Lettischen Republik erlassenen Gesetz „Über die Fortgeltung der vormaligen russischen Gesetze in Lettland“ vom 5. Dezember 1919 das bis dahin

geltende russische Recht in Kraft gelassen, das zuvor auf dem Gebiet Lettlands angewendet wurde. Für das Notariat bedeutete das die Fortgeltung des russischen Notariatsgesetzes „*Временное положение о нотариальной части*" vom 14. April 1866. Die Anwendung des Gesetzes erfolgte in der Republik Lettlands unter Nutzung nicht nur des Gesetzestextes, sondern auch der Rechtsprechung des Kaiserreichs. Das vom Kaiserreich erlassene Gesetz, das als provisorische, vorübergehende Lösung vorgesehen war, blieb auf dem Territorium Lettlands bis zum 14. Dezember 1937 in Kraft, als das Ministerkabinett der Republik Lettlands das „Notargesetz" verabschiedete.

5. Obwohl es das Konzept der Ulmanis-Diktatur war, eine ganz neue, nationale Regelung zu schaffen, wurde das Notargesetz von 1937 im Grunde genommen auf der Basis der vorangehenden Regelwerke für das Notariat erstellt, allerdings unter Berücksichtigung der noch am Ende des 19. Jahrhunderts laut gewordenen Kritik und des 1904 ausgearbeiteten Gesetzesentwurfs. Das neue Gesetz, mit dem in Lettland der im Russischen Kaiserreich erarbeitete Entwurf der Notariatsordnung in Kraft gesetzt wurde, zeichnete sich durch eine weitere Tendenz aus, nämlich die prägende Rolle des Justizministers für die Tätigkeit des Notariats. Die Verfasser des Gesetzes von 1937 erkannten dem Justizminister eine führende Rolle bei der Organisation des Notariats und der Aufsicht über das Notariat zu, was der im damaligen autoritären Staatswesen vorherrschenden Tendenz zur ungeteilten Machtkonzentration in den Händen der Exekutive entsprach.

6. Nach der Wiedererlangung der Unabhängigkeit der Republik Lettlands trat auch das Notargesetz von 1937 wieder in Kraft, das nach dem autoritären Staatsmodell auf die Dominanz der Exekutive ausgerichtet war. Auch wenn das heutige Lettland wesentliche Änderungen und Vervollständigungen der Notariatsnormen durchführte, sind doch noch nicht alle Probleme vollständig gelöst, welche die Rechtswissenschaftler schon Ende des 19. und anfangs des 20. Jahrhunderts benannt haben.

Dorfjustiz und Rechtsbewußtsein des russischen Bauerntums in der zweiten Hälfte des 19. Jahrhunderts (anhand der Materialien des Archivs der Russischen Geographischen Gesellschaft)

Alexander Rogatschewski

I. Geschichte des Gewohnheitsrechts in Rußland als Forschungsproblem

Die Geschichte des Gewohnheitsrechts in Rußland gehört zu den Themen, die einerseits zum traditionellen Kanon unserer rechtshistorischen Wissenschaft zählen, andererseits jedoch ungenügend erforscht sind. Dabei thematisierten russische Forscher das Gewohnheitsrecht relativ frühzeitig: Bereits in den 1840er Jahren sammelten die Korrespondenten der Russischen Geographischen Gesellschaft die Angaben über die lokalen Gewohnheiten der Bevölkerung verschiedener Gouvernements des Kaiserreiches.[1] Ungeachtet der Tatsache, daß das Gewohnheitsrecht eine beschränkte Anerkennung und Anwendung in den Gerichten fand, wurde es von den Rechtswissenschaftlern wenig beachtet. Man setzte die Begriffe „Recht" und „Gesetz" grundsätzlich gleich. Die russischen Nachfolger Savignys, d.h. die Vertreter der „historischen Schule der Rechtswissenschaft", betonten, wie wichtig es sei, das „Volksrecht" zu erkennen, und sie versuchten, eine Verbindung zwischen „Volksrecht" und staatlichem Recht herzustellen. Auch die russischen Rechtskundler (wie etwa K.D. Kawelin, W.I. Ssergejewitsch, M.F. Wladimirskij-Budanow, D.W. Ssamokwassow u.a.) beteiligten sich an dieser Polemik. Sie stuften Gewohnheiten als eine Quelle des geschriebenen Rechts ein. Auch erkannten sie die besonderen „inoffiziellen" Rechtsbeziehungen im Dorfe als Rechtskomplex an. Die Entwicklung des Gewohnheitsrechts war für sie jedoch nur unter dem Gesichtspunkt der Evolution der staatlichen Gesetzgebung bedeutsam. Dagegen interessierten sie sich nicht für die Probleme, die mit dem rechtlichen Alltag der Bauern verbunden waren.

Die Situation änderte sich nach der Aufhebung der Leibeigenschaft (1861). Diese große Reform des russischen Lebens wirkte sich in komplexer Weise auf das Rechtssystem aus. Gegen Mitte des 19. Jahrhunderts bestand die russische Gesellschaft aus zwei Hauptgruppen: den Bauern, welche die überwiegende Gruppe bildeten und deren Lebensweise von den staatlichen Gesetzen ignoriert wurde, und den Adelsleuten, Kaufleuten und Bürgern, deren Beziehungen durch Gesetze

---

[1] *Wladimir Berelowitch,* Aux origines de l'ethnographie russe: La Société de géographie des années 1840–1850: Cahiers du Monde russe et soviétique, Vol. XXXI. No. 2–3, Paris 1990, S. 265–274.

geregelt wurden. Die Spezifik der Gesellschaftsverfassung Rußlands hat die Entstehung zweier paralleler Rechtssysteme in einem Staate verursacht.

Diese Tatsache wurde auch in der 2. Hälfte des 19. Jahrhunderts deutlich. Die Bauernreform von 1861 und die Gerichtsreform von 1864 haben die Sonderstellung der Bauern nicht aufgehoben. Ganz im Gegenteil: Man legalisierte die Volksjustiz und sah ein, daß die Gesetzessammlung des Russischen Kaiserreiches (*Svod zakonov Rossijskoj imperii*) für die Problemlagen des Bauernlebens untauglich war. Laut Gesetz über die Aufhebung der Leibeigenschaft vom 19. Februar 1861 (Art. 21, 38, 107) durften die Bauern ihre Gewohnheiten bei der Lösung ihrer Vermögens-, Erb-, Vormundschafts- und sonstiger Sachen anwenden. Die sog. *Wolostgerichte*, d.h. die Gerichte der Territorialgemeinden, mußten die Gerichtsbarkeit im flachen Lande ausüben. Die zahlreichen Gerichtsurteile dieser Art wurden jedoch in die Gesetzessammlung nicht als Präjudizien eingetragen. Aus Mangel an qualifizierten Arbeitskräften war der Staat genötigt, 1864 auf lokaler Ebene ein zusätzliches System der Gerichte, die sog. *mirovye sudy* (buchstäblich „Friedensgerichte", die etwa den preußischen Schiedsämtern jener Zeit ähnelten) zu schaffen. Diese Gerichtsgremien sprachen nicht in sämtlichen Gegenden des Russischen Kaiserreiches Recht. 1889 wurden sie ganz abgeschafft und erst 1912 wiederhergestellt. Man erlaubte diesen Gerichten, Rechtsgewohnheiten anzuwenden.

Abgesehen von dieser staatlich anerkannten Gerichtsbarkeit bestanden im russischen Dorfe von alters her die nichtamtlichen, inoffiziellen Gerichte, wie Familien- und Schiedsgerichte, Gerichte der alten Leute und Nachbarn, Gerichte des Dorfältesten und der Dorfversammlungen. Sie stützten sich u.a. auf Gewohnheitsrecht und waren keinem förmlichen Verfahren unterworfen. Ihre Spruchpraxis wies keinen klaren Unterschied zwischen Zivil- und Strafverfahren auf. Meistens hatten sie schlichtende Funktion; manchmal jedoch waren ihre Urteile sehr scharf und kamen der Selbstjustiz nahe. Ungeachtet dieser Tatsache war ihre Autorität bei den Bauern häufig groß.[2]

Indem das Gewohnheitsrecht sozusagen legalisiert und sein Status erhöht wurde, stieg das Interesse der Rechtswissenschaftler und Staatsbeamten für diesen Problemkreis.[3] Die weitere Entwicklung der neu eingerichteten Gerichtsbarkeiten verlief unterschiedlich. Die Friedensgerichte erweckten die Sympathie des gelehrten Publikums, weil sie als Tätigkeitsfeld vieler progressiver Vertreter der Gesellschaft galten. Die Wolostgerichte empfand man als archaische Relikte. Die Friedensrichter hatten einen höheren Sozialstatus und sahen auf die Tätigkeit ihrer

---

[2] S. *Vjačeslav V. Tenišev*, Pravosudie v russkom krest'janskom bytu [Rechtspflege im russischen Bauernalltag], 2. Aufl. Moskau, 2010, S. 63–69.

[3] S. hierfür *Tat'jana I. Selina,* Teoretičeskaja postanovka aktual'nych problem obyčnogo prava v poreformennoj Rossii (vtoraja polovina XIX – načalo XX veka) [Die theoretische Stellung aktueller Probleme des Gewohnheitsrechts in Rußland nach der (Bauern)reform (zweite Hälfte des 19. bis Anfang des 20. Jahrhunderts)], Jevrazijskij juridičeskij žurnal [Eurasiatische juristische Zeitschrift], 2009 Nr. 5 (12), S. 13–22.

Wolostkollegen herab. Die liberal gesinnten Fachleute betonten den demokratischen und progressiven Charakter der neu eingerichteten Gerichtsbarkeiten. Es wurde jedoch auch darauf hingewiesen, daß das Gewohnheitsrecht nur schwach ausgebildet war und die Gefahr bestand, das ortsübliche Unrecht zum verbindlichen Gewohnheitsrecht zu erklären. Die Mitglieder der Wolostgerichte nahm man nicht als Vertreter der Gesellschaft, sondern als kleine örtliche, nur wenig alphabetisierte „Tyrannen" wahr.

Diese Zustände riefen Widerstand gegen die Tätigkeit der Wolostgerichte hervor. Etliche Autoren forderten, ihre Kompetenz zu beschränken und sie besser zu kontrollieren; andere empfahlen, diese Gerichtsbarkeit ganz abzuschaffen. Zwecks Erforschung der Lage und Verbesserung der Tätigkeit der Wolostgerichte hat die russische Regierung 1872 einen speziellen Ausschuß eingerichtet. Er bestand aus den Beamten der Justiz- und Innenministerien und wurde von Senator Luboschtschinski geleitet. Die Arbeit des Ausschusses weckte das Interesse der Publizisten und Experten für das Gewohnheitsrecht. Die Forscher betonten, wie schwierig es sei, diese Gerichte zu schaffen und zu leiten. Viele Bauern weigerten sich, als Richter zu fungieren: Diese Tätigkeit war ehrenamtlicher Natur, und es bestand die Gefahr, sich Feinde unter den Landesgenossen zu schaffen. Zudem waren die Richter der Wolostgerichte vom Wolost-Ältesten und vom Wolost-Sekretär abhängig. Es wurde jedoch deutlich, daß die tatsächliche Effektivität dieser Gerichte mit der wirtschaftlichen Lage der relevanten Kreise eng verknüpft war. In den ökonomisch bessergestellten Orten war das Gericht unabhängiger und ihre Gerichtsbarkeit für die Bauern besser; in den armen Gegenden war die Lage viel schlimmer.

Man wies außerdem darauf hin, daß die Bedeutung des Gewohnheitsrechts auch in den Wolostgerichten sank. Sogar bei der Regelung von Erbschaftssachen benutzten die Gerichte häufig den ersten Halbband des Bandes X der Gesetzessammlung, die Ordnung vom 19. Februar 1861 sowie die sonstigen Gesetze und Ordnungen. Es blieb in vielen Fällen im großen und ganzen unklar, welche Rechtsnorm ein Wolostgericht anwenden würde: entweder die Norm des Gewohnheitsrechts oder die „Ratschläge" des Wolost-Ältesten und des Wolost-Sekretärs. Auch betonte man andererseits, wie häufig das Wolostgericht in den Kompetenzbereich des Friedens- und Bezirksgerichts eindrang. Ungeachtet der Tatsache, daß die Sachen über Diebstahl, Raub, schwere Körperverletzung und dergleichen durch Versöhnung, d.h. Vergleich der Parteien nicht beendigt werden durften, zogen die Dorfältesten bzw. Wolostgerichte die Entscheidungskompetenz an sich.

Trotzdem war das Gewohnheitsrecht eine wichtige Grundlage für die Wolostgerichte. Das gilt sowohl für Zivil- als auch (bis 1889) für Strafsachen. Man wandte im Fall lückenhafter staatlicher Gesetzgebung Gewohnheitsrecht bei sämtlichen Handelsgerichten sowie beim Friedensrichter und Landeshauptmann (1889–1912) an. Außerdem hatte der Friedensrichter bis 1889 das Recht, die Sache bei jeder

Streitsumme „nach Gewissen" zu entscheiden, wenn beide Parteien darum baten; dabei wurden auch die gewohnheitsrechtlichen Normen angewandt.

Das Gesetz vom 12. Juli 1889 schrieb dann die obligatorische Anwendung des Gewohnheitsrechts in den Wolostgerichten vor. Diese Tatsache stimulierte die Erforschung der relevanten Gewohnheiten. Abgesehen von Privatinitiativen einzelner Juristen wurde diese Arbeit durch die Kaiserliche Russische Geographische Gesellschaft unterstützt, die 1889 ein Programm zur Erforschung der russischen juristischen Gewohnheiten publizierte.[4] Als Ergebnis der zahlreichen Studien sind viele Publikationen der lokalen Rechtsgewohnheiten aus verschiedenen Gouvernements sowie die reiche Sekundärliteratur (wie etwa die Darstellung S.W. Pachmans „Das zivile Gewohnheitsrecht in Rußland") zu nennen. Die rasche Entfaltung der Forschung spiegelte sich in der berühmten fünfbändigen annotierten Bibliographie zum Gewohnheitsrecht, die von Eugen Jakuschkin vorbereitet wurde. Sie enthält mehrere tausend Titel. Erst 100 Jahre später wurde diese Arbeit fortgesetzt.[5]

Die Rolle des Gewohnheitsrechts im Bauernleben und in der Tätigkeit der Wolost- und Friedensgerichte wurde von den russischen Juristen sehr unterschiedlich bewertet. Sie zählte zu den Hauptstreitpunkten der damaligen Rechtswissenschaft.

Russisches Gewohnheitsrecht im Urteil der russischen Rechtswissenschaftler (zweite Hälfte des 19. und Anfang des 20. Jahrhunderts)[6]

Problemkomplex	Autoren	Thesen
Verhältnis zwischen Gewohnheitsrecht und staatlicher Gesetzgebung	A.Ja. Jefimenko	Gewohnheitsrecht des Volkes und „kulturelles" Recht sind ganz unterschiedlich.
	S.W. Pachman	Gesetz und Gewohnheitsrecht weisen überhaupt keine prinzipiellen Unterschiede auf.

---

4 S.a. *Alessandro Stanziani*, Les enquêtes orales en Russie, 1861–1914, Annales. Histoire, Sciences Sociales, 55e Année, No. 1 (Jan.–Feb., 2000), S. 219–241.

5 *Jewgenij Jakuškin:* 1) Obyčnoe pravo. Materialy dlja bibliografii obyčnogo prava [Das Gewohnheitsrecht. Materialien zur Bibliographie des Gewohnheitsrechts], 1. Lief. 2. Aufl., Moskau, 1910; 2. Lief., Jaroslawl 1896; 3. und 4. Lief. Moskau, 1908–1906; 2) Obyčnoe pravo russkich inorodcev. Materialy dlja bibliografii obyčnogo prava [Das Gewohnheitsrecht russischer Fremdvölker. Materialien zur Bibliographie des Gewohnheitsrechts], Moskau 1899; *Alexej Nikišenkov,* Obyčnoe pravo narodov Rossii. Bibliografičeskij ukazatel' [Das Gewohnheitsrecht der Völker Rußlands. Ein Literaturverzeichnis], 1890–1998, Moskau 1998.

6 Die Tabelle faßt die Übersicht von T. W. Schatkowskaja (*Tatjana Šatkovskaja*, Zakon i obyčaj v pravovom bytu krest'jan vtoroj poloviny XIX veka [Gesetz und Gewohnheit in der rechtlichen Lebenshaltung der Bauern in der zweiten Hälfte des 19. Jahrhunderts], in: Voprosy istorii [Probleme der Geschichte], 2000, Nr. 11, S. 96–105) zusammen.

Ursachen der Unterschiede zwischen Gewohnheitsrecht und staatlicher Gesetzgebung	I. Werigin	3 Hauptunterschiede des Volksrechts und des staatlichen Rechts: der Charakter der Arbeit, die Idee der Vermögensverteilung und die Privatinitiative im Vermögensbereich
	I. Tütrümow, A.A. Leontjew	Die Unterschiede zwischen den Rechtsvorstellungen im Volk und den formellen Gesetzen sind durch die Besonderheiten der Entwicklung der Gesetzgebung, die ständische Bildung der Gesellschaft und die rechtliche Sonderstellung der Bauern bedingt.
	G. Baraz	Die Gesetze, die in der zweiten Hälfte des 19. Jahrhunderts erlassen wurden, enthalten keine Elemente, die „durch das russische Leben ausgearbeitet wurden" und somit „keinen Ausdruck des Volksrechts"; sie enthalten viele Institute aus sehr unterschiedlichen ausländischen Gesetzbüchern und sind deshalb den Rechtsvorstellungen des Volkes fremd.
Die Einführung des offiziellen Rechts im Dorf	I. Werigin, S.P. Nikonow, I.G. Orschanski u.a.	Das geschriebene Recht weist wichtige Gegensätze zu den Volksgewohnheiten auf und kann deshalb erst allmählich unter Berücksichtigung der Vorstellungen im Volk von Wahrheit und Gerechtigkeit eingeführt werden.
	Die Anhänger der „völkischen" Theorie („Narodniki") – u.a. K.R. Katschorowski	Die Einführung des offiziellen Rechts im Dorf hat „das schöne Gebäude der Gemeinde- und Familiengewohnheiten zerstört" und die traditionellen Rechtsvorstellungen der Bauern vernichtet.
	A.D. Bilimowitsch	Das Rechtsbewußtsein des Volkes entspricht den Prinzipien des geschriebenen Rechts und ist deshalb auf dessen Einführung vorbereitet.
	N. Drushinin	Das Bauernleben ist einfach, monoton und langweilig, darum können die allgemeinen Gesetzesnormen im Dorfe leicht eingeführt werden.
	G.A. Jewreinow	Das Gewohnheitsrecht hatte überhaupt keinen wesentlichen Einfluß auf das Bauernleben, weil die Bauern zumindest seit dem 11. Jahrhundert nach dem Gesetz lebten.

In der Sowjetzeit sank das Interesse der Wissenschaftler für das Gewohnheitsrecht. Die relevante Problematik verschwand nicht nur aus der Fachliteratur, sondern (was besonders schlimm war) auch aus den Lehrbüchern. Erst seit den 1980er Jahren tauchte dieser Problemkomplex in den Arbeiten von M.M. Gromyko, P.N. Syrjanow und W.A. Alexandrow wieder auf.[7] Diese Autoren waren keine Juristen,

[7] Zu den nennenswerten Werken dieser Art sind wohl zu rechnen: *Pavel N. Zyrjanov*, Obyčnoe graždanskoe pravo v poreformennoj obščine [Das zivile Gewohnheitsrecht in der (Bauern)gemeinde nach der (Agrar)reform], in: Ježegodnik po agrarnoj istorii [Jahrbuch zur Agrargeschichte]. Lief. VI., Wologda 1976, S. 91–101; *Vadim A. Aleksandrov*, Obyčnoe pravo krepostnoj derevni Rossii, XVIII–načalo XIX v. [Das Gewohnheitsrecht des russischen Leibeigenschaftsdorfes im 18. und Anfang des 19. Jahrhunderts], Moskau 1984; *Marina M. Gromyko*, Tradicion-

sondern Historiker. In erster Linie interessierten sie sich für die sozialen und soziokulturellen Aspekte des Gewohnheitsrechts.

Seit den 1990er Jahren kann man bereits von einer „Renaissance“ der Studien in diesem Bereich sprechen. Besonders wichtig ist eine ausführliche Edition der Materialien aus dem „Ethnographischen Büro“ des Fürsten Wjatscheslaw Tenischew (1843–1903), das 1897 bis 1901 in St. Petersburg wirkte und eine große Datenmenge zu den Volksgewohnheiten sammelte. Das Archiv des Büros befindet sich jetzt im Russischen Ethnographischen Museum in St. Petersburg, wo die ersten Bände inzwischen ediert sind.[8] Sie enthalten zahlreiche interessante Angaben zum Thema.

Heutzutage ist wohl eine Belebung der relevanten Forschung zu konstatieren, was auch in den Themen der Inaugural-Dissertationen und Habilitationsschriften zu beobachten ist.[9] Unter den modernen Arbeiten, in denen das russische Gewohn-

---

nye normy povedenija i formy obščenija russkich krest'jan XIX v. [Die traditionellen Verhaltensnormen und Kommunikationsformen russischer Bauern des 19. Jahrhunderts], Moskau 1986.

[8] Byt velikorusskich krest'jan-zemlepašcev. Opisanie materialov Ėtnografičeskogo bjuro kn. V.N. Teniševa. (Na primere Vladimirskoj gubernii) [*Boris M. Firsov/I.G. Kiselëva* (Hg.), Lebenshaltung der russischen Bauern-Ackersleute. Beschreibung der Materialien des Ethnographischen Büros des Fürsten W.N. Tenischew (Am Beispiel des Wladimirer Gouvernement)], St. Petersburg 1993; Russkie krest'jane. Žizn'. Byt. Nravy. Materialy „Ėtnografičeskogo bjuro“ knjazja V.N. Teniševa [*Izabella I. Šangina u.a.* (Hg.), Russische Bauern. Leben. Lebenshaltung. Sitten. Materialien des „Ethnographischen Büros“ des Fürsten W.N. Tenischew], St. Petersburg, Bd. 1 (Die Gouvernements Kostroma und Twer, 2004); Bd. 2 (Gouvernement Jaroslawl, Tl. 1–2, 2006); Bd. 3 (Gouvernement Kaluga, 2005); Bd. 4 (Gouvernement Nishni Nowgorod, 2006); Bd. 5 (Gouvernement Wologda, Tl. 1–4, 2007–2008); Bd. 6 (Die Gouvernements Kursk, Moskau, Olonez, Pleskau, Sankt Petersburg und Tula, 2008); Bd. 7 (Gouvernement Nowgorod, Tl. 1–4, 2009–2011).

[9] *Ludmila V. Vorob'ëva,* Poreformennaja russkaja krest'janskaja obščina kak juridičeskij fenomen, 1861–1905 gg. [Die russische Bauerngemeinde nach der (Bauern)reform als Rechtsphänomen, 1961–1905], Autorreferat der historischen Inaug.-Diss., Moskau, 2002; *Sergej Ju. Krasnov,* Obyčno-pravovoe regulirovanie imuščestvennych otnošenij u donskich kazakov vo vtoroj polovine XIX veka: istoriko-pravovoj aspekt [Die gewohnheitsrechtliche Regelung der Vermögensbeziehungen bei den Don-Kosaken in der zweiten Hälfte des 19. Jahrhunderts: Der rechtsgeschichtliche Aspekt], Autorreferat der juristischen Inaug.-Diss.,Wolgograd 2003; *Andrej V. Kirilin,* Krest'janskoe obyčnoe pravo v volostnych sudach i posudarstvennaja politika poreformennoj Rossii [Das bäuerliche Gewohnheitsrecht in den Wolostgerichten und die Staatspolitik Rußlands nach der (Bauern)reform], Autorreferat der historischen Inaug.-Diss., Moskau, 2004; *Leonid Zemcov*, Pravovye osnovy i organizacija dejatel'nosti volostnych sudov v poreformennoj Rossii (60–je – 80–je gg. XIX v.) [Rechtsgrundlagen und Organisation der Tätigkeit der Wolostgerichte in Rußland nach der (Bauern)reform (60er bis 80er Jahre des 19. Jahrhunderts)], Autorreferat der historischen Inaug.-Diss., Lipezk 2004; *Jelena I. Kuksenko,* Ėvolucija obyčnogo prava donskich kazakov, XVI–načalo XIX vv. [Evolution des Gewohnheitsrechts der Don-Kosaken, 16.–Anfang des 19. Jahrhunderts], Autorreferat der juristischen Inaug.-Diss., Rostow am Don 2005; *Anastasija G. Alborova,* Obyčnoe pravo rossijskich krest'jan vo vtoroj polovine XIX veka [Das Gewohnheitsrecht der russischen Bauern in der zweiten Hälfte des 19. Jahrhunderts], Autor-

heitsrecht erfolgreich erforscht wird, sind die Studien des Tambower Historikers Wladimir Besgin hervorzuheben. Er analysiert die wichtigsten Rechtsinstitute des Gewohnheitsrechts vor dem weiten Hintergrund des Bauernlebens vom 19. bis zum Anfang des 20. Jahrhunderts. Er war einer der ersten neueren russischen Wissenschaftler, die u.a. die große Menge der Archivalien wieder erschlossen. Zu seinen Verdiensten zählt auch der Versuch, das bäuerliche Recht auch im Hochschulunterricht darzustellen.[10]

Etliche Forschungen zum Thema wurden auch von den ausländischen Autoren vorbereitet.[11] Ihre Arbeiten bilden eine wichtige Ergänzung der vorangehenden Studien.

Ende der 1990er Jahre versuchte der moderne russische Sozialhistoriker Boris Mironow, das frühere Schrifttum zusammenzufassen und etliche Thesen über den ganzen Problemkomplex Gewohnheitsrecht vs. geschriebenes Recht aufzustellen. Er weist auf drei Besonderheiten der für das 18. und 19. Jahrhundert typischen Situation hin. Erstens: Seit dem 18. Jahrhundert war die Gesellschaft ständisch organisiert, jeder Stand bekam sein eigenes Gerichtssystem, früher jedoch waren die Bauern und die Bürger (*meščanstvo*) den gemeinsamen Rechtsnormen unter-

---

referat der juristischen Inaug.-Diss., Nishni Nowgorod 2007; *Tat'jana V. Šatkovskaja,* Obyčnoe pravo rossijskich krest'jan vtoroj poloviny XIX–načala XIX veka: istoriko-pravovoj aspekt [Das Gewohnheitsrecht der russischen Bauern in der zweiten Hälfte des 19. bis Anfang des 20. Jahrhunderts: Der rechtsgeschichtliche Aspekt], Autorreferat der juristischen Habilitationsschrift, Rostow am Don 2009.

10 *Vladimir B. Bezgin,* Obyčnoe pravo russkoj derevni (vtoraja polovina XIX – načalo XX vv.) [Das Gewohnheitsrecht des russischen Dorfes (zweite Hälfte des 19.–Anfang des 20. Jahrhunderts)], Tambow 2000; *ders.,* Krest'janskaja povsednevnost' (tradicii konca XIX – načala XIX veka) [Der Bauernalltag (die Traditionen am Ende des 19. und am Anfang des 20. Jahrhunderts)], Tambow 2004; *ders.,* Pravovye obyčai i pravosudie russkich krest'jan vtoroj poloviny XIX–načala XX vv. [Die Rechtsgewohnheiten und Rechtspflege der russischen Bauern in der zweiten Hälfte des 19. bis zum Anfang des 20. Jahrhunderts], Tambow 2012.

11 *Moshe Lewin,* Customary Law and Russian Rural Society in the Post-Reform, Russian Review, Vol. 44, No. 1 (Jan. 1985), pp. 1–19; *Christine D. Worobec*, Reflections on Customary Law and Post-Reform Peasant Russia, a.a.O., pp. 21–25; *Michael Confino*, Russian Customary Law and the Study of Peasant, a.a.O., pp. 35–43; *Stephen P. Frank,* Popular Justice, Community and Culture among the Russian Peasantry, 1870–1900, Russian Review, Vol. 46, No. 3 (Jul. 1987), pp. 239–265; *Corinne Gaudin*, Les zemskie načal'niki au village: Coutumes administratives et culture paysanne en Russie, 1889–1914, Cahiers du Monde russe, Vol. 36, No. 3 (Jul.–Sep. 1995), pp. 249–272; *Cathy A. Frierson*, 'I Must Always Answer to the Law...' Rules and Responses in the Reformed Volost Court, The Slavonic and East European Review, Vol. 75, No. 2 (Apr. 1997), pp. 308–334; *Jane Burbank*, Insult and Punishment in Rural Courts: The Elaboration of Civility in Late Imperial Russia, Études rurales, No. 149/150, Justice et sociétés rurales (Jan. –Jun. 1999), pp. 147–171; *dies.,* Russian Peasants Go to Court: Legal Culture in the Countryside, 1905–1917, Bloomington/Indianapolis, 2004; *Gareth Popkins*, Code versus Custom? Norms and Tactics in Peasant Volost Court Appeals, 1889–1917, Russian Review, Vol. 59, No. 3 (Jul. 2000), pp. 408–424.

stellt gewesen. Später wurde die Stadt zum Geltungsbereich des geschriebenen Rechts, und das Dorf blieb eine Zone, in der das Gewohnheitsrecht herrschte. Zweitens: Die Erweiterung der neueren Rechtsideen auf das Dorf wurde dadurch gehemmt, daß die Bauern wenig alphabetisiert waren und vielen Vorurteilen sowie dem Aberglauben unterlagen. Drittens: Die Kronbehörden versuchten, die rechtliche Sonderstellung der Bauern gezielt zu konservieren, um den Einfluß der Stadt auf das Dorf zu beschränken und die Ordnung auf dem flachen Lande durch die Erhaltung der traditionellen Institute des Gewohnheitsrechts (wie etwa die Neuverteilungsgemeinde, die Gemeindegarantie u.a.) zu kontrollieren. Nach 1861 wurde diese Politik fortgesetzt; die Risiken, die eine solche Absonderung der Bauern von der allgemeinen Rechtsordnung enthielt, traten erst Anfang des 20. Jahrhunderts an das Tageslicht, als die stolypinsche Agrarreform die wesentlichsten Überreste des Gewohnheitsrechts im Dorfe beseitigte.[12]

Es ist notwendig, die Erforschung des Gewohnheitsrechts fortzusetzen, weil sie viele Besonderheiten in der Geschichte der Völker Rußlands und in der Entwicklung des Landes erklärt.

II. Die Sammlung von Ponomarjow und ihre Bedeutung

Zu den vielversprechenden Quellen über die Geschichte des Gewohnheitsrechts der Russen und etlicher anderer Völker des Kaiserreiches gehört eine interessante Archivsammlung, die bis heute weithin unerschlossen bleibt. Es handelt sich um die reiche Sammlung zum Thema, die im Archiv der Russischen Geographischen Gesellschaft in St. Petersburg aufbewahrt wird. Diese Aufzeichnungen wurden von Ssemjon Michajlowitsch Ponomarjow, einem begabten Forscher der Volksgewohnheiten und Folklore, angelegt. Sein Leben war kurz: Er starb 1889, als er etwa 24 Jahre alt war. Trotzdem ist es ihm gelungen, eine große Menge der Materialien über das Volksleben und die geistige Kultur russischer Bauern vor und nach der Aufhebung der Leibeigenschaft zu sammeln. Er hat etwa 150 Orte im Samarer, Orenburger und Ufaer Gouvernement besucht. Weitere Daten sammelte er im Übersiedlermittelpunkt in Orenburg nach den Angaben der Bauern, die über Orenburg nach Ufa und Sibirien fuhren. Er hat nach diesen Angaben 19 Artikel und viele kleine Zeitungsmiszellen geschrieben, aber der Hauptteil der Materialien blieb unediert.

Die in Frage kommende Sammlung besteht meistens aus Heften, deren Format im allgemeinen dem Format der heutigen Schulhefte ähnelt. Darin verfaßte Ponomarjow auf einer Seite jedes Blattes, meistens mit einem Bleistift, seine Eintragungen, die gewöhnlich gut lesbar sind. Teilweise wurden sie thematisch grup-

---

[12] S. hierzu *Boris N. Mironov,* Social'naja istorija Rossii periode imperii (XVIII – načalo XX v.). Genezis ličnosti, demokratičeskoj sem'i, graždanskogo obščestva i pravovogo gosudarstva [Die Sozialgeschichte Rußlands: Die Epoche des Kaiserreiches. Die Genese der Persönlichkeit, der demokratischen Familie, der Zivilgesellschaft und des Rechtsstaates], Bd. 2, Sankt Petersburg 1999, S. 67, 76 f.

piert und betitelt; trotzdem sind etliche interessante Fragmente zum Thema auch an unerwarteten Stellen auffindbar. Die Stücke rechtlichen Inhalts sind mit den Angaben über die Bräuche und Sitten einzelner Gegenden des Kaiserreiches hier und da gemischt.

Kurz nach Ponomarjows Tod geriet sein Nachlaß in das wissenschaftliche Archiv der Geographischen Gesellschaft (1890). Leider blieb er lange unerforscht. Seit den 1950er Jahren wurde diese Sammlung von der Leningrader Philologin Pelageja Schirjaewa (1903–1986) untersucht. Sie hat einen biographischen Beitrag mit der ersten Übersicht des Nachlasses veröffentlicht.[13] Um das Jahr 1981 hat sie eine dreibändige Sammlung der erwähnten Materialien aus dem Bestand Ponomarjows erstellt, die durch das Institut für russische Literatur der Akademie der Wissenschaften der UdSSR publiziert werden sollte.[14] Dieses Vorhaben wurde indessen nicht veröffentlicht. Die vollständig fertige Arbeit blieb „wegen Überlastung des Vorrats" des Verlagshauses „Nauka" („Wissenschaft") unveröffentlicht.[15] Später wurde die Publikation durch den Tod der Forscherin verhindert.[16]

Aus dem Exposé des künftigen Buchs, das in demselben Bestand des Archivs erhalten ist, wird ersichtlich, daß die Ausgabe in erster Linie für die Volkslieder und die sonstigen Stücke der Folklore (insgesamt über 1600 Nummern) bestimmt war. Es war auch geplant, etliche Eintragungen über die Volksgewohnheiten und die Justiz der Gutsbesitzer im dritten Bande zu veröffentlichen.[17] Diese Materialien aber erschöpfen die ganze Menge der Ponomariow'schen Angaben über das Gewohnheitsrecht der Russen und der anderen Völker Rußlands nicht.

---

[13] *Pelageja G. Širjaeva*, Semën Michajlovič Ponomarëv (iz istorii russkogo fol'klora XIX veka) [Ssemjon Michajlowitsch Ponomarjow (aus der Geschichte der russischen Folklore des 19. Jahrhunderts)], in: Russkij fol'klor [Russische Folklore], 4. Lief., Moskau/Leningrad 1959, S. 174–195; *dies.*, Fol'klorno-ėtnografičeskoe sobranie Semëna Michajloviča Ponomarëva [Folklore- und volkskundliche Sammlung von Ssemjon Michajlowitsch Ponomarjow], in: Izvestija Vsesojuznogo geografičeskogo obščestva [Nachrichten der Geographischen Allunionsgesellschaft], Bd. 94, 1962, Nr. 4, S. 343–347.

[14] Das Buch bekam den Titel: „Fol'klorno-ėtnografičeskie materialy, sobrannye S.M. Ponomarëvym ot krest'jan, jechavšich v 1880–je gody čerez Orenburg v Ufu i Sibir'. V 3–ch tt. Vstup. st., sost., primečanija *P.G. Širjaevoj*, otv. red. A.A. Gorelov" [Folklore- und volkskundliche Materialien, die von S.M. Ponomarjow von den Bauern, die in den 1880er Jahren über Orenburg nach Ufa und Sibirien fuhren, gesammelt wurden. In 3 Bänden; Einleitung, Zusammenstellung und Anmerkungen von *P.G. Schirjaewa*, verantwortlicher Hg. A.A. Gorelow], Leningrad 1981 (Archiv der Russischen Geographischen Gesellschaft (St. Petersburg), Bestand 12 (S.M. Ponomarjow), Findbuch 2. Akte 31, Bl. 12).

[15] A.a.O., Bl. 1.

[16] Der Nachlaß P.G. Schirjaewas war dem Institut für russische Literatur der Akademie der Wissenschaften der UdSSR übergeben worden und wird dort bis heute verwahrt (freundliche Mitteilung des Sohnes der Forscherin, Herr Albert Schirjaew).

[17] Archiv der Russischen Geographischen Gesellschaft (St. Petersburg), Bestand 12 (S.M. Ponomarjow), Findbuch 2. Akte 31, Bl. 14.

Im vorliegenden Beitrage werden etliche Materialien dargestellt, die sich auf Dorfjustiz und Rechtsbewußtsein des russischen Bauerntums nach der Aufhebung der Leibeigenschaft (1861) beziehen. In seinen Aufzeichnungen konzentrierte sich Ponomarjow auf das materielle Recht,[18] die prozeßrechtlichen Eintragungen sind nicht zu zahlreich. Trotzdem umfaßt seine Sammlung auch interessante Daten zu den prozessualen Aspekten des Bauernrechtslebens sowie etliche Nebenfragen, die mit der Rechtspsychologie jener Zeit verbunden sind. Die angeführten Angaben sind insofern besonders wertvoll, weil sie meistens über die informelle Dorfjustiz des 19. Jahrhunderts berichten, die in den amtlichen Papieren selten auffindbar ist.

Es wurden von mir sieben Akten (Hefte) des Bestandes ausgewertet; am Ende des Beitrags befindet sich eine ausführliche Liste dazu. Im Folgenden werden die Archivalien grundsätzlich mit Aktennummer und Blatt zitiert. Fast alle Fragmente sind undatiert. Die relevanten Ortschaften werden meistens bei den jeweiligen Eintragungen angedeutet; in wenigen Ausnahmefällen werden sie von mir unter Berücksichtigung der damaligen administrativen Gliederung (Ort – falls vorhanden –, Kreis und Gouvernement oder Gebiet) ergänzt.

III. Gerichtsverfassung und Dorfjustiz (allgemeines)

In den Ponomarjow'schen Eintragungen sind etliche Angaben allgemeinen Inhalts erhalten, welche die örtlichen Gewohnheiten und Vorstellungen der Bauern über die Gerichtsverfassung darstellen. Ein Dorfgericht wurde als „Bastschuhgericht" bezeichnet und dem Wolostgericht gegenüberstellt. Ein Vorteil des ersteren wurde darin gesehen, daß es so oft tagte, wie es notwendig war, das letztere hatte dagegen nur einmal im Monat eine Sitzung. Ein „Bastschuhgericht" bestand aus dem Dorfältesten und den „alten Leuten" (3:4–5, Studenez, Kr. Sadonsk, Gouv. Woronesh) oder aus dem Dorfältesten und 5 „hurtigen Leuten", die als „Zeugen" gewählt worden waren; sie richteten im Haus des Klägers oder des Beklagten (3:5–6, Mischutino, Kr. Schazk, Gouv. Tambow).

---

[18] Die materiellrechtlichen Stellen wurden von mir früher teilweise in folgenden Publikationen untersucht: *Alexander L. Rogačevskij*, K istorii obyčnogo prava v Rossii a XIX v. (iz archiva Russkogo Geografičeskogo obščestva). I. Kljatva i božba [Zur Geschichte des Gewohnheitsrechts in Rußland im 19. Jahrhundert (aus dem Archiv der Russischen Geographischen Gesellschaft), I. Eid und Schwur], in: Juridičeskaja mysl' [Juristisches Denken] 2001, Nr. 3, S. 12–16; II. Zaščita česti i dostoinstva [Schutz der Ehre und Würde], in: a.a.O., 2002, Nr. 2, S. 5–8; III. Imuščestvennye posjagatel'stva [Vermögenseingriffe], in: a.a.O., 2003, Nr. 3, S. 11–24; Ėtnografičeskie svedenija o jevrejach v čerte osedlosti i Orenburž'je vo vtoroj polovine XIX v. (Iz archiva Russkogo Geografičeskogo obščestva) [Die ethnographischen Angaben über die Juden innerhalb der Ansiedlungsgrenze und im Orenburgischen in der zweiten Hälfte des 19. Jahrhunderts (aus dem Archive der Russischen Geographischen Gesellschaft)], in: Jevrejskij muzej. Sbornik statej [*Walerij A. Dymschiz/Viktor Je. Kelner* (Hg.), Jüdisches Museum. Ein Sammelband], St. Petersburg 2004, S. 203–212.

Im Fall eines nichtvorhandenen oder abwesenden Dorfältesten war es möglich, die Nachbarn als Richter einzuladen; dafür wurde ihnen aufgetischt (3:7, Troizkoe, Kr. Tschern', Gouv. Tula).[19] Eine Bewirtung des Dorfältesten mit Wein und Wodka und die Schenkung des Geldes und der Handtücher vor der Gerichtssitzung war auch üblich (3:10, Schenkursk, Gouv. Archangelsk).

Ein 50jähriger Greis durfte weder im Gericht sitzen noch an der Gemeindeversammlung teilnehmen (im letzteren Fall nahm seine Frau an der Versammlung teil). Sogar als Zeuge durfte er nicht auftreten und die Papiere unterzeichnen (2:174, Studenez, Kr. Sadonsk, Gouv. Woronesh). Nach anderen Angaben hatte ein Mann im Alter von 25 bis 60 Jahren das Recht, an der Dorfversammlung teilzunehmen (2:176, Kr. Lipezk, Gouv. Tambow).

Im Verfahren der Dorfgerichte unterschied man die geringfügigen Zivil- und Strafsachen kaum; gleiches gilt für die Trennung der Voruntersuchung und der eigentlichen Beweisaufnahme. Wenn keine Zeugen des Geschehens vorhanden waren, lief der Geschädigte in das allernächste Haus, um sein Unglück zu melden (3:5, Kr. Tschern', Gouv. Tula). Ein Verleumder wurde bestraft: mit Geldstrafe und Wodka für die Gemeinde (7:12, Lossina, Kr. Lipezk, Gouv. Tambow), mit Ruten, härter als ein echter Dieb (3:3, Lubimowka, Kr. Bogorodizk, Gouv. Tula) oder gar mit derselben Strafe, die dem Angeschuldigten zukam, zumindest jedoch mit Prügelstrafe, und danach war er „wie ein Dieb" bemakelt (7:12–13, Chornowka, Kr. Mglin, Gouv. Tschernigow).

Wegen Nichtvorhandenseins von Räumen für die Verhafteten wurden diese in den Bauernhäusern eingesperrt und bewacht. Die Speisen wurden ihnen aus dem Haus oder von dem Zehntmann geliefert; im letzten Falle mußten sie 3 Kopeken für jeden Laib Brot zahlen (3:1, Lossina, Kr. Lipezk, Gouv. Tambow).

IV. Gericht oder Selbstjustiz?

In etlichen Eintragungen wird das Dorfgericht auch als „öffentliche Selbstjustiz" bezeichnet. Es wird dabei darauf hingewiesen, daß die Bauern mit der Zeit dazu neigten, den Verurteilten nicht zu schlagen, wie es ursprünglich üblich gewesen war, sondern Geld von ihm einzutreiben. Im Fall schwererer Verbrechen wurden die Verbrecher jedoch nach Sibirien verbannt (6:39, Ssemjonowka, Kr. Isjum, Gouv. Charkow).

Man war der Ansicht, ein ordentliches Gerichtsverfahren sei keineswegs in allen Fällen notwendig. Beispielsweise unterlag ein Holzdieb oft der Selbstjustiz; er wurde mit der Hetzpeitsche geschlagen (6:27, Gouv. Orenburg). Der Pferdediebstahl stach besonders hervor, weil der Verlust des Arbeitsviehs das Überleben

---

[19] Es wurde auch anerkannt, daß die Nachbarn das Recht hatten, ein Zivilverfahren zu initiieren. Z.B. wenn ein Vater die Kühe der verstorbenen Frau vertrank, durften die Nachbarn sich „für Hab und Gut der Dirne" ins Zeug legen (3:156, Lossina, Kr. Lipezk, Gouv. Tambow).

der Bauernfamilie bedrohte. In solchen Fällen wurden die erwischten oder vermeintlichen Pferdediebe an Ort und Stelle häufig ohne weiteres getötet.[20]

Die Strafgewalt des Dorfgerichts reichte manchmal weiter als die des Wolostgerichts, da das erstere die durch Gesetz vorgeschriebenen Strafen überschritt: die Bauern konnten z.B. bei leichten Vergehen mit 50 Ruten züchtigen (7:20, Tschern', Gouv. Tula). Die „uneigennützige Sünde" (ohne Gewinn für den Verbrecher) strafte man dabei härter als eine „Sünde mit Absicht"; einem Diebstahl für sich oder für ein Pferd wurde geringere Gefahr zugeschrieben (6:120, Kr. Schenkursk, Gouv. Archangelsk). Einen Diebstahl geringwertiger Sachen mußte man andererseits strenger und härter strafen, da eine solche Tat als eine Vorstufe zu den schwereren Verbrechen angesehen wurde (6:62, Bogoslowka, Kr. Tschern', Gouv. Tula).

Man sah in der Verfolgung der Verbrecher in erster Linie eine Sache der Verwandten des Opfers. Die Gründe für die Einleitung eines Verfahrens waren durch den Charakter des Verbrechens bedingt und wurden durch Massenpsychologie und Aberglauben entscheidend geprägt. Eine Einmischung der Behörden war in den Augen der Beteiligten (sogar bei schweren Strafen) gar nicht immer zulässig. Zwei Beispiele: Ein Totschlag eines Sohnes durch die Eltern, „besonders für eine wahre Sache" [*„osobenno za pravdu"*[21]], wurde als rechtmäßig eingestuft (14:58, Ssaposhok, Gouv. Rjasan). Ein Bauer tötete eine Frau, die eine „Puppe" (d.h. eine anthropomorphe Figur zwecks Zauberei) auf seinem Landstrich gemacht hatte. Danach vergingen zehn Jahre; den Behörden aber wurde nichts mitgeteilt, weil der Totschlag sich als „gerecht" erwiesen hatte (14:75, Paporotka, Kr. Bogorodizk, Gouv. Tula).

Auch in den Fällen, die unstrittig als Verbrechen galten, strebten die Parteien häufig an, ohne Beteiligung eines staatlichen Gerichts auszukommen. Die Erwägungen dafür waren unterschiedlicher Natur. So war in Sterlitamak (Gouv. Ufa) eine Witwe getötet worden, die eine Tochter hinterließ. Die Waise vereinbarte mit den Totschlägern, daß diese sie künftig unterhalten und anzuvermählen hatten (14:62). Die Verwandten versuchten, eine Versöhnung im Falle des Totschlages (als Sonderfall ist bei Ponomarjow auch die Vergiftung erwähnt) mit Geld zu erreichen, um kein „großes Gericht" anzufangen (14:62–63, Kr. Arsamas, Gouv. Nishni Nowgorod; besonders auch Uralgebiet). Eine solche Versöhnung war

---

[20] Eine Reihe ausdrucksvoller Zeugnisse aus derselben Sammlung wurde von mir früher in genannten Publikationen angeführt: *Alexander L. Rogačevskij*, K istorii obyčnogo prava (oben Fn. 18), Teil III.

[21] Das Konzept „Pravda" (buchstäblich „Wahrheit") gehörte zu den Schlüsselkonzepten der russischen Rechtspsychologie und Volkskultur. S. hierfür *Christoph Schmidt*, Von Gottes und Rechts wegen oder zu einigen Charakteristika von Gerechtigkeit in Rußland. Ein Kommentar, Jahrbücher für Geschichte Osteuropas, N.F. Bd. 53. H. 4 (2005), S. 565–568; *Irina V. Paščenko*, Ėvolucija kategorij russkogo srednevekovogo pravosoznanija [Evolution der Kategorien des russischen mittelalterlichen Rechtsbewußtseins], Autorreferat einer Inaug.-Diss., Rostow am Don 2008.

möglich, wenn der Mörder die Witwe des getöteten Ehemannes mit einem Haus ausstattete. Dabei versuchte der Totschläger, vor allem den Pfaffen zu beschenken[22] (14:63, Tumanowo, Kr. Arsamas, Gouv. Nishni Nowgorod).

Beim Streben, ohne Gerichtsverfahren auszukommen, konnten nicht nur praktische, sondern auch superstitiöse Gründe eine Rolle spielen: Ein Junge tötete ein altgläubiges Mädchen. Die Altgläubigen wollten Rache an dem „Sibierer" üben. Das ermordete Mädchen erschien jedoch ihrer Mutter im Traum und bat, dem Totschläger zu verzeihen. Sie erklärte, daß das vieljährige Verfahren sie im Jenseits gequält habe. Die Mutter kam mit ihrer Verzeihung zum Totschläger und brachte Nüsse als Mitbringsel. Als sie der Mutter des Mörders erklärte, wer sie war, wurde ihre Gesprächspartnerin ohnmächtig. Die Besucherin und der Mörder haben einander niedergeworfen und geküßt (7:29–30, Kuragino, Kr. Gorodischtsche, Gouv. Pensa).

Die Einmischung der Staatsbehörden und somit die Kompetenzabgrenzung des (inoffiziellen) Dorfgerichts und des Wolostgerichts wurde wohl auch durch die Frequenz der Delinquenz bestimmt: „Zwei Übeltaten verzeiht man, für die dritte ins Gefängnis" (3:2, Kr. Jelez, Gouv. Orjol).

Auch im Fall eines staatlichen Verfahrens forderten die Prozeßteilnehmer weder Schadensersatz noch Strafe, sondern die Versöhnung der Parteien, was mitunter auch von dem (An)kläger anerkannt wurde. Gewöhnlich diente das gemeinsame Zechen zur Versöhnung. Wenn eine Gemeindeversammlung als Gericht fungierte, schenkte der Angeklagte Wodka aus und damit war die Sache zu Ende. Wenn er kein Geld hatte, wurde ihm befohlen, Stiefel, Kleidung oder Vieh zu verkaufen und ein Viertel bis zwei Eimer (also etwa drei bis 24 Liter) Wodka zu schenken. „Die Gemeinde verfolgt nur den *Frieden*, um sich zu versöhnen; die Gemeinde braucht Frieden, und der Dieb trinkt, und der Beleidigte trinkt" (15:46–47, Kr. Jaransk, Gouv. Wjatka). Diese Gewohnheit war in vielen Territorien des Russischen Kaiserreiches üblich: Ponomarjow erwähnt in diesem Zusammenhang auch das Orenburger Gouvernement, den Sterlitamaker Kreis des Ufaer Gouvernements, das Dongebiet. Überall gab es Ankäufer für die genannten Sachen (15:46).[23] Manchmal zahlte in einer solchen Situation ein reicher Mann für den Wein; am nächsten Tag nahm er im Haus des Bestraften eine Sache, die für diesen unentbehrlich war (wie etwa ein Joch oder einen Rollwagen) und die er bis zur Bezahlung bei sich zurückbehielt (15:47, Bujez, Kr. Jepifan', Gouv. Tula). Die obsiegende Partei schenkte auch ein Viertel Wodka für die unterliegende Partei, die letztere schenkte

[22] Ponomarjow verweist auch darauf, daß es im Voruralgebiet üblich war, den Verwandten [des Getöteten] für das Verschweigen 50 Kopeken bis 25 Rubel zu zahlen (14:63).

[23] Die Verteilung der relevanten Strafsumme wurde in etlichen Gegenden deutlicher bestimmt. So in Bogoslowka (Kr. Tschern', Gouv. Tula): Wenn eine Geldstrafe entrichtet wurde, bekam der Geschädigte ein Drittel davon, die Restsumme wurde vom Gericht der alten Leute vertrunken (3:2).

ebenso „einen kleinen Teil“, und die beiden tranken (3:10, Troizkoe, Kr. Tschern’, Gouv. Tula). Bei jeder Versöhnung im Dorfgericht verbeugten der Kläger und der Beklagte sich tief und küßten einander (3:5, Studenez, Kr. Sadonsk, Gouv. Woronesh).

V. Die Beweismittel

Das Beweismittelsystem, das im Bauernrechtsleben üblich war, wird in der untersuchten Sammlung ungleichmäßig beleuchtet. Teilweise sind solche Beweismittel rational begründet, teilweise vom Aberglauben geprägt. Von den gewöhnlichen Prozeduren wie etwa Haussuchung, Verhör des Tatverdächtigen und der Zeugen und ähnliche Verfahrensweisen ist selten die Rede. Ponomarjow schreibt, daß es als zulässig galt, zum „gesichteten“ Dieb zwecks Haussuchung direkt zu gehen; trotzdem begann man das Suchen gewöhnlich vom dritten Haus davor (2:4, Kr. Sadonsk, Gouv. Woronesh). Die Rolle der Zeugen wird eher beiläufig reflektiert. So betont Ponomarjow die Bedeutung des Zeugenbeweises beim Streit um Vieh. Im Vorverkaufsvertrag mußte der Zeuge nicht nur das Geschäft im eventuellen Gerichtsprozeß beweisen; als Nachbar sollte er beobachten, daß das Vieh keinem Dritten unter Übergehung des ersten Käufers verkauft wird. Mißlang die Überwachung, mußte er selbst im Gericht als Mitschuldiger eines Verbrechers Rede und Antwort stehen und wurde durch Verhaftung bestraft (21:48–49, Kr. Lipezk, Gouv. Tambow). Manchenorts geschah eine originelle Interpretation der Verjährung: Solange die Zeugen das Geschehen im Gedächtnis behielten, trat keine Verjährung ein; vergaßen sie das Geschehen, wurde das Verfahren wegen Verjährung eingestellt (3:9, Kr. Tschern’, Gouv. Tula).

Es wird auch ein altertümliches Verfahren, und zwar die sog. allgemeine Umfrage (*poval’nyj obysk*) beschrieben, die bei Strafsachen üblich war. Erweckte jemand einen Verdacht, begann das Gericht etwa zehn Häuser davor die Umfrage, zum Haus des Verdächtigen allmählich heranrückend. „Dabei“ (d.h. neben seinem Hause) stand jemand und „achtete“. Danach ergriff man den Tatverdächtigen und schlug ihn manchmal. Die Prügel wurden jedoch eher als eine Vorgehensweise der „Dummköpfe“ betrachtet; der kluge Mann mußte den Verbrecher mit gesetzlichen Mitteln verfolgen (2:4–5, Kr. Semljansk, Gouv. Woronesh).

Manchmal werden weitere rational begründete Beweismittel erwähnt. Ponomarjow berichtet z.B. über die weitverbreitete Gewohnheit, die Muttermilch bei sämtlichen Frauen des Dorfes zu untersuchen, wenn eine Leiche eines kleinen Kindes aufgefunden wird (2:42–45, Kr. Schenkursk; Rostow; Olechino, Kr. Totma, u.a.).

Unter den Beweismitteln ist auch eine psychologische Probe des Tatverdächtigen aufzufinden. Dem mutmaßlichen Mörder wurde ein Säbel angeboten: ist er schuldig, wird er sich bis zum Blut verwunden, da seine Hände zittern; der Unschuldige jedoch wird sein Blut nicht vergießen (2:45–46, Nowaja Leguschtschewka, Kubangebiet). In etlichen Genossenschaften der Handwerker wurden den

Mitgliedern bei Diebstahl Binsenstengel angeboten und befohlen, in einer Stunde wiederzukommen. Man versprach, daß bei dem Diebe der Stengel sich verlängern würde. Als der Dieb ankam, war sein Stengel abgeknabbert (2:64, Donezbezirk, Gebiet des Don-Kosakenheeres). Wenn man einen Dieb suchte, schrie man: „Hände aufheben!“. Alle hoben ihre Hände, danach fragte man: „Dieb, hast Du auch aufgehoben?“. Der Dieb antwortete, „Ich habe auch aufgehoben“ und dadurch verriet er sich (2:64, Dongebiet). Fand man eine Leiche, befahl man allen Dorfbewohnern, sie zu überschreiten. Verweigerte jemand dies zu tun oder zitterte er, wurde er für schuldig befunden (2:47, Uschika, Kr. Mglin, Gouv. Tschernigow; Schenkursk, Gouv. Archangelsk).

Ein weitverbreitetes Mittel, Verbrecher aufzufinden, war die Wahrsagerei. Die Kunstgriffe waren dabei sehr unterschiedlich. Gewöhnlich war es die Sache einer Wahrsagerin, die dafür neun Scherben (2:73, Kr. Schazk, Gouv. Tambow), Spielkarten (2:74, Teteri, Kr. Maloarchangelsk, Gouv. Orjol), Garnspindel (2:71, Kr. Sadonsk, Gouv. Woronesh) oder Spiegel (2:74–75, Kr. Arsamas, Gouv. Nishni Nowgorod) benutzte. In Lossina (Kr. Lipezk, Gouv. Tambow) wurde folgende „Methode“ praktiziert: Suchte man einen Dieb, nahm die Wahrsagerin ein Tuch, dessen vier Ecken in ihrer Faust zusammengeballt waren. Sie bat die Versuchspersonen (worunter offensichtlich ein Verdächtiger war), die Ecken herauszuziehen. Wer die kürzere Ecke erhielt, wurde als schuldig betrachtet, da er „kürzer“ zur Schuld war. Dann ging man zur Sicherheit zu ihm zwecks Haussuchung (2:71).

Häufig war die Wahrsagerei mit schädigender Magie verknüpft, die angeblich einen Verbrecher zu erkennen half. Es wurde z.B. empfohlen, bei Diebstahl in das Wasser zu starren. Dort sollte ein Gesicht erscheinen, das dem Diebe gehört. Stieß man in sein Auge, sollte das Auge beim Diebe ausfließen (2:77, Kr. Totma, Gouv. Wologda). Wurde ein Teil der gestohlenen Sache in die Ofenmündung eingearbeitet, sollte der Dieb eintrocknen (2:65, 2:69, Kr. Lipezk, Gouv. Tambow; Teteri, Kr. Maloarchangelsk, Gouv. Orjol). Zwecks Identifizierung der Diebe wurde auch ein Blasebalg benutzt. Ein Teil der gestohlenen Sache konnte in den Blasebalg gelegt werden; der Dieb sollte sich aufblähen (2:68–69, Samarajka, Kr. Liwny, Gouv. Orjol). Legte man den Blasebalg mit dem Fragment der Sache unter den Toten, sollte der Dieb dadurch sterben (2:68, Bogatyri, Kr. Juchnow, Gouv. Smolensk). In Lossina (Kr. Lipezk, Gouv. Tambow) glaubte man, daß die Benutzung des Blasebalgs nur dann helfen könnte, wenn der Suchende kein Dieb ist und die fremde Sache niemals verheimlichte (2:63).

Wenn Geld verschwand, legte man eine Menschensehne in den Ofen; im Feuer zog sich die Sehne zusammen und ebenso sollte der Dieb gequält werden. Dann sollte er das Geld heimlich zurückgeben (2:66, Gouvernements Pensa und Ssaratow). Ein anderes Mittel, das gestohlene Geld zurückzuerhalten, wurde im Schenkursker Kreis (Gouv. Archangelsk) praktiziert. Man legte einen Stein mit einem Köder an eine menschenleere Stelle; die Mäuse überfielen den Dieb, unter seiner Kleidung schlafend. Ermüdet sollte der Dieb das gestohlene Geld zurückgeben

(2:70). Im Archangelsker Gouvernement war es auch üblich, ein Wichtelmännchen auf einen Dieb loszulassen. Das Wichtelmännchen verursachte beim Dieb ein Reißen, das ihn bis zur Erstattung des Geldes quälen sollte (2:70–71, Ishma und Mesen, Kr. Mesen; Kr. Schenkursk).

Die Vorstellung, es existiere eine magische Verknüpfung des gestohlenen Vermögens mit dem Rest desselben, tritt in den erforschten Aufzeichnungen deutlich hervor. Wurde eine Leinwand aus der Abbleichstelle gestohlen, legte man ein Stück der verbliebenen Leinwand unter die Glocke, um dem Diebe Kopfschmerzen zu verursachen (2:70, Kr. Karatschew, Gouv. Orjol). Legt man ein Fragment der verschwundenen Sache unter den Boden, wird der Dieb unfähig, diese Stelle zu verlassen (2:67, Kasakowo, Kr. Jelez, Gouv. Orjol). Im Fall, daß kein Rest der gestohlenen Sache mehr vorhanden war, sollte es möglich sein, die nächstliegende Sache unter einen Quetschstein zu legen. Der Dieb sollte gequält werden, eintrocknen und seine Zunge unbeweglich werden (2:65, Kr. Sadonsk, Gouv. Woronesh).

Die Kunstgriffe der Verbrecher wurden zu jener Zeit manchmal als eine Art Magie betrachtet, was in der in Frage kommenden Sammlung auch belegt ist. Ponomarjow erwähnt, daß die Bauern dem Werwolf, der sich als ein Hund erwies, eine Pfote abgenommen hätten; danach suchten sie im Dorf einen Dieb ohne Hand (2:1, Tscheschujki, Kr. Mglin, Gouv. Tschernigow). Als Mittel für die Erkennung eines Werwolfes wurde Wasser empfohlen, da darin kein Wolf, sondern der Mensch sich spiegeln sollte; deswegen glaubte man, Werwölfe trinken niemals mit den echten Wölfen zusammen (2:54, Ort näher nicht angedeutet).

Beim Totschlag wurden auch magische Mittel benutzt. So bat man den mutmaßlichen Mörder, den Getöteten zu küssen; wenn auf den Lippen des Verdächtigen das Blut hervortrat, galt dies als Schuldindiz (2:46–47, Neschegowka, Kr. Mglin, Gouv. Tschernigow; 2:62, Kr. Mariupol, Gouv. Jekaterinoslaw). Es gab auch den Volksglauben, daß der Tote die Hand des Mörders bis zu dessen Geständnis festhält, nachdem der Mörder zum Händehalten aufgefordert wurde (2:46, Kr. Mglin, Gouv. Tschernigow; Chatolino, Kr. Roslawl, Gouv. Smolensk). Man glaubte, daß das Grab den Getöteten nicht annahm, d.h. die Leiche nicht verweste, bevor der Mörder überführt sei. Erst nach dem Gerichtsurteil war eine Bestattung möglich (14:73, Gouv. Orjol).

Sehr häufig benutzte man im Rechtsverfahren den Eid als Beweismittel.[24] In den Ponomarjow'schen Aufzeichnungen ist eine interessante Sammlung der Eidformeln erhalten, die unterschiedliche Aspekte der damaligen Mentalität spiegeln. Bei etlichen Eidesleistungen waren Elemente des christlichen Kultus präsent, die entweder in die Schwurformeln eingingen oder als Bestandteil des Brauchs hervortraten. Es handelte sich u.a. um Kreuz und Osterei (2:28, Kostomarowka, Kr. Tschern', Gouv. Tula), Ikonen (2:9, Lossina-Luka, Kr. Lipezk, Gouv. Tambow;

[24] S. *Tenišev*, Pravosudie (oben Fn. 2), S. 139–146; *Semën V. Pachman*, Obyčnoe graždanskoe pravo v Rossii [Das zivile Gewohnheitsrecht in Rußland], Moskau 2003, S. 344–347.

2:18, Kr. Tschaussy, Gouv. Mogiljow) oder das Glockengeläut als Begleitung der Eidesleistung (2:11, Archangelsk; 2:14, Orenburg und die umliegenden Dörfer; 2:29, Gouv. Tschernigow; Kr. Tschern', Gouv. Tula).

Häufiger jedoch trug die Eidesleistung sehr archaische, heidnisch geprägte Züge. Als wichtiges Objekt diente die Erde, was besonders bei Streitigkeiten um Boden zu beobachten war. Die Echtheit der Flurgrenzen wurde mit Eidesleistung begleitet, die im Falle des Meineides „schwarz wie nasse Erde werden" (2:17, Kr. Isjum, Gouv. Charkow). In Chornowka (Kr. Mglin, Gouv. Tschernigow) versammelten sich die Bauern dreier Dörfer, als die Flurgrenze beschädigt worden war. Einer der Bauern schnitt ein Stück Rasen ab, legte es auf seinen Kopf und machte drei tiefe Verbeugungen mit dem Rasen auf dem Kopf. Dann ging er weiter; so weit er ging, gehörte ihm der Boden. Diejenigen, die einen falschen Schwur geleistet hatten, starben in einem Jahr (2:34). Oft wurde auch das Schlucken einer Erdscholle praktiziert (2:17, Kr. Belebej, Gouv. Orenburg; 2:23–24, Sapolje, Kr. Tschaussy, Gouv. Mogiljow; 2:37, Sainsk, Kr. Menselinsk, Gouv. Archangelsk). Unter den relevanten Aufzeichnungen befindet sich eine Episode, die in Scharowka (Kr. Bogoduchow, Gouv. Charkow) stattfand. Beim Strafverfahren wegen Totschlags aßen die Bauern die Erde, einer davon verschluckte sich. Danach hat er seine Schuld eingestanden (2:62–63).

Es wurden auch etliche weitere Objekte als Elemente der Eidesleistung benutzt: ein Espenast (2:10–11, Sainsk, Kr. Menselinsk, Gouv. Archangelsk), ein trockener Stock (2:13, Kr. Kurmysch, Gouv. Simbirsk), ein Stock, der aus der Wurzel einer Eberesche geschnitten wurde, die im Wald am Ameisenhaufen wuchs (2:23, Wyssokowo, Kr. Wjatka, Gouv. Wjatka), Stücke Brot mit Salz (2:10, Ortschaft näher nicht angedeutet).

Die Bauern glaubten, daß Gott das Leben des Meineidigen verkürzt (2:34, Kr. Mglin, Gouv. Tschernigow). Im Dorf Iwanowka (Kr. Schazk, Gouv. Tambow) wurde das Urteil erst drei Tage nach der Eidesleistung vollstreckt, da binnen dieser Zeit Gott den Meineidigen strafen mußte (2:27).[25]

In einigen Gegenden war auch eine Art „Gottesgericht" zu beobachten. In unklaren Fällen wurde der gefesselte Tatverdächtige (evtl. mit dem Stein am Halse) in den Fluß geworfen; taucht er auf, ist er unschuldig, sonst wird sein Verbrechen geprüft (2:58, Kr. Orenburg, Gouv. Orenburg, 1840er und 1850er Jahre, Mordverdacht; 2:53–54, Chornowka, Kr. Mglin, Gouv. Tschernigow, Diebstahlverdacht). Ein anderes Mittel war das Einsperren in ein heißes Bad mit Kohlenmonoxyd: Der schuldige Mensch starb und der unschuldige überlebte (2:55, Chornowka, Kr. Mglin, Gouv. Tschernigow).

---

[25] Ausführlicher dazu s. auch in meinem Beitrag: *Rogačevskij*, K istorii obyčnogo prava (oben Fn. 18), Teil I.

In der Sammlung Ponomarjows wird auch die Folter erwähnt. Die Folter wurde in Rußland durch den geheimen Erlaß Katharinas II. vom 8. November 1774 abgeschafft. Kaiser Alexander I. bestätigte das Verbot am 27. September 1801. Trotzdem wurde sie im Rechtsalltag hier und da weiter praktiziert. Die gesammelten Materialien lassen vermuten, daß bei Totschlag und Diebstahl die Folter angewandt wurde. Die erwähnten Foltermittel und -arten sind unterschiedlich. Eine Folter mit Hetze war verbreitet. Man praktizierte z.B. das Aufhängen kopfunter und Brennen mit glühenden Kohlen an den Fersen (2:53, Nowossel'je, Kr. Krasnyj, Gouv. Smolensk); es wurden auch glühendheiße Eisen oder eiserne Erzeugnisse verwendet (2:54, Chornowka, Kr. Mglin, Gouv. Tschernigow; 2:59, Lubimowka, [Kr. Bogorodizk], Gouv. Tula; 2:59–60, Pronkino, Kr. Buguruslan, Gouv. Samara). Die „großen Möglichkeiten" des russischen Winters wurden ebenfalls ausgenutzt: Die Angeklagten wurden bei Kälte am Pfahl in Ketten ausgestellt (2:59, Kr. Arsamas, Gouv. Nishni Nowgorod, Praxis vor der Bauernbefreiung) oder barfuß in einem Hemd (offensichtlich im Winter) für drei Stunden. Konnte der Tatverdächtige durchhalten, war er unschuldig. In anderen Fällen wurde der Verdächtige im unbeheizten Raum für zwei Wochen eingesperrt und bekam nur ein Pfund (=409 g) Brot für diese Zeit (2:54, Chornowka, Kr. Mglin, Gouv. Tschernigow).

Unter den Quälereien erwähnt Ponomarjow auch den sog. *Tschekljak*. Die Gliedmaßen des angeblichen, aber nicht geständigen Mörders wurden hinter seinem Rücken zusammengebunden. In den dadurch gebildeten Ring wurde ein Stock durchgezogen und danach der Leib gedreht (2:60–61, Schanewa, Kr. Jaransk, Gouv. Wjatka). Etliche weitere Foltermethoden sind im Zusammenhang mit Diebstahlverdacht belegt. Es handelt sich u.a. um die Peinigung mit einem (glühenden?) Putzstock (2:60, Korotajewka, Kr. Jaransk, Gouv. Wjatka), um das Zerschneiden der Arme mit einem Messer (2:55, Gouv. Stawropol, für die Diebstahlverdächtigen genutzt), um die Ernährung mit übersalztem Essen (2:61, Kr. Semljansk, Gouv. Woronesh). In Chornowka (Kr. Mglin, Gouv. Tschernigow) gab es einen Bock, d.h. eine Karre mit Nägeln; darauf wurden die angeblichen Diebe nackt gesetzt und durch die Straßen umhergefahren, um ein Geständnis zu erpressen (2:55).

VI. Zwischenbilanz

Die angeführten Angaben erschöpfen im wesentlichen den Inhalt der Stellen, die bei Ponomarjow die prozeßrechtliche Problematik spiegeln. Das Bild des bäuerlichen Rechtsbewußtseins, das sie darstellen, scheint ambivalent zu sein. Einerseits belegen sie die Anhänglichkeit der Bauern an die traditionelle gesellschaftliche und rechtliche Ordnung des damaligen Dorfes. Ihre Ansichten sind oft archaisch und magisch geprägt. Häufig bevorzugen sie, ihre Probleme ohne Heranziehung der Kronbehörden zu lösen. Der Individualismus und die Achtung der Interessen eines Privatbesitzers, sogar seitens der Gerichtspersonen, sind eher gering entwickelt. Die Wiederherstellung des Friedens in der Gemeinde tritt wohl als das höchste Ziel hervor. Die Entschädigung für die Verluste des Betroffenen, geschweige denn die Anwendung eines abstrakten staatlichen Gesetzes, steht deshalb oft nicht im Vordergrund. Andererseits ist zu berücksichtigen, daß die Epoche, in der die relevanten Aufzeichnungen gemacht wurden, eine Lebenswende für das ganze Land war. Eben zu dieser Zeit beginnt auf dem Lande ein schmerzhafter Prozeß der zunehmenden gesellschaftlichen Spaltung, der von der Entwicklung des Eigentumsgefühls und dem allmählichen Zerfall der patriarchalischen Familienbeziehungen begleitet wurde. Außerdem waren die Träger der Rechtstradition im Dorfe überwiegend die älteren Leute, die vorangehende Generation war von der historischen Bühne noch nicht abgetreten. Deshalb sieht das Bild des bäuerlichen Rechtslebens etwas archaischer aus, als es tatsächlich der Fall war.

Alles in allem bin ich geneigt, die Meinung zu akzeptieren, daß das Gewohnheitsrecht jener Zeit als eine dynamische Synthese der Rechtsideen, Werte, Anschauungen, Institute und Beziehungen des Bauernstandes, als eine Sonderverbindung gegenüber dem „zivilisierten" Staat (der über eigene Instrumente wie Gesetzgebung und Gerichtssystem verfügte) auftritt.[26] Es scheint mir, daß die erörterten Quellen diese Ansicht stützen. Die Fortsetzung der Studien (die nun nach langer Pause wiederaufgenommen ist) läßt hoffen, daß das allgemeine Bild der russischen neuzeitlichen Rechtskultur differenzierter und detaillierter wird.

Liste der benutzten Archivalien
Archiv der Russischen Geographischen Gesellschaft (St. Petersburg)

Bestand 12 (S.M. Ponomarjow).
Findbuch 1.
(Die Hefte sind vermutlich von S.M. Ponomarjow betitelt).

Nr. 2. Haussuchung. Eidesleistung. Besichtigung einer Dirne. Folter.

Nr. 3. Gerichtsverfahren.

Nr. 6. Diebstahl.

Nr. 7. Kriminalität.

Nr. 8. Urteile der Wolost- und Kosakensiedlungsgerichte.

Nr. 14. Preisgebung [zwecks Opferbringung]. Ausspeisung und Hilfe durch die Gemeinde. Ehebruch u.a.

Nr. 15. Spitznamen. Nachbarschaft. Justiz der Gutsbesitzer. Beitreibung. Verführung.

Nr. 21. Festspiele am Tage [u.a.].

---

[26] S. *Svetlana/S. Krjukova*, Pravovaja kul'tura russkich krest'jan v Rossii XIX v.: problemy i interpretacii [Die Rechtskultur russischer Bauern in Rußland des 19. Jahrhunderts: Probleme und Interpretationen], Ėtnografičeskoe obozrenie [Ethnographische Rundschau] 2003, Nr. 1, S. 98–123, hier S. 99.

Das einheimische Privatrecht im Usus modernus der Kieler Spruchfakultät

Frank L. Schäfer

I. Eine ertragreiche Geschichtsquelle – Kieler Spruchfakultät

Die Spruchfakultäten der Universitäten des Heiligen Römischen Reichs sind eine überaus ertragreiche Quelle für ein wichtiges Problem der Privatrechtsgeschichte.[1] Sie spielen eine zentrale Rolle bei der Antwort auf die Frage, inwiefern die Rechtspraxis während der Epoche des *Usus modernus pandectarum* neben dem gemeinen römischen Recht einheimische deutsche Rechtsnormen berücksichtigte. Die klassische Antwort fällt auf der Grundlage der gedruckten Entscheidungssammlungen der Spruchfakultäten dahin aus, die Rechtspraxis habe vor dem 19. Jahrhundert das römische Recht gegenüber dem einheimischen Recht bevorzugt.[2] Demgegenüber tendiert die Forschung in jüngerer Zeit zu einem gegenteiligen Ergebnis, das ein deutlich ausgewogeneres Verhältnis zwischen römischem und einheimischem Recht in der Rechtspraxis attestiert.[3] Allerdings kann sich die Forschung für diese

---

[1] Übersicht bei *Peter Oestmann*, Art. Aktenversendung, HRG, 2. Aufl., Bd. 1, Berlin 2008, Sp. 128–132; aus der neueren Spezialliteratur: zu Privatgutachten *Ulrich Falk*, Consilia. Studien zur Praxis der Rechtsgutachten in der frühen Neuzeit, Frankfurt a.M. 2006; zum regionalen Umfeld *Kjell Åke Modéer*, Aktenversendung und Greifswalder Juristenfakultät zur Zeit der Eröffnung des Wismarer Tribunals, in: Dirk Alvermann/Jürgen Regge (Hg.), Justitia in Pommern (Kolloquium aus Anlaß des 350. Jahrestages der Errichtung des Wismarer Tribunals, Greifswald, 2003), Münster 2004, S. 73–86; *Ralph Weber*, Spruchaktenpraxis und Verfahren der Aktenversendung der Rostocker Juristenfakultät 1570–1841/77 – ein Überblick über Bestand und Verfahren, in: Hans-Georg Knothe/Marc Liebmann (Hg.), Gerichtskultur im Ostseeraum. Vierter Rechtshistorikertag im Ostseeraum, 18.–20. Mai 2006 in Greifswald, Frankfurt a.M. u.a. 2007, S. 189–226; weitere neuere Arbeiten von *Chantal Jaeger*, Die Gutachtertätigkeit der Juristenfakultät Zürich, Zürich u.a. 2008; *Angela Kriebisch*, Die Spruchkörper Juristenfakultät und Schöppenstuhl zu Jena – Strukturen, Tätigkeit, Bedeutung und eine Analyse ausgewählter Spruchakten, Frankfurt a.M. u.a. 2008, alle m.w.N.

[2] Beispielhaft aus Kieler Sicht *Anton Sebastian Struve*, Dissertatio academica de commodis et incommodis transmissionis actorum, Kiel 1744, S. 25, unter Berufung auf eine Gerichtsordnung der Herzogtümer Bremen und Verden, welche die Aktenversendung für das einheimische Recht untersagte. Weitere Nachweise bei *Frank L. Schäfer*, Juristische Germanistik. Eine Geschichte der Wissenschaft vom einheimischen Privatrecht, Frankfurt a.M. 2008, S. 221 Fn. 1.

[3] *Anja Amend-Traut*, Wechselverbindlichkeiten vor dem Reichskammergericht. Praktiziertes Zivilrecht in der Frühen Neuzeit, Köln u.a. 2009, S. 422–429; *Nils Jörn*, Lübisches, Magdeburger, Hamburger, Stader, Bremer, Römisches oder Schwedisches Recht – nach welchem Recht wurde am Wismarer Tribunal geurteilt?, in: Marju Luts-Sootak/Sanita Osipova/Frank L. Schäfer (Hg.), Einheit und Vielfalt in der Rechtsgeschichte im Ostseeraum. Sechster Rechtshistorikertag im Ostseeraum, 3.–5. Juni 2010, Tartu und Riga, Frankfurt a.M. u.a. 2012, S. 95–107; *Peter Oestmann*, Rechtsvielfalt vor Gericht: Rechtsanwendung und Partikularrecht im Alten Reich, Frankfurt a.M. 2002, zusammenfassend S. 627–631; *Schäfer*, Germanistik (oben Fn. 2), zusammenfassend

These bislang nur auf das Reichskammergericht, die Untergerichte in Frankfurt am Main und Lübeck, auf das Wismarer Tribunal sowie auf die Prozessgesetzgebung stützen. Zu fragen ist nun, ob sich für die Spruchfakultäten abseits der Oberfläche der gedruckten Sammlungen[4] in den überlieferten Aktengebirgen ebenfalls zumindest für die zweite Hälfte des 18. Jahrhunderts eine Tendenz hin zum einheimischen Recht nachweisen lässt.

Als Einstieg sollen die ungedruckten Rechtssprüche der Spruchfakultät der Christian-Albrechts-Universität zu Kiel dienen. Die Rechtssprüche haben im Gegensatz zu anderen Universitätsakten den letzten Weltkrieg überdauert. Sie befanden sich ursprünglich an der Rechtswissenschaftlichen Fakultät bzw. in der Universitätsbibliothek und gelangten dann 1974 bzw. 1976 in das Landesarchiv Schleswig-Holstein in Schleswig.[5] Dort sind die Sprüche zusammen mit Dubletten, Rechnungssachen, Protokollen und internen bzw. externen Schriftwechseln der Spruchfakultät verwahrt. Die herausragende Bedeutung der Archivalien folgt bereits aus dem Umstand, dass aus der gesamten Tätigkeit der Spruchfakultät lediglich einige Sprüche aus dem 17. Jahrhundert in Form gedruckter und damit allgemein zugänglicher Sammlungen überliefert sind.[6] Im Detail nehmen die Kieler Sprüche im Landesarchiv rund 60 Foliobände und 30 Aktenbündel ein.[7] Der mit Ausnahme der Fachtermini in deutscher Sprache abgefasste Bestand ist recht vollständig.[8] Er reicht von 1683, also nur wenige Jahre nach Gründung der Universität,

---

S. 261 f.; *Jan Schröder*, Recht als Wissenschaft: Geschichte der juristischen Methodenlehre in der Neuzeit (1500–1933), 2. Aufl., München 2012, S. 119.

4 Vgl. *Falk*, Consilia (oben Fn. 1), S. 8–13, zum Problem der Authentizität gedruckter Entscheidungen.

5 Findbuch: Abt. 47.4–47.8, unveröffentlicht, Landesarchiv Schleswig-Holstein (LA-SH), ohne Jahr; *Wolfgang Prange*, Findbuch des Bestandes Abt. 400.5: Von der Universitätsbibliothek Kiel übernommene Handschriften, Schleswig 1975, S. 50.

6 *Erich Mauritius*, Consiliorum Kiloniensium specimen, 1. Aufl., Kiel 1669, mit rund 30 Kieler Sprüchen; *Heinrich Michaelis*, Responsorum, sive deductorum juris, Kiloniensium aliorumque selectorum, Lübeck 1673, mit 11 Kieler Sprüchen und Privatgutachten. Details bei *Eugen Wohlhaupter*, Die Spruchtätigkeit der Kieler juristischen Fakultät von 1665–1879, ZRG GA 68 (1938), S. 752 (768); *Heinrich Gehrke*, Die privatrechtliche Entscheidungsliteratur Deutschlands: Charakteristik und Bibliografie der Rechtsprechungs- und Konsiliensammlungen vom 16. bis zum Beginn des 19. Jahrhunderts, Frankfurt a.M. 1974, S. 196 f. (mit zu Wohlhaupter abweichenden Zahlen).

7 LA-SH, Abt. 47.5 Nr. 13–109, davon die eigentlichen Sprüche unter Nr. 25–109; ferner Abt. 400.5 Nr. 755–760, Nr. 763 f. Andere Zahlenangaben noch bei *Rainer Weiss*, Aus der Spruchtätigkeit der alten Juristenfakultät in Kiel: Rechtsgeschichtliche Betrachtung, Inauguraldiss. Kiel, Heidelberg 1965, S. 6, vor der Verlegung nach Schleswig.

8 Die Akten zu anderen Spruchfakultäten sind weitaus lückenhafter, siehe *Heiner Lück*, Die Spruchtätigkeit der Wittenberger Juristenfakultät. Organisation – Verfahren – Ausstrahlung, Köln u.a. 1998, S. 9 f., zu Wittenberg im 18. Jahrhundert.

mit einer Lücke von 1714 bis 1745[9] bis zum Ende der Aktenversendung mit den Reichsjustizgesetzen von 1877/79. Dabei weist die Spruchfrequenz eine abnehmende Tendenz auf. Während für das 17. und 18. Jahrhundert mehr als einhundert Sprüche pro Jahr überliefert sind, verringerte sich die Aktivität der Kieler Spruchfakultät im 19. Jahrhundert bis hin zu einer einstelligen Spruchzahl pro Jahr. Mit dieser Frequenz liegt Kiel beim Fakultätenvergleich eher im unteren Bereich.[10] Die Gesamtzahl der in Schleswig archivierten Sprüche dürfte mindestens 7.000 Stück betragen.[11]

Die Rechtsgeschichte befasste sich nur vereinzelt mit der Kieler Spruchfakultät,[12] obwohl diese in einem Gebiet mit besonders hoher Komplexität des Partikular- und Verfassungsrechts residierte und somit aus historischer Sicht besonders interessant erscheint.[13] Die rechtshistorische Forschung untersuchte wie zu fast allen anderen Spruchfakultäten des Reichs grundsätzlich nicht das materielle Privatrecht, sondern abseits dessen die institutionelle und prozessuale Seite der Spruchfakultät. Eine große Ausnahme bildet eine bislang in der neueren Forschung übergangene Kieler Dissertation unter der Aufsicht Robert Scheyhings, die sich auf die Akten von 1780 bis 1810 konzentriert.[14] Die Studie nimmt die Meinung vorweg, man habe in der Rechtspraxis des Usus modernus das einheimische Recht gegenüber dem römischen Recht nicht substantiell benachteiligt, sondern im

---

[9] Die allgemeine Lücke reicht bis 1752, der Zeitraum ab 1746 wird immerhin durch Sprüche des Germanisten Johann Carl Heinrich Dreyer (LA-SH, Abt. 400.5, Nr. 755: Responsa Dreyeriana argum. Iuris Germanici Vol. I [Cod. MS. S.H. 580]) abgedeckt. Dazu *Henning Ratjen*, Johann Carl Heinrich Dreyer und Ernst Joachim von Westphalen. Beitrag zur Geschichte der Kieler Universität und der juristischen Literatur, Kiel 1861, S. 95–98.

[10] Übersicht bei *Falk*, Consilia (oben Fn. 1), S. 21–24; *Karl Kroeschell*, Deutsche Rechtsgeschichte, Bd. 3, 5. Aufl., Köln u.a. 2008, S. 51. Sie weisen in Einzelfällen bis zu 850 Eingänge von Rechtsfällen pro Jahr nach. Die gesamte Fallzahl wird für die sächsischen Spruchfakultäten sogar auf einen sechsstelligen Bereich geschätzt.

[11] *Weiss*, Spruchtätigkeit (oben Fn. 7), S. 17, schätzt die Anzahl auf mindestens 4.000 Sprüche.

[12] Grundlegend *Wohlhaupter*, ZRG GA 68 (1938), S. 752–787; des Weiteren *Erich Döhring*, Geschichte der juristischen Fakultät (Geschichte der CAU zu Kiel 1665–1965, Bd. III/1), Neumünster 1965, S. 49–61; *Sören Krusemark*, Die Spruchtätigkeit der Kieler Juristenfakultät zu Hexenprozessen 1665–1710, Hausarbeit M.A. Kiel 1992; *Weiss*, Spruchtätigkeit (oben Fn. 7). Aus dem 19. Jahrhundert: *Ratjen*, Dreyer (oben Fn. 9), bes. S. 95–105; aus dem Alten Reich: *Nicolaus Heinrich Kusel,* Disputatio iuridica inauguralis de inrotulatione actorum, Kiel 1671 (Präsident Magnus v. Wedderkop); *A.S. Struve*, Dissertatio (oben Fn. 2).

[13] Exemplarisch die Rechtslandkarte im Anhang bei *Otto Kähler*, Das Schleswig-Holsteinische Landesrecht. Eine Darstellung des in Schleswig, Holstein und Lauenburg noch geltenden Sonderrechts, 2. Aufl., Glückstadt 1923. Übersicht zum Rechtspartikularismus a.a.O., S. 16–31; ferner *Werner Schubert*, Recht und Gerichtsverfassung in Schleswig-Holstein vor 150 Jahren, in diesem Tagungsband; zur ebenso komplexen verfassungshistorischen Lage *Frank L. Schäfer*, Partikularismus, Nation und Sprache in der Verfassungsgeschichte der Herzogtümer Schleswig und Holstein, Festschrift Diethelm Klippel, Tübingen 2013, S. 485–501.

[14] *Weiss*, Spruchtätigkeit (oben Fn. 7), bes. S. 78–125.

Gegenteil dem römischen Recht vorgezogen. Die vorliegende Analyse der Kieler Spruchfakultät soll an diese Studie anknüpfen und die Datenbasis für die vorgetragenen Thesen erweitern. Dazu wurden sämtliche Kieler Sprüche im Landesarchiv bis zum Ende des Alten Reichs im Jahr 1806 anhand der typischerweise hervorgehobenen Literatur- und Rechtsquellenzitate auf die Anwendung des einheimischen Privatrechts, z.B. des Sachsenspiegels oder des lübischen Rechts, hin durchgesehen.

II. Herrschaft der Statutentheorie – gedruckte Sammlungen

Die klassische Meinung, der zufolge die Rechtspraxis dem gemeinen römischen Recht gegenüber dem einheimischen Recht den Vorrang einräumte, hat einen wahren Kern. Die rund 200 gedruckten Konsiliensammlungen, d.h. die Sammlungen der Sprüche der Spruchfakultäten sowie der Privatgutachten,[15] erwecken für das 17. Jahrhundert sowie für die erste Hälfte des 18. Jahrhunderts in der Tat einen solchen Eindruck.

Zentrales Instrument zur Bevorzugung des gemeinen römischen Rechts war die auf die mittelalterliche italienische Jurisprudenz zurückgehende Statutentheorie. Obwohl sie für die Spruchfakultäten äußerst wichtig war, erschließt sich ihr genauer Inhalt nicht aus Dissertationen oder anderen Monographien, sondern primär aus der Zusammenschau der Spruchpraxis. Lediglich eine Dissertation des Hallenser Professors Simon Peter Gasser (1676–1745) befasste sich in monographischer Form mit der Statutentheorie.[16] Die Schrift ist in der Tradition der Hallenser Fakultät, die sich mit Christian Thomasius (1655–1728) und Johann Gottlieb Heineccius (1681–1741) als Vorreiterin der juristischen Germanistik als Wissenschaft des einheimischen Rechts verstand, als Generalkritik angelegt.

Die Statutentheorie enthielt Regeln auf der Rechtsquellen- und Methodenebene und wurde von weiteren, prozessualen Regeln umrahmt.[17] Die herrschende Meinung des Usus modernus gestand zwar ein, das gemeine römische Recht sei zu spezielleren Rechtsquellen (Lokal-, Stadt- und Landrechte) subsidiär. Doch habe man das römische Recht *in complexu* rezipiert, so dass es die Geltungsvermutung für sich habe (*fundata intentio*). Einheimische Gesetze und einheimisches Gewohnheitsrecht sollten dagegen im Zweifel bewiesen werden müssen. Immerhin erleichterte man den Beweis durch eine Geltungsvermutung für Gesetze aufgrund bewiesener Publikation. Ein wesentliches Hilfsmittel waren hier speziell für die Kieler

---

15 Übersicht bei *Gehrke*, Entscheidungsliteratur (oben Fn. 6), bes. S. 57–77, 167–244.

16 *Simon Peter Gasser*, Dissertatio in qua exminatur brocardicum vulgare: statuta ex iure communi esse interpretanda, 1. Aufl., Halle 1731, 2. Aufl. 1757. Zu Gasser *Theodor Inama von Sternegg*, in: ADB, Bd. 8, Leipzig 1878, S. 401 f. Wichtig sind auch die Ausführungen bei Riccius' Handbuch zu den Stadtrechten (näher bei Fn. 34) sowie bei *Christian Heinrich Eckhard*, Hermeneutica iuris, 1. Aufl., Jena 1750, 2. Aufl. 1779 (Methodenlehrbuch).

17 Im Detail *Schäfer*, Germanistik (oben Fn. 2), S. 221–266, mit umfangreichen Nachweisen zu den Spruchsammlungen, zur Gesetzgebung sowie zur heutigen Literatur.

Spruchfakultät die reichlich vorhandenen Gesetzessammlungen.[18] Ferner war notorisches, d.h. gerichtsbekanntes Gewohnheitsrecht nicht beweisbedürftig. Im Detail unterteilte sich die Statutentheorie in folgende methodische Unterelemente: Bei unklarem Wortlaut sollten Statuten, d.h. alle Gesetze und Gewohnheitsrechte, nach dem Recht der Nachbarterritorien bzw. nach römischem Recht auszulegen (Auslegungsgebot) und dem römischen Recht möglichst anzunähern sein (Annäherungsgebot). Auch sollten Statuten nicht erweiternd angewendet (Analogie- bzw. Extensionsverbot zulasten des speziellen einheimischen und zugunsten des gemeinen römischen Rechts) oder von einem Ort ohne Rezeptionsnachweis auf einen anderen Ort übertragen werden (Übertragungsverbot). In diesen Fällen sollte eine Lücke allein über das römische Recht geschlossen werden.

Die vielzitierte Einleitung des Greifswalder Juristen David Mevius (1609–1670) von 1642 in dessen Kommentar zum Lübecker Stadtrecht[19] weicht von diesem Schema nur geringfügig ab, auch wenn dieses Werk zu Recht als wichtige Wegmarke hin zur juristischen Germanistik gilt. Mevius wollte das Lübecker Stadtrecht zunächst aus sich selbst heraus ohne Rücksicht auf das römische Recht auslegen. Er modifizierte somit das Auslegungsgebot als erstes Element der Statutentheorie. Bei den anderen Elementen der Statutentheorie folgte er indessen der restriktiven Linie des Usus modernus. Beispielsweise schwächte er den Vorrang des sächsischen Rechts vor dem gemeinen römischen Recht ab, indem er das sächsische Recht ungeprüft nur zur Auslegung des Lübecker Stadtrechts, nicht aber zur Lückenfüllung heranziehen wollte.

Die letztere Unterscheidung erweist sich als stilprägend für die Spruchfakultäten. Auch wenn die germanistischen Hochburgen in Halle und Göttingen bei der Auslegung in vielen Fällen von der Statutentheorie abwichen und wie Mevius den Sachsenspiegel (als privat niedergeschriebenes mittelalterliches, aber in vielen Teilen des Reichs notorisches, d.h. gerichtsbekanntes Gewohnheitsrecht) dem römischen Recht vorzogen, so unterschieden auch diese Spruchfakultäten dezidiert zwischen bloßer *Auslegung* von Statuten und *Lückenfüllung*. Im ersteren Fall sprach die Vermutung für das einheimische Partikularrecht, im zweiten Fall nicht.[20] Mit dieser Differenzierung bewegten sie sich wie Mevius noch im Gesamtrahmen

---

[18] Dazu *Kähler*, Landesrecht (oben Fn. 13), S. 33–35, 40 f.

[19] *David Mevius*, Commentarii in Jus Lubecense, zitiert nach der Ausgabe Frankfurt/Leipzig 1700, Quaestio Decima: De Juris Lubecensis interpretatione, S. 41–43. Dazu und zum Folgenden *Schäfer*, Germanistik (oben Fn. 2), S. 54–57. Zu Mevius aus neuerer Zeit stellvertretend *Stephan Buchholz*, Zum Usus modernus bei David Mevius, in: Nils Jörn (Hg.), David Mevius (1609–1670). Leben und Werk eines pommerschen Juristen von europäischem Rang, Hamburg 2007, S. 71–80; *Hans-Georg Knothe*, David Mevius (1609–1670) – ein herausragender Jurist des Usus modernus Pandectarum, ZEuP 2010, S. 536–561; *Kai Wöllert*, David Mevius und sein „Commentarius von Wucherlichen Contracten“ – ein Beispiel von Jurisprudenz als angewandte Wissenschaft in Umbruchzeiten, in: Festschrift Hans Wolfsteiner, Köln/München 2008, S. 207–221.

[20] Wie hier bereits *Weiss*, Spruchtätigkeit (oben Fn. 7), S. 87–90.

der Statutentheorie. Denn die Statutentheorie ging Hand in Hand mit der prozessrechtlichen Beweislast gegen das einheimische Recht. Eine allzu leichte Anwendung eines eigentlich ortsfremden Rechtssatzes kraft Vermutung seiner Rezeption hätte das Übertragungsverbot als Element der Statutentheorie konterkariert. Die Statutentheorie öffnete damit aus Sicht der Germanistik dem römischen Recht die Tür. Es darf allerdings nicht übersehen werden, dass auf diese Art und Weise zugleich das lokale einheimische Recht am Streitort vor einer Vermischung mit ortsfremden Rechtssätzen geschützt wurde. Die Statutentheorie sicherte somit die Rechtssetzungskompetenz der Landes- und Stadtherren, behinderte aber zugleich die vergleichende Verknüpfung der einheimischen Partikularrechte im Sinne des Deutschen Privatrechts als gemeines einheimisches Recht.

III. Abseits der Statutentheorie – Kieler Spruchfakultät

1. Institutioneller und personeller Rahmen

Die Kieler Spruchfakultät stand zumindest seit der Mitte des 18. Jahrhunderts der Statutentheorie deutlich skeptischer gegenüber. Die Spruchfakultät an der Juristischen Fakultät der Universität Kiel kooperierte mit regionalen Obergerichten wie der Regierungskanzlei zu Glückstadt als Obergericht für Schleswig, dem Obergericht zu Gottorf für Holstein, dem Adeligen Landgericht[21] sowie bei der Anwendung des lübischen Rechts mit dem bis in das 18. Jahrhundert aktiven Lübecker Oberhof. Es gab in Schleswig und Holstein aber keinen allgemeinen Zwang zur Aktenversendung an eine Spruchfakultät. Vielmehr musste eine Fakultät nur in Problemfällen befragt werden.[22] Die Kieler Spruchfakultät bezog ihre Akten fast ausschließlich aus dem norddeutschen Raum bis Braunschweig-Lüneburg und Brandenburg als südliche Grenzen. Die Aktenversendung unterlag während des 18. und 19. Jahrhunderts mit der Professionalisierung der Gerichte und dem Ausbau der Landesherrschaft immer größeren Restriktionen. Die Entwicklung in Schleswig und Holstein entsprach hier der in anderen Reichsteilen.[23] Im ersten Schritt beschränkten die Landesherren im Verlauf des 18. Jahrhunderts die Aktenversendung aus den Gerichten und Ämtern der Herzogtümer auf die lokale Spruchfakultät in Kiel.[24]

---

[21] Übersicht bei *Niels Nicolaus Falck*, Handbuch des Schleswig-Holsteinischen Privatrechts, Teil 3, Altona 1835, S. 216–254; zum 19./20. Jahrhundert *Werner Schubert*, Recht und Gerichtsverfassung in Schleswig-Holstein vor 150 Jahren, in diesem Tagungsband; *ders.*, Zur Geschichte der Justizverfassung in Schleswig-Holstein im 19. und 20. Jahrhundert, Frankfurt a.M. 2012.

[22] Siehe Stadtrecht Husum von 1608, Pars IV Tit. 25 Art. 2: beim Zweifel der Richter; Landgerichtsordnung der Herzogtümer Schleswig und Holstein von 1636, Pars III Tit. 24 § 8: bei besonderer Schwierigkeit oder Wichtigkeit des Falls; Hofgerichtsordnung des Herzogtums Holstein-Schaumburg von 1639, Pars II Tit. 26 § 12: bei Uneinigkeit der Hofräte. Dazu bereits *Wohlhaupter*, ZRG GA 68 (1938), S. 752 (760–762).

[23] Siehe parallel z.B. zu Kursachsen und den anderen sächsischen Ländern *Kriebisch*, Spruchkörper (oben Fn. 1), S. 156–189, 199–207, mit Nachweisen aus der Gesetzgebung.

[24] Details bei *Wohlhaupter*, ZRG GA 68 (1938), S. 760–762.

Daher befasst sich das Gros der Akten mit Rechtsfällen aus Schleswig und Holstein. Im zweiten Schritt wurde die Aktenversendung gänzlich untersagt. Am Anfang stand ab 1735 ein temporäres Verbot für die Versendung aus dem Kreis Norderdithmarschen,[25] 1834 für das Oberappellationsgericht Kiel,[26] bis am Ende das Gerichtsverfassungsgesetz 1879 die Aktenversendung für das gesamte Deutsche Reich beendete.

Die überlieferten Sprüche beginnen mit einem vom Dekan Nikolaus Martini (1632–1713) unterzeichneten Rechtsgutachten vom 20. Oktober 1683.[27] Der Aufbau ist dreigeteilt: *facti species* (Sachverhalt), *responsum* (Entscheidung) und *rationes decidendi* (tragende Entscheidungsgründe). Es fehlen *rationes dubitandi* (Zweifelsgründe). Die Spruchfakultät begutachtete einen Erbschaftsstreit um Schmuck. Einheimische Rechtssätze bzw. Rechtsquellen lagen der Entscheidung nicht zugrunde. Das einheimische Privatrecht trat erstmals 1707 in einem Spruch zu den erbrechtlichen Folgen aus einer Gütergemeinschaft nach Hamburger Stadtrecht ans Tageslicht der Spruchpraxis.[28]

Die Morgenröte des einheimischen Rechts in den Sprüchen setzte in Kiel parallel zu Forschung und Lehre ein: Um 1700 richtete zunächst der Universalhistoriker Samuel Reyher (1635–1714) Kolloquien und vergleichende Vorlesungen zu norddeutschen Partikularrechten sowie zum dänischen Recht aus. Christoph Heinrich Amthor (1677–1721) stieg kurze Zeit später im Jahr 1712 auf den Lehrstuhl für *ius patrium*, eine der ältesten Professuren für einheimisches Privatrecht im Reich. Unter Amthors Nachfolgern ragten in der Zeit bis um 1800 Johann Carl Heinrich (Henrich) Dreyer (1723–1802) als Vordenker der Germanischen Rechtsgeschichte und Ludwig Albrecht Gottfried Schrader (1751–1815) als Autor des ersten „Handbuch[s] der vaterländischen Rechte in Schleswig und Holstein" heraus.[29] Inwiefern sich in den folgenden Jahrzehnten nach 1713 das einheimische Privatrecht in den Sprüchen im Detail stärker materialisierte, bleibt leider im geschichtlichen Dunkel, da bis 1752 die allgemeinen Aktivitäten des Spruchkollegiums nicht überliefert sind. Lediglich Dreyer verewigte sich als Berichterstatter für die Zeit von 1746 bis 1767 in einem eigenen Band zur Kieler Spruchfakultät, der sich anders als die

---

[25] Konstitution v. 14.7.1735; dazu *Ratjen*, Dreyer (oben Fn. 9), S. 102.

[26] Verfügung, betreffend die provisorische Gerichtsordnung für das Schleswig-Holstein-Lauenburgische Oberappellationsgericht in Kiel für die Herzogthümer Schleswig und Holstein, § 11, in: Schleswig-Holsteinische Anzeigen, 32. Stück, 11.8.1834, Sp. 1169 (1173).

[27] LA-SH, Abt. 47.5 Nr. 25 (A. Relationes, Sententiae et Responsa, Facultatis Jurid. Kil. ab Anni 1683 die. 10 Octobris ad Anni 1690 die. 29. Aprilis elaborata a Schultio, Martini, Musaeo, Strykio), Bl. 1r–2r.

[28] LA-SH, Abt. 47.5, Nr. 36, Bl. 23r ff. v. 1707.

[29] Zu diesen Personen *Schäfer,* Germanistik (oben Fn. 2), S. 177, 180, 291 f.; ferner ausführlich zu Dreyer *Ratjen*, Dreyer (oben Fn. 9), S. 52–156; sehr kritisch zu Dreyer *Ahasver v. Brandt*, NDB, Bd. 4, Berlin 1959, S. 122 f. Zu weiteren Germanisten *Döhring*, Geschichte (oben Fn. 12), S. 72, 82 f., 96 f.; *Schäfer*, a.a.O., S. 96, 177 f., 202 f., 214 f.

übrigen Konvolute im Landesarchiv durchgehend mit dem einheimischen Privatrecht beschäftigte.[30] Die anderen Kieler Germanisten verfügen über kein vergleichbares Vermächtnis.[31] Mit dem Wiedereinsetzen der allgemeinen Spruchakten zum Jahr 1752 sind Fälle zum einheimischen Privatrecht dann fester Bestandteil des Repertoires der Spruchfakultät. Im Vergleich zum gemeinen römischen Recht und zum Strafrecht verbleibt ihr Anteil aber vergleichsweise gering.

Inhaltlich dominieren für das 18. Jahrhundert aus Sicht der heutigen, engen Definition des Privatrechts das Familien- und Erbrecht bzw. Schnittmengen wie die Gütergemeinschaft im Erbgang. Schuldrechtliche Materien wie Kaufrecht oder die Verwahrung als Treuhand im weiteren Sinne[32] finden sich seltener. Die Spruchakten des 19. Jahrhunderts enthalten dann aufgrund ihrer geringen Anzahl naturgemäß nur sehr selten einheimisches Privatrecht.[33] Bei den Autoren des gemeinen römischen Rechts zitieren die Sprüche des 18. Jahrhunderts neben den deutschen Autoritäten des 17. und 18. Jahrhunderts oft den flämischen Juristen Mathias Wesenbeck (1531–1586), der im 16. Jahrhundert wirkte. Beim einheimischen Privatrecht wird im 18. Jahrhundert der Göttinger Germanist Christian Gottlieb Riccius (1697–1784) mit seinem Handbuch zu den Stadtrechten auffallend häufig herangezogen.[34] Unter den Verweisen auf das Deutsche Privatrecht dominierte zunächst das Lehrbuch von Johann Rudolf Engau (1708–1755), dann folgten die Werke der Göttinger Germanisten Johann Heinrich Christian v. Selchow (1732–1795) und Justus Friedrich Runde (1741–1807).[35]

2. Bindungswirkung der Rechtssprüche

Der Einfluss der Spruchfakultäten im Rechtsprechungssystem des Alten Reichs zeigt sich besonders in der Frage, inwiefern den Sprüchen einer Spruchfakultät Bindungswirkung gegenüber denjenigen Institutionen und Personen zukam, welche

---

[30] Siehe oben Fn. 9.

[31] Die im LA-SH unter Sig. Abt. 400.5 Nr. 763 f. für den Zeitraum von 1815 bis 1824 überlieferten beiden Bände des Germanisten Niels Nicolaus Falck enthalten keine für die Forschung relevanten Stellungnahmen zum einheimischen Privatrecht.

[32] Zu letzterer *Johann Carl Heinrich Dreyer*, Urteil v. Juli 1746 für die Spruchfakultät Kiel, in: LA-SH, Sig. Abt. 400.5 Nr. 755, unpaginiert, zu Lib. 3 Tit. 3 Lübecker Stadtrecht von 1586 (De deposito – von treuer Hand).

[33] Hervorgehoben sei das Urteil Schultz ./. Erben Neuendorf v. 31. März 1813, Referent Prof. Brinkmann, an das Stadtgericht zu Ribnitz in Mecklenburg, LA-SH, Abt. 47.5, Nr. 60, Entscheidung Nr. 4. Entscheidungsgrundlage dieser Konkurssache war lübisches Recht. Ferner ein in der Literatur dokumentierter Erbschaftsfall, dazu *Conrad Plitt*, Das Lübeckische Erbrecht nach dem Gesetze vom 10. Februar 1862, das Erbrecht der Eheleute und der Blutsfreunde, die letztwilligen Verfügungen, so wie die Erbgüter betreffend, 2. Aufl., Wismar 1872, S. 12 f.

[34] *Christian Gottlieb Riccius*, Zuverlässiger Entwurff von Stadt-Gesezen oder Statutis, vornehmlich der Land-Städte, Frankfurt a.M. 1740. Zu ihm, wenn auch ohne Hinweis auf dieses entscheidende Werk, *Ernst Landsberg*, ADB, Bd. 28, Leipzig 1889, S. 409 f.

[35] Zu diesen Autoren und Werken *Schäfer*, Germanistik (oben Fn. 2), S. 109–115, m.w.N.

die Fallakten an eine Spruchfakultät zur Stellungnahme gesendet hatten.[36] Zumindest für die Kieler Spruchfakultät lassen sich eindeutige Aussagen treffen.

Die Rechtssprüche sind zunächst von den privat angefertigten Stellungnahmen eines einzelnen Professors einer Rechtsfakultät oder eines sonstigen Gelehrten abzugrenzen. Eine solche Stellungnahme zu einem Rechtsfall wurde entweder auf Vorlage eines Gerichts oder einer Person zu einem Rechtsfall abgegeben. Es handelt sich stets um Privatgutachten, die für den Auftraggeber unverbindlich waren. Hinter den Rechtssprüchen einer Spruchfakultät als offizielles Organ einer Rechtsfakultät verbergen sich dagegen sehr unterschiedliche Konstellationen.

Zum einen unterscheiden sich die Sprüche nach dem Urheber. Teils trat die Spruchfakultät als Kollegium auf, teils wurde ein einzelner Professor als Berichterstatter für die Spruchfakultät hervorgehoben. Zum anderen differiert die Bindungswirkung der Sprüche. In der Kieler Spruchfakultät bezeichnen der deutsche Begriff „Urtheil" sowie der lateinische Begriff *sententia*[37] für die anfragende Instanz verbindliche Entscheidungen. Ein im Eingangsteil des Spruchs genanntes Gericht legte der Spruchfakultät in einem laufenden Gerichtsverfahren einen Rechtsfall mit der Bitte vor, ihn anhand bestimmter Leitfragen zu entscheiden. Die Kieler Spruchfakultät entschied dann unter dem Namen des anfragenden Gerichts („erkennen wir nach eingeholtem Rat für Recht"). Das Gericht hatte daraufhin kein eigenständiges Urteil mehr anzufertigen, sondern übernahm die Entscheidung der Spruchfakultät als verkündungsreifes Urteil. Dieses Auftreten der Kieler Spruchfakultät im Namen des anfragenden Gerichts indiziert die Bindungswirkung seiner Entscheidungen.[38] Unverbindlich war ein Urteil nur bei Unkenntnis des anzuwendenden Partikularrechts.[39] Hingegen verwendete die Spruchfakultät den lateinischen Begriff *responsum* und äußerst selten das deutsche Wort „Rechtsgutachten", um unverbindliche Gutachten zu bezeichnen. In dieser Spruchkategorie fehlt bei der Stellungnahme der entscheidende Hinweis, dass die Spruchfakultät im Namen eines Gerichts entschied.[40] Ein solches Gutachten konnte von einzelnen Personen, aber auch von hoheitlichen Instanzen, also auch von Gerichten, bei der Kieler Rechtsfakultät in Auftrag gegeben werden. Für das 17. und das frühe 18. Jahrhundert enthalten die Kieler Akten darüber hinaus Sprüche, die mit dem lateini-

---

[36] Zur Frage der Bindungswirkung zusammenfassend *Kriebisch*, Spruchkörper (oben Fn. 1), S. 19–24, mit Nachweisen aus der Gesetzgebung.

[37] Ebenso die Einordnung zu *sententia* bei *Lück*, Spruchtätigkeit (oben Fn. 8), S. 202.

[38] Allgemeine Meinung für Kiel, siehe *Wohlhaupter*, Die Spruchtätigkeit der Kieler juristischen Fakultät von 1665–1879, ZRG GA 68 (1938), S. 752 (762 f.); im übergeordneten Rahmen *Lück*, Spruchtätigkeit (oben Fn. 8), S. 36, mit Hinweis auf den Reichsabschied von 1570.

[39] *Weiss*, Spruchtätigkeit (oben Fn. 7), S. 18, m.w.N.; ebenso *Oestmann*, Art. Aktenversendung, HRG, 2. Aufl., Bd. 1, Berlin 2008, Sp. 128 (130).

[40] Siehe *Kriebisch*, Spruchkörper (oben Fn. 1), S. 20 f., mit Schwankungen in der Praxis der Jenaer Spruchfakultät.

schen Begriff *relatio* tituliert werden. Darunter sind Vorentwürfe eines Berichterstatters zu verstehen, wie sie vom Reichskammergericht bekannt sind.

Die Kieler Typologie der Rechtssprüche unterscheidet sich von einigen anderen Spruchfakultäten im Alten Reich. Der Begriff *consilium*, der sowohl für ein unverbindliches Gutachten als auch übergreifend für jegliche verbindliche oder unverbindliche Stellungnahme einer Fakultät oder einzelnen Person zu einem Rechtsfall stehen kann,[41] taucht in den Akten der Kieler Spruchfakultät nicht auf.[42] Er muss sich in den Kieler Verhältnissen folglich auf die im Landesarchiv nicht dokumentierten Privatgutachten der Professoren abseits der Spruchfakultät beschränken. Auch ist an anderen Spruchfakultäten die Terminologie zumindest in den gedruckten Sammlungen weitaus weniger klar bzw. die einzelnen Begriffe haben abweichende Bedeutungen. Teilweise werden dort die Termini *consilium* und *responsum* synonym für alle Sprüche einer Rechtsfakultät benutzt oder die Begriffe verschoben, indem man mit *consilium* ein Rechtsgutachten der Spruchfakultät und mit *responsum* ein Urteil der Fakultät bezeichnet.[43] Die Bindungswirkung eines Spruchs lässt sich daher nur durch einen Blick auf die Formulierungen in konkreten Sprüchen einer einzelnen Fakultät messen.[44]

3. Beispiel 1 – Verfügungsbeschränkung durch Beispruchsrecht

Die Frage nach der Bindungswirkung muss durchaus bei der inhaltlichen Aussagekraft einzelner Sprüche der Kieler Rechtsfakultät mitbedacht werden. Um den Umgang der Spruchfakultät mit dem einheimischen Privatrecht zu skizzieren, sollen aus der Vielzahl der Sprüche drei Regelungsprobleme und ihre Lösungen im einheimischen Privatrecht herausgegriffen werden.

Das erste Beispiel handelt auf der Grundlage des Sachsenspiegels von zwei Rechtsgutachten zum sog. Beispruchsrecht.[45] Ein Rechtsgutachten aus dem Dezember 1753 befasste sich mit der Wirksamkeit eines Kaufvertrags im herzoglichen Amt Reinbeck (heute Stadt Reinbek im Landkreis Stormarn) im südlichen Holstein

---

[41] Statt aller *Gehrke*, Entscheidungsliteratur (oben Fn. 6), S. 63–70. Umgekehrt jetzt *Renate Schulze*, Justus Henning Böhmer und die Dissertationen seiner Schüler. Bausteine des Ius Ecclesiasticum Protestantium, Tübingen 2009, S. 7. Sie benutzt für die Spruchfakultäten den Oberbegriff *Responsum*. Siehe ferner *Falk*, Consilia, 2006, S. 1: Er hält die Begriffe *consilium* und *responsum* für austauschbar.

[42] Schiefe Terminologie daher bei *Wohlhaupter*, ZRG GA 68 (1938), S. 752 (755), der für Kiel begrifflich zwischen *consilium* (bloße Gutachten) und *sententia* (Urteile) unterscheiden möchte.

[43] Dazu *Gehrke*, Entscheidungsliteratur (oben Fn. 6), S. 68, m.w.N. Wie in Kiel die Spruchfakultät Jena (*Kriebisch*, Spruchkörper [oben Fn. 1], S. 230–238: Urteile und Gutachten [dort auch *responsum* genannt]) und Wittenberg (*Lück*, Spruchtätigkeit [oben Fn. 8], S. 202 f.).

[44] Der Sache nach ebenso *Kroeschell*, Rechtsgeschichte, Bd. 3 (oben Fn. 10), S. 50.

[45] Dazu *Kähler*, Landesrecht (oben Fn. 13), S. 201; aus der neueren Literatur z.B. *Adrian Schmidt-Recla*, Kalte oder warme Hand? Verfügungen von Todes wegen in mittelalterlichen Referenzquellen, Köln u.a. 2011, z.B. S. 37–40; *Werner Ogris/Christian Neschwara*, Art. Erbenlaub, HRG, 2. Aufl., Bd. 1, Berlin 2008, Sp. 1360 f.

über eine Mühle zwischen einer Witwe und ihren Stiefkindern nach fürstlich-holsteinischen Gesetzen und Landesgebräuchen.[46] Das nach der Sentenz „Stadtrecht bricht Landrecht und Landrecht bricht gemeines Recht“ vorrangige lokale Recht enthielt für diesen Fall keine spezielle Regel, so dass sich die Frage einer subsidiären Anwendung des Sachsenspiegels stellte. Der Sachsenspiegel, Landrecht, Buch 1 Art. 52 knüpfte die Veräußerung des Grundeigentums durch den künftigen Erblasser an die Zustimmung seiner (potentiellen) Erben an (sog. Erbenlaub). Die Erben konnten Herausgabe des Grundeigentums vom Erwerber verlangen, wenn sie die Zustimmung nicht erteilt hatten. Das Beispruchsrecht sicherte damit den Erbgang in der Familie gegen Verfügungen über Grund und Boden, welche dem Erbe die wirtschaftliche Substanz entzogen hätten.

Erben der Witwe wären im konkreten Fall ohne Einkindschaft nicht die Stiefkinder, sondern die Verwandten der Witwe gewesen. Aus heutiger Sicht ist das Beispruchsrecht als gesetzliche, im Erbrecht verankerte Verfügungsbeschränkung zugunsten der Erben einzuordnen. Das deutsche BGB kennt eine solche gesetzliche Beschränkung nicht, sondern nur eine Beschränkung durch Verfügung von Todes wegen zugunsten von Nacherben. Das Beispruchsrecht unterscheidet sich vom heutigen Erbrecht auch in einem anderen Punkt. Es bewirkte nach dem kausalen Einheitsprinzip, d.h. der vertraglichen Einheit von schuldrechtlichem Geschäft und dinglicher Verfügung zugleich die Unwirksamkeit des Kaufvertrags. Der heutige Nacherbe ist nach § 2113 BGB nur auf dinglicher Ebene geschützt.

Die Spruchfakultät prüfte ausführlich, ob das Sachsenrecht – gemeint war der Sachsenspiegel – im Amt Reinbeck eine verbindliche Rechtsquelle war und somit dort das Beispruchsrecht zur Anwendung kommen konnte. Das Rechtsgutachten der Fakultät enthüllt, dass diese Frage im Usus modernus für Holstein offenbar umstritten war. In den *rationes dubitandi*, den die Entscheidung nicht tragenden Gründen, nannte die Spruchfakultät die Argumente, die für die Anwendung des Sachsenspiegels sprachen. Das Rechtsbuch habe in Holstein die *fundata intentio* für sich. Zum Beleg führte die Spruchfakultät folgende Rechtsquellen an: den Bordesholmer Vergleich von 1522 zwischen Christian II., König von Dänemark, Norwegen und Schweden (1481–1559), und Herzog Friedrich I. von Gottorf (1471–1533),[47] die Holsteinische Landgerichtsordnung von 1573[48] sowie die damals gel-

[46] LA-SH, Abt. 47.5 Nr. 39, S. 174–204.

[47] Bei *Niels Nicolaus Falck* (Hg.), Sammlung der wichtigsten Urkunden, welche auf das Staatsrecht der Herzogthümer Schleswig und Holstein Bezug haben, Kiel 1847, S. 36 (40): „Idt schall lock im Hertochdom tho Holsten na eren olden Gewahnheiten unde Statuten, ock na dem Sachsenspegel gericht und geordelet werden […].“

[48] […] Landtgerichts Ordnung / zu befürderunge der ordentlichen Justitien und Rechtens in unsern Fürstenthumben Schleßweig Holstein und Stormarn, Ausgabe Hamburg 1573, Pars II Tit. 3 (unpaginiert): „[…] nach Sechsischen Rechten“.

tende Holsteinische Landgerichtsordnung von 1636.[49] Die letztere Ordnung normierte:[50]

> „Jedoch soll die Rechtliche Erkäntnus nicht / wie in den Schleswigischen Sachen / auf das Lowbuch / sondern weil das Fürstenthumb Hollstein kein beschrieben Recht hat / auff den alten kundtbahren Landsgebrauch / so der Vernunfft und Billigkeit nicht zu wieder / Oder auch des heiligen Reichs Ordnungen und *Constitutionen* nicht entgegen / gegründet / In Mangel aber einer solchen beständigen rechtmässigen Gewohnheit / soll nach den Sachsen Rechten / dergestalt / wie Wir deßwegen das jenige / so der Vernunfft und Billigkeit *conforme*, auch unsern Fürstenthumben am nützlichsten seyn wird / extrahiren und abfassen zu lassen / im Werck begriffen / geurtheilt / Wäre aber derselbe Fall darauff gesprochen werden soll / darin nicht enthalten / so soll als in *casu omisso* der *disposition*, gemeiner beschriebenen Recht gefolget / und die Urtheil darauff gegründet werden […].“

Die Landgerichtsordnung von 1636 schränkte im Gegensatz zur älteren Landgerichtsordnung aus dem 16. Jahrhundert nach dem Wortlaut die Anwendung des Sachsenspiegels auf einen amtlichen Auszug aus dem Rechtsbuch ein. Wie die Spruchfakultät feststellte, war ein solcher Extrakt „bis zu dieser Stunde“ indessen nicht angefertigt worden. Die Spruchfakultät wischte in den Zweifelsgründen die unterlassene Anfertigung beiseite: Der Sachsenspiegel sei weiterhin geltendes Recht, bis ein solcher Extrakt tatsächlich angefertigt worden sei.[51] Die Fakultät führte für diese These ein ganzes Bündel an Gründen an: Erstens werde das Rechtsbuch nicht nur beim Adel, sondern auch bei allen anderen Personen „auf dem Lande und in den Aembtern“ herangezogen. Zweitens bestätigten bedeutende Kieler Autoritäten (Dreyer, Reyher sowie Kurator Ernst Joachim v. Westphalen [1700–1759], der ehemals in Rostock gelesen hatte[52]) die Geltung des Sachsenspiegels in Holstein. Drittens zog die Spruchfakultät Art. 2 der für Reinbeck maßgebenden hochfürstlichen Kanzleiordnung von 1708 heran, der die subsidiäre Anwendung des „alte[n] Sachsen-Recht[s]“ anders als die Landgerichtsordnung ohne Einschränkung anordnete. Viertens argumentierte man, das sei „von jeher *juris Germanici universalis* gewesen“[53] und verwies damit auf die junge Disziplin des Deutschen Privatrechts. Die Spruchfakultät unterstrich diesen Punkt mit einem vergleichenden Schluss aus den Stadt- und Landrechten in Schleswig und Holstein sowie aus dem lübischen Recht.[54] Ein derartiger Vergleich der Rechte benachbarter Territorien war typisch sowohl für die Statutentheorie als auch für das Deutsche Privatrecht in der Mitte des 18. Jahrhunderts.

---

[49] Revidirte Landgerichts-Ordnung […] in Unsern Fürstenthumben Schleswig Hollstein […] Verfasset und publiciret Anno 1636, Ausgabe Gückstadt 1665, Pars II Tit. 3 § 3.

[50] A.a.O., S. 35.

[51] LA-SH, Abt. 47.5 Nr. 39, S. 182.

[52] Ausführlich zu Westphal *Ratjen*, Dreyer (oben Fn. 9), S. 1–62.

[53] LA-SH, Abt. 47.5 Nr. 39, S. 185.

[54] Der Sachsenspiegel galt subsidiär z.B. im Bereich des Dithmarscher Landrechts sowie des lübischen Rechts in Holstein, siehe *Kähler*, Landesrecht (oben Fn. 13), S. 19, m.w.N.

In den tragenden Entscheidungsgründen, den *rationes decidendi*, lehnte die Spruchfakultät freilich die Anwendung des Sachsenspiegels ab und entschied sich somit gegen das Beispruchsrecht, d.h. für die Wirksamkeit des Kaufvertrags. Die *fundata intentio* für eine Norm aus dem Sachsenspiegel sei abzulehnen, da das Rechtsbuch mangels Extrakt, wie ihn die Landrechtsordnung von 1636 vorsehe, in Holstein nicht „*in toto suo complexu*" rezipiert worden sei.[55] Daher müsse man im Einzelfall die Praxisgeltung von Normen aus dem Sachsenspiegel beweisen – was im Ergebnis nicht gelang. Die Fakultät zitierte zur Frage der Beweislast bei einer mangelnden Rezeption *in complexu* ausgerechnet den germanistischen Wegbereiter Johann Georg v. Kulpis (1652–1698) und den frühen Rintelner Germanisten Henrich Ernst Kestner (1671–1723), die mittelalterliche Rechtsquellen in der Neuzeit hatten anwenden wollen.[56] Die Fakultät kehrte damit die allgemeine Stoßrichtung dieser Autoren um, die dem römischen Recht die Geltung *in complexu* abgesprochen hatten, um das einheimische Recht zu fördern.

Daneben bediente sich die Spruchfakultät vieler weiterer Argumente: Erstens sei der grundsätzliche Ausschluss des Sachsenspiegels auch im benachbarten Herzogtum Sachsen-Lauenburg üblich. Zweitens müsse sogar Dreyer eingestehen, dass der Sachsenspiegel in Holstein nur einen „*usum dogmaticum*, und keinen *usum legalem* habe, auch nicht *ex verbis*, sondern *ex observantia* beurtheilet werden müsse."[57] Dreyer habe später zwar eine andere Meinung vertreten, doch habe er diese nur in einem Privatgutachten geäußert. Drittens könne die historische Rechtslage im 16. Jahrhundert nicht als Argument herangezogen werden, weil die maßgebliche Landgerichtsordnung von 1636 technisch gesehen einen Doppelschritt gehe: Sie setze den Sachsenspiegel im ersten Schritt außer Kraft und erfordere im zweiten Schritt für die Geltung des Sachsenspiegels in der Zukunft die Übernahme von Normen aus dem Spiegel in einen Extrakt. Die Wirksamkeit des ersten Schritts, d.h. der Außerkraftsetzung, sei unabhängig davon, ob der Landesherr im zweiten Schritt besagten Extrakt angefertigt habe. Die fragliche Stelle in der Landrechtsordnung sei daher wie folgt zu lesen:

> „daß nach dem Sachsen-Recht dergestalt,[58] wie die Landes-Herrschafft deswegen dasjenige, nach der Vernunfft und Billigkeit conform, auch Ihren Fürstenthümern am nützlichsten seyn werden, extrahiren, und abfaßen zu lassen im Werk begriffen wären, geurtheilet werden solle."[59]

[55] LA-SH, Abt. 47.5 Nr. 39, S. 189.

[56] Zu ihnen *Schäfer*, Germanistik (oben Fn. 2), S. 62–64, 137.

[57] LA-SH, Abt. 47.5 Nr. 39, S. 190 unter Verweis auf *Johann Carl Heinrich Dreyer*, De usu genuino iuris Anglo-Saxonici in explicando iure Cimbrico et Saxonico liber singularis, Kiel 1747, S. 89 f.

[58] Unterstreichungen im Original.

[59] LA-SH, Abt. 47.5 Nr. 39, S. 194.

Viertens habe man, wie Dreyer selbst ausführe,[60] bereits vor 1636 derjenigen Seite im Prozess die Beweislast für die Geltung einer Norm aus dem Sachsenspiegel aufgebürdet, die sich darauf berufen habe. Aus der Kanzleiordnung von 1708 folge nichts Gegenteiliges, da sie für die Anwendung des Sachsenspiegels wiederum auf die Landgerichtsordnung verweise („vermöge der Landgerichtsordnung").

In der Bewertung erweist sich das Kieler Gutachten als einseitig und gegenüber dem Sachsenspiegel voreingenommen. Obwohl die zeitgenössischen Germanisten (zur Mitte des 18. Jahrhunderts) und die Rechtspraxis zu Recht die Wiederbelebung längst vergangener mittelalterlicher Rechtsdenkmäler ablehnten, stand die Fortgeltung des im Sachsenspiegel niedergelegten Rechts in der Neuzeit in vielen Landstrichen im heutigen Nord- und Ostdeutschland außer Frage. Die Gesetzgebung setzte auch nach 1636 für Holstein in Einzelschritten Normen des Sachsenspiegels außer Kraft und ersetzte sie durch zeitgemäße Lösungen. Im Umkehrschluss ging die Gesetzgebung somit von der grundsätzlichen Weitergeltung des mittelalterlichen Rechtsbuchs aus. Ebenso dokumentierte die Literatur des 19. und des 20. Jahrhunderts einhellig die Anwendung des Sachsenspiegels im Herzogtum Holstein.[61] Es war lediglich die Frage umstritten, ob unter das „Sachsenrecht" im Sinne der Prozessordnungen auch die neuere sächsische Gesetzgebung wie die kursächsischen Konstitutionen von 1572 fallen sollte.[62] Wie tendenziös das Gutachten verfasst ist, beweist im Detail der Verweis auf die Rechtslage im Herzogtum Sachsen-Lauenburg. Lauenburg gehörte zwar von 1689 bis 1705 zum Herzogtum Braunschweig-Lüneburg. Dort hatte die Kanzleiordnung in der Tat die Anwendung des Sachsenspiegels untersagt. Doch verpflichtete die nach der Trennung im Herzogtum Lauenburg wieder einschlägige Hofgerichtsordnung von 1681 (sowie spätere Gesetze) die Gerichte wieder zur Anwendung des Sachsenspiegels.[63]

Es kann daher nicht verwundern, dass sich ein drei Jahre jüngeres Rechtsgutachten der Kieler Spruchfakultät vom 2. Oktober 1756 auf die Seite des Sachsenspiegels schlug und damit zum „Normalzustand" zurückkehrte.[64] Im Sachverhalt des zweiten Gutachtens hatte eine Frau, die ohne eheliche leibliche Erben verstorben war, ihrem Ehemann ihr Grundeigentum in Preetz im heutigen Holsteiner Landkreis Plön vermachen wollen. Die Intestaterben der Frau versuchten gegen diesen letzten Willen wiederum aus ihrem Beispruchsrecht vorzugehen.

---

[60] *Dreyer*, De usu (oben Fn. 57), S. 89.

[61] Statt aller aus dem 20. Jahrhundert *Kähler*, Landesrecht (oben Fn. 13), S. 19; *Eugen Wohlhaupter*, Rechtsquellen Schleswig-Holsteins, Bd. 1 (einziger Bd.), Kiel 1938, S. 80 f.; aus dem 19. Jahrhundert *Niels Nicolaus Falck*, Handbuch des Schleswig-Holsteinischen Privatrechts, Teil 1, Altona 1825, S. 404–408, m.w.N.

[62] Dazu *Kähler*, Landesrecht (oben Fn. 13), S. 19 f.

[63] Im Detail *Cornelia Adler*, Eheverträge im Amt Lauenburg. Studien zur Rechtsgestaltung durch Vertrag in einem Partikularrecht, Berlin 2010, S. 30 f.

[64] LA-SH Sig. Abt. 47.5 Nr. 41, Kirchhoff ./. Friedrichsen, unpaginiert.

Die Spruchfakultät stellte ihre Argumente nunmehr um und erzielte dadurch das gegenteilige Ergebnis. Sie vertauschte einfach die *rationes decidendi* mit den *rationes dubitandi*. In den Zweifelsgründen sind daher die Argumente gegen den Sachsenspiegel zu lesen: Die Landgerichtsordnung von 1636 habe den Sachsenspiegel außer Kraft gesetzt und mache eine erneute Geltung von der Verfassung eines Extrakts abhängig. Bislang habe der Landesherr einen solchen Extrakt aber nicht angefertigt. In den tragenden Entscheidungsgründen entschied sich die Fakultät dann für die gegenläufige Deutung der Landgerichtsordnung und verwies auf die fortbestehende Rechtspraxis sowie auf vergleichender Grundlage auf das Deutsche Privatrecht. Im Ergebnis sprach sich das zweite Rechtsgutachten damit für die Intestaterben aus.

Ein solcher Widerspruch zwischen zwei Stellungnahmen derselben Fakultät ist bemerkenswert. Da beide Gutachten exakt dieselben Argumente verwenden und lediglich die Zuordnung zu den tragenden Entscheidungsgründen bzw. Zweifelsgründen austauschen, muss eines der beiden Gutachten ein Gefälligkeitsgutachten sein.[65] Angesichts der Tatsache, dass die Literatur des 19. und des 20. Jahrhunderts im Rückblick für die Frühe Neuzeit einhellig die Geltung des Sachsenspiegels im Herzogtum Holstein dokumentiert, trifft dieser Befund auf das etwas ältere erste Gutachten zu. Es ist freilich zu berücksichtigen, dass es sich eben nicht um verbindliche Urteile, sondern nur um unverbindliche Gutachten handelte. Hier hatte die Spruchfakultät wohl einen größeren Spielraum für „flexible“ Standpunkte als bei Urteilen. Der Widerspruch sollte nicht von Dauer sein. Der Streit um das Beispruchsrecht erledigte sich am Ende des 18. Jahrhunderts. Der Landesherr schaffte im Zuge der Bodenmobilisierung in beiden Herzogtümern das Beispruchsrecht in der Gestalt einer gesetzlichen Verfügungsbeschränkung zum Jahr 1796 bzw. 1798 ab.[66]

4. Beispiel 2 – Erbschaft von Halbgeschwistern

Das nächste Beispiel ist ebenfalls dem Erbrecht entnommen. Den Auftakt bildet ein Urteil der Kieler Spruchfakultät aus dem Jahr 1753.[67] Bürgermeister und Rat der Stadt Burg auf Fehmarn[68] hatten die Kieler Rechtsfakultät um ein Urteil zur gesetzlichen Erbfolge von Halbgeschwistern gebeten, d.h. von Geschwistern, die anders als vollbürtige Geschwister nur einen gemeinsamen Elternteil haben. Dieses Regelungsproblem betrifft zunächst einen kinderlosen Erblasser, wenn zugleich die Eltern vorverstorben sind und die Geschwister des Erblassers erben sollen. Es fragt sich dann, ob die Halbgeschwister des Erblassers wie seine Vollgeschwister zu behandeln sind. Das Problem ist nicht nur in der Gegenwart mit sog. Patchworkfamilien präsent, sondern war angesichts der hohen Mortalitätsrate und häufiger

---

[65] Überblick zur Parteilichkeit im Gutachtenmarkt bei *Falk*, Consilia (oben Fn. 1), S. 56–63.

[66] *Kähler*, Landesrecht (oben Fn. 13), S. 201, m.w.N.

[67] LA-SH Sig. Abt. 47.5 Nr. 39, Rauert ./. Erben Hultermann, S. 198 ff.

[68] Nicht zu verwechseln mit der Gemeinde Burg im heutigen Landkreis Dithmarschen.

Wiederverheiratung gerade in der Vergangenheit von hoher praktischer Bedeutung. Nach dem auf dem Parentelsystem aufbauenden heutigen deutschen Erbrecht sind Halbgeschwister nach § 1925 BGB Erben in der zweiten Ordnung neben den Vollgeschwistern. Sie rücken nur – bildlich gesprochen – „mit einer Hand" in die Hälfte des Elternteils ein, den sie mit dem Erblasser gemeinsam haben.[69] Das führt in vielen Fällen zur Halbierung des Erbteils. Das vorliegende Urteil betraf indessen nicht die zweite Ordnung, sondern mit den Halbgeschwistern der Eltern des Erblassers die dritte Ordnung. Nach § 1926 BGB vermindert sich hier ebenfalls der Erbteil der Halbgeschwister.

Der Fall vor der Kieler Spruchfakultät war weitaus schwieriger als im BGB zu lösen. Er spielte in der Stadt Burg, die wie die ganze Insel Fehmarn von 1581 bis 1713 zum herzoglichen Anteil an Schleswig, danach zum königlich-dänischen Herzogtum Schleswig im dänischen Gesamtstaat gehörte.[70] Im Gegensatz zum Umland galt in Burg nicht das Fehmarnsche Landrecht von 1558,[71] sondern kraft unbestrittener Bewidmung seit dem 14. Jahrhundert lübisches Recht.[72] Das lübische Erbrecht modifizierte das Dreiliniensystem, das zwischen absteigenden Verwandten, Vorfahren in gerader Linie und Seitenverwandten differenzierte:[73] Zunächst sollten die Abkömmlinge erben, dann die Eltern und Geschwister, erst danach die Großeltern und zuletzt entferntere Seitenverwandte nach der Gradesnähe. Im Detail war für die Halbgeschwister in der zweiten Ordnung allgemein anerkannt, dass sie nach lübischem Recht im Erbenrang hinter die Vollgeschwister zurücktraten, d.h. neben Vollgeschwistern nicht erbten. Höchst umstritten war hingegen nach lübischem Recht, ob sich der Vorrang der Vollgeschwister auf die vorliegende Konstellation in der dritten Ordnung ausdehnte. Ein paralleler, jüngst edierter Rechtsstreit in der Stadt Lübeck, der 1756 mit einem Urteil des Reichs-

---

[69] Parömie nach *Karlheinz Muscheler*, Erbrecht, Bd. 1, Tübingen 2010, Rn. 1322, mit ausführlicher Darstellung in Rn. 1321–1326, 1333; siehe auch *Kähler*, Landesrecht (oben Fn. 13), S. 535: „mit halber Hand".

[70] *Kähler*, Landesrecht (oben Fn. 13), S. 14; *Wohlhaupter*, Rechtsquellen (oben Fn. 61), Bd. 1, S. 65.

[71] Dazu *Wohlhaupter*, Rechtsquellen (oben Fn. 61), Bd. 1, S. 70 f.

[72] *Wohlhaupter*, Rechtsquellen (oben Fn. 61), Bd. 1, S. 72 f. Ergänzt durch Verordnungen, siehe Corpus statutorum Slesvicensium, oder: Sammlung der in dem Herzogthum Schleswig geltenden Land- und Stadt-Rechte, nebst den für die Gegenden erlassenen neueren Verfügungen, Bd. III/2, Schleswig 1812, S. 265–297.

[73] Zu den verschiedenen Systemen zusammenfassend *Gottfried v. Schmitt*, Entwurf eines Rechtes der Erbfolge für das Deutsche Reich nebst dem Entwurfe eines Einführungsgesetzes. Vorlage der Redaktoren, 1879, S. 557–572, in: Werner Schubert (Hg.), Die Vorlagen der Redaktoren für die erste Kommission zur Ausarbeitung des Entwurfs eines Bürgerlichen Gesetzbuches, Erbrecht, Teil 1, Berlin/New York 1984, S. 673–688. Speziell zur Erbfolge nach lübischem Recht *Götz Landwehr*, Erbfolgeordnung und Verwandtschaftszählung. Ein Diskussionsbeitrag anhand des sächsisch-magdeburgischen und des lübischen Rechts, in: Festschrift Heinz Holzhauer, Berlin 2005, S. 32–50.

kammergerichts endete, dokumentiert eindrucksvoll den Streitstand im 18. Jahrhundert.[74] Auch die Partikularrechte in Schleswig und Holstein boten zum Problem verschiedene Lösungen an, vom kompletten Gleichrang der Halbgeschwister über einen halben Erbteil bis hin zum Nachrang.[75]

Die Kieler Spruchfakultät erörterte zunächst Lib. 2 Tit. 2 Art. 1 des lübischen Rechts in der berüchtigten Ballhorn-Ausgabe von 1586. Die Norm setzte nach dem Rechtssprichwort „Das halbe Glied geht zurück" die Halbgeschwister im Rang hinter die Vollgeschwister. Ähnlich legte Art. 22 fest: „Vol-Brüder und Schwester-Kinder, nehmen Erbe vor halb-Brüdern und Schwestern [...]".[76] Die offenen Formulierungen in der Ausgabe des Stadtrechts von 1586 hätten zumindest einer Ausdehnung des Vorrangs der Vollgeschwister auf die dritte Ordnung nicht zwingend entgegengestanden.

Zeitgenössische Autoren bezweifelten allerdings, ob die Ausgabe von 1586 überhaupt den verbindlichen Normtext stellte. Es war unter den Juristen strittig, ob nicht ältere Codices des lübischen Rechts in den Tochterstädten gelten sollten.[77] Beispielhaft ist ein in den Schleswiger Akten enthaltenes gedrucktes Gutachten Dreyers.[78] Er wies auf eine Anordnung in der Landgerichtsordnung von 1636 hin.[79] Danach sollten die holsteinischen Städte „glaubwürdige", d.h. authentische Ausgaben des Lübecker Stadtrechts vorhalten. Damit, so Dreyer, könne nicht die Druckausgabe von 1586 gemeint sein; vielmehr beziehe sich die Anordnung auf aus der Zeit davor stammende handschriftliche Ausgaben. Maßgebend seien etwa für Kiel die im Stadtarchiv aufbewahrten Manuskripte des mittelalterlichen Lübecker Rechts. Man wird Dreyer im Rückblick einen gewissen Hang zur Ironie nicht absprechen können, da er den ursprünglichen Kieler Codex des lübischen Rechts

---

[74] *Peter Oestmann* (Hg.), Ein Zivilprozeß am Reichskammergericht: Edition einer Gerichtsakte aus dem 18. Jahrhundert, Köln u.a. 2009, insbes. in der Einleitung S. 5 f., zu der anlässlich des Lübecker Rechtsstreits veröffentlichten Fachliteratur. Auf der Edition baut auf *Matthias Doms*, Rechtsanwendung im Usus modernus. Eine Fallstudie zum Erbrecht der halben Geburt, Inaugural-Diss. Münster 2010.

[75] *Kähler*, Landesrecht (oben Fn. 13), S. 530–537. Danach gab es unterschiedlich große Erbteile bei Voll- und Halbgeschwistern im Nordstrander und Eiderstedter Landrecht, Husum und Friedrichstadt, den kompletten Vorrang der Vollgeschwister nach Sachsenspiegel, lübischem Recht, Land- und Marschrecht sowie nach Dithmarscher Landrecht. Im Übrigen wurde nicht zwischen Voll- und Halbgeschwistern differenziert. – Speziell zur Rechtslage in Burg *Heinrich Carl Esmarch*, Das im Herzogthume Schleswig geltende bürgerliche Recht, Schleswig 1846, S. 325 f.

[76] Halbgeschwister in (nach heutiger Terminologie) zweiter Erbenordnung waren damit nicht vollständig von der Erbenfolge ausgeschlossen (vgl. Lübecker Stadtrecht 1586 Lib. 2 Tit. 2 Artt. 18 f.), sondern standen im Rang lediglich eine Stufe unter den Vollgeschwistern.

[77] Zur Kontroverse *Falck*, Privatrecht, Teil 1 (oben Fn. 61), S. 396–400; *Kähler*, Landesrecht (oben Fn. 13), S. 20 f., jeweils m.w.N.

[78] *Dreyer*, Rechtliche Bedencken, in: LA-SH, Sig. Abt. 400.5 Nr. 755, unpaginiert, zu Lib. 1 Tit. 10 Art. 6 (Verfügungsverbote bei Erbgütern). Dazu *Ratjen*, Dreyer (oben Fn. 9), S. 96.

[79] Pars I Tit. 4 § 1.

nach Kopenhagen (jetzt Kopenhagener Codex) und dafür den ursprünglichen Lübecker Codex nach Kiel (jetzt Kieler Codex) gebracht haben soll.[80]

Die Kieler Spruchfakultät vertrat in ihrem Urteil aus dem Jahr 1753 dieselbe Ansicht und verwarf die Ausgabe von 1586 als verbindliche Autorität. Sie lag damit auf der Linie mit Reskripten aus dem Jahr 1765 für die großfürstlich-gottorfischen Städte in Holstein, die dem alten lübischen Recht vor 1586 den Vorzug einräumten.[81]

Die Fakultät führte auf dieser Grundlage aus, die Manuskripte vor 1586 enthielten zwar an einigen Stellen Hinweise auf bloße Halbgeschwister, doch sei den Quellen kein unterschiedlicher Rang in der Erbfolge zu entnehmen. In der gesetzlichen Erbenfolge sei nur allgemein von Geschwistern die Rede.[82] Die Fakultät musste daher den Begriff „Geschwister" durch Auslegung konkretisieren bzw. die Normen, welche die Halbgeschwister erwähnten, dahin auslegen, ob ihnen eine erbrechtliche Differenzierung entnommen werden sollte. Aus Methodensicht handelte es sich wohl nicht um eine Lückenfüllung durch Analogiebildung, sondern noch um eine Auslegung im Rahmen der Wortlautgrenzen.

Zunächst zog die Fakultät die Grundsätze des Naturrechts („*secundum principia Juris naturalis* zu verstehen und zu erklären") heran,[83] dann das Soester Recht (*ius sufatensium)* als Mutterrecht für Lübeck. Sogar die Beschreibungen der germanischen Sitten in Tacitus' Germania wurden konsultiert. Tacitus habe bei seiner Beschreibung der Germanen ganz bewusst nicht zwischen „voller und halber Geburth" unterschieden, obwohl er die gegenteilige Rechtslage im römischen Recht gekannt habe.[84] Die Fakultät führte unter Berufung auf den Germanisten Heineccius aus, diese Gewohnheit habe sich bis auf den heutigen Tag fortgesetzt. Im Ergebnis kam den Halbgeschwistern nach der Lesart der Kieler Fakultät in der gesetzlichen Erbfolge mangels Sonderregelung derselbe Rang wie den vollbürtigen Geschwistern zu. Diese Argumentation hätte sich sogar auf die Halbgeschwister in der zweiten Ordnung übertragen lassen.

Ausdrücklich lehnte die Spruchfakultät eine Anwendung des gemeinen römischen Rechts auf das ältere lübische Recht ab. Das war eine konsequente Ent-

---

[80] Siehe *v. Brandt*, NDB, Bd. 4, Berlin 1959, S. 122 f. Erhalten ist heute in Kiel der Lübecker Kanzleicodex, auch Kieler Codex genannt, um 1282, weitergeführt bis ca. 1350, 2003 aus der ehemaligen Sowjetunion zurückgegeben, 96 Bl., Stadtarchiv Kiel, ohne Sig., Angabe nach www.handschriftencensus.de/1492.

[81] Dazu *Kähler*, Landesrecht (oben Fn. 13), S. 20. Burg lag zu dieser Zeit im königlichen Herzogtum Schleswig, so dass die Reskripte für die Stadt nicht galten. *Kähler*, a.a.O., S. 28, nimmt für Burg die Geltung nach der Fassung von 1586 an.

[82] Zu den konkreten Normen in den mittelalterlichen Manuskripten *Doms*, Rechtsanwendung (oben Fn. 74), S. 138–140, m.w.N.

[83] LA-SH Sig. Abt. 47.5 Nr. 39, Rauert ./. Erben Hultermann, S. 204 f.

[84] A.a.O., S. 211.

scheidung, weil das schleswigsche Prozessrecht explizit die Allegation auf das gemeine Recht und damit auf das römische Recht verbot.[85] Damit unterschied sich die Rechtslage deutlich vom Herzogtum Holstein und der Stadt Lübeck, die beide die subsidiäre Geltung des gemeinen römischen Rechts anordneten.[86] Konkret sprach sich die Fakultät gegen die Auslegung des lübischen Rechts nach der Novelle 118 aus dem Jahr 543 aus, welche die Vollgeschwister in der Erbfolge vor die Halbgeschwister setzte. Im Gegensatz zum heutigen Verständnis der Novelle[87] wollte damals eine bedeutende Rechtsmeinung deren Regelungsbereich und folglich (nach heutiger Terminologie) den Vorrang der Vollgeschwister nicht auf die Erben zweiter Ordnung beschränken, sondern sie auf die dritte Ordnung erstrecken.[88] Die Auslegung nach dem gemeinen römischen Recht hätte also zu einer Ausdehnung des Vorrangs der Vollgeschwister jenseits der zweiten Ordnung führen können.

Die Kieler Spruchfakultät referierte, der Rostocker Professor Ernst Cothmann (1557–1624), David Mevius und Reichshofrat Nikolaus Christoph Freiherr v. Lyncker (1643–1726) wollten das gemeine römische Recht heranziehen, weil das ältere lübische Recht den Fall nicht eindeutig entscheide („*cum statuta stricte sint interpretanda, nec de casu ad casum extendenda*"). Dies sei aber der falsche Weg. Die Spruchfakultät argumentierte:

> „Da gleichwohl dieses alles auf das längst verworffene Brocardicum [allgemeine Rechtsregel], *quod statuta ex Jure Civili Romano sint interpretanda, limitanda et restringenda*, hinaus lauffe; allermaßen so wohl der Vernunfft, als der Intention der Gesetzgeber nach man unmöglich bey denen in *Statutis* etwa bemerkten speciellen Fällen nur stehen bleiben; in andern *casibus* aber, wo gleichwohl *paritas rationis*, oder wo *per alia argumentuo mens est intentio Statutentium* hervor leuchtet, kaum *ad Jus peregrinum* recurriren, und […] keine *analogiam statuti*, noch die diesen zum Grunde gediente […] Gewohnheiten gelten lassen könne."[89]

Die Fakultät verwarf damit die Lückenfüllung des lübischen Rechts nach römischem Recht und damit auch die bevorzugte Auslegung des lübischen Rechts mit römischem Recht. Sie hielt an der Statutentheorie nur in den Teilen fest, die das einheimische Recht nicht einschränkten. Für ihre Ansicht zitierte die Fakultät die

[85] Siehe *Kähler*, Landesrecht (oben Fn. 13), S. 24 f., mit Nachweisen aus der fürstlichen Kanzleiordnung von 1708 und der Obergerichts-Resolution von 1746. Eine Ausnahme galt nur für das Eiderstädter Landrecht, das Husumer Stadtrecht und das Friedrichstädter Stadtrecht.

[86] Zu Holstein *Kähler*, Landesrecht (oben Fn. 13), S. 18; zu Lübeck *Oestmann*, Edition (oben Fn. 74), S. 63, Fn. 370, mit Hinweis auf den Lübecker Kassarrezess von 1665.

[87] Siehe nur *Heinrich Honsell/Theo Mayer-Maly/Walter Selb*, Römisches Recht, 4. Aufl., Berlin 1987, S. 447; *Max Kaser/Rolf Knütel*, Römisches Privatrecht, 19. Aufl., München 2008, § 67 Rn. 23: Vollgeschwister (neben anderen Personen), dann halbbürtige Geschwister, zuletzt alle übrigen Seitenverwandten nach der Gradesnähe. Im letzten Fall wurde also nicht mehr nach halber oder voller Geburt differenziert.

[88] Dazu ausführlich *Doms*, Rechtsanwendung (oben Fn. 74), S. 71–88.

[89] LA-SH Sig. Abt. 47.5 Nr. 39, S. 208 f.

Dissertation Gassers sowie das Methodenlehrbuch des Jenenser Professors Christian Heinrich Eckhard (1716–1751).[90]

Dieses Verdikt gegen die Statutentheorie war kein Einzelfall, wie ein weiteres Urteil vom 6. September 1783 zum lübischen Recht belegt.[91] Die Kieler Rechtsfakultät antwortete Bürgermeister und Rat der Reichs- und Hansestadt Lübeck zur Auslegung des Injuriendelikts nach Lib. 4 Tit. 4 Art. 1. Die Fakultät urteilte unter Hinweis auf den Lübecker Partikularrechtler Joachim Lucas Stein (1711–1785):

> „das *vulgatum*: *iura statutaria stricte sunt interpretanda ex ita, ne nimis a iure communi discrepent* [...] als irrig und falsch verworfen wird, daher dann hier so wie in andern Fällen die gewöhnlichen Regeln der rechtlichen Auslegungskunst anzuwenden und bey den gemachten Voraussetzungen keine *restrictiones* anzunehmen sind".[92]

Ein zweites Urteil der Kieler Rechtsfakultät vom März 1755 zu Halbgeschwistern bestätigte das erste Verdikt.[93] Die anfragenden Richter zu Burg auf Fehmarn hatten wiederum einen Fall auf Fehmarn zu Halbgeschwistern in der dritten Ordnung zu entscheiden, diesmal aber für das Burger Umland auf Fehmarn. Entscheidungsgrundlage war nicht das Fehmarnsche Landrecht, sondern eine Verordnung aus dem Jahr 1563. Sie führte bei der Geschwistererbfolge die Halbgeschwister nicht separat auf,[94] so dass die Halbgeschwister denselben Rang wie die Vollgeschwister einnahmen. Dieses Ergebnis hätte sich über die weit verstandene Novelle 118 des gemeinen römischen Rechts korrigieren lassen. Die Spruchfakultät wies dazu einleitend auf Mevius hin und stellte die These in den Raum, das Landrecht sei *prima facie* nach dem gemeinen römischen Recht auszulegen („*statuta ex Jure statuta communi sint interpretanda*").[95]

Die Spruchfakultät ging im weiteren Argumentationsstrang aber über das gemeine römische Recht hinweg und blieb beim Gleichrang der Halbgeschwister. Sie gab bei der Auslegung dem einheimischen Recht der Nachbarterritorien den Vorzug. Unter erneuter Berufung auf Mevius benutzte man die Formel „*cum tamen in interpretatione statutorum magna vir fit legum adiorum populorum ejusdem provinciae*". Die Fakultät bewegte sich an dieser Stelle durchaus noch im Rahmen der Statutentheorie, wenn man die Problemlösung als bloße Auslegung der Verordnung und nicht als Lückenfüllung durch Analogie bewertet. Zudem war das

---

[90] Zu beiden oben bei Fn. 16.

[91] LA-SH Sig. Abt. 47.5 Nr. 51 II, Schroeder ./. Hildebrand, S. 807–828.

[92] LA-SH Sig. Abt. 47.5 Nr. 51 II, S. 823 f. Wobei anzumerken ist, dass Stein in seiner Haltung gegenüber dem gemeinen römischen Recht schwankte; siehe *Schäfer*, Germanistik (oben Fn. 2), S. 178 f. Zu Stein *Adolf Hofmeister*, in: ADB, Bd. 35, Leipzig 1893, S. 641 f.

[93] LA-SH, Sig. 47.5 Nr. 40, Frobös ./. Brodersen, ohne Paginierung.

[94] Verordnung, wie es in Erbfällen auf dem Lande Fehmarn gehalten werden solle v. 12.2.1563, §§ 9 f., in: Corpus Statutorum Slesvicensium, oder: Sammlung der in dem Herzogthum Schleswig geltenden Land- und Stadt-Rechte, Bd. 1, Schleswig 1794, S. 698 f. Dazu *Kähler*, Landesrecht (oben Fn. 13), S. 532.

[95] LA-SH, Sig. 47.5 Nr. 40, ohne Paginierung.

gemeine Recht – wie die Fakultät selbst hervorhob – gegenüber den nächstgelegenen Stadt- und Landrechten subsidiär. Erster nachbarlicher Bezugspunkt war somit das lübische Recht der Stadt Burg und damit wiederum Lib. 2 Tit. 2 Art. 22 des lübischen Rechts. Ferner verwies die Fakultät auf das Hamburger Stadtrecht sowie auf das Jütische Low.

Im Ergebnis lag die Kieler Rechtsfakultät auf der Linie des Reichskammergerichts, das sich ebenfalls gegen einen Vorrang der Vollgeschwister in der dritten Ordnung aussprach.[96] Inhaltlich argumentierte die Kieler Fakultät aber deutlich restriktiver. Ihre Argumente hätten zumindest für das lübische Recht in Holstein und für Fehmarn sogar in der zweiten Ordnung gegen einen Vorrang der Vollgeschwister gesprochen. Die Kieler Spruchfakultät griff anders als in der Frage des Sachsenspiegels für Holstein hier bedenkenlos auf mittelalterliche Rechtsquellen bis hin zum germanischen Recht zurück.

5. Beispiel 3 – Gütergemeinschaft

Das letzte und dritte Beispiel bewegt sich mit der Erbfolge bei einer Gütergemeinschaft unter Ehegatten an der Schnittstelle von Familien- und Erbrecht. Die Kieler Spruchfakultät urteilte am 2. März 1789 über einen Fall des Stadtgerichts Neubrandenburg im Kurfürstentum Brandenburg.[97] Nach einer kinderlosen Ehe stritt sich der verwitwete Ehemann mit den Verwandten der verstorbenen Ehefrau um die Höhe des jeweiligen Erbteils aus dem Anteil der verstorbenen Gattin an der Gütergemeinschaft. Das war kein Einzelfall in der Rechtspraxis. Die Quotelung zwischen dem überlebenden Ehegatten und den Verwandten des verstorbenen Ehegatten bildete ein klassisches Problem des Usus modernus bzw. des Deutschen Privatrechts, mit dem sich zahlreiche Abhandlungen beschäftigten.[98] Die Kieler Spruchfakultät führte deshalb aus, es gebe kaum eine Materie mit einer größeren Meinungsvielfalt als die Gütergemeinschaft.

Das gemeine römische Recht mit seinem Dotalrecht blieb bei der Falllösung von vornherein abseits, da die Gütergemeinschaft allgemein als originär einheimisches Rechtsinstitut galt.[99] Wie in den anderen Beispielen stützte sich die Spruchfakultät im Ausgangspunkt auf das einschlägige Partikularrecht. Entscheidend sei nicht die Meinung der Rechtslehre, die oft an der Rechtspraxis vorbeigehe, sondern die spezifischen Landesgesetze, Statuten und Gewohnheiten. In Neubrandenburg galt die *Constitutio Joachimica* („Constitution des Kurfürsten Joachim 1.“),[100] eine

[96] Ebenso der Sache nach im 19. Jahrhundert *Esmarch*, Recht (oben Fn. 75), S. 326.

[97] LA-SH, Sig. Abt. 47.5 Nr. 55, Intestaterben Catharina Maria Dudey ./. Moritz Christian Dudey, unpaginiert. Referent: Adolf Dietrich Weber.

[98] Zu den Varianten in der Lösung statt aller *Schäfer*, Germanistik (oben Fn. 2), S. 276–279, m.w.N.

[99] Paradigmatisch zur Qualität als einheimisches Recht in einem anderen Fall *Dreyer*, Urteil v. 1748 für die Spruchfakultät Kiel, in: LA-SH Sig. Abt. 400.5 Nr. 755, S. 237–317.

[100] LA-SH, Sig. Abt. 47.5 Nr. 55, unpaginiert.

Teilgesetzgebung des Kurfürsten von Brandenburg aus dem Jahr 1527 zum Erbrecht. Auf dieser Grundlage stufte die Fakultät den Güterstand bzw. die dingliche Rechtslage zwischen den Ehegatten nicht als bloßes Miteigentum bzw. als römische *societas*, sondern als Gütergemeinschaft ein. Allerdings enthielt die Joachimica keine ausdrückliche Regelung für die beschriebene Konstellation einer kinderlosen Ehe. Es hätte für die Fakultät somit nahegelegen, die Lücke durch Sätze des Deutschen Privatrechts bzw. des Naturrechts oder durch Normen benachbarter Stadt- und Landrechte aufzufüllen. In der Tat erwog die Fakultät in den *rationes dubitandi* im Anschluss an die naturrechtliche Diskussion, eine Gütergemeinschaft sei eine moralische Person, bei welcher dem überlebenden Ehegatten das gesamte Erbe zustehe. In den *rationes decidendi* hingegen verfolgte die Fakultät eine konservativere Linie. Sie judizierte, entscheidend sei mangels einer landesgesetzlichen Regelung das lokale Recht, hier das lokale Gewohnheitsrecht. Da die Parteien nach Ansicht der Fakultät für das Gewohnheitsrecht keinen überzeugenden Beweis und Gegenbeweis erbringen konnten, verfasste sie kein Schlussurteil, sondern gab den Klägern lediglich auf, ausreichende Beweise zu den ihnen günstigen Erbrechtsnormen vorzubringen.

Für die Bewertung des Urteils ist festzuhalten, dass die Kieler Spruchfakultät hier wieder einmal uneinheitlich entschied. Während sie beim Recht auf Fehmarn keine Bedenken hatte, vergleichend bei der Normauslegung die Lösungen in umliegenden Stadt- und Landrechten heranzuziehen, zog sie sich zu Brandenburg auf die Position zurück, entscheidend sei mangels einer Regelung im Landesrecht das lokale Gewohnheitsrecht. Das war jedoch keine gegen das einheimische Privatrecht gerichtete Position. Vielmehr gewichtete die Fakultät die Sentenz „Stadtrecht bricht Landrecht und Landrecht bricht gemeines Recht" resp. den Satz *lex specialis derogat legi generali* stärker als den Wunsch nach einer abschließenden Entscheidung durch Rechtsvergleich. Entscheidend könnten drei Momente gewesen sein: erstens der angesprochene Unterschied zwischen Auslegung und Lückenfüllung. Im Fall der Auslegung gestattete auch die Statutentheorie ohne weiteres die vergleichende Einbeziehung der Nachbarrechte, im Fall der Lückenfüllung nur ausnahmsweise, wenn der Beweis der Rezeption am Ort des Rechtsfalls gelungen war. Zweitens könnte die Kieler Spruchfakultät die Regel im Gedächtnis gehabt haben, dass ohne ausreichende Kenntnis des Partikularrechts verfasste Rechtssprüche unverbindlich sind. Eine Zurückverweisung lag daher in jedem Fall näher als eine abschließende Entscheidung. Und drittens war nach Ansicht der Kieler Fakultät die Lösung in einem Gewohnheitsrecht fernab der Landesgrenzen zu suchen, das mangels Notorietät erst näher zu erforschen war.

IV. Fazit – Neubewertung der Spruchtätigkeit im Usus modernus

Die Auswertung der Sprüche der Kieler Spruchfakultät bestätigt die These, dass sich die Spruchfakultäten im Heiligen Römischen Reich in der zweiten Hälfte des 18. Jahrhunderts, d.h. in der Spätphase des Usus modernus pandectarum, dem einheimischen Partikularrecht zuwandten. Im Detail ist festzuhalten:

1. Die einheimischen Gesetze und Verordnungen der Frühen Neuzeit wurden in Kiel an ihrem originären Geltungsort ohne weitere Prüfung, d.h. der Sache nach von Amts wegen angewendet. Die Normanwendung von Amts wegen umfasste Auslegung und Analogiebildung. Das war die konsequente Folge des Satzes „Stadtrecht bricht Landrecht und Landrecht bricht gemeines Recht" bzw. von *lex specialis derogat legi generali*.

2. Die Statutentheorie sicherte die Vorherrschaft des römischen Rechts in der Rechtsanwendung. Die Kieler Rechtsfakultät gab sie in ihren tragenden Elementen, d.h. der vorzugsweisen Auslegung einer Norm nach römischem Recht bzw. dem Analogieverbot zulasten des einheimischen Partikularrechts, spätestens ab der Mitte des 18. Jahrhunderts auf. Sie ging hier weit über die Korrekturen bei Mevius hinaus. Übrig blieben von der Statutentheorie zwei Elemente: erstens die Skepsis gegenüber der Lückenfüllung durch fremde Partikularrechte; zweitens die Normauslegung mittels Rechtsvergleich mit den benachbarten Partikularrechten. Diese Artefakte der Statutentheorie bevorzugten allerdings nicht das römische Recht.

3. Ambivalent war allein das Verhältnis zu einheimischen Rechtsquellen aus dem Mittelalter. Die juristischen Germanisten kritisierten ab der Mitte des 18. Jahrhunderts den Rückgriff auf solche Quellen. Die Kieler Fakultät schwankte hier. Teilweise griff sie auf mittelalterliche Stadtrechte und sogar auf Tacitus' Germania zurück, teilweise lehnte sie die Anwendung des Sachsenspiegels als wichtigstes mittelalterliches Rechtsbuch ab.

4. Möglicherweise favorisierte die Kieler Spruchfakultät aufgrund ihrer exponierten Position in der neuen Wissenschaft der juristischen Germanistik das einheimische Recht bereits in großen Teilen der ersten Hälfte des 18. Jahrhunderts. Allerdings sind für diese wichtige Zeit die Spruchakten der Fakultät in großen Teilen nicht mehr vorhanden, so dass sich die These nicht verifizieren lässt.

5. Zumindest für die Zeit vor 1700, d.h. in der Hochphase des Usus modernus, bleibt das einheimische Privatrecht bereits quantitativ in den Kieler Sprüchen eine Randerscheinung. Man könnte die These aufstellen, Gerichte und Privatpersonen hätten die Rechtsfakultät erst gar nicht um Rechtsrat gefragt, weil die juristische Germanistik als Wissenschaft des einheimischen Rechts erst um 1700 entstand und vor dieser Zeit keine Expertise für das einheimische Recht an den Universitäten vorhanden gewesen war. Gegen diese These spricht allerdings der gleichbleibend hohe Zufluss durch Aktenversendung an die Spruchfakultät während des 17. und 18. Jahrhunderts. Plausibler ist die These, dass sich die Kieler Fakultät wie viele andere Fakultäten des Heiligen Römischen Rechts der juristischen Germanistik zuwandte und damit in ihrer Spruchtätigkeit auf der Ebene der Rechtsquellen und Methodenlehre die Regeln zugunsten des einheimischen Privatrechts änderte.

6. Nicht vergessen werden darf zum Schluss, dass auch im 18. Jahrhundert die Sprüche mit Elementen zum einheimischen Privatrecht eine kleine Minderheit in der Spruchtätigkeit darstellten. Die Literatur hat dafür eine bedenkenswerte These

aufgestellt: Die Spruchfakultäten hätten das einheimische Privatrecht nur dort zitiert, wo es sich in den Lösungen vom gemeinen römischen Recht unterschieden habe.[101] Folgt man dieser These, war das Entscheidungsvolumen zum einheimischen Privatrecht in der Rechtsgeschichte wesentlich höher als es der Wortlaut der Sprüche vermuten lässt. Dagegen war das einheimische Privatrecht nur in wenigen Fällen tatsächlich entscheidungserheblich.

---

[101] *Weiss*, Spruchtätigkeit (oben Fn. 7), S. 115–118, zum Hamburger Stadtrecht: „Mit gemeinem [...] Recht übereinstimmende Rechtssätze wurden dagegen kurzerhand ohne Zitierung der Fundstelle in hamburger Kodifizierungen dem gemeinen Recht entnommen; selten wird auf die Übereinstimmung des hamburger mit dem gemeinen Recht hingewiesen."

Recht und Gerichtsverfassung in Schleswig-Holstein vor 150 Jahren

Werner Schubert

In kaum einem anderen Teil des Deutschen Bundes bzw. Dänemarks war die Zersplitterung und Uneinheitlichkeit des Rechts auf allen Gebieten so groß wie in den Herzogtümern Schleswig und Holstein, als diese 1867 als eigene Provinz zu Preußen kamen. Versuche, wenigstens die Gerichtsverfassung und das Prozessrecht auf der Basis der Öffentlichkeit und Mündlichkeit sowie des Anklageprozesses zu reformieren, waren fehlgeschlagen. Die letzte Gesamtdarstellung des bürgerlichen Rechts im Herzogtum Schleswig war 1854[1] erschienen. Das Handbuch des Schleswig-Holsteinischen Privatrechts von Falck war noch bis 1848 erschienen,[2] so dass die seit 1854 ergangenen, nicht unwichtigen, wenn auch nur geringfügigen Teilreformen des Zivilrechts nicht mehr in eine systematische Darstellung des Privatrechts Schleswig-Holsteins Eingang fanden.

Auch über die Prozessrechte und die Gerichtsverfassung der beiden Provinzen existieren keine Darstellungen, welche die letzten Reformverordnungen für dieses Rechtsgebiet berücksichtigten.[3] Im Folgenden soll die Gerichtsverfassung, das Prozessrecht und wichtige Gebiete des bürgerlichen Rechts dargestellt werden, wie sie sich bis 1864/65 entwickelt hatten, als Schleswig-Holstein unter preußische bzw. österreichische Verwaltung kam. Dabei ist zu berücksichtigen, dass sich das Zivilrecht in Schleswig und Holstein unterschiedlich entwickelt hatte. Verordnungen, die in einem Landesteil galten, wurden nicht immer inhaltsgleich für den anderen Landesteil in Kraft gesetzt.

---

1 *Heinrich Carl Esmarch*, Das im Herzogthum Schleswig geltende bürgerliche Recht, 2. Aufl., Schleswig 1854; und vgl. auch die Nachschriften von Vorlesungen von *Paul Roth*, Das Schleswig-Holsteinische Privatrecht, 1860/61 und 1862/63 (mit Ergänzungen für die preußische Zeit), im Jur. Seminar der Univ. Kiel vorhanden.

2 *Nikolaus Falck,* Handbuch des Schleswig-Holsteinischen Privatrechts, Teil IV, Altona 1825–1848 (unvollendet); *Paul Detlev Christian Paulsen,* Lehrbuch des Privatrechts in den Herzogtümern Schleswig und Holstein, 2. Aufl., Kiel 1842.

3 Insoweit war teilweise überholt das Werk von *August Wilhelm Samuel Francke,* Der gemeine Deutsche und Schleswig-Holsteinische Civilprozeß, Hamburg, Kiel 1839–1843. – Für das Strafverfahren vgl. *Heinrich Carl Esmarch,* Praktische Darstellung des Strafverfahrens im Herzogthum Schleswig, Schleswig 1840–1843. – Für die Justizverfassung vor den preußischen Reformen vgl. den Bericht des preußischen Justizbeamten Krüger von 1967 (bei *Werner Schubert,* Zur Geschichte der Justizverfassung in Schleswig-Holstein, Frankfurt a.M. 2012, S. 1–115).

I. Das in Schleswig und Holstein geltende Recht

Otto Kähler stellte für *Holstein* folgende Allgemeinregeln auf:[4]

> „In den Städten galt Lübsches Recht, dahinter Sachsenrecht, dahinter Gemeines Recht. – In Dithmarschen galt Dithmarsisches Landrecht, dahinter Sachsenrecht, dahinter Gemeines Recht. – In den Schauenburgischen Landen galt nur Gemeines Recht. In allen übrigen Landesteilen galt Sachsenrecht, dahinter Gemeines Recht."

In der Regel lasse sich erkennen, dass der Satz: „Stadtrecht bricht Landrecht, Landrecht bricht Gemeines Recht" auch in Holstein Anerkennung gefunden habe. Unter gemeinem Recht war nicht nur das römische, sondern auch das deutsche Recht und Teile des kanonischen Rechts zu verstehen. Das gemeine Recht galt an erster Stelle für die Angehörigen der Universität Kiel, für die Schauenburgischen Lande, für Altona, Pinneberg und die Grafschaft Rantzau. Als Sachsenrecht war der Sachsenspiegel anzusehen, dem allerdings spezielle Rechte vorgingen. Zu diesen gehörten das Lübsche Recht von 1586, das vor allem in den vier Städten Kiel, Rendsburg, Itzehoe und Oldesloe galt. Das Dithmarscher Landrecht von 1567/1642 war in plattdeutscher Sprache abgefasst und richtete sich weitgehend nach dem Lübschen Recht. Zum Gebiet des Sachsenrechts gehörten ferner das Land- und Marschenrecht, die Neumünsterschen Kirchspielsgebräuche und die Bordesholmer Amtsgebräuche. Anders als für Holstein existierte in *Schleswig* kein allgemein geltendes Recht. Von Ausnahmen abgesehen hatte keinen Eingang gefunden das gemeine Recht, das in den Urteilen nicht allegiert werden durfte. Lediglich als *ratio scripta* wurde das römische Recht herangezogen. Zu den wenigen Rechten, in denen das gemeine Recht subsidiär galt, gehörten das Eiderstedter Landrecht von 1572/91, das Husumer Stadtrecht von 1582/1608 und das Friedrichstädter Stadtrecht von 1633. Das Friesische Recht (Nordstrander Landrecht) galt in der Landschaft Nordstrand und in den vier Marschharden des Amtes Tondern. Die übrigen Landesteile von Schleswig gehörten zum Rechtsgebiet des Jütschen Lov von 1240 – das Gesetzbuch Christians V. von 1683 war nicht eingeführt worden. Folgende Spezialrechte gingen dem Jütschen Lov vor: Das Lübsche Recht in Tondern und Burg, das Fehmarnsche Landrecht von 1558, die Stapelholmer Konstitutionen von 1623, das Flensburger, Apenrader, Haderslebener und Eckernförder Stadtrecht. In den dänischen Landesteilen, die bis 1920 zu Preußen gehörten, galt das dänische Recht, also insbesondere noch das Gesetzbuch Christian V. von 1683.

II. Die Gerichtsverfassung in den Herzogtümern[5]

In *Holstein* existierten neben dem Oberappellationsgericht in Kiel (begründet 1834; bis 1850 für beide Landesteile zuständig) fünf Oberdikasterien (Holsteinisches

---

4 *Otto Kähler,* Das Schleswig-Holsteinische Landesrecht, Glückstadt 1908, S. 12 ff.

5 Zum Folgenden preuß. Justizministerialblatt 1867, 123 ff. (*Holstein*), 186 ff. (*Schleswig*); vgl. ferner *August Wilhelm Samuel Francke,* Der gemeine deutsche und Schleswig-Holsteinische Civilprozeß, 2. Aufl., Teil 1, Hamburg 1844, S. 68 ff., 83 ff.

Obergericht, Holsteinisches Landgericht, Oberkonsistorium, Land-Oberkonsistorium und Ober-Kriminalgericht – sämtlich in Glücksburg), einige wenige Mittelgerichte und die erstinstanzlichen, nicht von der Verwaltung getrennten Gerichte. Als besondere Gerichte sind zu nennen die Konsistorien (geistliche Gerichtsbarkeit), die akademischen Konsistorien in Kiel und die Klosterkonvente bzw. das Zönobialgericht für die Angehörigen der adeligen Klöster. In geringfügigen und summarischen Sachen oblag die Entscheidung der Rechtsstreitigkeiten den Amtsschreibern, Amtsvögten, Bürgermeistern und anderen Amtsinhabern.

In den Städten bildete der Magistrat das ordentliche Gericht erster Instanz. In den Ämtern, Landschaften und adeligen Marschgütern bestanden ursprünglich Volksgerichte unter Leitung eines königlichen Beamten. Die unter einem Dingvogt stehenden Laienrichter (Holsten, Hausleute, Dingmänner, Schöffen) hatten „rechtlich durchgängig alleinige Stimme" (Urteilsfinder); doch waren um 1860 die Volksgerichte sehr selten und durch landesherrliche Gerichte ersetzt worden, und zwar weitgehend durch Prorogation. Die Regierung legte den Ständen 1859 den Entwurf eines Gesetzes, über die „Aufhebung der im Herzogthum Holstein bestehenden Dinggerichte und die Übertragung der diesen zustehenden Gerichtsbarkeit an andere Gerichtsbehörden" vor. Hiernach sollten vor allem die in den Ämtern Rendsburg, Wandsbek, Trittau und Tremsbüttel noch bestehenden Dinggerichte aufgehoben werden. Das Obergericht in Glückstadt hatte zu dieser Frage am 22.11.1858 ein ausführliches Gutachten erstattet, in dem es die Aufhebung der Dinggerichte befürwortete. Die vom Obergericht von den Untergerichten eingeholten Berichte wünschten „mit Entschiedenheit die Aufhebung der Dinggerichte". Im Bericht aus Trittau vom 25./28.2.1858 heißt es:

> „Wer es vor Augen hat, wie sehr der Processgang durch die regelmäßig nur einmal im Jahre stattfindenden Dinggerichte verzögert wird, wie oft die Provokation ans Ordinarium von säumigen Schuldnern zur Hinhaltung der Gläubiger benutzt worden [...] und wie leicht im Dinggericht die Urtheilsfinder in die Lage kommen, sich das Erkenntniß suggeriren zu lassen, oder aber eine unjuristische Entscheidung abzugeben, – der kann nur mit Freuden die Aussicht begrüßen, diese aus dem Mittelalter überkommene, überlebte Einrichtung verschwinden zu sehen, und es wird die Aufhebung der Dinggerichte als eine Wohlthat für die unter diesem schwerfälligen und langsamen Processgange leidenden angesehen werden müssen".[6] Es sei auch einleuchtend, „dass die Dinggerichte, welche regelmäßig nur ein- oder zweimal im Jahr gehalten werden, ein sehr geeignetes Mittel bieten, den Proceß in die Länge zu ziehen".

Im Übrigen fühlten sich die Kläger oft zu einem für sie ungünstigen Vergleich genötigt, um eine Entscheidung des Dinggerichts zu vermeiden. Die Holsteinische Ständeversammlung lehnte die Gesetzesvorlage ab, weil mit ihr nicht die von ihr wiederholt geforderte Legalisierung der Justizverfassung von Teilen Holsteins verbunden war.

---

[6] Zitiert nach der Akte des Landesarchivs Schleswig, Rep. 80, Nr. 1282. Die Gesetzesvorlage findet sich in der Zeitung für die Verhandlungen der 10. Holsteinischen Provinzialversammlung 1859, Beil. I, S. 177–195; vgl. auch Beil. II, 11 ff. und Verh., S. 116 ff., 124, 353.

Die Gerichtsbarkeit auf den adligen Gütern übten ein vom König bestätigter Gerichtshalter und zwei Beisitzer aus.[7] An das Obergericht in Glückstadt gelangten die Rechtsstreitigkeiten der Personen, die einem eximierten Gerichtsstand unterlagen (Adelige, Doktoren, Ober- und Landgerichtsadvokaten, höhere Beamte). Volksgerichte zweiter Instanz bestanden nur noch in sehr wenigen Bezirken. Das Holsteinische Obergericht (Glückstadt) war die zweite Instanz in allen Rechtssachen, während das nur vierteljährlich tagende Landgericht die zweite Instanz für die privilegierten Rechtssachen bildete. Strafsachen kamen in den Landdistrikten vor die Oberbeamten, in den Städten vor die Magistrate. Strafen über ein Jahr Zuchthaus konnten nur durch das Oberkriminalgericht ausgesprochen werden. Rechtsmittel gingen an das Oberappellations- und an das Kriminalobergericht.

Das *Oberappellationsgericht zu Kiel*[8] war 1834 aufgrund des Art. 12 der Bundesakte begründet worden, wonach jeder Bundesstaat mit einer Einwohnerzahl von 300.000 an verpflichtet war, ein oberstes Gericht als dritte Instanz zu errichten. Dies traf auch für Holstein mit 362.000 Einwohnern (1817) zu, das zum Deutschen Bund gehörte. Seit 1819 gingen beim Bundestag in Frankfurt/Main Beschwerden über verweigerte und gehemmte Rechtspflege ein. In Kopenhagen versuchte man die Frage der Errichtung eines obersten Gerichts dilatorisch zu behandeln, stellte aber einen 14 Punkte umfassenden Entwurf über die für das Obergericht maßgebenden Gesichtspunkte auf. Hiernach sollte das Oberappellationsgericht die höchste Instanz in Zivil- und Kriminalsachen darstellen und in keinem Fall als *forum privilegiatum* in erster Instanz entscheiden. Die Verhandlungen sollten schriftlich aufgrund einer eigenen Gerichtsordnung erfolgen. Die „Erkenntnisse" waren nach Ziffer 5 der Grundsätze zu begründen. Das Gericht sollte aus dem Präsidenten und acht Räten bestehen. *Brockdorff,* seit 1802 Präsident des Holsteinischen Obergerichts in Glückstadt, stellte 1820 in einem Gutachten zu den Grundsätzen fest, dass die bisher in Holstein unbekannte Trennung der Justiz von der Administration durch die Errichtung eines Oberappellationsgerichts unerlässlich werde. 1827 lagen Entwürfe zur Bildung eines Oberappellationsgerichts für Holstein und für eine Gerichtsordnung vor, die hauptsächlich vom späteren Nachfolger Brockdorffs, von Johann Paul Höpp (damals in der schleswig-holsteinischen Kanzlei in Kopenhagen) stammten. Der König genehmigte am 10.11.1826, dass „für das Herzogthum Holstein ein Oberappellationsgericht, dem zugleich die Funktion einer höchsten Rechtsinstanz für das Herzogthum Lauenburg beizulegen wäre, errichtet" werden sollte. Sitz des Gerichts sollte Kiel sein mit der Einschränkung,[9] dass es für die Berufung in Strafsachen nicht zuständig sein sollte.

---

7 Schleswig-Holsteinische Anzeigen 1805, Sp. 905 ff.

8 Zum Folgenden *Werner Schubert,* 175 Jahre Obergerichtsbarkeit in Schleswig-Holstein, SchlHA 2009, S. 308 ff. m.w.N.

9 *Paul Richter,* Zeitschrift der Gesellschaft für Schleswig-Holsteinische Geschichte 58 (1929), S. 529 f.

Erst nach der französischen Julirevolution gab König Friedrich VI. der Kanzlei auf:[10]

> „Dass gleichzeitig mit der Einführung von Ständen für jedes Herzogthum insbesondere, nicht nur für die schon länger für das Herzogthum Holstein beabsichtigte Trennung der Administration von der Justiz zur Ausführung gebracht, sondern auch auf das Herzogthum Schleswig erstreckt, und zu dem Ende für beide Herzogthümer ein gemeinschaftliches Oberappellationsgericht, welches zugleich für das Herzogthum Lauenburg die höchste Instanz bildet, errichtet werden soll."

Eine neue, aus *O. J. von Moltke, Brockdorff* und dem Kanzler des Gottorfer Obergerichts *Spies* gebildete Kommission aktualisierte die Entwürfe von 1826/27. Der Versuch von *Spies,* ein mündliches Verfahren durchzusetzen, stieß auf den Widerstand von *Brockdorff,* der dringend davor warnte:

> „In unsern Zeiten muß man mit der Belebung des Gemeinsinns und der Theilnahme an öffentlichen Angelegenheiten vorsichtig seyn. Es geht damit wie mit der Aufklärung, alles hat seine Grenze, und muß nicht übereilt werden."

Einig war man sich darüber, dass entgegen den früheren Vorschlägen das Oberappellationsgericht auch für Kriminalsachen zuständig sein sollte. Kontrovers war die Frage, ob Schleswig oder Kiel Sitz des neuen Gerichts sein sollte.

> *Moltke* setzte sich für Schleswig ein, da es von „größter politischer Wichtigkeit" sei, „die festere Verbindung des Herzogthums Holstein (mit der Monarchie) auch für die Zukunft zu beachten". Gegen Kiel spreche, „dass Holstein zu Deutschland gehöre und stets deutsch fühlen werde; ‚ein solches Gefühl werde sich unvermerkt dem Gerichtshof mitteilen und dieser ein rein deutscher werden'. Außerdem könne der König nicht zugeben, dass ein höchster Gerichtshof des Herzogtums Schleswig im Namen des deutschen Bundes als Austrägalinstanz (Schiedsgericht) auftrete, dem könne dadurch abgeholfen werden, dass er seinen Sitz außerhalb Deutschlands habe."

Die drei anderen Kommissionsmitglieder waren sich darüber einig, die Verbindung Holsteins mit Dänemark für die Zukunft zu sichern; eine Verlegung nach Schleswig könne „doch leicht die entgegengesetzte Wirkung" haben:[11]

> „Eine dritte Instanz außerhalb des Bundesgebietes könnte zu unangenehmen Erörterungen im Bundestag führen. Auch erwarteten sie vorteilhaften Einfluss des Gerichts als Examinationskollegium auf Sitten und Fleiß der Studenten, erhofften sich Nutzen für die Gerichtsräte durch die Universitätsbibliothek und günstige Wirkungen für Theorie und Praxis durch Gedankenaustausch mit den Professoren der Universität".

Endlich könnten „die juristischen Professoren zu außerordentlichen Beisitzern" ernannt werden, an jedem anderen Orte fehle es dazu an „geeigneten Männern".

Die ordentlichen Zivilgerichte erster Instanz im Herzogtum *Schleswig* bildeten in den Städten der Magistrat und auf dem Lande die sog. Dinggerichte mit Beisitzern (freie Landeigentümer, sog. Bonden, Sandmänner, Reffninger, Synsmänner,

---

[10] Zitiert nach *Reiner Witt*, SchlHA 1988, Sonderheft, 29.

[11] Zitiert nach *Andreas Scharf*, in: Volquart Pauls (Begr.), Geschichte Schleswig-Holsteins, Bd. 7, 2. Lieferung, Neumünster 1980, S. 102.

Dingmänner, Dinghörer, Rathmänner, Hardesmänner) unter dem Vorsitz eines Hardesvogts.[12] Die Dingmänner waren im Laufe der Zeit weitgehend zu stimmlosen Beisitzern (Solemnitätszeugen) geworden. Im Amt Flensburg gaben die Gerichtsbeisitzer noch ihre Zustimmung regelmäßig „durch Stillschweigen“ zu erkennen. 1854 wurden im Herzogtum Schleswig – nicht jedoch in Holstein – der eximierte Gerichtsstand und die Patrimonialgerichtsbarkeit aufgehoben und stattdessen zum Teil neue Gerichtsbezirke geschaffen unter Leitung eines Hardesvogts.[13] Seit 1850/54 bildete für Schleswig die zweite und höchste Instanz das Appellationsgericht in Flensburg,[14] das aus einem Präsidenten und acht Räten bestand. An Entscheidungen mussten fünf Gerichtsmitglieder mitwirken. Untergerichte in Strafsachen waren wie in Holstein die Vögte (zusammen mit Beisitzern), in den Städten der Magistrat, und zwar seit 1854 in jeder Kriminalsache ohne Rücksicht auf die Höhe der zu erkennenden Strafe (bis dahin nur bei einer Verurteilung ab zehn Jahren Gefängnis). Zweite und dritte Instanz war das Obergericht in Flensburg.

III. Das Prozessrecht in den Herzogtümern

Der Zivilprozess beruhte auf dem gemeinen Prozessrecht,[15] wie es durch die Reichskammergerichtsordnung und den Jüngsten Reichsabschied von 1654 ausgestaltet worden war. Hinzu kamen noch Teilregelungen vor allem in der revidierten Landgerichtsordnung für das Herzogtum Schleswig und Holstein von 1636 und die Schauenburgische Hofgerichtsordnung von 1639 sowie weitere Einzelverordnungen. Grundlage des Prozesses bildeten die schriftlichen Klage- und Exzeptionsrezesse; im Ganzen war das Verfahren ein schriftlich-mündliches. Nach der Verhandlung über die Klage und die Exzeptionen wurde mündlich re- und dupliziert. Vor Einreichung der Klage war eine Bescheinigung darüber zu erbringen, dass ein Güteversuch durch den Oberbeamten stattgefunden hat. Die Verhandlungen waren grundsätzlich öffentlich. Für die Oberdikasterien in Schleswig und Holstein erging 1834 eine Verfügung „betreffend eine Instruction und Gerichtsordnung für die dem Schleswig-Holsteinischen-Lauenburgischen Oberappellationsgericht zu Kiel unmittelbar untergeordneten Landesdicasterien des Herzogthums Schleswig (Holstein)“,[16] die auch Teile des Verfahrens regelte. Hiernach fanden öffentliche Sitzungen statt zur Entscheidung der im Wege des ordentlichen Prozesses mündlich zu verhandelnden Sachen. Der Entscheidung, an der vier Richter mitwirken mussten, ging ein schriftliches Referat und in der Regel auch ein

[12] *Francke,* Civilprozeß (oben Fn. 5), S. 89.

[13] Gesetz vom 6.2.1854, in: Chronologische Sammlung der Verordnungen, Verfügungen etc. für das Herzogthum Schleswig, 1854, S. 95 ff.

[14] Patent vom 6.2.1854, in: Chronologische Sammlung 1854, Sp. 99 ff.; vgl. auch *Lorenzen,* SchlHZ 1962, S. 256, Fn. 40.

[15] Zum Folgenden *Francke,* Civilprozeß (oben Fn. 5), S. 17 ff.

[16] SchlHZ 1834, S. 889 ff.

Korreferat voraus. Sämtliche Entscheidungen mussten mit Urteilsgründen versehen sein.

Das Oberappellationsgericht erhielt eine eigene provisorische Prozessordnung mit 120 Bestimmungen, die grundsätzlich am gemeinrechtlichen schriftlichen Prozess festhielt:[17] „Bis Uns ein Bedenken des Oberappellationsgerichts über die Ausführung Unserer allerhöchsten Absicht, bei demselben baldthunlichst ein öffentliches und mündliches Verfahren eintreten zu lassen, vorgelegt ..., geschieht die Verhandlung in allen zu Entscheidung des Oberappellationsgerichts gelangenden Sachen im Wege des schriftlichen Verfahrens (§ 9).“ Das Gericht hatte die Pflicht (§ 10), „bei allen Entscheidungen, welche es abgiebt, die Gründe der Entscheidungen in das Erkenntniß einzurücken, oder solche dem Urtheile in einer besonderen Anlage beizufügen“. Relationen und Correlationen waren mit einem vollständigen Aktenextrakt schriftlich auszuarbeiten, und zwar innerhalb von drei bzw. zwei Wochen. Jedes Urteil musste in der Regel „wenigstens innerhalb drei Monaten, und die Entscheidung in Straf- sowie in den im unbedingten Mandatsprozesse schwebenden Sachen, die vor allem zu fördern sind, jedesmal in einer kürzeren Frist nach Eingang der letzten Processchrift abgegeben werden“ (§ 45)“.

Die Zulässigkeit des letztinstanzlichen Rechtsmittels war von einem Beschwerdewert von 400 Reichstalern abhängig, wobei die Appellation suspensive Wirkung hatte. An keine Revisionssumme war das außerordentliche Rechtsmittel der Nichtigkeitsbeschwerde geknüpft; sie war zulässig, wenn „in der Person des Richters, oder der Partheien, oder hinsichtlich des Verfahrens ein wesentlicher Mangel statt gefunden hat (§ 77).“ Die „Einführung der Appellation“ hatte „mittelst einer Schrift zu erfolgen, welche nebst der Geschichtserzählung, einer kurzen Proceßgeschichte und der Rechtfertigung der beobachteten Formalien, eine bestimmte Angabe der Beschwerden, die Ausführung derselben und den Antrag auf Abänderung des angefochtenen Urtheils oder Bescheides enthalten“ (§ 99) sollte.

Jede Partei konnte „neue rechtliche Deductionen ihrer Ansprüche“ (§ 105) liefern. Sie war jedoch nicht befugt, „neue Thatsachen oder neue, durch den Ablauf des Beweistermins in der früheren Instanz präcludirte Beweismittel vorzubringen“. Wenn das „eingewandte Rechtsmittel nach dem Ermessen des Oberappellationsgerichts dergestalt gemißbraucht“ wurde, „daß dasselbe die angebrachte Beschwerde in der Entscheidung als frevelhaft zu bezeichnen sich veranlaßt findet“, war die Partei, die sich dieses Missbrauchs schuldig machte, eine nach richterlichem Ermessen zu bestimmende Strafe bis zum Betrag von 200 „Bankthalern“ zu verurteilen (§ 108).

Mitte und Ende der 50er Jahre war geplant, für das Appellationsgericht eine revidierte Gerichtsordnung zu erlassen, mit der sich der zuständige Ausschuss der

[17] SchlHA 1834, Sp. 1169 ff., 1217 ff., 1257 ff., 1297 ff., 1329 ff.

8. Holsteinischen Provinzialständeversammlung befasst hat.[18] Von Ausnahmen abgesehen war in Zivilsachen mündlich zu verhandeln: „In dem zur Verhandlung angesetzten Termine sind den Parteien bloß mündliche Vorträge gestattet. Weder schriftliche Recesse über die zu haltenden mündlichen Vorträge sind zulässig, noch soll dem Gesuche einer Partei irgend einen Theil des Vortrages in das Protocoll aufzunehmen, stattgegeben werden" (§ 96). In jedem Falle „muss der mündliche Vortrag selbstständig sein; das Ablesen ist nicht gestattet. Jedoch darf der Redner durch schriftliche Notizen seiner Rede zu Hülfe kommen, auch aus Urkunden, Briefschaften und Rechnungen, worauf er sich beruft, vorlesen oder vorlesen lassen" (§ 97 Abs. 3). Das Referat und Korreferat sollten künftig wegfallen,[19] insgesamt eine Regelung, die über das Revisionsrecht der CPO von 1877 hinausging.

Die Ständeversammlung begrüßte die Einführung des mündlichen Verfahrens, das sich wegen seiner unverkennbaren Vorzüge „nach und nach in fast allen Deutschen Ländern Bahn gebrochen" habe: „Bei dem mündlichen Verfahren sprechen beide Parteien in der von ihnen für geeignet gehaltenen Weise und durch die von ihnen selbst gewählten Organe gleichzeitig zu allen Richtern; bei dem schriftlichen Referiren tragen 2 Mitglieder des Gerichts den übrigen diejenigen Momente vor, die nach ihrer individuellen Ansicht die entscheidenden sind; die Vortheile des unmittelbaren und lebendigen, des gleichmäßigen Eindruckes, welche mit der mündlichen Verhandlung verbunden sind, gehen bei dem rein schriftlichen Verfahren verloren, und die bei einem collegialisch besetzten Gerichte zur selbständigen Prüfung und Entscheidung erforderliche selbständige Auffassung des Thatbestandes und der in Betracht kommenden Rechtsnormen leidet immer, wenn sie durch ein Gerichtsmitglied vermittelt werden soll." Das neue Verfahren, das dem Gericht vielleicht ein größeres Ansehen hätte verschaffen können, trat nicht mehr in Kraft. Über die Praxis des Gerichts – einige Urteile wurden in Seufferts Archiv veröffentlicht – fehlen bisher eingehendere Untersuchungen.

Für *Holstein* ergingen noch am 14.7.1863 vier Gesetze, die den Zivilprozess teilweise reformierten. Zum einen wurde das Beweisverfahren – wohl unter Beibehaltung des Beweisurteils – neu geregelt.[20] Das zweite Gesetz[21] regelte die Folgen des „Ungehorsams" der Parteien in der ersten Instanz, das dritte Gesetz regelte die

---

[18] Der Entwurf ist wiedergegeben in den Beilagen zur Zeitung für die Verhandlungen der achten Holsteinischen Provinzial-Landesversammlung 1855–1856, 1. und 2. Beiheft, S. 73 ff. (Entwurf, 73 Bestimmungen), S. 112 ff. (Motive). – Erneute Vorlage des Entwurfs 1859, Ständezeitung 1859, Beil. I, S. 96 ff.

[19] Demgegenüber wünschten die Stände die Beibehaltung des Referats, ein Antrag, dem die Regierung in der neuen Vorlage von 1859 nicht nachkam, den die Stände jedoch wiederholten (vgl. Ständezeitung 1859, S. 505 ff., 543 ff., Beil. I, 96, Beil. II, 129).

[20] Gesetz- und Ministerialblatt für das Herzogthum Holstein, 1863, S. 178 ff.; Ständezeitung 1859, Beil. I, S. 559 ff.

[21] Gesetz- und Ministerialblatt für das Herzogthum Holstein, 1863, S. 186 ff.; Ständezeitung 1859, Beil. I, S. 91 ff.

Wiedereinsetzung in den vorigen Stand, das vierte Gesetz die Handhabung der den Parteien gesetzten Fristen.[22] Bedeutsam erscheint, dass ein Versäumnisurteil erst nach dem zweimaligen Ausbleiben einer Partei im Termin erging.

Der inquisitorische Strafprozess wie auch das materielle Strafrecht richtete sich teilweise noch nach der Carolina von 1532, die allerdings durch Verordnungen und gewohnheitsrechtlich erheblich modifiziert worden war. So wurden 1843 die sog. Verdachtsstrafen abgeschafft.[23] Initiativen der Ständeversammlungen ab 1836/37, den Strafprozess zu modernisieren und ein neues Strafgesetzbuch zu erlassen, hatten keinen Erfolg.[24] Aufgrund des Art. 118 des Staatsgrundgesetzes für die Herzogtümer vom 15.9.1848 sollte „regelmäßig der Anklageprozess stattfinden".[25] Die Vorlagen der damaligen Regierung zu einer Strafprozessordnung und eines Gerichtsverfassungsgesetzes für die Herzogtümer am 16.9.1850[26] waren nicht mehr behandelt worden.

IV. Personen- und Familienrecht

1. Personenrecht

Der privilegierte Gerichtsstand für den Adel und Beamte war im Herzogtum Schleswig durch eine Bekanntmachung vom 29.7.1850/6.2.1854[27] beseitigt worden. Jedoch bestanden für die Ritterschaft hinsichtlich der gutsherrlichen Verhältnisse, des Erbrechts und der Vormundschaft einige Abweichungen vom allgemeinen Recht. Ferner hatte der Adel das Recht zur „Hauscopulation ohne vorgängiges Aufgebot". Mündigkeit trat mit Vollendung des 21. Lebensjahres ein. Die eigentliche Geschlechtsvormundschaft über unverheiratete Frauen war schon im 18. Jahrhundert weggefallen. Geblieben ist die *cura sexus*, so dass Frauen auch nach erlangter Mündigkeit sich nicht allein zu umfangreicheren Leistungen verpflichten konnten.[28] Geschäfte des täglichen Lebens fielen nicht hierunter. Die Geschlechtsvormundschaft wurde erst durch ein preußisches Gesetz vom 21.1.1869 aufgehoben,[29] ohne dass dies auf die eheliche Vormundschaft Einfluss haben sollte. Nicht unter die *cura sexus* fielen die der Ritterschaft angehörigen verheirateten und

---

[22] Ständezeitung für Holstein 1863, Beil. I, S. 75 f., 77 ff.

[23] Verordnung betr. die Bedingungen und Wirkungen des Anzeigenbeweises vom 27.3.1843, in: *Theodor Reinhold Schütze* (Hg.), Sammlung der das Schleswigsche Strafrecht betreffenden Gesetze und Verordnungen, Kopenhagen 1856, S. 260 f.

[24] Für Holstein vgl. *Horst-Alex Schmidt,* in: Heribert Ostendorf (Hg.), Strafverfolgung und Strafverzicht. Festschrift zum 125jährigen Bestehen der Staatsanwaltschaft Schleswig-Holstein, Köln 1992, S. 8 ff.

[25] Zitiert nach *Schmidt,* a.a.O., S. 11.

[26] Hierzu *Schmidt,* a.a.O., S. 11 ff.

[27] Chronol. Sammlung (oben Fn. 13), 1848–1850, S. 73 f.; 1854, 95 ff.

[28] *Esmarch*, Recht (oben Fn. 1), § 48 (S. 110 ff.).

[29] Preuß. Gesetzessammlung 1869, S. 289 f.

unverheirateten Frauen sowie die Klosterdamen. Die Gleichstellung der Juden mit der übrigen Bevölkerung erfolgte erst durch ein Gesetz vom Februar 1854/Juli 1863.[30] Nach diesen Gesetzen waren die Juden allen bürgerlichen Gesetzen unterworfen; sie genossen volle Niederlassungs- sowie Berufswahlfreiheit und konnten Grundstücke ohne Beschränkung erwerben. Ihre Ehesachen wurden von den weltlichen Gerichten entschieden. Die Leibeigenschaft war bereits durch eine Verordnung vom 19.12.1805[31] aufgehoben worden. Das Gesinde war persönlich frei, unterlag jedoch den Bestimmungen der Gesindeordnung von 1840.[32] Der Gesindevertrag konnte schriftlich oder mündlich geschlossen werden; im letzteren Fall wurde er nur verbindlich durch die Annahme eines Gottes- oder Handgeldes von Seiten der Dienstboten (§ 121). Die Herrschaft war verpflichtet,[33] „nach bester Einsicht für das leibliche und sittliche Wohl des Gesindes zu sorgen, dasselbe nicht ungebührlich von dem Besuche des öffentlichen Gottesdienstes abzuhalten, und unconfirmirte Dienende zum Schulbesuch anzuhalten; auch den Dienstboten mit den täglichen Lebensbedürfnissen auf eine verantwortliche Weise zu versehen, und den bedungenen Lohn zur Verfallzeit, d.h. im Zweifel halbjährig, zu bezahlen". Beide Parteien konnten den Vertrag jederzeit „ohne Angabe von Gründen" kündigen.

Wie weit Körperschaften der staatlichen Genehmigung bzw. Anerkennung bedurften, war umstritten. Dagegen war für Stiftungen und Fideikommisse die staatliche Konfirmation erforderlich.[34] Veräußerungen von Immobilien an die „tote Hand" waren ohne königliche Genehmigung nach einer Verordnung Christians VII. vom 17.5.1799 unwirksam:[35]

> „Wir wollen und befehlen hiedurch allergnädigst, dass in gedachten Herzogthümern und Landen itzkünftige keine Veräußerung oder Uebertragung von adelichen oder andern Landgütern, Grundstücken und Immobilien irgend einer Art in die todte Hand, oder an eine autorisirte und beständige Gesellschaft oder Commüne, sie geschehe unter Lebendigen oder auf den Todesfall und in welcher Form sie wolle, ohne ausdrückliche landesherrliche Zulassung Statt haben und bestehen, sondern dieselbe, wenn dergleichen dennoch vorgenommen wurde, von keiner Kraft und Gültigkeit seyn, und diese durch keine Verjährung erlangen solle".

---

[30] Chronol. Sammlung (oben Fn. 13), S. 124 ff.; Gesetz- und MinBlatt (oben Fn. 20), 1863, S. 117 ff.

[31] Die Leibeigenschaft war bereits durch VO vom 19.12.1805 aufgehoben worden (Chronol. Sammlung der in den Jahren 1748–1848 ergangenen Verordnungen und Verfügungen, Glückstadt 1805, S. 441).

[32] Wiedergegeben bei *Kähler,* Landesrecht (oben Fn. 4), S. 181 ff.

[33] *Esmarch*, Recht (oben Fn. 1), S. 330.

[34] *Kähler*, Landesrecht (oben Fn. 4), S. 54 ff.

[35] *Kähler*, Landesrecht (oben Fn. 4), S. 61.

2. Familienrecht

Ein Eheversprechen (Verlöbnis) begründete seit einer Verordnung von 1853/56[36] keine Klage mehr auf Vollziehung der Ehe oder auf Leistung dessen, was für den Fall des Rücktritts versprochen war. Trat ein Teil vom Verlöbnis zurück, musste er dem anderen Teil den wirklichen Schaden ersetzen. Ehen waren bis 1854/63 verboten zwischen Christen und Juden oder anderen nicht zur christlichen Religion sich bekennenden Personen. Ehen zwischen Lutheranern und Katholiken waren zulässig mit einem Dispens unter der ausdrücklichen Bedingung, „dass die künftigen Eheleute sich von einem evangelisch-lutherischen Prediger copuliren lassen, und sich noch vor der Copulation verbindlich machen, ihre Kinder ohne Unterschied des Geschlechts, von einem evangelischen Prediger taufen, und in der evangelischen Lehre erziehen zu lassen“.[37] Gleiches galt für Mennoniten, die nicht in Friedrichstadt wohnten. Söhne und Töchter, die sich erstmals verheiraten wollten, durften sich nicht „ohne ihrer Aeltern Vorwissen und Einwilligung in ein Ehegelöbniß einlassen, und solches durch die Trauung vollziehen“. Das Gesetz über die Religionsübung von 1863[38] stellte den Brautleuten, wenn sie verschiedenen Kirchen angehörten, die Wahl des Geistlichen, der die Trauung vollziehen sollte, frei. Es wurden die Bestimmungen von 1757 aufgehoben und den Geistlichen untersagt, „den Brautleuten gemischter Confession vor der Copulation ein mündliches oder schriftliches Versprechen abzunehmen, daß sie ihre Kinder in einer bestimmten Confession erziehen lassen“ (§ 6). Für Juden erfolgte die Trauung weiterhin nach dem jüdischen Ritus.

Eine Ehe konnte von den Consistorien geschieden werden[39] wegen Ehebruchs, Misshandlungen, „welche Leben und Gesundheit des misshandelten Ehegatten Gefahr drohen, oder wegen lebensgefährlicher Nachstellungen“, wegen böslichen Verlassens und wegen Verurteilung des anderen Ehegatten zu lebenslangem Zuchthaus. Unversöhnlicher Hass wurde nicht als Scheidungsursache angesehen. Jedoch konnten die Ehegatten als bloße landesherrliche Gnadensache die Aufhebung der Ehe beantragen.

Dem Mann stand in Fragen der religiösen Erziehung der Kinder die Entscheidung zu. Der Wille der Mutter kam nur in Betracht, wenn der Vater der Kinder verstorben war. Diese erlangten die religiöse Mündigkeit mit dem Erreichen des gesetzlichen Konfirmationsalters von 16 Jahren bzw. bei Mädchen des vollendeten

---

[36] Gesetz vom 7.9.1853 für Schleswig (Chronol. Sammlung 1854, S. 223); VO vom 14.4.1856 für Holstein (Gesetz- und MinBlatt 1856, S. 136).

[37] VO vom 14.7.1863 für Holstein (Gesetz- und MinBlatt 1863, S. 163 ff.); vgl. für Schleswig die VO vom 23.4.1863 (Sammlung, 1864, S. 58).

[38] Vgl. die in Fn. 37 nachgewiesenen Verordnungen.

[39] *Esmarch*, Recht (oben Fn. 1), S. 50 ff., Zitat 51.

15. Lebensjahrs.[40] Hinsichtlich des *unehelichen Kindes*[41] standen der Mutter keine vormundschaftlichen Rechte zu. Das Kind bekam vielfach den Familiennamen des Vaters, jedoch bestand insoweit kein Gewohnheitsrecht.[42] Die Möglichkeit der Einrede des Mehrverkehrs war nur in Holstein anerkannt.

Das *eheliche Güterrecht* war äußerst zersplittert.[43] In Betracht kamen das Lübsche Güterrecht, die Schleswiger Rechte (mit allgemeiner Gütergemeinschaft), das Dithmarscher und Fehmarische Güterrecht sowie die Güterrechte des Sachsenspiegels, der Schauenburgischen Landesteile, des Land- und Marschrechts, des Nordstrander Landrechts, des Jütischen Lov sowie das Güterrecht einzelner Personenklassen.

Das sächsische Güterrecht nach dem Sachsenspiegel sah vollständige Gütertrennung mit Verwaltung des Frauenvermögens durch den Mann vor, der die Frau hinsichtlich ihres Vermögens vertrat. Dem Zugriff der Gläubiger unterlag das Vermögen der Frauen nicht. Die überlebende Ehefrau erhielt vom Nachlass des Mannes ein Viertel oder ein Drittel, je nachdem Kinder vorhanden waren oder nicht. Der überlebende Mann erhielt den gesamten beweglichen Nachlass der Frau und vom übrigen Vermögen der Frau ein Viertel. – Auch das Lübsche Güterrecht beruhte auf der Gütertrennung mit Verwaltungs- und Nutzungsrecht des Ehemannes. Die Frau war nicht geschäftsunfähig, konnte jedoch über ihr Vermögen nicht ohne Zustimmung ihres Mannes verfügen. Bei beerbter Ehe (Vorhandensein von Kindern) wurden die Güter der Frau und des Mannes als Einheit behandelt; sie hafteten insgesamt auch für die Schulden des Mannes. Nach dem Tod eines Ehegatten blieb der überlebende Ehegatte mit den Kindern „in ungeteiltem Nachlass sitzen; das Verhältnis wurde, obwohl eine Gütergemeinschaft nicht eintrat, ähnlich der fortgesetzten Gütergemeinschaft behandelt".[44] Es konnte jedoch eine Vermögensteilung erfolgen, die entweder das gesamte beiderseitige Vermögen betraf (Totalteilung) oder nur das Vermögen des verstorbenen Ehegatten; letzteres war in den Holsteinischen Städten gewohnheitsrechtlich die Regel. Von dem Vermögen des Verstorbenen erhielt der Überlebende die sog. statutarische Portion, wozu zahlreiche partikulare Besonderheiten existierten. Für die Schauenburgischen Landesteile (insbesondere die Herrschaft Pinneberg) galt zunächst das System der Gütergemeinschaft, das jedoch durch das der Gütereinheit verdrängt worden war.

---

[40] *Kähler*, Landesrecht (oben Fn. 4), S. 565 (Verfügung von 1767 für Schleswig, von 1799 für Holstein).

[41] Vgl. *Esmarch*, Recht (oben Fn. 1), S. 61 ff. (für Schleswig).

[42] *Kähler*, Landesrecht (oben Fn. 4), S. 560; durch VO vom 4.7.1863 (Gesetz- und MinBlatt 1863, 145) wurden für das Gebiet des Lübschen Rechts die unehelichen Kinder den ehelichen Kindern der Mutter erbrechtlich gleichgestellt.

[43] *Kähler*, Landesrecht (oben Fn. 4), S. 568 ff.

[44] *Kähler*, Landesrecht (oben Fn. 4), S. 600.

Das Güterrechtssystem des jütschen Low[45] stellte eine Errungenschafts- und Fahrnisgemeinschaft dar. Die Frau stand unter ehelicher Vormundschaft des Mannes, so dass sie ohne Zustimmung ihres Mannes über ihr Gut (auch das Sondergut) weder verfügen noch entsprechende Verpflichtungsgeschäfte eingehen konnte. Beide Ehegatten konnten mit ihren Kindern in „ungeteilten Gütern sitzen bleiben". Nach Beendigung der Gütergemeinschaft fand die Teilung der Güter statt. Der Mann erhielt sein Sondergut, das während der Ehe durch Geschäft unter Lebenden erworbene Land („Kaufland") und ferner den „besten Kindesteil von dem gemeinschaftlichen Gut und von dem der Frau gesondert gehörenden Lande". Weit verbreitet waren die Schleswiger Rechte mit allgemeiner und fortgesetzter Gütergemeinschaft.

V. Erbrecht

Nach dem gesetzlichen Erbrecht im *Herzogtum Schleswig* erhielten die männlichen Erben doppelt so viel wie die weiblichen Erben (Bruderteil, Schwesterteil), während im Landesteil *Holstein* Kopfteilung unter Geschwistern eintrat.[46] Im größten Teil Schleswig-Holsteins bestand die Eigentümlichkeit der sog. väterlichen Aussage.[47] Diese bestand „in dem Rechte des überlebenden Ehemanns, bei der Abtheilung mit Abkömmlingen, namentlich im Falle seiner Wiederverheiratung, den Kindern statt der Erbtheile am mütterlichen Nachlasse durch einseitige, auf Verlangen zu beeidigende Aussage eine Abfindung zu bestimmen". Hiermit war das Recht verbunden, „den mütterlichen Nachlass zu behalten und auch die festgesetzten Abfindungen der Kinder erst zu einem gewissen Zeitpunkte auszukehren".

In Schleswig bestand seit 1663 „Testierungsfreiheit" (ab 21 Jahren);[48] die Testamente bedurften jedoch der landesherrlichen Konfirmation, die seit einer Verordnung vom 4.2.1854[49] von wenigen Ausnahmen abgesehen nicht mehr notwendig war: „Jeder, der Dispositionsbefugniß über sein Eigenthum hat und bei gesunder Vernunft ist, soll künftig berechtigt sein, durch eine letztwillige Verfügung über sein gesammtes freies Eigenthum, mit Ausnahme des gewöhnlichen Pflichttheils der Leibeserben und Ascendenten nämlich der Hälfte von dem freien Eigenthum des Erblassers, wenn 5 oder mehrere, und den dritten Teile, weniger als 5 pflichttheilsberechtigte Erben vorhanden sind, rechtsgültig zu disponiren, ohne dass es Unserer Allerhöchsten Confirmation der letztwilligen Verfügung bedarf." Das holographische Testament einer Frau bedurfte der Unterschrift ihres Curators. Nicht eigenhändig unterschriebene oder mündlich erklärte Testamente bedurften

45 *Kähler*, Landesrecht (oben Fn. 4), S. 674.

46 *Kähler*, Landesrecht (oben Fn. 4), S. 701 ff.

47 *Kähler*, Landesrecht (oben Fn. 4), S. 725 m. Zitat 725.

48 *Kähler*, Landesrecht (oben Fn. 4), S. 743 f.

49 Chronol. Sammlung 1854, S. 91 f.

der öffentlichen Beurkundung in Gegenwart zweier männlicher Zeugen. Minderjährige konnten über ihr Vermögen nicht letztwillig verfügen.

Auch im *Herzogtum Holstein* bestand schon früh Testierfreiheit (ab 16 Jahren),[50] wofür im Wesentlichen das römischrechtliche Testamentsrecht subsidiär galt. Das holographische Testament als solches war unbekannt. Daran änderte auch die Verordnung für Holstein über die Form letztwilliger Verfügungen vom Sept. 1859[51] nichts. Für nicht eigenhändig geschriebene Testamente galt § 2: „Ist die letztwillige Disposition von dem Disponenten (der Disponentin) nicht eigenhändig geschrieben, so soll der Disponent oder die Disponentin in Gegenwart eines der streitigen oder freiwilligen Gerichtsbarkeit betrauten Beamten oder eines Notars nebst zweien, sowohl dem Testator als dem hinzugezogenen Beamten oder Notar, bekannten Zeugen welche schreibkundige, mündige und zur Ablegung eines gerichtlichen Zeugnisses geeignete Männer sein müssen, unter Vorzeigung der letztwilligen Verfügung, erklären, dass hierin sein (ihr) letzter Wille enthalten sei, sowie darauf in Gegenwart der oben genannten Personen, als reine Frauensperson mit ihrem Curator, die letztwillige Disposition mit resp. seiner oder ihrer oder ihres Curators Namensunterschrift versehen“ (§ 2). Sofern ein eigenhändig geschriebenes Testament vorlag, hatte der nebst zwei Zeugen zugezogene Beamte oder Notar auf dem Testament zu attestieren, „dass die letztwillig disponirende Person, welche sich nach dem Ergebniß der mit ihr gepflogenen Unterredung bei gesunder Vernunft befunden, und nach ihrer eigenen Erklärung ihre letztwillige Disposition eigenhändig geschrieben, datirt und unterschrieben habe ... und dass darauf zur Beurkundung dessen dieser Attest von dem Beamten oder dem Notar sowie von den beiden zugezogenen, sowohl dem Testator nach dessen eigener Erklärung als auch die unterzeichneten Beamten und Notar bekannten Zeugen in Gegenwart der disponirenden Person eigenhändig unterschrieben, auch von Ersterem untersiegelt sei“ (§ 3). Nach dem Recht beider Herzogtümer waren gemeinschaftliche Testamente nicht nur unter Ehegatten, sondern auch unter anderen Personen zulässig. Erbverträge waren in beiden Landesteilen anerkannt.[52]

---

[50] *Kähler*, Landesrecht (oben Fn. 4), S. 747 ff.

[51] Gesetz- u. MinBlatt 1859, S. 305 ff.; vgl. auch Zeitung für die Ständeverhandlungen 1859, S. 309 ff., 415 ff.

[52] Nach einer von der Ständeversammlung 1863 angenommenen, aber nicht mehr in Kraft gesetzten Gesetzesvorlage sollte in Holstein die Bestimmung des Sachsenspiegels II 2 Art. 9, wonach eheliche Kinder „kein Erbe nehmen“ sollten, aufgehoben und alle unehelichen Kinder (und damit auch die Ehebruchs- und Blutschandekinder) im Herzogtum Holstein gegenüber der Mutter und gegenüber ihren mütterlichen Verwandten den ehelichen Kindern gleichgestellt werden (Ständezeitung für Holstein 1863, S. 124 ff., 148 ff., 161; Beil. I, 136; Beil. II, 16 ff.; auch die Akte im Landesarchiv Schleswig, Rep. 80, 1248).

VI. Sachenrecht

Schleswig-Holstein stand in der Gesetzgebung, so die Motive[53] zu dem Gesetz vom 3.1.1873 über die Ablösung der Reallasten in der Provinz Schleswig-Holstein, „in der Gesetzgebung über die Regelung der gutsherrlich-bäuerlichen Verhältnisse und Ablösung der Reallasten" hinter den übrigen Teilen des preußischen Staats zurück. Außer der Aufhebung der Leibeigenschaft durch ein Kanzleiedikt vom 30.4.1805 war „auf diesem Gebiet im Wesentlichen nichts weiter geschehen, als dass in Schleswig in den Königlichen (Domanial-)Distrikten die Umwandlung des Erbpacht- und Erbfest-Besitzes in Eigenthum und die Kapitalabfindung des Kanons auf Antrag des Pflichtigen gesetzlich ermöglicht ist". Trotz der Aufhebung der Leibeigenschaft behielten die „angesessenen Leibeigenen" nur diejenigen beschränkten Rechte, „welche ihnen bis zur Freilassung zustanden, und es wurden nur ihre Dienstverhältnisse näher bestimmt". Im Zusammenhang mit dem Patent von 1805 hatten die Besitzer vieler adliger Güter „die Gutsfelder parzellenweise und die bäuerlichen Landstellen teils zu Eigentum, teils zu Erbpacht, gegen einen Kanon oder Grundzins unter gänzlicher Beseitigung des früheren Rechtsverhältnisses veräußert." Neben den bäuerlichen Gütern (Bondengüter) bestanden noch zahlreiche Erbpacht- und Festehöfe. In Holstein und für nicht fiskalische Erbpachtgüter auch in Schleswig existierte kein Gesetz, womit die Eigentumsübertragung zu erzwingen war. Auch die Umwandlung der Zehnten in „feste Körner-Abgaben" war bisher nicht erfolgt. 1863 waren in Schleswig über 1100 dienstpflichtige, erblich besessene Stellen, in Holstein 3305 solche Stellen nicht reguliert. Das preußische Ablösungsgesetz vom 3.1.1873[54] hob das geteilte Eigentum auf und erklärte alle Abgaben zum 20- oder 25-fachen Betrag für ablösbar: „Bei den zu Erbzins, Erbfeste oder Erbpacht besessenen Grundstücken und Gerechtigkeiten wird das Obereigenthum und das Heimfallsrecht des Berechtigten und andererseits die Verpflichtung desselben zur Vertretung der auf den pflichtigen Realitäten haftenden Steuern hiermit kraft Gesetzes ohne Entschädigung aufgehoben. Die aus dem Obereigenthum entspringenden Berechtigungen auf Abgaben oder Leistungen oder ausdrücklich vorbehaltene Nutzungen bleiben aber fortbestehen, und zwar mit denselben Vorzugsrechten in dem Vermögen der Verpflichteten, welche sie bisher darin hatten. Sie unterliegen der Ablösung nach den Vorschriften dieses Gesetzes."

Für die Übertragung des Eigentums an beweglichen Sachen galt das Traditionsprinzip. Dabei wurde vorausgesetzt, dass zwischen Veräußerer und Erwerber ein Verpflichtungsgeschäft vorlag. Die Regel des lübschen Rechts: „Hand muss Hand warten oder wahren" galt nur in Burg und Tondern sowie in einigen Gebieten Holsteins (sonst Verjährung Jahr und Tag).[55] Bei einem Kauf ging das Eigentum

---

[53] Sten. Berichte, Haus der Abgeordneten, 11. Legislaturperiode, 2. Session 1871, Bd. 2, S. 755 ff., Zitat 760.

[54] Preuß. GS 1873, S. 3 ff.

[55] *Esmarch,* Recht (oben Fn. 1), S. 140.

nur über, wenn der Kaufpreis bezahlt oder gestundet war. Grundstücksveräußerungen bedurften eines schriftlichen, meist gerichtlich angefertigten Kontrakts. Hinsichtlich der Übergabe bestand in einigen Gegenden die Lachbietung oder Verschöterung.[56] Dies bedeutete, dass das Grundstück an drei Gerichtstagen lachgeboten wurde. Wenn keine Einwendungen erhoben worden waren, wurde dem Erwerber das Eigentum zugesprochen. Dieser erhielt darüber den sog. Schötebrief.

Nach den Motiven zum Gesetz vom 27.5.1873 über das Grundbuchwesen und die Verpfändung von Seeschiffen in der Provinz Schleswig-Holstein bestand „das dringendste Bedürfniß, unverzüglich mit der Reform des Immobiliarsachenrechts vorzuschreiten, unter den neu erworbenen Provinzen für die Provinz Schleswig-Holstein".[57] Es herrsche „in der Praxis eine große Ungleichförmigkeit, vielfach auch Unsicherheit über die Bedingungen des Eigenthumserwerbs". Dem Hypothekenrecht, das wesentlich auf der Grundlage des römischen Rechts beruhte, fehlten „die für die Sicherung des Realkredits unentbehrlichen Prinzipien der Publizität und Spezialität. Gesetzliche und stillschweigende Hypotheken bestehen noch, ebenso können durch Vertrag Generalhypotheken bestellt werden. Die Rechtsverhältnisse der Grundstücke im Konkurse endlich benachtheiligen die Rechte der hypothekarischen Gläubiger nicht allein insofern, als dieselben genöthigt sind, in den Konkurs einzutreten und aus der Gesamtmasse ihre Befriedigung zu erwarten, sondern auch dadurch, dass ihnen eine große Zahl absolut privilegirter Forderungen vorgeht, deren Mehrzahl mit dem Grundeigenthum des Kridars in keiner Verbindung steht". Noch mehr als die materiellrechtliche Seite des Rechts befand sich „seine formelle in einem durchaus genügenden, unsicheren und selbst lokal abweichenden Zustande": „Ueber das Schuld- und Pfandprotokollwesen gibt es eine große Zahl in wesentlichen Punkten voneinander abweichender Gesetze und Verordnungen".

Die Einführung von Schuld- und Pfandprotokollen[58] hatte den Zweck gehabt, „dem unleidlichen Nachtheil, den die in dem herrschend gewordenen Römischen Pfandsystem vorkommenden privilegirten Hypotheken dem Kredit zufügen, abzuhelfen. Sie sprechen zwar den Satz aus, dass die protokollirten Pfandrechte den nicht eingetragenen, wenn auch mit einem Privilegium versehenen, vorgehen und dass folgeweise die Rangordnung unter den protokollirten sich lediglich nach der Eintragung bestimmt, aber sie weichen sehr von einander ab in dem Wege, auf welchem sie im Übrigen ihr Ziel, den Kredit zu befestigen, zu erreichen streben."

---

[56] D.h. nach einer dreimaligen öffentlichen Proklamierung des Eigentums bekam der Erwerber den gerichtlichen Schötebrief (*Esmarch*, Recht [oben Fn. 1], S. 142 f.).

[57] Sten. Berichte, Herrenhaus, Anlagenband Session 1871/73, Bd. 2 (Anlagen), S. 122 ff., Zitate 125 f.

[58] Die Verpflichtung zur Anlegung solcher Protokolle beruhte auf einer VO vom 10.2.1813; hierzu gab es eine Vielzahl von Protokollordnungen (aufgeführt bei *Kähler*, Landesrecht [oben Fn. 4], S. 250 ff.).

Im Einzelnen gab es Protokolle mit Namen und Realfolien. Die Idee, welche den Namensfolien zugrunde lag, war darin zu sehen,

> „dass den Schuldnern die Möglichkeit hat gewährt werden sollen, Pfandrechte zu bestellen, über deren Priorität vor allen nicht in das Protokoll eingetragenen ein Zweifel nicht obwalten kann. Dabei ist die Ermittelung der Gegenstände, namentlich auch der Grundstücke, welche der Verfügung der Schuldner unterliegen, wie auch des Werths dieser Grundstücke den betheiligten Gläubigern überlassen geblieben. Die Schwierigkeit, welche es nach diesem System hat, die auf einem öfter veräußerten Grundstück haftenden protokollirten Pfandrechte zu ermitteln, musste im Laufe der Zeit immer mehr wachsen, und dadurch der Kredit, den die Verpfändung eines Grundstücks annähernd bis zu dessen jeweiligem Werth zu schaffen vermag, beeinträchtigt werden. Um diesem Übelstand zu begegnen, ist es bei der Mehrzahl der gesetzlich nach Namen zu führenden Schuld- und Pfandprotokolle in Gebrauch gekommen, auf die Folien der Grundbesitzer die Grundstücke welche sie besitzen, nebst der protokollirten Beschwerung, welche aus der Zeit der früheren Gesetze auf den Grundstücken haftet, auszuführen."

Damit hatte die Praxis die Namenfolien in Realfolien umgewandelt.

Von Anfang an existierten Realfolien für die den Landgerichten unmittelbar unterworfenen Güter und Besitztümer. Fast gleichzeitig wurden Realfolien für die „Untergehörigen" der adligen Güter sowie für die Städte eingeführt. Für einige wenige Besitzungen gab es überhaupt keine gesetzlichen Grundlagen für die Führung der Schuld- und Pfandprotokolle.

VII. Modernisierung und Vereinheitlichung des Rechts in Schleswig-Holstein

Preußen und das Deutsche Reich machten den überkommenen Rechten in Schleswig und Holstein zwischen 1867 und 1900 weitgehend ein Ende. Maßgebend für die für Schleswig-Holstein erlassenen Verordnungen von 1867 waren die Berichte des Berliner Richters *Hermann Krüger*,[59] der im Frühjahr 1867 im Auftrag des Justizministeriums die neue Provinz besuchte und detaillierte Berichte über das dortige Recht vorlegte. Die Verordnung vom 26.6.1867 „über die Trennung der Rechtswege von der Verwaltung, die Aufhebung der Privatgerichtsbarkeit und des eximirten Gerichtsstandes, sowie über die Gerichtsverfassung in den Herzogtümern Schleswig und Holstein"[60] sowie weitere Verordnungen[61] stellte die Justiz und die Provinz auf völlig neue Grundlagen: Trennung der Gerichtsbarkeit von der Verwaltung, Beseitigung der, soweit noch vorhandenen, Patrimonial- und Gemeindegerichtsbarkeit, Einführung des Anklageverfahrens und der Staatsanwaltschaft,

---

[59] Geh. StA Berlin-Dahlem, Rep. 84 a, Nr. 24010–I 175. Jetzt bei *Werner Schubert*, Zur Geschichte der Justizverfassung in Schleswig-Holstein im 19. und 20. Jahrhundert. Quellen und Studien, 2012.

[60] Preuß. GS 1867, S. 1073 ff.

[61] GS 1867, S. 1073 ff.

durchgehende Öffentlichkeit und Mündlichkeit des Zivil- und Strafverfahrens, Mitwirkung von Geschworenen und Schöffen in Strafsachen, Aufhebung des eximierten Gerichtsstandes und Ausbau der Kollegialverfassung in erstinstanzlichen Zivilsachen.

Als Vorbild für die neuen Einrichtungen diente im Wesentlichen die hannoversche Gerichtsverfassung von 1850/59, für die vor allem eine Zweiteilung der erstinstanzlichen Zivilgerichtsbarkeit kennzeichnend war. Nach § 11 der Verordnung vom 26.6.1867 wurde die Gerichtsbarkeit ausgeübt durch Amtsgerichte und kollegial eingerichtete Kreisgerichte, durch ein Appellationsgericht und durch den obersten Gerichtshof. Nach dem „Plan für die Organisation der Gerichte in den Herzogtümern Schleswig und Holstein“[62] waren insgesamt 86 Amtsgerichte mit 103 Amtsrichtern vorgesehen. Dies bedeutete, dass die meisten Amtsgerichte mit nur einem Richter besetzt waren. Für Schleswig-Holstein, Nassau und Kurhessen erging am 24. Juni 1867 ferner eine „Verordnung über das Verfahren in Civilprozessen“,[63] die den reformierten landrechtlichen Zivilprozess von 1846 (schriftliches Verfahren mit mündlicher Schlussverhandlung) in den neuen Landesteilen einführte. Dies bedeutete für Schleswig-Holstein keine grundlegende Umgestaltung des Zivilprozesses, da die Verordnung von 1846 auf dem gemeinen Recht beruhte. Das Rechtsmittel der Oberappellation, jetzt Revision genannt, wurde, wenn auch in sehr eingeschränktem Maße, beibehalten. Der Strafprozess richtete sich nach einer neu erlassenen Strafprozessordnung,[64] die auf dem nur unwesentlich umgearbeiteten preußischen StPO-Entwurf von 1865 beruhte. Die einfachen Strafsachen waren durch die „Polizeigerichte“ des Amtsgerichts abzuurteilen, die aus dem Einzelrichter und zwei Schöffen bestanden, eine Einrichtung, die aus der hannoverschen Justizverfassung stammte.[65] Oberste Instanz für die neuen Landesteile war das Oberappellationsgericht in Berlin, das 1874 mit dem Obertribunal vereinigt wurde. Die neue Gerichtsverfassung ist in Schleswig-Holstein, zumindest was die Verteilung der Gerichte angeht, im Wesentlichen wohl auf Zustimmung gestoßen, da Preußen mit den 86 Amtsgerichten und fünf Kreisgerichten in Altona, Kiel, Itzehoe, Schleswig und Flensburg – hinzu kam später noch Lauenburg – den Besitzstand der Gemeinden weitgehend gewahrt hatte.

Zur neuen Gerichtsverfassung schrieben am 17.7.1867 die Schleswiger Nachrichten:[66] „Man wird ihr im allgemeinen seinen Beifall nicht versagen können; die endliche Trennung der Justiz von der Verwaltung und die gänzliche Aufhebung des bevorzugten Gerichtsstandes, die Beseitigung der Patrimonialgerichtsbarkeit

---

[62] *Christian von Stemann,* Sammlung der Gesetze, Verordnungen und Verfügungen, welche den bürgerlichen Proceß in Schleswig-Holstein betreffen, Kiel 1868, S. 72 ff.

[63] GS 1867, S. 885 ff.

[64] GS 1867, S. 921 ff.

[65] Eingeführt wurden auch die Allgemeine Deutsche Wechselordnung, das ADHGB und das preuß. Genossenschaftsgesetz von 1867 (GS 1867, S. 669 ff., 1133 ff., 501 ff.).

[66] *Schmidt*, in: Ostendorf, Strafverfolgung (oben Fn. 24), S. 19.

und die Bildung größerer abgerundeter Gerichtsbezirke im Gegensatz zu der früheren regellosen Zerrissenheit, die Beseitigung des Sportelwesens und endlich die Einführung der Staatsanwaltschaft sind lauter entschiedene Fortschritte, deren heilsame Bedeutung für das Land nicht hoch genug angeschlagen werden kann." Ferner führte Preußen noch 1867 die Allgemeine Deutsche Wechselordnung, das Allgemeine Deutsche Handelsgesetzbuch (einschließlich des Handelsregisters)[67] und das Genossenschaftsgesetz von 1867 ein. Ein weiteres wichtiges, für Schleswig-Holstein geltendes Gesetz war das bereits erwähnte Gesetz vom 3.1.1873 über die Ablösung der Reallasten, nach dessen § 2 das geteilte Eigentum bei Bauerngütern aufgehoben wurde. Das Gesetz vom 27.5.1873 über das Grundbuchwesen und die Verpfändung von Seeschiffen[68] in der Provinz Schleswig-Holstein führte das neue preußische Grundstücksrecht von 1872 ein. Die bereits erwähnten Schuld- und Pfandprotokolle auf der Basis von Namensfolien entsprachen nach Meinung des Gesetzgebers nicht den Anforderungen des Grundkredits:[69]

> „Sie enthalten Vieles, was auf die Grundstücke und deren dingliche Belastung keine Beziehung hat, generelle und Mobiliarhypotheken, selbst Schuldverschreibungen ohne Hypothek, um ihnen durch die Protokollirung ein Vorzugsrecht beizulegen, und sie gewähren keinen Anhalt dafür, mit Zuverlässigkeit das verpfändete Objekt, das Grundstück und alle auf dasselbe bezüglichen Rechtsverhältnisse vollständig zu erkennen. Es kann daher von einer Fortbenutzung solcher Folien, selbst in einer verbesserten Gestalt, nicht die Rede sein."

Auch die nach Realfolien angelegten Protokollbücher eigneten sich nicht zur Weiterbenutzung:

> „Dagegen spricht die Verschiedenheit der Gesetze, nach denen sie jetzt zu führen sind, die daraus hervorgehenden zahlreichen Abweichungen in ihrer äußeren, formellen Einrichtung, die durch die Justizorganisation von 1867 geänderten Eintheilung der Gerichtsbezirke, so dass fast alle Schuld- und Pfandprotokollbücher für Distrikte angelegt sind, welche mit den jetzigen Bezirken der Amtsgerichte nicht zusammenfallen, die Bücher auseinandergerissen werden müssten."

1874 wurde die staatliche Standesbeurkundung und damit auch die obligatorische Zivilehe eingeführt.[70] 1875 erhielt Preußen ein neues Vormundschaftsrecht,[71] das – anders als bisher in Schleswig-Holstein – den Vormund gegenüber den Vormund-

---

[67] Vgl. bei Fn. 65.

[68] GS 1873, S. 241 ff.

[69] Sten. Berichte (oben Fn. 57), S. 126 (Motive).

[70] GS 1874, S. 207 ff.; hierzu *Werner Schubert,* Zur Vorgeschichte und Entstehung der Personenstandsgesetze, ZRG GA 97 (1980), S. 56 ff.

[71] RGBl. 1875, S. 23 ff.; hierzu *Schubert*, a.a.O., S. 76 ff.

schaftsbehörden wesentlich freier stellte als bisher. 1883 folgte eine grundlegende Änderung des Rechts der Grundstückszwangsversteigerung.[72]

Von den Reichsgesetzen sind zu erwähnen das Personenstandsgesetz von 1875,[73] das nicht nur die obligatorische Zivilehe reichseinheitlich einführte, sondern auch die materiellen Erfordernisse der Eheschließung regelte. 1879 wurde durch die Reichsjustizgesetze (Gerichtsverfassungsgesetz, Civilprozessordnung, Strafprozessordnung und Konkursordnung) das preußische und damit auch das 1867 in Schleswig-Holstein eingeführte Justizrecht zum Teil grundlegend umgestaltet.[74] Dies bedeutete, dass sich die Richter der Provinz Schleswig-Holsteins nach 12 Jahren erneut auf ein geändertes Straf- und Zivilprozessrecht umstellen mussten, während die Gerichtsverfassung im Wesentlichen erhalten blieb. Das bisher nicht zusammenhängend geregelte Advokatenrecht wurde durch die Rechtsanwaltsordnung von 1878 grundlegend umgestaltet und vereinheitlicht. Das außerordentlich vielfältige materielle bürgerliche Recht wurde am 1.1.1900 weitgehend durch das Bürgerliche Gesetzbuch verdrängt, verbunden mit Änderungen des Handels-, Prozess- und Konkursrechts.

[72] Hierzu *Werner Schubert,* in: Horst Heinrich Jakobs/ders. (Hg.), Die Beratung des BGB, Sachenrecht IV, Gesetz über die Zwangsversteigerung und die Zwangsverwaltung, Berlin 1983, S. 22 ff.

[73] GS 1875, S. 431 ff.; hierzu *Werner Schubert,* Das altpreußische Recht der freiwilligen Gerichtsbarkeit und dessen Reform und Vereinheitlichung unter dem Justizminister Leonhardt (1867–1879) unter besonderer Berücksichtigung des Vormundschaftsrechts, in: Jörg Wolff (Hg.), Das Preußische Allgemeine Landrecht, Heidelberg 1995, S. 237 ff., 245 ff.

[74] Hierzu *Werner Schubert*, SchlHA 1988, Sonderheft, S. 34 ff.

The Danish Supreme Court 1661–2011

Ditlev Tamm[1]

The Danish Supreme Court is an old, but still functioning, national institution, and is possibly the oldest continuous highest court of law in Europe, perhaps even the world. Naturally there are other law courts whose history can indirectly be traced much further back in time to an institution dealing with the King and his judgments. The Danish Supreme Court has a pre-history of this kind as well, but if one measures the foundation of an institution from the point at which it received its new name and foundational charters, then the Danish Supreme Court is in a class of its own in terms of age.

As an institution, the Supreme Court is tied to a shift in power and a constitutional change, namely the introduction of absolutism. Because of this change the Supreme Court has attained a special position in relation to other corresponding highest courts of law in Europe. A wide range of these were also introduced in connection with constitutional changes, but normally these were constitutions which introduced democratic or constitutional governance and clearly defined the status of the Court as a third power of state. The age of the Danish Supreme Court indicates that the court did not have the same status by means of a Constitution. Rather its place within the national legal system was defined under changing constitutions.

The history of the Court is the history of numerous legal decisions which solidified what constituted valid law in Denmark, but it is also the history of a law court which defined itself in relation to legislative and executive powers. The long history of the Supreme Court also means that it bears a heavy legacy. The history told in this chapter concerns the history of the Supreme Court during the past 350 years. The primary focus here lies precisely upon pointing out this aspect, that the court has a long history, and how it adjusted to modern conditions from its origins in absolutism.

As stated, the Supreme Court, as an institution, is closely linked to the introduction of absolutism in Denmark. Its origin as a branch of the King's power, not as an independent seat of power, is of great significance for our understanding of the history of the Supreme Court. The framework for the exercise of power was especially broad in Denmark and gave the King a very strong position as an absolute monarch. The balance of power was decisively seized around the year 1660 from a government in which the King ruled alongside a royal council which became a form of government where the King alone possessed all the power. In October 1660 the King was hailed in Copenhagen as an hereditary monarch. On 10 January 1661, the King sent out the document which is seen as the birth certificate of absolutism, the so-called Act of Hereditary Autocracy (*enevoldsarveregeringsakt*). One month

1 I thank Jeff Love and Christopher Goddard for valuable help with the translation of this article.

later, on 14 February 1661, the Supreme Court was established by a statute concerning "the administration of the Supreme Court in Denmark".

In the statute it says that:

> "Whereas the administration of justice (*Justitien*) is, following the matter of religion, the most important and fitting basis upon which all governments should be established. Therefore we shall, with the utmost graciousness, have at once from the beginning of our change in government, according to our royal wishes, how the Supreme Court, from which no appeal might occur, is to be established and organized for the benefit of our Danish realm, and to this end present our most gracious ordinance to be followed by all our faithful subjects and let it be promulgated and proclaimed from this moment.
>
> First, we desire that the aforementioned Supreme Court shall hereafter be run and administered by a certain number of people, of which one half shall be from the nobility and the other half from the learned and the ordinary citizen classes, which shall be nominated and sent by us ourselves …"

It was further confirmed that two secretaries should be attached to the court

> "one from the nobility and one from the ordinary citizen class, who always, when the court is in session, should maintain proper procedure over it, as provisions and writings indicate" and "a Justice Clerk, who shall proclaim all acts and documents on behalf of the court".

The most exhaustive history of the court is the book which commemorated its 300th anniversary in 1961.[2] The outer history of the court, its relationship to the government, penal law, and legal personnel are described there, but a more detailed treatment of the meaning of the court for the development of Danish jurisprudence is still lacking. As early as 1888 Sophus Vedel wrote about the early history of the court, and Troels G. Jørgensen, president of the court during the years 1936–1944, also contributed to the history of the Supreme Court from the perspective of his own time in the court.[3] In 1986 *Ugeskrift for retsvæsen* issued a special edition for the 25 years which ran between 1961 and 1986.[4]

On 4 March 1661, the King himself presided over the first Supreme Court case, together with nine nobles and nine ordinary citizen judges or 'assessors', as they were called. Law and power were closely knit, even if the King had long since showed the same interest in the newly established Supreme Court as previous kings, who had ruled together with the royal council, had showed in taking part in the highest judicial authority. Even though the Supreme Court as an institution was new and a child of absolutism, its function in exercising the law, as the 'supreme court', was far from new.

---

2 *Povl Bagge/Jep Lauesen Frost/Bernt Hjejle*, Højesteret 1661–1961, København 1961.

3 *Sophus Vedel*, Den dansk-norske Høiesterets Historie under Enevælden fra 1661 indtil 1790, Kjøbenhavn 1888; *Troels G. Jørgensen*, I Justitias Tjeneste: Erindringer, København 1970.

4 *Torben Jensen/W.E. von Eyben/Mogens Koktvedgaard*, Højesteret 1661–1986, særudgave af Ugeskrift for Retsvæsen, København 1986.

The Supreme Court's predecessor was actually the King and the Royal Council. The most active monarch as a judge was Christian IV (1588–1648), while the first absolute king, Frederik III (1648–1670), did not take part in court activities to the same extent and not at all after he became absolute monarch in 1660. The Supreme Court was a branch of absolute government, but the old-fashioned patriarchal royal power of taking an active role in the execution of justice was now replaced by a more distant centre of power which primarily exerted its authority through others. An administrative apparatus was formed around the King. This administration conveyed decisions in which the King personally took part, and the Supreme Court was a piece of that system. 'Justice' ranked immediately after religion as a foundation of the state, but in the hierarchy the highest legal power was placed on the same footing as the highest administrative areas which also appeared in the first years of absolutism. Just as the Supreme Court was a continuation of the King's Council, so too was the administrative authority which controlled the judicial system, the so-called Danish Chancery, a continuation of the administration before absolutism, organized in a different way. Specifically, it was a so-called *collegium*, where not one person but several made decisions. In this way it was also just as in the Supreme Court, where the *collegium* comprised eighteen members. On the other hand, it was not expected that the task of giving judgment in court demanded a person's complete attention. On the contrary, judges often had other various professions aside from being a Supreme Court judge, just as it is for judges today. One or two things have happened over the course of the Supreme Court's history since 1661, but the inheritance of absolutism continues to influence the organization of the Court, which was largely established in a statute of 1771 and continues to be foundational for court activities.

The origin in early absolutism and a strong retention of traditions and procedure with old roots are special attributes of the Danish Supreme Court. Deliberations had been conducted orally since the days of the King's Council as Supreme Court, and the Court continued to maintain that tradition at a time when other legal arenas were changing to written treatment of cases. In this regard the Danish Supreme Court is somewhat unusual, and what follows will highlight these remarkable features through an historical perspective. It would not be fair to claim that the Court has stood still in those many years, and there have been many external influences. Not least important is the international trend which has led to a situation in which the Supreme Court, as well as Danish law, belongs to a world where authorities other than Danish, including the Court itself, lead the way in certain areas of the law. The Supreme Court has set foot into the global world in this manner, especially within recent years, but the path to this point was also affected by changes which came together to form the Court we recognize today.

Still, there is reason to underscore the fact that the Supreme Court was once part of an absolute power. Other Nordic Supreme Courts have another history. The Norwegian Supreme Court was founded in 1814 as part of the establishment of a new Norwegian state, and the two Finnish Supreme Courts, The Supreme Court

(*Högsta Domstolan*) and The Supreme Administrative Court (*Högsta Förvaltningsdomstolan*), which both celebrated their 90th anniversary in 2009, also have their foundations tied to the country's independence. The Swedish Supreme Court (*Högsta Domstolen*), founded in 1789, is connected to Gustav III's attempt to introduce absolutism, but it received a new foundation in the Swedish governmental reform in 1809 and thereby a new position.

The absolutist Supreme Court did not have the mandate to protect the rights of citizens and guarantee the state of law that it does today. One did not speak of judicial power, but rather about 'Justice' ("*Justitien*"), which the reigning king took care of in the same way as other civil duties. Therefore the history of the Supreme Court is, in many ways, a history of how a law court, which was at the same time part of an absolute power, came to move towards asserting its independence and live up to its independent duties. In order to find the red thread in the work of the Supreme Court, it is necessary to present some historically decisive events.

The King was present at the opening of the Supreme Court in March 1661. The case being deliberated concerned defamatory remarks by the governor of Norway, former royal councillor Niels Trolle, against a certain Jørgen Løvenclau, who had been Commissioner General (*Generalproviant-kommissær*) in Norway but was dismissed by Trolle. Løvenclau, in return, had a series of grievances against Trolle for negligence in connection with the war in Norway. The case was investigated by a special commission. After the commission had concluded their investigation, Trolle brought the case before the Supreme Court, which, in its first judgment on 5 March 1661, absolved Trolle of all charges and, in the course of the proceedings, stripped Løvenclau of his honours and title. Løvenclau continued his polemics against Trolle and, furthermore, declared the judgment of the Supreme Court to be unjust. It was not the last time that the word 'unfair' would be associated with a Supreme Court judgment, but neither at that time nor later did such accusations make any significant impression on the Court or on the public. A half year passed until the Court had any further activity in September 1661. The next case was also unusual. Unlike the case between Trolle and Løvenclau, it shook Danish history. This case was brought by the King's treasurer (*generalfiskal*) against a nobleman, Kaj Lykke, who had indicated in a letter to a lover that the queen had a very free relationship with her retinue. The letter stemmed from a period before the introduction of absolutism, but it first appeared later during a revenge move against Kaj Lykke, who had fled to Sweden. It proved to be a clever decision when the Supreme Court condemned him to death for *lèse-majesté* (*majestætsfornærmelse*), even though the case did not involve the King or concern national security, but rather was an indication of the status of the queen. The Court had received permission to read the letter, which had not been published, and therefore it reached a decision which certainly pleased the absolute monarch but which also proclaimed that the Supreme Court did not view its mandate as opposing authority. So it was in an absolute state, and although the Court later obtained legally independent status in relation to the King, the Supreme Court had no opportunity to oppose the powers of state under absolutism.

Yet another political case during the reign of Frederik III was the case against Corfitz Ulfeldt, who was dealt with by the entire contingent of 26 judges in July 1663. He was accused of treason. Like Kaj Lykke he had fled the country and was sentenced to death.

That the Supreme Court was not, in reality, an independent state power but rather part of the absolute power, was clearly expressed partially in the constitution of absolutism, the King's Law or *Lex Regia* from 1665, and partially by the fact that the Court did not justify its decisions. Judgments of the Supreme Court were pronounced in the King's name as declarations and did not require any further justification other than that this was the royal will.

With respect to the *Lex Regia* the case is a little more complicated. The text was composed by the King's librarian, Peter Schumacher. It was a work which showed that he not only understood that absolutism meant a new era, but also that a new era required an entirely new and powerful language. The text of the law is an elegant expression of Danish baroque style. As has been noted, it was a monumental work of art, unique in Europe in terms of law texts. Absolutism was also known in other places, but no other monarch dared to promulgate a law concerning absolutism itself. The reality is that, just as the King's Law defines itself as *Lex Regia* and thus elegantly refers to the law in which the Roman people transferred power to the emperor, so also is the *Lex Regia* granted by the wielder of power in person.

The text is almost a lesson in constitutional law, and its theoretical application is influenced by contemporary constitutional theory, where words like 'fundamental law', 'sovereignty' and 'royal privileges' play an important role. One reckoned the power of judgment among royal privileges at the time, but the *Lex Regia* does not specifically discuss judicial power. The nearest we come is art. IV of the *Lex Regia* which mentions the King's 'highest power and authority' to 'appoint and dismiss all officials, high and low, regardless of what name or title they might have ...' Judges simply did not appear as a separate category of 'officials' at that point in time. In the country and the cities the district and city sheriffs generally had official duties. There were not many provincial judges, and for a long time most of the Supreme Court justices were only at the Court part-time and had other positions as their primary job.

In reality, the Supreme Court itself was on its way towards establishing itself as a special kind of judicial power, but it was still a good while before recognition that judicial power was something special appeared in the absolute system. The situation had been different under the old regime prior to 1660/61, where power or 'sovereignty' was associated with the King and the royal council.

At that time the King had considered it an important responsibility to protect the law and rights, and he himself took part in judicial activities. After 1660/61 judicial power became but one among many forms through which royal power manifested itself and was far from the most important. The Supreme Court was a *collegium* on the same level as other centrally controlled administrative units, and, as stated before, it would take some time before the image of judicial power changed.

It would be unfair to condemn the Supreme Court's efficacy based on its experiences during the early years. In England Chief Justice Coke attempted, without success, to make the judicial courts independent from the King, James I. It was only in 1760 that English law protected judges against dismissal at the King's whim. Implementing the idea that law courts should be independent of the higher powers of state belongs to the 18th century or a later period. Only in 1809 did the Swedish Supreme Court become independent of the King's influence over appointments and dismissals. A court as old as the Danish Supreme Court has baggage which does not widely conform to modern notions of the highest judicial power. Therefore a look back into the history of the Danish Supreme Court also becomes an encounter with a piece of Denmark's history from a time before modern conceptions of court activities.

During most of the first hundred years of its operation, the Supreme Court had no actual president, but the Court's head is mentioned as 'the highest delegate' up until 1758. The first person appointed to this position was a former member of the old royal council, Peder Reedtz, who was also chancellor and therefore head of the Chancery. Reedtz's successor as highest delegate was Peder Griffenfeld, who became the new chancellor in 1674 with the death of Reedtz. Along with the position came the new title of royal chancellor. As chief secretary in the Chancery, Griffenfeld had already in 1670 arranged for new instructions which ensured the Chancery a position as the highest among the new *collegia*. In the following years it was also that very Chancery whose responsibility for judicial functions made it alternately the ally and opponent of the Supreme Court in the realm of Danish jurisprudence. The statute in which the head of the Chancery was also made head of the Supreme Court is reminiscent of the situation in England, where the Lord Chancellor was, for a lengthy period, head of the highest English court, the House of Lords legal branch, until 2009. Griffenfeld was only active within the Court a few times during his period of service. A chief justice was appointed alongside him. The post was vacant for long periods, and charge of the Court was taken by the eldest judge in the Court.

Griffenfeld's period in the Supreme Court ended as abruptly as his other duties with his fall in 1676. Already in 1674, a justice as functioning president was appointed alongside him, and this arrangement continued until 1758, at which time this justice became the actual president of the Court. The office was specifically given a name in 1683, and another important step on the way towards an independent presidential office was that the justice received a separate salary as from 1705 and that the position was not connected to any other public duties. However, since the appointment of Willum Worm as justice and Mathias Moth as chief secretary in 1690, day-to-day charge of the Chancery was such that the two institutions essentially functioned independently of one another with a symbolic authority above them. Another matter is that the Chancery, like the Justice Ministry, had close contacts with the Supreme Court and assisted with administration and processing. Under later chancellors, joint management of the Chancery and the highest court was re-established, but the position of the *justitarius* became stronger from 1740.

In the early days of the Court it was the King who convened the delegates who met for each individual case. A stable core of judges included Peder Reedtz, Otto Krag, who had studied law abroad when he was younger, and Ove Skade as the judges from the nobility, as well as two judges, professor Henrik Ernst and Peder Lassen, along with the mayor of Copenhagen, Hans Nansen or Peter Bülche, who was not a lawyer but had studied medicine in Germany and Holland. With this core of judges, at least three of whom were competent lawyers, with the remainder possessing a wealth of administrative experience, the Court had a clear legal advantage in relation to other courts in Denmark. The practice of having the chancellor convene the Court judges began in 1663, and it seems to have been the custom that the civil judges were considered fixed judges within the Court and were expected to organize meetings concerning case matters. Peder Lauridsen Scavenius, professor of Law at the University of Copenhagen, also belonged to the fixed circle of judges starting in 1662. The remaining Danish law professors, such as Peder Hansen Resen, Cosmus Bornemann, Chr. Reitzer, Christian Bagger, Andreas Hojer, Henrik Stampe, Peder Kofod Ancher and I.E. Colbjørnsen (while B.G. Obelitz, John Erichsen, C.M.T. Cold, Laurids Nørregaard and later Schlegel, F. T. Hurtigkarl, M.H. Bornemann, Kolderup-Rosenvinge, P.G. Bang and I.E. Larsen were appointed as extraordinary deputies to the Court) were appointed as members of the Court in the following years leading up to the end of the 18th century at a time when law exams did not yet exist or were only partially implemented in such a way that the Court had control over legal proficiency. Provincial judges could also be appointed as members of the Supreme Court, for example, Villum Lange, a provincial judge in Jutland, in 1661, Tage Thott, a provincial judge in Zeeland, in 1700 and Jørgen Brahe, a provincial judge in Fyn, in 1700. As early as during the reign of Christian V the so called advocate general (*generalprokurør*), chief legal adviser to the government, became a member of the Court in order to support the King's interests. Likewise the original demand for balance between noble and civil was repealed, and legal competence was strengthened in a civil-dominated court.

A long series of Supreme Court judges were also active in the great law code endeavour which was set in motion in 1661 at the same time as the foundation of the Supreme Court. This resulted in the issue of the Danish Code in 1683 and then four years later in 1687 the accompanying Norwegian Code, which was essentially a copy of the Danish Code with a few Norway-specific regulations.[5] Just as the Danish Code finally created a unity of law in Denmark, the two law codes together meant that one might also speak of a *de facto* unity of law in Denmark and Norway. With this law the foundation was laid for Dano-Norwegian jurisprudence, as well as Dano-Norwegian Supreme Court case law based on Dano-Norwegian legislation. Two Supreme Court judges are of special importance for the Danish Code. One was a lawyer, Peder Lassen, who reworked drafts of the law, especially during its early stages. Meanwhile, the person who came to be of crucial importance for the Danish Code was Rasmus Vinding, who, besides being an assessor in the Supreme Court during the years 1661–1681, was a professor of Greek and later history and geography. He had already expressed sympathy for an inherited monarchy early on, and after the introduction of absolutism he later secured a good relationship with the ruling powers, first and foremost with Griffenfeld. When he eventually received the task of revising a draft upon which the final draft of the law was based, it certainly did not harm his position with regard to legal work. One could rightfully object to the Danish Code as being more backward-looking than forward-looking, but there is scarcely a doubt that without Vinding's influence the project would not have been finished at that time. Another Supreme Court judge and later justice, Caspar Schøller, was, together with Mathias Moth, responsible for bringing the Norwegian law project to completion.

The absolute kings displayed only a moderate interest in appearing at court. Frederick III appeared only rarely, while Christian V frequently took part during the first months after he assumed power, afterwards essentially confining himself to appearing at the Court's ceremonial opening. And so it continued. The Court was referred to by lawyers as "The Mightiest, Most Gracious Hereditary Lord and King", but the seat, as the aforementioned practice indicates, stood empty. On the other hand, if it suited him, the King could alter Supreme Court decisions after they had been made. It was also stipulated that certain cases should be put before the King prior to rendering a judgment. Thus the King had a definite influence on court decisions, both directly and indirectly, so judges knew that the King had the last word.

In the history of the Supreme Court, Christian VI's repeal of a Supreme Court decision is referred to as the last example in which the King directly interfered in court decisions. The case concerned an official's authority to refuse legal counsel, and one could discuss whether the judgment actually concerned the competence of the Court. In any event, the King repealed the judgment which went against a certain Prefect (*stiftamtmand*) Gersdorff, who was close to the royal household. The chief justice, Didrik Seckmann, protested as politely as possible when he

---

[5] *Ditlev Tamm*, The History of Danish Law, Selected Articles and Bibliography, København 2011, pp. 69 sq.

simultaneously conceded that "Your Majesty's delegates in the Supreme Court are human, and are subject to all human frailties", just as he admitted that a mistake can occur in the Supreme Court as well as anywhere else.

The history of the Supreme Court in the 18th century is mostly a history of adaptation of an increasingly outdated penal code which stood in book six of the Danish Code and the Norwegian Code. Concerning private law, the story deals with how the many lacunae in the Danish Code were filled through procedure, in particular through use of natural principles. The Danish historian and author Ludvig Holberg described the situation thus: "Danish laws are so brief that if the judge is not acquainted with Natural Law, he is often in a pinch …".[6] Once the judges had a legal education, natural law increasingly became the foundation for a long series of decisions about questions for which the Danish Code held no provisions.[7] As an example one can cite a judgment from 1759 in which it was established that intent or negligence defined as culpa should be the basis for assessment of damage compensation. The Norwegian-born judge Falsen formulated the question thus: "The question now becomes who among the partners was in culpa."

There are still large gaps in our knowledge of Supreme Court procedure in the years from the establishment of the Court up until the first collection of judgments at the beginning of the 19th century began to make the policies of the Court available. A hallmark of Supreme Court judgments is that they were without precedent. In order to determine views which underpin individual decisions, it is necessary to go to the deliberation protocols. Judgments were not made public, so it was up to the memory of individual judges whether the Court could follow a fixed policy. There are also examples where the Court deviated from earlier decisions on to a new course without having even noticed that it was doing so. It is not possible here to summarize in detail Supreme Court policy at various times. It should only be mentioned that the Court's significance for jurisprudence was limited by the fact that judgments were not publicly known. The study of court policy did not feature among 18th century concepts of legal methodology. The starting point was awareness of the law and of natural rights as presented in authoritative foreign works, which were supplemented during the 18th century by more accessible Danish and Norwegian products. Theory was one thing, practice another, and at that point it did not make any great difference that university professors took part in legal work.

A turning point came about with Anders Sandøe Ørsted (1779–1860), who in 1810 became a judge in the Supreme Court after having been a judge in the Royal and City Court (*Hof- og Stadsretten*) since 1801. Ørsted was editor of a series of legal journals which established the particularly Danish tradition of uniting court publications with legal journals containing articles, reviews, and so on. The career path from the Royal and City Court in Copenhagen to the Supreme Court was listed

---

[6] *Ludvig Holberg*, Værker Bind 12, København 1969–71, p. 109.

[7] *Thøger Nielsen*, Studier i ældre dansk formueretspksis, København 1951.

in the guidelines from 1771, which for a long time solidified the framework for court positions. In those guidelines a law exam became an entry requirement, and a judge was required to have for some years been an "Assessor in the Royal and City Court or in the guise of another judicial office and there obtained for himself practical knowledge and experience in the application of the laws in future circumstances ...". This practice therefore established a routine career path which has long left its mark, especially in the practice that judges are primarily recruited among people with judicial experience. Ørsted was the one who combined practical judicial experience with knowledge of foreign law and legal theory and, on that basis, provided Danish law with a practically oriented direction. In his own writings he does not often cite judgments, but it is clear that his remarks were written specifically with the intent that laws could, in a broad sense, be 'applied' to practical cases.

The inability of the Court to take positions on questions concerning the relationship between citizens and the public is also part of the old Supreme Court image. The ordinance of the city government (*magistratsinstruks*) from 1795, which Christian Colbjørnsen was responsible for, explicitly states that administrative authorities were not subject to review by the Courts. Only after the constitution of 1849, and to a larger extent early in the course of the 20th century, did the Supreme Court begin taking positions with regard to administrative disputes. In that area the Supreme Court has continued to be the highest court of law in Denmark, whereas other countries have introduced special administrative courts.

In contrast to the constitutions of many other countries, the Danish Constitution of 1849 did not discuss the Supreme Court in detail. There is mention of "The kingdom's highest law court" in connection to the Royal Court, and in a provision in § 63, sect. 2, the idea of founding administrative courts was sunk by the requirement that the decisions of such courts should be brought before "the kingdom's highest law court". The point of an administrative court system is precisely that it is a parallel system with respect to the highest law court. It can be introduced and function in a different way than as a general Supreme Court.

But a new age was ushered in with the Constitution, including among other things a Parliament which did not easily allow itself to be influenced by old, absolute institutions such as the Supreme Court. However one now spoke of the Court as an 'Honorary Supreme Court', and the King's seat had been removed. The fine old hierarchy in which one could not publicly criticize the authorities was now history, so when the Supreme Court judges, who accounted for half of the Court of Impeachment in 1855, acquitted the Ørsted Cabinet, the decision was viewed as reactionary and anti-constitutional, and there were repercussions. "The accused are free, but the Supreme Court is convicted" is how it stood in the press, and the reaction of the new government was to dismiss five court judges who were over 65 and appoint a president outside of the Court's own ranks, namely I.E. Larsen, professor of law, who then died in 1856 and was succeeded by P.G. Bang, who came from the post of Prime Minister. Only in 1861 was a president selected from the Court's own ranks once again. A further consequence of the 1855 decision had positive effects. The Court was given the choice between public voting in cases or providing its decisions with justification and chose the latter. Afterwards there was an ongoing discussion about whether the argumentation of the Supreme Court was sufficiently outlined, but from that time there was a rapid development from the first short, reluctant justifications up to modern standards. During the following several years, court decisions came forth as unanimous, since dissent was not reported. Allowing judgments to appear without mention of dissenting opinions is a way to strengthen the authority of the Court, as was known from southern European countries. It was first decided in 1937 that judges should report dissent and the count of dissenting judges, but anonymity of judges was first repealed in 1958. From that point the names of majority and minority judges were reported.

Clearly the disclosure of court justifications was of great importance for the Court's effectiveness as part of the legislative process. It was difficult to determine why the Court believed as it did if its decisions were not justified, and only in those instances where the Supreme Court upheld decisions from an earlier authority with reference to the justification made by the lower court could one see upon what the Supreme Court had placed emphasis. By the end of the 19th century they were still lacking most of the legislation which we view as fundamental to Danish courts, and much was therefore not regulated and must have been established through procedure. A new penal code appeared in 1866, but judicial reform was first implemented in 1919 and with it the principles of orality and immediacy, which were admittedly more restrictive for district courts and High Courts than for the Supreme Court, which had had a tradition of oral procedures for centuries. In the area of private law, there was still no Statute of Sale (*Købeloven*), Statute of Contract (*Aftaleloven*), or statutes on marriage and divorce or the many other laws which were part of the Nordic legal milieu during the first decades of the 20th century and served as a legal foundation for Danish courts. In a broad sense, the Court may have helped form the general principles of law, as the force of the Danish Code did not lie only in formulating more general principles. The importance of the Supreme Court is clearly demonstrated by the words of Julius Lassen, who spoke of his work collecting legal documents in his 1917 farewell address:

> "I chose the path … of explicating and classifying the Danish judgments which are held in the records (*Domssamlingerne*). At times I had to go back to these and consult the Protocols of the Court".

Legal practice was now a visible part of the basis for Danish jurisprudence. As another example of the importance attached to judgments (not least those of the Supreme Court) during the latter half of the 19th century, one can name Carl Goos' systemization of a very large number of sentences in his book on criminal law.

Some years earlier during the keynote address at the university in 1899, law professor Julius Lassen made himself the spokesman for both a new legal code intended as a replacement for the Danish Code from 1683 and for a more conservative view of the role of the judges. Among his arguments for implementing a new legal code was that codification of the law would remove a portion of the uncertainty which was inherent in a legal situation where judges have great freedom to reach their own decisions, especially necessary where legislative regulation is lacking. Julius Lassen's picture of the lawmaker judge was only moderately positive:

> "The judge's sense of justice is affected by irrelevant considerations, sympathies and antipathies, which, unbeknownst to the judge, lead to a shift in his perception of the proper standard favourable to the one party and unfavourable to the other. No one can declare himself to be completely free from such things lying beneath the threshold of consciousness, and irrelevant considerations can influence his capacity for decision."

Against that background, but naturally also with reference to the newly finished German civil code which came into force the following year, Julius Lassen promoted the introduction of a Nordic civil law code. As is well known, this was never done, but from a broad perspective one still has an impressive string of Nordic laws in the area of contract and tort law and personal and family law, which also later came to shape the basis of the Danish court. Moreover, it gave the Supreme Court more of a role as an interpreter of the law and less as an independent creator of legislation.

A much more detailed regulation of criminal justice was introduced with a new penal code in 1866, with new criminal offences added to it, or rather one might say that many of the broad formulations in the older penal legislation were now replaced by more precise legislation. Hitherto penal legislation had been based on the sixth book of the Danish Code from 1683 with various newer statutes, the most recent being some criminal laws concerning property crimes and arson, which A.S. Ørsted articulated according to modern principles. But there had been a serious need for a modern penal code, so that when the law finally came in 1866 it naturally had significance for the Supreme Court. It now became necessary to take positions on how the new law should be interpreted in practice. Criminal cases therefore came to play a large role at the end of the 19th century. One of the new pieces of legislation concerned pornography, and it became the thankless job of the Supreme Court to determine what the boundaries were during a less liberal era. Furthermore, the victims of this legislation were renowned *literati* such as the famous Danish authors Herman Bang and Gustav Wied and the French authors Guy de Maupassant and Crébillon, whose spicy but rather innocent novel about what a sofa can experience became considered lewd in the understanding of the penal code. The limit for penalization of pornographic writings instilled during the bloom of Victorianism lasted such a long time that it formed the perceptual basis in Denmark for what constituted pornographic writing. The 1930 penal code perpetuated the standard of the 1866 law, and even in the 1960s the Supreme Court took a position on punishment of obscene writings, probably for the last time. The reason for this occasion was that a publisher had rereleased an English novel from the 18th century by the author John Cleland with the title *Fanny Hill. Memoirs of a Woman of Pleasure*. Publication of the book had previously been considered punishable, and a run of prints had been confiscated. But by 1964 things had progressed so far that the District Court and a portion of the Eastern High Court (*Østre Landsret*) had considered the book permissible. On this occasion the defence had shared the same point of view as the prosecution: that acquitting the publisher meant that the penal code provision on pornographic literature had no efficacy. The majority of the Supreme Court probably agreed when in their justification for acquittal they referred to the widespread sexual freedom at the time, which meant that a conviction would have been viewed as obsolete.

Another example of a decision bound by current events at the end of the 19th century is a series of judgments in cases attached to political antagonism in Denmark, closely linked to the question of which chamber of the Parliament (*Rigsdagen*) should be the dominant one. The Supreme Court had played a political role earlier, and many cases concerning the limits of free speech under later absolutism had helped form the impression of a court which could function as the long arm of the government. In his work on the history of the Supreme Court 1661–1961, Georg Nørregaard wrote that by no means did the Supreme Court act as a slave to the government or the Chancery.[8] Indeed, the court did not slavishly follow the prosecution. On the contrary, it took an independent position which could lead to acquittal or conviction. Nevertheless, contemporary liberals had an image of a court which stood on the side opposed to progress, enlightenment and justifiable and necessary criticism. The harsh reaction to the acquittal of the Ørsted Cabinet by the Supreme Court judges in 1856, namely the dismissal of five judges, including the president of the Court, can only be seen as an expression of a belief that the Supreme Court had a load of reactionary decisions in its baggage and would have difficulty in keeping up with the times, not least in the new era under democracy.

It is natural to examine cases involving freedom of the press in the final years of absolutism as political cases, and it might have been easier for the Court to begin completely anew as a new law court with a foundation in the new constitution. Thus Parliament and the Supreme Court would have been on an equal footing. Yet the Court did not, in fact, manage to avoid being thrown into a political conflict once again, such as what occurred during the 1880s during parliamentary struggles between the two dominant political parties. At that time the Parliament consisted of two chambers: the upper chamber (*Landstinget*) and the second chamber (*Folketinget*). In 1866 a new political force emerged, in the shape of a group of conservative landowners who were capable of action and who acquired decisive importance in the upper chamber following a change in the rules on suffrage. This so-called privileged suffrage was agreed in the "revised constitution" of 1866.

---

8 *Bagge/Frost/Hjejle*, Højesteret 1661–1961 (supra fn. 2).

During the 1870's a fierce constitutional struggle developed along similar lines in relation to Bismarck's battle against the Prussian House of Lords (*Herrenhaus*) in the 1860s. At the root of the problem was the fact that the revised constitution did not provide for a common organ that could have acted as a mediator when the two chambers were unable to reach agreement. When the liberal farmers' party gained a majority in the second chamber in 1872, a new era started, since the farmers' success was soon followed by a demand for the King to appoint his government from members of the majority groups in the second chamber. The King, however, insisted on his right enshrined in the constitution to form his government as he wished, and he was supported by the upper chamber in this opinion. The farmers attempted to hinder the government by refusing to accept both the annual budget act and later legislation in general. The government's response was simply to declare these types of act to be provisional legislation, since a provision in the Constitution allowed the King to enact provisional legislation "in particularly urgent cases, when the Parliament is not assembled." Harmony between the two chambers was not achieved until 1894, and it was to take until 1901 before the parliamentary principle that the King should appoint a government composed of the members of the majority grouping in the lower chamber was recognized.

The Supreme Court however indirectly came to take positions in this constitutional struggle in a series of criminal cases about whether the government's use of provisional laws could be considered constitutional.

The Supreme Court often handled cases more mildly and issued milder punishments than did lower authorities, but decisions were also often given with strong dissent. There were even judges who wanted to strike down provisional laws as unconstitutional. It is difficult to demonstrate the relationship between political beliefs and taking positions on cases, since only a few of the Court's judges were profiled politically, but one can generally trace a certain amount of scepticism toward provisional policies which, however, did not find expression in decisions. The reality was that the judges supported the Estrup policies, if not with a high degree of enthusiasm. There were two particular Supreme Court decisions on these matters which caused a sensation. One was a prison sentence for a leading politician belonging to the liberal farmers, Christen Berg, who was convicted of conspiring to hinder an official from performing his duty when he agreed to have a police chief rather roughly removed from a podium where he was meant to speak. For this the Supreme Court imposed a prison sentence. On the question of the provisional law's legitimacy, a decision from 1886 concerning the social-democratic editor Sigvald C.C. Olsen was of particular importance. The case centred on an infraction of a provisional penal law from 2 November 1885, which stipulated a penalty for criticizing the government. The Supreme Court did not want to set aside the provisional penal law. Instead it accepted the law and stated further that a private bill with the same content as the provisional law and subsequently thrown out of the second chamber had no significance for deliberation of the law's validity. In this way the liberal farmers' party had tried to demonstrate that as such the provisional penal law would not have been approved by the second chamber. The Supreme Court presented the purely formal consideration that this particular law had not in fact been thrown out of the second chamber, where the law had not been submitted. The point of view was sufficiently correct, but it is difficult to ignore that the Supreme Court was not prepared to oppose the government. The president of the Supreme Court in those years, Buch, also received the prestigious Danish Order of the Elephant for his efforts, a highly unusual distinction for a Supreme Court president that has since not been repeated.

Additionally, it can be noted that the Supreme Court basically recruited judges from the higher courts, and, as previously stated, very few had political experience. Since 1861 there was also a fixed custom to recruit the president from among the judges. In that way the Court ensured its competence as well as a professional approach to selection of judges; but at the same time this was a limitation because so few judges had experience outside of courtroom activities. The method by which judges were recruited for the Supreme Court helped maintain the Court as a function of the state, which considered judicial powers as a professional section of the state government whose task it was to deliver judgments on legal questions and adhere to them.

Should anyone doubt whether the Court's fundamental attitude was to uphold the status quo, one can listen to Niels Lassen, the Court president in 1911, who said in a speech during the opening of the Court's 250th anniversary: "Conservatism belongs with old age, and we in the Supreme Court are getting on a little in years".

The question of how innovative or conservative judges should be in relation to the establishment of law is a classic question within jurisprudence. In the same 1911 speech Niels Lassen also turned to the prevailing opinion in the past of law courts as "classification machines" (*subsumptionsautomater*), where decisions were reached through a type of logical deduction: "For example, the law says: When a man has stolen, he shall be punished; the accused has stolen x – therefore he shall be punished. The law is the theory, the following cases the statement, the ruling the conclusion". This was not only the opinion of the president. The Courts might often have erred on the side of liberality in questionable circumstances, where one might ask "but where should we find norms for decisions?" The answer might have been "within ourselves". Niels Lassen advocated active, legislative judges, but he certainly did not think so to such a degree that the Courts should actively assert themselves over the other two bodies of state. The consequence of the Supreme Court overruling those provisional laws would have been enormous, and at that time, as in others where the Supreme Court followed the government on controversial cases, it chose to lean towards the other powers of state. One could also formulate it thus: the Supreme Court's view of its role through the years has been to interpret the powers of state as a unity in which the Supreme Court has its function, which entailed a duty to monitor other powers of state. However, this duty did not extend to raising doubts concerning the agents of the other state powers.

One period in Supreme Court history which still in 1661 was a delicate subject is the occupation between 1940 and 1945 and the position of the Supreme Court during the Ocuupation and with regard to post-war trials during the following years. The role of the Supreme Court was disputed during the occupation, not least during the initial years, and still remains so. In its simplest form, the problem was how the Court should position itself towards special legislation adopted by Parliament for actions directed against the occupying powers. A law of 1941 set certain penalties for actions which were capable of seriously damaging Denmark's foreign relations. According to that law, an 18-year old man who had sought to flee to Sweden was sentenced to prison for one year and six months, while the High Court had moved for acquittal. In its justification, the Court stressed "the gravity of current conditions is leading toward a closing of the country's borders". From the deliberations it is clearly evident that the judges viewed the case as a means to accommodate the occupying powers and desired to set an example by imposing a harsh sentence. The same thing happened during a case against the historian, Vilhelm la Cour, who expressed his criticism of the occupying powers through a series of lectures, accusing Denmark of being "the little canary of robbers and murderers" and expressing doubt about whether Germany would be victorious. The judgment passed on him was made harsher from four months detention to seven months in prison. The Court's voting protocols for this case also show how they wanted to increase sentences in order to show that the law was to be taken seriously. This is even more clearly visible in the judgment on the captain who sailed the conservative politician Christmas Møller to Sweden, whence he was further taken to London. In this case the sentence was increased from three years to six years imprisonment.

In a case against the editor P. de Hemmer Gudme, which was discussed in closed proceedings, the Supreme Court broadly expanded the definition of the concept of 'public' and sentenced him to four months detention. One man who had housed a German deserter received an increased sentence from 40 days to three months in jail. In a decision on the illegal print industry, the punishment was reduced from eight years in jail to six years, but otherwise the Supreme Court tendency moved in the direction of increased sentences.

A reading of the voting protocols in these six extraordinary cases elicited by special circumstances during the occupation shows a Supreme Court which took its duties seriously as the highest government agency and as a participant in appeasement policies. There is nothing which indicates that judges distanced themselves from their roles of judging people who fought for the nation's freedom. The deliberations overwhelmingly demonstrate that it was important to set examples, and several opinions show that the judges did not show any particular sympathy toward those who pursued their own struggle in the conflict against governmental efforts to maintain appeasement policies. Within this picture one must also include legislation which was primarily intended to ensure that these cases remained in the Danish courts, but there is nothing which indicates that the

Supreme Court deliberated over how problematic it actually was to hand down harsh sentences in those instances where those condemned actively displayed that they were against the occupying powers. The Supreme Court's judgments in these cases are not a part of the most honourable chapter in the history of the Court. No one can claim that the Danish Supreme Court positioned themselves on the side of the resistance, as in Norway, but it is still disheartening to read deliberations which unilaterally and repeatedly back up the official policies and do not express the least sympathy for or concern about harsh penalties for people who were fighting for the country's freedom and who dared to speak their minds.

Naturally the Court's ruling in the case concerning the arrest of Danish communists in June 1941, which included communist members of Parliament, also belongs in the picture. The behaviour of Supreme Court president Troels G. Jørgensen was particularly unfortunate with respect to this matter. He took an active part in efforts to advance a special act for the arrest of communists, and when the law came into being in August 1941, the Supreme Court president published an article in which he concluded that the law did not concern constitutional rights of freedom. At the time this was one of the dubious questions about which others had a different opinion, and it was certainly not the right time for a member of the Supreme Court to express himself on a question which was to be tried by the Court shortly thereafter. In a ruling on 8 September 1941, the Supreme Court also upheld the arrests with the brief reasoning that objections to the law "are found to lack grounds". This was an easy way of getting around the question, and it did not evoke respect for the Court in resistance circles. Confidence in the Court president and his ability to judge was also weakened. Seen through this perspective, it is no wonder that the Court judges were not happy about their president. One can speculate about it, but a reading of the Court's deliberations clearly shows that the president did not stand alone with his vision of the Supreme Court in its role as an active supporter of the occupation government. He simply stated publicly what the others merely said in deliberations.

Opposition to the Supreme Court's role during the occupation played a part in the post-war trials following the occupation. The post-war trials were arranged in such a way that the Supreme Court came to have a decisive importance in a series of cases which formed the overall framework. The vast majority of the nearly 14,000 criminal cases were handled by district and High Courts, and the Supreme Court itself dealt with decisions in fewer than 200 cases, most of which involved the death penalty. Statistics show that the Supreme Court upheld the majority of judgments which were put before them. In ca. 10% of cases they increased the penalty, and in ca. 25% they reduced the earlier sentence. The role of the Supreme Court during the post-war trials can be illustrated by two judgments delivered in the months of November and December 1945 and which came to be of lasting importance for the duration of the post-war trials. On 28 November 1945, the Supreme Court took a position on the question of culpability for participation as a voluntary soldier in the *Frikorps Danmark*, the Danish Volunteer Army, who had fought on the Eastern Front against the Soviets. The district court had acquitted the defendant in one case where the accused claimed that he believed that the government's affiliation with the *Frikorps* could be seen as "authorization" in the legal understanding, and would thus entail no criminal penalties. The High Court had rejected that view and declared a legal minimum sentence of four years imprisonment. The Supreme Court's action was to reduce the sentence to two years imprisonment. Because of this, the judgment became one of the most important judgments, as well as one of the most crucial with regard to the post-war trials. The law had set a minimum sentence of four years in order that only serious cases were brought before the courts. With the establishment of a penal framework of two years imprisonment for 'German war service", the Supreme Court ensured that all cases of a similar kind where a sentence of four years would be given without consideration would now come before the Court. With a revision of the law in 1946 the minimum penalty was reduced to one year, commensurate with the practice set by the Supreme Court. There was no uniformity at all in these cases, and those sentenced to two years were part of a compromise where some judges wanted to sentence them to four years, while others simply wanted to acquit.

Another noteworthy decision was the Supreme Court judgment on 5 December 1945, which authorized the death penalty for journalist and SS-member Flemming Helweg-Larsen. There was no talk of a miscarriage of justice. Helweg-Larsen had been complicit in committing a murder, he had been a German war correspondent, and he had also been involved in the arrest of Danish Jews. He was sentenced according to the provision in the penal code concerning murder in 'German interests'. The legal problem was whether the murder counted as being in 'German interests' or rather as a private act of vengeance. Regardless of the circumstances, this meant the death penalty, which was the first offence placed at that level during the post-war trials. One murder was sufficient to warrant the death penalty, and it ended up leading to a long series of death sentences during the early post-war years. It also resulted in a practice which could not be maintained when exceptionally grave cases concerning terrorising gangs, murder and torture carried out by Danes in the service of the Germans appeared. How to deal with murder accessory cases during the post-war trials became the first matter upon which the Supreme Court took a position, but the Supreme Court showed an inflexibility which backfired. Later there were pardons in far more serious cases, and at this point the Supreme Court was responsible for setting a misguided course during the post-war trials.

Two further cases where the Supreme Court took a position in relation to the post-war trials should be mentioned here. A portion of the Supreme Court decisions involved economic collaboration, involving the economic collaborationists (*værnemagere*) who had worked as industrialists or contractors for the Germans during the occupation. They were sentenced under a special act. The criterion for the penalty was whether their cooperation was 'excessive'. In June 1949 the Supreme Court took a position on this question in relation to a criminal case against an entrepreneurial company which had actively carried out German orders and expanded to meet German requirements. However, the Supreme Court here chose to weigh these factors against the clearly expressed wishes of the Danish government during the occupation which stated that Danish firms should undertake that sort of work. District and High Courts cast a sympathetic eye on a firm if its profit interests were clear, but the Supreme Court chose to place emphasis on compliance with official policies. The decision also meant that a series of older cases with convictions could be reopened. The case was instrumental in creating a disparity whereby large businesses with large profits were acquitted, while smaller craftsmen and enterprises which could not shield themselves by keeping work in Danish hands according to governmental wishes were convicted.

The case against the German plenipotentiary Dr. Werner Best and two others responsible for German terror tactics in Denmark, SS-leader Pancke and police chief Bovensiepen, should be mentioned as a final example of the Supreme Court's handling of post-war trial cases. You may argue, that if any German war criminal had deserved the death penalty introduced for war crimes, it was these three, but things did not turn out that way. The District Court sentenced Best and Bovensiepen to the death penalty. However at the High Court, the punishment was commuted to life in prison for Bovensiepen and only five years imprisonment for Dr. Best. The High Court judgment over Dr. Best is probably one of the most criticized and flawed decisions in Danish legal history and rests upon a very limited understanding of the nature of war crimes, the personality of Best and his position in the Nazi-system and his liability for the action taken against Danish Jews in 1943.[9] The High Court's incorrect assessments of Best is recognized as such today. Due to procedural rules the Supreme Court was bound by the High Court decision as to the assessment of facts. The punishment however was raised to a sentence to twelve years imprisonment, which might also be seen and by many was seen as far too mild a sentence for one of the central figures within the Third Reich's reign of terror.

With these four judgments the Supreme Court actively managed to give the post-war trials a skewed course and to create the not entirely inaccurate "myth" that the small fish were convicted and the big ones escaped, or at least got off with less. The judgments illustrate how difficult it is for a court with a long history of traditional application of the law to step into a more extraordinary position and set a course on the basis of more or less arbitrary cases which came before the Court.

The Post-War Trial judgments now lie far back in the past, and it has been fifty years since the Supreme Court celebrated its first 300 years. At the 325th jubilee in 1986 a publication was produced containing a series of articles on court decisions on a range of new case subjects during recent years. Among the more spectacular judgments from those years which were highlighted on that occasion, and which

---

9 See about Werner Best the biography by *Ulrich Herbert*, Best: Biographische Studien über Radikalismus, Weltanschauung und Vernunft, 1903–1989, Bonn 1996.

gave rise to some publicity, one can mention a case concerning the Free City of Christiania from 1978. This case acquired significant importance not only for the Free City remaining where it is, but also for establishing the right of the state to make decisions on the region. For this the Supreme Court referred to § 3 of the Constitution concerning the division of legislative, executive and judicial authority. This prevented the Court from taking a position on human and social concerns and to grant the people of Christiania the right to the area when no clear promises existed.

Characteristic of the Danish Supreme Court from an international perspective is the Court's universal competence in all types of judicial decisions. The Court's historical inheritance naturally plays a role here as well. New constitutions in several countries during the 20th century have introduced constitutional courts. Other regions have also recognized a special administrative jurisdiction, where cases concerning the relationship between citizens and public affairs are ultimately decided by special administrative courts. There are usually several cases outside the scope of these kinds of Supreme Courts, but the Danish Supreme Court naturally sets limits on the number of cases which can be heard against public authorities.

A general overview of Supreme Court cases in recent years will give an impression of tendencies in the most recent Supreme Court practice. The provision in § 3 of the Constitution became a hot topic again in 1999 when the Court broke with more than a hundred years of reticence when a case involving a question of the law's constitutionality came to trial. A series of cases from the period around 1920 were much discussed at the time. They involved replacement of rent charges (*grundbyrder*), tenant farmer rights (*fæste*) and conversion of entailed estates into fee simples (*len*), and the Supreme Court denied that the oppressive economic conditions resulting from the legislation were a breach of a constitutional provision protecting ownership rights. In these cases the discussion was about protecting ownership rights, and it is probably not too much to say that the Supreme Court's denial that the rulings constituted a breach of constitutional ownership protections came close to a denial that that provision in the Constitution had any meaning beyond being a liberal phrase.[10]

In the so-called "Tvind-judgment" of 1999, the question was whether the law's treatment of a series of named independent schools, some of which could not receive public subsidies, was a breach of § 3 of the Constitution, since the law concluded that the question of subsidies be brought before the Court.[11] It can certainly be debated whether a possible challenge to a right to a subsidy should be a right granted by the Constitution, and that a law which infringes this right can be considered to be unconstitutional. The result, however, was unanimously reached by the Supreme Court and thereby brought Denmark's Supreme Court into the

[10] U.1921.148H, U.1921.644H and U.1921.168H.

[11] U.1999.841H.

company of supreme courts which had enforced so-called "judicial review" so prominently introduced in the US Supreme Court in 1803 through the landmark decision in "Marbury v. Madison". In recent years the Supreme Court has also made decisions within the area of constitutional law which have caught the public eye.

In the so-called "Maastricht case" in 1998, the Supreme Court took a position on whether implementation of the treaty of The European Community (The EC Treaty) in Denmark as amended by the Treaty of the European Union (The Union Treaty) had properly taken place in line with § 20 of the Constitution, or whether implementation required a constitutional amendment with respect to § 88.[12] The question before the Court was a rather serious one, and earlier such a case would probably have been rejected because the claimants would not have been recognized as having a legitimate interest. The fact that this case came before the Court is one expression of how the Supreme Court positions itself more openly to debating constitutional questions. The decision included the question whether Denmark had relinquished powers to EU entities to such an extent that it violated the constitutional requirement that such transfers of sovereignty can only occur to a certain extent. The Supreme Court reached the expected conclusion: no constitutional violation had taken place, and, among other reasons, justified it thus:

> "With regard to the question whether release of sovereignty under the Act of incorporation (*tiltrædelsloven*) has such a form that it goes against the constitutional requirement for a democratic form of governance, it is to be pointed out that relinquishing parts of parliamentary legislative ability to an international organization will entail a certain degree of interference with the Danish democratic form of governance. This is taken into consideration with respect to the formulation of the strict requirements of adoption according to § 20 sect. 2. With regard to the EC Treaty, legislative power in the first instance is given over to the Council, in which the Danish government, under the authority of Parliament, can exercise its influence. It should be considered a matter for the Parliament to take a position on whether the government's membership in EC cooperation should be subject to more extensive democratic control. Therefore, in this matter the Supreme Court finds no substantive reason to consider the Accession Act unconstitutional."

This case also included an examination of which duties belonged to Parliament and which belonged to the Supreme Court. These cases highlight an important trend and mark yet another way in which the Supreme Court operates among the international community. The interest in foreign political affairs and the Supreme Court's willingness to hear such cases shows that constitutional questions have gained a new meaning and that the Supreme Court is not as reluctant as before when it comes to taking positions on a question whose basis is political, such as Denmark's acceptance of the treaty involving the European communities. Similar questions have been tested before the German constitutional court, which is composed very differently from the Supreme Court. There also remains the important question

[12] U.1998.800H.

whether the Supreme Court is sufficiently structured to be the forum where decisions should be made on whether conditions for continued membership in the EU are to take place.

In connection to the Supreme Court's position towards constitutional questions, one can also mention a decision from 2006,[13] where the Supreme Court took a position on whether it was justified for a municipality (*kommune*) to have provided social benefits to a recipient who had not taken part in a work activity. The prosecution referred to the regulations of the ECHR (European Convention on Human Rights) forbidding forced labour and ILO Conventions as evidence that such a request could not be made, but the Supreme Court supported the municipality for, among other reasons, the point of view that the Danish rules concerning obligatory activities for recipients of social services (*aktiveringsregler*) were in agreement with fundamental objectives underlying international ILO regulations.

In 1999 the Supreme Court took a position on the meaning of § 79 of the Constitution concerning freedom of assembly in a case which stemmed from a 1996 law which allowed the possibility to forbid certain persons from remaining in certain places which could be perceived as gang hangouts. In its justification for upholding the intervention, the Supreme Court referred to the concrete purpose of the law to protect others from the dangers associated with gang unrest, and pointed out that it was not the goal of the law to hinder expression of political opinions, which § 79 of the Constitution is intended to protect.[14]

The majority of Supreme Court decisions do not concern more spectacular questions about the Constitution. Currently, a new aspect of the Supreme Court's work is the significance accompanying the ECHR as a universal benchmark of civil liberties. The topic emerged when the European Human Rights Court ruled on the so-called 'Green Jacket Case' in 1994.[15] The Court justified the actions of a TV journalist who gave young, so-called 'green jackets' the opportunity to express racist opinions on Danish television in violation of Danish criminal law. In 1988 the Supreme Court confirmed a High Court judgment convicting the journalist, but the Human Rights Court ruled that grounds of freedom of expression should take precedence.[16] The case has been mentioned in a series of later decisions, usually without being integral to the case, where one party has raised questions concerning the ECHR, especially on whether its provisions for equality or case procedure have been met.

It would be incorrect to conclude that the Supreme Court is on its way to becoming a constitutional court on the basis of these decisions. By far the largest part of Supreme Court decisions involves more daily concerns where the Supreme

[13] U.2006.770H.

[14] U.1999.1798H.

[15] Jersild v. Denmark, Application no. 15890/89.

[16] U.1989.339H.

Court takes a position in its capacity as the highest appellate court. The Supreme Court continues to play an important role in that area, although it is important to emphasize that a vast number of important conflicts do not come before the Supreme Court at all. Many large and important cases are, and probably will continue to be, resolved through private arbitration. Here one should also mention that because the new court system allows many cases to begin in district courts, special permission is required in order to bring the case before the Supreme Court. A similar system for the highest court exists in several countries, and we will see what sort of impact will be generated by the Supreme Court's opportunity to concentrate on more fundamental questions. The Court's role as a resolver of conflicts is decreasing rather than increasing. However, the Supreme Court obviously still has the 'last word' when it comes to significant questions of interpretation, and this applies essentially to all parts of the legal system. I circulated a questionnaire among my university colleagues to gain an impression of which judgments are perceived to hold particular import for diverse disciplines during recent years. Here I will mention a set of examples drawn from the results which illustrate the breadth of the Court's duties.

In the US one speaks of so-called 'landmark cases', a designation referring to those decisions reached by the American federal Supreme Court which often have a special importance and where hitherto valid principles have been set aside to establish an entirely new path of interpretation. The phenomenon has something to do with the American Supreme Court's importance to societal development and the nature of some divisions lying in the grey area between law and politics, a phenomenon unknown in Denmark. In Denmark we do not meet with cases on separate or divided schools for coloured persons, a position on abortion rights, criminalization of homosexuality, the right to bear arms, or presidential election recounts. In Denmark we are not familiar with the distinctive way of referring to periods in legal history by who was president. Here at home it is noted who is chosen as president, but neither the president nor the judge's name is usually recognized in public. As for the press, the closest one has come to the American system was probably when there were references to 'Pontoppidan's court' when Niels Pontoppidan was president of the Supreme Court. This probably had something to do with the fact that it was at the end of the 1990s when the judgments on the Constitution, including the 'Tvind Judgment', were handed down. Insofar as anyone might have a sense of activism being represented in that period, the Court has its own statements and activities in the first ten years of the 21st century which contradict such a trend.

Supreme Court cases fall within a broad spectrum of subjects. In the vast majority of cases, Supreme Court decisions go unnoticed outside of specialist circles, but certain cases attract more general interest, above all the constitutional cases mentioned above. One example is a Supreme Court judgment of 2005 in which it ruled that a chain store had the right to insist that employees not wear headscarves in customer service departments. The Supreme Court upheld a provincial court decision according to which such a clothing regulation must be regarded as objectively justified.[17]

One question which occasionally arises in connection with the Court's handling of administrative disputes is whether the Court can be viewed as particularly state-friendly and, furthermore, whether it has a tendency to give an advantage to the public. The question can, among other things, also be raised in view of the Supreme Court's position toward social services. Among the questions upon which the Court has taken a position in recent years is whether the grant of increased disability pensions should be calculated from the point when the application is made or from the point when the pension is granted with no retroactive force. In a judgment of 1999 the Court ruled that the point from which benefits could first be calculated was the first of the month after which the pension was awarded.[18] On the other hand, the Court ruled in another judgment that the Court's, and therefore also the Supreme Court's, review of whether medical requirements for receiving social pensions of a certain size should also be included in evaluations of a discretionary nature.[19] In that instance the Supreme Court ruled that the Court had the right to an intensive review of whether conditions were sufficient for receiving a pension.

With respect to these cases concerning social benefits there is a need to emphasize that in several foreign court systems (e.g. Swedish or Finnish courts), the decision on such matters would be one for special administrative courts, which often handle a long series of similar cases and which differ from the general Supreme Court of those countries in terms of both working methods and approach.

The Supreme Court has also to some extent taken a position on cases to do with treatment of patients in hospital. One much discussed case concerns use of a certain solidifying mixture, Boneloc, in prosthetic hips.[20] The mixture was shown to not have the expected durability. The question in the case was whether the public was responsible for a patient who did not pay attention to warnings that there were problems with Boneloc. The patient received compensation from the Patients' Board of Appeals (*patientankenævnet*). For the Court, the case was a matter of whether the Ministry of Health was responsible for the Board of Health not having intervened in a timely fashion. Both a High Court and the Supreme Court acquitted the ministry of compensation claims where the Court did not find sufficient grounds for inaction or that the patient had not been adequately informed about the risks concerning the mixture involved in the operation.

According to the Danish system, which does not recognize administrative courts, it is only rarely that the Supreme Court can review administrative decisions. On the other hand, examinations are quite intensive in certain cases. One example

[17] U.2005.1265H.

[18] U.2000.179H.

[19] U.2000.645H.

[20] U.2000.515H.

is a recent judgment from 2005 in which the Supreme Court took a position regarding the extent of sick leave allowances for mothers on maternity leave. The Court decided that allowances should be calculated on the basis of leave allowance and not prior earnings. In a case from 2007, the Supreme Court took a position on which regulations should apply to child benefits allotted to single adoptive parents and a position stating that regulations governing single parents do not apply to single adoptive parents.[21]

Over time the Supreme Court has played a large role in establishing general administrative legal principles within the area of traditional administrative law; the Court has also taken positions on decisions encompassing a broad spectrum of areas related to public administration. Tax cases play a special role, but the Court has also taken positions on cases involving employment, immigration and general administrative legal principles, such as the requirement of justification, obligatory consultation, the limits of discretion and the principles of proportionality and equality. In two decisions from 2005,[22] the Court took a position on whether the formal requirements relating to layoffs were also valid for establishing a voluntary redundancy scheme. In that case the Court was inclined to take a more flexible, labour-oriented point of view instead of focusing on administrative law regulations. The Supreme Court reached the conclusion that regardless of whether administrative law provisions took precedence, they could not interfere with a negotiated resignation contract in public employment. The decision went against a statement by the parliamentary ombudsman who had expressed support for the mandatory nature of administrative law.

In another decision from 2005, the Supreme Court upheld a High Court judgment which ruled in a case concerning allocation of additional local funds.[23] The ruling was that there had been a legally negotiated system which did not fall under administrative law. Through these cases the Court was responsible for establishing a boundary between public regulations and private law.

New disciplines in which Supreme Court practice plays a role have developed in recent years. One such area is stock market law, where the Court has, for example, taken a position on a question concerning so-called insider trading[24] and liability for trading advice.[25] One might also mention a much discussed case concerning an advocate's disclosure of confidential information to *Fondsbørsen,* the Danish Stock Exchange. The information concerned criminal activities, and the disclosure was not viewed as a violation of the lawyers' code of good conduct (U 2002, p. 1531). The Supreme Court and others have taken positions on cases within

---

[21] U.2005.341H.

[22] U.2005.537 and 622H.

[23] U.2005.2111H.

[24] U.2005.984H.

[25] U.2005.2354H.

another new discipline, Information Technology law, on banning domain names from transmitting works protected by copyright, though Supreme Court activities generally play a lesser role in the formation of law in this area.

Competition law (*konkurrenceretten*) is a discipline in which public law and private law meet. Decisions on competition law can be appealed before the Competition Law Tribunal (*Konkurrenceankenævnet*) with a Supreme Court judge as foreman, who usually has the last word. The Supreme Court's importance in this field is somewhat limited. By contrast, the Court has taken a position on several cases involving marketing law (*markedsføringsloven*) involving advertising or misuse of other business practices. Many of these cases are clear-cut and have a strong bearing as a precedent.

A vast majority of Supreme Court decisions fall within the traditional disciplines of jurisprudence which we recognize from private law. Supreme Court impact, however, has not been evenly distributed among these areas. The Supreme Court has long played a more peripheral role in family and inheritance law. It has made a series of important decisions on marriage, contributions, and property ownership between spouses, but in recent years there have been relatively few cases. The situation in Denmark differs from that in Norway, whose Supreme Court still handles many family and inheritance law cases.

In recent years, the Supreme Court has settled many more concrete cases within the general field of obligations law. The Court took a position on a set of contractual questions, on the interpretation of liability limits in sale contracts, on the definition of 'a declaration of intent', on raising the compensation for ballet composers[26] if a ballet does not take place, on financing requirements, on withdrawal of cancellation, on guarantees involving sale of used cars, on delays, remediation, the obligation to investigate, and so on.

A reading of Supreme Court judgments from recent years confirms the impression of a court which is definitely not specialized. The span of cases runs from major constitutional questions on Denmark's status within the international community through public responsibility in more daily contractual situations, to situations involving financing, to use of staple goods. It is nearly impossible to determine in which direction the trend is going on the basis of development of Supreme Court duties. There seems to be a trend towards a more active court from around the year 2000. It also appears that the Court principally takes positions on, for example, cases involving public services. It might be that private law is less visible, probably because of a visible trend towards lower priority in traditional disciplines such as family and inheritance law and obligations law among legal professionals, while other disciplines, such as development of society in a more technological direction, are making themselves more pronounced. Of particular

---

[26] U.2000.656H.

importance for the role of the Supreme Court are developments which have taken place since the elimination of Supreme Court attorney examinations in 1958. These formerly meant that only a few lawyers could go through the procedure. Court cases only play a limited role today in the world of jurisprudence, where the basis for the efficacy of large legal firms is not processes but advice. On the other hand there is an increased awareness of the Court's role as a protector of the Constitution and individuals.

The Supreme Court is turning 350. The contention of this paper is that age is not automatically an advantage for a court, and certainly not when its history goes all the way back to the first years of absolutism. We are so accustomed to considering the Supreme Court as the third, "least dangerous" power of state that it is difficult to see the Court in an historical perspective which deals with it first finding its place as part of an all-powerful state power and, since then, as a participant in a democratic society. It has not always been easy, and this brief discussion of the Court's history points to examples where the Court did not always have the most fortunate 'last word'. The Court has renewed itself in recent years. Recruitment policies have changed, and experience beyond judicial experience is represented in the Court. However, the Supreme Court is still discrete, which might be the Court's most outstanding attribute. Judicial appointments do not attract much public attention with discussions on the views of current judges about this and that in society. There is no doubt that appointments come about purely from professional legal criteria. The Supreme Court also shows its obligations and limitations. The Court respects the boundary between jurisprudence and politics and has no authority in areas where decisions would be political. It is a long way from the Danish Supreme Court to the US Supreme Court or other courts in the world which display their importance in more spectacular fashion. The strength of the Danish Supreme Court is that one knows that the 'last word' is spoken from professional consideration and as much legal competence as can be found within the country. The Supreme Court's most important good is probably that the Court has the people's confidence. Ministers and members of parliament come and go, but the Supreme Court remains. That is the true power of the Court.

Dualismus der Verwaltungsgerichtsbarkeit in der II. Republik Polen – Justiz im Spiegel der preußischen und österreichischen Einflüsse

Anna Tarnowska

I. Das Erbe der Rechtsgeschichte

Der Beitrag befasst sich mit dem Thema Erbe in der Rechtsgeschichte. Allerdings soll nicht vom Erbe als Institution des Erbrechts, sondern vom Erbe als Konsequenz eines internationalen Rechtstransfers von einem Territorium in ein anderes und der Beständigkeit eines solchen Transfers unter geänderten politischen Bedingungen die Rede sein. Die Zweite Republik Polen war eine Schöpfung des Versailler Vertrags von 1919. Die Polen in den ehemals russischen und österreichischen Gebieten hatten ihre Souveränität schon im November 1918 proklamiert. Nach 123 Jahren erschien Polen wieder auf der Landkarte Europas.

II. Historischer Hintergrund: die drei polnischen Teilungen

Der neue polnische Staat bestand aus Territorien, welche die mächtigen Nachbarn Preußen, Österreich und Russland durch drei Teilungen in den Jahren 1772, 1792 und 1795 annektiert hatten. Die Teilungsmächte planten, die annektierten Territorien möglichst rasch zu konsolidieren und ihrer Herrschaftsordnung anzupassen.[1] Dieses Ziel erreichten sie. Allerdings blieben innerhalb der annektierten Gebiete bestimmte territoriale Unterschiede bestehen. Das zeigt sich beispielhaft in den von Russland annektierten Gebieten: In Zentralpolen galt eine andere Rechtsordnung (die 1815 für das „Königreich Polen", Kongresspolen, oktroyierte Verfassung) und gab es eine andere Verwaltungsorganisation als in den östlichen, direkt in das Zarenreich (als sog. westliche Provinzen) eingegliederten Gebieten.

Dasselbe galt für die östlichen, „polnischen" Provinzen des Königreichs Preußen (Posen, Westpreußen, Schlesien). In der Provinz Posen traten viele neue Regelungen mit großer Verspätung oder gar nicht in Kraft. So trat die *Provinzialordnung* von 1875 erst 1889 in Kraft; die *Kreisordnung* von 1828 wurde erst 1904 novelliert, während in den anderen Ostprovinzen schon die neue *Kreisordnung* seit 1872 galt. Die Verwaltung blieb teilweise archaisch und ständisch. Es sei nur ein Beispiel genannt: Das Präsentationsrecht, d.h. das Recht der Kreistage zur Ernennung des Landrats, wurde in der Provinz Posen nach der königlichen Begründung „wegen der politischen Unzuverlässigkeit des Adels"[2] bereits 1833 suspendiert. Dagegen

---

1 Vgl. ausführlicher *Manfred Alexander*, Kleine Geschichte Polens, Stuttgart 2003, S. 163–270.

2 Kabinettsorder v. 2. Februar 1833; vgl. *Georg Lammermann*, Die Entwicklung der rechtlichen Stellung des preußischen Landrats, Göttingen 1939, S. 29–31.

blieb das Präsentationsrecht in den Provinzen Westpreußen und Schlesien trotz bedeutender polnischer Minderheiten bestehen.

Schon im freien Polen koexistierten vor diesem historischen Hintergrund drei Strafgesetzbücher (deutsch, russisch, österreichisch) und vier bürgerliche Gesetzbücher (BGB, ABGB, russische Vorschriften nach *Svod Zakonov* und sogar die Regelungen des Code Napoléon, die Polen aus den napoleonischen Kriegen von 1806 bis 1812 geerbt und dann in Kraft belassen hatte).[3]

III. Rechtsvereinheitlichung im polnischen Staat

Die drei ehemals den Großmächten Preußen, Österreich und Russland zugeordneten Teilungsgebiete des neugeborenen Staates mussten wirtschaftlich und rechtlich zusammengefügt werden. Die anfänglichen schwachen Zentralbehörden standen vor einer riesigen Aufgabe. Die neue Wahlordnung führte für den Januar 1919 einen freien und erstmals in der polnischen Geschichte völlig allgemeinen Modus zur Parlamentswahl ein.[4] Zu diesem Zeitpunkt dienten der „Vorläufige Staatschef“[5] Józef Piłsudski und die von ihm ernannte Regierung als oberste Staatsorgane. Im Februar 1919 traf der „konstituierende Sejm“ erste Verfassungsentscheidungen. Er beschloss, dem bisherigen Staatschef Józef Piłsudski weiter das Amt des Staatsoberhaupts anzuvertrauen und ihn unter die Kontrolle des Sejms zu stellen. Wie nicht anders zu erwarten war, hatte der Beschluss einen vorläufigen und apodiktischen Charakter.[6]

Die territorialen Behörden stellten ein buntes und sehr zersplittertes Mosaik dar. Gestalt und Grundsätze des Verwaltungssystems unterschieden sich je nach Region, angefangen mit der Verwaltungshierarchie: In den ehemaligen preußischen Provinzen waren die Behörden in vier Stufen (Gemeinde, Kreis, Regierungsbezirk, Provinz) organisiert, woanders in drei – speziell in Galizien, wo die Organisation über Gemeinden und Kreisen mit einer obersten Verwaltungsstufe für das Kronland Galizien abschloss.

Die Vereinheitlichung der Verwaltung war ein Prozess, der bis zum Zweiten Weltkrieg nicht abgeschlossen wurde. Selbstverständlich könnte man einfach auf

---

[3] Vgl. *Herbert Küpper*, Einführung in die Rechtsgeschichte Osteuropas, Frankfurt a.M. 2005, S. 282–290.

[4] Dekret o ordynacji wyborczej z 28 listopada 1918 r. [Dekret über die Wahlordnung vom 28. November 1918]; Dziennik Praw Państwa Polskiego [Rechtsblatt des Polnischen Staates], künftig: Dz.P.P.P. Nr. 18, Pos. 46).

[5] Polnisch: Tymczasowy Naczelnik Państwa [Vorläufiger Staatschef]; seit 20. Februar 1919 Naczelnik Państwa. Vgl. auch *Alexander*, Geschichte (oben Fn. 1), S. 285.

[6] Uchwała Sejmu Ustawodawczego z dnia 20 lutego 1919 r. o powierzeniu Józefowi Piłsudskiemu dalszego sprawowania urzędu Naczelnika Państwa [Beschluss v. 20. Februar 1919 über die Einsetzung von Józef Piłsudski in das Amt des Staatschefs, sog. „kleine Verfassung”]; Dz.P.P.P. Nr. 19 Pos. 226).

die wichtigsten Schritte verweisen, doch blieben einige Partikularismen gesetzlich in Kraft und waren damit tief in der Praxis verankert.

Damit sind vor allem die ehemals preußischen Territorien gemeint. Als der polnische Staatspräsident 1928 die Vereinheitlichung der Gestalt der Territorialbehörden und der Regierungsverwaltung anordnete,[7] verblieb die Selbstverwaltung in ihrem zersplitterten Zustand. Nur in den Woiwodschaften von Posen und Pommerellen (ehemals Westpreußen) bündelten die Woiwodschafts-Landtage (ehemals preußische Provinziallandtage) das staatliche Handeln, und ihre Kompetenz umfasste die Änderung alter preußischer Vorschriften. Die Regierung weigerte sich, in den anderen Landesteilen solche Landtage ins Leben zu rufen, da sie eine Schwächung der territorialen Staatsbehörden, sog. Woiwoden, auf dieser Stufe befürchtete. Dieser Zustand dauerte bis zum Zweiten Weltkrieg.

Das Zusammenlegungsgesetz von 1933[8] reformierte die Organisation der Selbstverwaltung in Gemeinden und Kreisen und vereinheitlichte weitgehend die unterschiedlichen Verwaltungssysteme. Die Selbstverwaltung auf der Ebene der Woiwodschaften blieb davon unberührt: im Westen als umgewandelte preußische Organe, in anderen Regionen existierte diese Ebene wie schon erwähnt grundsätzlich nicht.

IV. Einflüsse ausländischer Rechtsordnungen

Selbstverständlich ist die Analyse des ausländischen Einflusses auf die verschiedenen Aspekte der Verwaltungsvereinheitlichung ein höchst interessantes Forschungsgebiet. Die österreichischen und preußischen Spuren sind besonders deutlich sichtbar;[9] auf russische Vorbilder berief sich der polnische Gesetzgeber dagegen nur sehr selten. Als seltenes Beispiel für den russischen Einfluss ist die Oberste Kontrollkammer zu nennen. Das russische Verwaltungsmodell entsprach nicht mehr den Anforderungen an die moderne Verwaltung und nicht den Regeln des Rechtsstaats, obwohl das russische materielle Recht, wie z.B. das moderne Strafgesetzbuch von Taganzew, noch bis 1932 beibehalten wurde.

Die Staatsorgane, vor allem das seit 1921 aus zwei Kammern (Sejm und Senat) zusammengesetzte Parlament, standen also immer vor der Frage, welche Elemente

---

[7] Rozporządzenie Prezydenta RP z z 19 stycznia 1928 r. o organizacji i zakresie działania władz administracji ogólnej [Verordnung des Präsidenten Polens über Organisation und Tätigkeitsbereich der allgemeinen Verwaltungsbehörden v. 19. Januar 1928]; Dziennik Ustaw Rzeczypospolitej Polskiej [Gesetzblatt der Republik Polen], künftig: Dz.U.R.P. Nr. 11, Pos. 86).

[8] Ustawa z 23 marca 1933 r. o częściowej zmianie ustroju samorządu terytorialnego [Gesetz über die teilweise Abänderung der Verfassung der territorialen Selbstverwaltung vom 23. März 1933]; Dz.U.R.P. Nr. 35, Pos. 294).

[9] Diesem Problem widmete die Autorin eine monographische Arbeit: Z dziejów unifikacji administracji II RP: rola przepisów pruskich, Toruń 2012, 324 Seiten [*Anna Tarnowska*, Zur Geschichte der Verwaltungsvereinheitlichung der Zweiten Polnischen Republik: die Rolle der preußischen Vorschriften].

der „geerbten“ Verwaltung dem neuen Staat am besten dienen würden. Eine der bedeutendsten Weichenstellungen im Bereich des Verwaltungsaufbaus bzw. des Grundrechtsschutzes war die Wahl des Verwaltungsgerichtsmodells. Es ist eine wohlbekannte Tatsache, dass zwei der drei Teilungsmächte – Österreich und Preußen – die Verwaltungsgerichtsbarkeit bereits in den siebziger Jahren des 19. Jahrhunderts erfolgreich eingeführt hatten. Sie hatten sich aber für sehr unterschiedliche Modelle entschieden.

Die Errichtung eigenständiger Verwaltungsgerichte in Preußen begann 1872 gleichzeitig mit dem Erlass der Kreisordnung.[10] Der Aufbau vollzog sich in zwei Etappen: erstens mit der Einführung von Verwaltungsgerichten in den fünf östlichen preußischen Provinzen in den Jahren 1872 bis 1876 nach Maßgabe der Kreisordnung, der Provinzialordnung,[11] des Gesetzes über die Verwaltungsgerichtsverfassung und das Verwaltungsprozesses vom 3. Juli 1875,[12] des Zuständigkeitsgesetzes vom 26. Juli 1876,[13] und dann zweitens mit der Ausweitung der Verwaltungsgerichtsbarkeit auf alle preußischen Provinzen auf der Grundlage des Gesetzes über die allgemeine Landesverwaltung vom 30. Juli 1883[14] sowie des neuen Gesetzes über die Zuständigkeit der Verwaltungs- und Verwaltungsgerichtsorgane vom 1. August 1883.[15]

Die Verwaltungsgerichtsbarkeit in Preußen war mehrstufig – die erste Instanz bildeten die Kreisausschüsse (bzw. Stadtausschüsse), eigentlich Organe der Selbstverwaltung. Die Berufung lag in der zweiten Instanz bei den Bezirksverwaltungsgerichten, die 1883 unter Beibehaltung der Gerichtsfunktionen in Bezirksausschüsse umgewandelt wurden. Den letzteren schrieb der Gesetzgeber aber einen Doppelcharakter zu, weil die Ausschüsse auch als Organe der Bezirksverwaltung, also als Regierungsverwaltung, tätig waren. Der wichtigste Funktionsunterschied lag im Verfahren – als Organ der Verwaltung erkannten die Bezirksausschüsse die

---

[10] Kreisordnung für die Provinzen Preußen, Brandenburg, Pommern, Posen, Schlesien und Sachsen vom 13. Dezember 1872 (Gesetz-Sammlung für die Königlichen Preußischen Staaten, künftig: GS, S. 661), mit den Veränderungen v. 19. März 1881 (GS, S. 179).

[11] Provinzialordnung für die Provinzen Ost- und Westpreußen, Brandenburg, Pommern, Schlesien und Sachsen v. 29. Juni 1875 (GS, S. 355), mit den Veränderungen v. 22. März 1881 (GS, S. 233).

[12] Gesetz betreffend die Verfassung der Verwaltungsgerichte und das Verwaltungsstreitverfahren (GS, S. 375), mit den Veränderungen v. 2. August 1880 (GS, S. 328).

[13] Gesetz betreffend die Zuständigkeit der Verwaltungsbehörden und Verwaltungsbehörden im Geltungsbereiche der Provinzialordnung vom 29. Juni 1975 (GS, S. 297).

[14] Gesetz über die allgemeine Landesverwaltung v. 30. Juli 1883 (GS, S. 195).

[15] Gesetz über die Zuständigkeit der Verwaltungs- und Verwaltungsgerichtsbehörden v. 1. August 1883 (GS, S. 237). Vgl. auch *Niklas Hubertus Paul Nowatius*, Die Einführung der Verwaltungsgerichtsbarkeit in Preußen durch die Kreisordnung von 1872 unter besonderer Berücksichtigung der Verdienste von Eduard Lasker, Bonn 2000, pass. Klassisch bleibt die Arbeit von *Ulrich Stump*, Preußische Verwaltungsgerichtsbarkeit 1875–1914. Verfassung – Verfahren – Zuständigkeit, Berlin 1980, pass.

Sachen im Beschlussverfahren, als Verwaltungsgerichte im Streitverfahren. Nur das OVG, das Oberverwaltungsgericht in Berlin, verfügte formal betrachtet über volle gerichtliche Unabhängigkeit. Für die Praxis kann dies freilich bezweifelt werden, wie der Fall „Die Weber"-Aufführung belegt.[16]

Der spätere Bundesverwaltungsgerichtspräsident Ludwig Frege sah das OVG idealistisch als

> „Hüterin der Rechtsstaatlichkeit [...]. Aus seinen Urteilen ist deutlich ersichtlich, dass seine [...] von einem starken Gerechtigkeitswillen getragene Rechtsprechung geleitet war von dem Bestreben, dem Schwachen gegenüber dem Mächtigen zu seinem Recht zu verhelfen".[17]

Als dritte Instanz erkannte das OVG in einer ausschließlich hauptamtlichen Besetzung, je zur Hälfte bestehend aus Richtern und höheren Verwaltungsbeamten.

In der Zusammenschau war die preußische Verwaltungsgerichtsbarkeit in den niedrigeren Instanzen nicht durchgehend mit Juristen besetzt und in ihren Entscheidungen nicht unabhängig. Die Berufungsinstanzen hatten im dreistufigen System Revisionscharakter. Ferner ist zu erwähnen, dass die Zuständigkeit der Gerichte auf einer Kombination von enumerativen Elementen und einer partiellen Generalklausel zur Anfechtung polizeilicher Verfügungen aufbaute.

In Österreich wurde nach einem langwierigen Gesetzgebungsverfahren[18] 1875 bzw. 1876 eine einstufige Verwaltungsgerichtsbarkeit[19] ins Leben gerufen, deren geistiger Vater Karl von Lemayer, späterer Vizepräsident des Verwaltungsgerichtshofs (VwGH), war. Der österreichische Verwaltungsgerichtshof entschied auf der Grundlage einer umfassenden Generalklausel mit taxativ, d.h. erschöpfend aufgezählten Ausnahmen und ausschließlich mit Berufsrichtern, d.h. ohne Laienanteil. Der VwGH begann seine Rechtsprechung mit 271 Beschwerden im ersten Jahr; zum Ende der Monarchie betrug doch die Zahl der Beschwerden knapp 10.000.[20] Zu Recht schreibt heute Andrzej Dziadzio von der Tätigkeit des VwGH als von

---

[16] Vgl. auch ausführlicher *Martin Pagenkopf*, Das Preußische OVG und Hauptmanns „Weber". Ein Nachtrag zum 125. Geburtstag von Gerhart Hauptmann, Bonn 1988, pass.

[17] Zitiert nach: *Hansgeorg Bräutigam*, Ein Jahrhundert Verwaltungsgerichtsbarkeit in Berlin, Berlin 1975, S. 22.

[18] Die Rechtsgrundlage für die Ankündigung der neuen Institution war noch Art. 15 des Grundgesetzes über richterliche Gewalt v. 21. Dezember 1867. Vgl. *Adam Wandruszka/Peter Urbanitsch* (Hg.), Die Habsburgermonarchie 1848–1919, Bd. 2. Verwaltung und Rechtswesen, Wien 1975, S. 692–702.

[19] Die Gesetz v. 22. Oktober 1875 betreffend die Errichtung eines Verwaltungsgerichthofes (RGBl. 1876, S. 88).

[20] Vgl. vor allem *Thomas Olechowski*, Der österreichische Verwaltungsgerichtshof: Geschichte der Verwaltungsgerichtsbarkeit in Österreich – das Palais der ehemaligen Böhmisch-Österreichischen Hofkanzlei, Wien 2001, S. 79–113.

„einem eigenartigen Damoklesschwert gegenüber antikonstitutionellen Neigungen der Staatsbürokratie“.[21]

Besonders hervorzuheben ist, dass die österreichische Obrigkeit den nationalen Minderheiten wesentlich breitere Karrieremöglichkeiten im Staatsdienst als in Preußen eröffnete. Viele Polen studierten – auch auf Polnisch – an den Universitäten in Krakau und Lemberg. Der polnische Anteil in der kaiserlichen Hochbürokratie war sichtbar. Kasimir Graf Badeni wurde 1895 sogar zum Ministerpräsidenten ernannt. Auch beim Verwaltungsgerichtshof gewannen die Polen juristische Erfahrungen. Unter den Richtern des VwGH ließen sich 11 Polen zählen, darunter Adam Budwiński[22] und vor allem Jan Sawicki, der seit 1909 als Senatspräsident im VwGH amtierte.[23]

Daher wurden diese beiden höchst unterschiedlichen Modelle auf den zukünftigen polnischen Territorien praktiziert – das preußische im Westen (Województwo Poznańskie [Woiwodschaft Posen] und Województwo Pomorskie [Woiwodschaft Pomerellen]), das österreichische im Süden (in vier Woiwodschaften; von Kraków [Krakau], Lwów [Lemberg], Stanisławów und Tarnopol). Jedes hatte Vorteile und Nachteile und musste den Praxistest bestehen. In einem neuen Staat, der beide Modelle vorfand, musste aber schnell eine verbindliche Entscheidung für ein einheitliches Modell getroffen werden. Selbstverständlich orientierte sich der Gesetzgeber an den beiden aus der Praxis bekannten Systemen, nicht an anderen nur im Ausland praktizierten und somit nur theoretisch bekannten Systemen wie dem englischen oder französischen.

V. Verfassungsrechtliche Vorgaben

Ein erster Schritt wurde in der Märzverfassung von 1921[24] gemacht, deren Art. 73 die Verwaltungsgerichtsbarkeit regelte. Die Norm lautete: „Zum Zweck der Rechtsprechung über die Gesetzmäßigkeit von Verwaltungsakten im Bereich sowohl der Regierungs- als auch der Selbstverwaltungs-Administration errichtet ein gesondertes Gesetz eine sich in ihrer Organisation auf die Zusammenarbeit von staatsbürgerlichem und richterlichem Mitwirken stützende Verwaltungsgerichtsbarkeit mit einem Obersten Verwaltungsgerichtshof an der Spitze“. Die Vorschrift sah also die Schaffung einer mehrinstanzlichen Verwaltungsgerichtsbarkeit („mit einem

---

[21] Vgl. *Andrzej Dziadzio*, Die Angelegenheiten aus Galizien in der Rechtsprechung der österreichischen Verwaltungsgerichtsbarkeit im 19. und 20. Jahrhundert, in: Zoran Pokrovac (Hg.), Rechtsprechung in Osteuropa. Studien zum 19. und frühen 20. Jahrhundert, Rechtskulturen des modernen Osteuropa, Frankfurt a.M. 2012, S. 538–539.

[22] Auch Redakteur der Sammlung: Erkenntnisse des k.u.k. Verwaltungsgerichtshofes, zusammengestellt auf Veranlassung von Dr. Adam Freiherrn von Budwiński, Band 1 bis 41, 1876–1918.

[23] Vgl. auch *Stanisław Grodziski/Andrzej Partyka*, Die Polen in der österreichischen Rechtspflege 1772–1914, in: Zeszyty Naukowe UJ. Prace Historyczne [Wissenschaftliche Hefte der Jagellonen-Universität. Geschichtliche Arbeiten], 1978, H. 37, S. 99.

[24] Verfassung der Republik Polen v. 17. März 1921 (Dz.U.R.P. Nr. 44, Pos. 267).

Obersten VGH an der Spitze") vor. Zweitens wurde die Rolle des staatsbürgerlichen Elements betont, d.h. die Einbeziehung der ernannten oder gewählten Laienmitglieder in die richterlichen Kollegialorgane, deren genauer Name und Struktur in der Verfassung offen geblieben war. Immerhin deutete die Verfassungsnorm eine Präferenz für das preußische Modell an.

VI. Der Oberste Verwaltungsgerichtshof

Das polnische Gesetz vom 3. August 1922[25] gestaltete die oberste Gerichtsinstanz – den Obersten Verwaltungsgerichtshof – aus. Der OVGH wurde als abschließende Instanz festgelegt, zuständig für die Rechtsprechung über die Rechtmäßigkeit von Anordnungen und Entscheidungen der Verwaltungsbehörden und Selbstverwaltungsbehörden (mit einigen Ausnahmen). Seine Urteile waren im Sinne eines Kassationsgerichts endgültig.

Von der Zuständigkeit des OVGH waren ausgenommen:

1. alle Angelegenheiten, die zur Zuständigkeit der ordentlichen Gerichte und der Sondergerichte gehörten,

2. Ermessensentscheidungen der Verwaltungsbehörden in den Grenzen des Ermessens,

3. Ernennung zu öffentlichen Ämtern und Stellungen, soweit nicht gesetzliche Rechte der Besetzung oder der Präsentierung von Kandidaten verletzt waren,

4. alle Angelegenheiten der Vertretung des Staates und der Staatsbürger gegenüber fremden Staaten und Behörden und die hiermit unmittelbar im Zusammenhang stehenden Angelegenheiten,

5. alle militärischen Angelegenheiten mit Ausnahme der Angelegenheiten der Versorgung und Ergänzung des Heeres,

6. alle Disziplinarsachen,

7. andere Sachen nach Sondervorschriften,

8. eigentlich auch die Gültigkeit ordnungsmäßig verkündeter Gesetze, doch nahm der OVGH mangels eines Verfassungsgerichtshofs die Prüfungskompetenz

---

[25] Ustawa z 3 sierpnia 1922 r. o Najwyższym Trybunale Administracyjnym [Gesetz über den Obersten Verwaltungsgerichtshof v. 3. August 1922]; Dz.U.R.P., Nr. 67, Pos. 600; mit Änderungen v. 25. März 1926 (Dz.U.R.P. Nr. 37, Pos. 237). Siehe auch: Rozporządzenie Prezydenta PP z 31 lipca 1923 r. w przedmiocie regulaminu Najwyższego Trybunału Administracyjnego [Verordnung des Präsidenten der Republik Polen zum Gegenstand des Reglements des OVGH v. 31. Juli 1923], Dz.U.R.P. Nr. 80, Pos. 630) und Rozporządzenie Prezydenta RP z 25 maja 1928 r. w sprawie wydania regulaminu Najwyższego Trybunału Administracyjnego [Verordnung des Präsidenten der Republik Polen im Betreff des Reglements des OVGH v. 25. Mai 1928], Dz.U.R.P. Nr. 77, Pos. 537).

zunächst für sich in Anspruch. Erst die neue Aprilverfassung von 1935[26] verwehrte dem OVGH ausdrücklich ein solches Prüfungsrecht.

Diese Ausnahmenliste ähnelte der österreichischen; eine weitere bemerkenswerte Ähnlichkeit war die Tatsache, dass der OVGH wesentliche Grundlagen für die Gesetzgebung im Bereich des Verwaltungsverfahrens geschaffen hat. Die Verwaltungsverfahrensverordnung wurde 1928 verabschiedet.[27] Wie in Österreich gliederten sich die Entscheidungen des OVGH in zwei große Gruppen: Administrativ- und Steuerrecht. Die Klage war binnen zweier Monate seit Zustellung der anzufechtenden Anordnung oder Entscheidung zu erheben. Der Kläger musste durch einen Anwalt vertreten sein.

Der polnische OVGH setzte sich aus dem Ersten Präsidenten, den Präsidenten und den Richtern zusammen. All diese Personen mussten eine juristische Ausbildung vorweisen; darüber hinaus musste die Hälfte der Richter (seit 1932 ein Drittel[28]) die Befähigung zum Richteramt haben.[29] Die Verwaltung des OVGH oblag dem Ersten Präsidenten.

Der Gesetzesbeschluss vom 3. August 1922 regelte die niederen Instanzen nicht. Auch blieb die von der Verfassung aufgeworfene Frage einer staatsbürgerlichen Partizipation unbeantwortet. Warum? Der bekannte polnische Rechtshistoriker Lesław Pauli weist darauf hin:

> „Hier spielten also nicht nur ideologisch-politische Rücksichten die Rolle, sondern eine andere Gruppe von Ursachen, Rücksichten von sofortig-praktischer Natur mit einbeschlossen. Angesichts der organisatorischen, finanziellen und technischen Schwierigkeiten,[30] welche eine schnelle Lösung im vollen Bereich verhinderten, entschloss man sich zur Anwendung eines Palliativs. Anstelle eines ausgebauten Apparates nach französisch-preußischem Muster, dessen Schaffung die März-Verfassung vorsah, wurde ein vereinfachter, wenn auch nicht so vortrefflicher Apparat nach dem österreichischen

---

[26] Ustawa Konstytucyjna z 24 kwietnia 1935 r. [Verfassungsgesetz v. 24. April 1935], Dz.U.R.P. Nr. 30, Pos. 227).

[27] Rozporządzenie Prezydenta RP z 22 marca 1928 r. o postępowaniu administracyjnem [Verordnung des Präsidenten der Republik Polen über Verwaltungsverfahren v. 22. März 1928], Dz. U.R.P. Nr. 36, Pos. 341).

[28] Rozporządzenie Prezydenta RP z 27 października 1932 r. o Najwyższym Trybunale Administracyjnym [Verordnung des Präsidenten der Republik Polen über den Obersten Verwaltungsgerichtshof v. 27. Oktober 1932]; Dz.U.R.P. Nr. 94, Pos. 806).

[29] Zum Thema OVGH vgl: *Dorota Malec*, Najwyższy Trybunał Administracyjny 1922 – 1939 w świetle własnego orzecznictwa [Der Oberste Verwaltungsgerichtshof 1922–1939 im Licht seiner Rechtsprechung], Warszawa/Kraków 1999, passim; *dies.*, Der Oberste Verwaltungsgerichtshof und seine Rechtsprechung in den Jahren 1922–1939, in: Zoran Pokrovac (Hg.), Rechtsprechung in Osteuropa (oben Fn. 21), S. 541–596; auch viele kleinere Arbeiten der Autorin.

[30] Auf diese Beschränkungen berief sich Jan Sawicki, Sądy administracyjne w Polsce [Verwaltungsgerichte in Polen], Dziennik Urzędowy Departamentu Sprawiedliwości [Amtsblatt des Justizdepartments], Dział Nieurzędowy 1920, S. 177–188; 234–240, vor allem S. 181.

Typus geschaffen, welche aber eine kleinere Personalbesatzung und bescheidenere finanzielle Mittel beanspruchte".[31]

Eine nicht zu unterschätzende Rolle spielten die polnischen Richter, die früher am VwGH in Wien tätig gewesen waren. Sie wollten natürlich ihre Erfahrungen einbringen.[32] Hier ist der Name Jan Sawicki zu wiederholen; sein Entwurf bildete die Grundlage für das Gesetz.

Für die ehemaligen österreichischen und russischen Landesteile sollte der polnische OVGH als einziges Verwaltungsgericht dienen. Dagegen hielt das Gesetz für die ehemals preußischen Landesteile der Woiwodschaften Pomerellen, Posen und Schlesien das preußische System aufrecht. Art. 35 des Gesetzes über das OVGH legte fest:

„Bis zur Bildung einer Verwaltungsgerichtsbarkeit auf niederer Ebene auf dem gesamten Gebiet der Republik Polen bleibt die im ehemaligen preußischen Landesteil bestehende Verwaltungsgerichtsbarkeit (Rechtsprechung in Verwaltungsstreitverfahren) unberührt mit der Änderung, dass die Kompetenzen [der obersten Instanz] an den Obersten Verwaltungsgerichtshof übergehen [...]".

Nach dieser Regelung war der Kreisausschuss das erstinstanzliche Verwaltungsgericht. Als zweite Instanz wurden statt der Bezirksräte Woiwodschafts-Verwaltungsgerichte in Toruń (Thorn), Katowice (Kattowitz) und Poznań (Posen) errichtet.[33] Gegen ihre Entscheidungen konnte Berufung an den Obersten Verwaltungsgerichtshof eingelegt werden. Der OVGH spielte also eine entscheidende Rolle als Klammer zwischen beiden Systemen. In dem einen System war er das einzige Gericht, in dem anderen Gericht dritter Instanz.

VII. Weitere Veränderungen

Die Verwaltungsgerichtsverfassung in den westlichen Territorien Polens wurde in den nächsten Jahren weiter verändert bis hin zur vollen richterlichen Unabhängig-

---

[31] *Lesław Pauli*, Die Verwaltungsgerichtsbarkeit in Polen zwischen den beiden Weltkriegen (Rechtsvergleichende Bemerkungen über ihre Entstehung und ihr Organisationsmodell), in: Andor Csimadia (Hg.), Entwicklungsfragen der Verwaltung im Mitteleuropa. Aus Materialien der internationalen Konferenz über Verwaltungsgerichte in Pécs (18.–20. Mai 1972), Pécs 1972, S. 214.

[32] A.a.O.

[33] Rozporządzenie Ministra byłej Dzielnicy Pruskiej z 21 lutego 1920 r. [Verordnung des Ministers für die ehemaligen Preußischen Landesteile vom 21. Februar 1920], Dziennik Urzędowy Ministerstwa byłej dzielnicy Pruskiej [Amtsblatt des Ministeriums für die ehemaligen Preußischen Landesteile] Nr. 10, Pos. 81); Rozporządzenie Wojewody Śląskiego z 1 sierpnia 1922 r. w przedmiocie utworzenia Wojewódzkiego Sądu Administracyjnego [Verordnung des Woiwoden von Schlesien v. 1. August 1922 wegen Schaffung eines Woiwodschaftsverwaltungsgerichts], Dziennik Ustaw Śląskich [Schlesisches Gesetzblatt] Nr. 12, Pos. 42). Vgl. ausführlicher *Anna Tarnowska*, Die niedere Verwaltungsgerichtsbarkeit im Polen der Zwischenkriegszeit. Die Rechtsprechung der Woiwodschaftsgerichte im ehemals preußischen Landesteil, in: Zoran Pokrovac (Hg.), Rechtsprechung in Osteuropa (oben Fn. 21), S. 619–673.

keit und zur organisatorischen Eigenständigkeit der Woiwodschafts-Verwaltungsgerichte, worüber die altpreußischen Bezirksausschüsse niemals verfügt hatten. Mehrfach aber bewies das Ministerium des Innern seine juristische Ignoranz, als es fälschlicherweise die Richter der Woiwodschafts-Verwaltungsgerichte als Beamte des Innenministeriums qualifizierte. Diese Frage blieb vor dem OVGH ungelöst.[34]

Immer mehr preußische Vorschriften traten außer Kraft, dementsprechend verkleinerte sich der Rechtsprechungsumfang der westlichen Verwaltungsgerichte. Man kann wohl behaupten, dass die vollständige Vereinheitlichung des materiellen Verwaltungsrechts zu Ende gedacht in aller Konsequenz das Ende der niederen Verwaltungsgerichte bedeuten würde, weil nach den Vorschriften des Gesetzes – aufgrund der Generalklausel – für alle neuen Rechtsstreitigkeiten der OVGH zuständig war.

VIII. Bewertung

Dieser Dualismus war der Preis, den der neue Staat zu Lasten von Rechtssicherheit und Gerechtigkeitssinn zahlen musste. Der Gesetzgeber nahm Rücksicht auf praktisch-orientierte Zustände, berief sich aber gleichzeitig auf die Traditionen und Erfahrungen der Teilungszeit. Obwohl das komplizierte System theoretisch als ein Provisorium anerkannt wurde, erfuhr es keine wesentliche Reform bis zum Zweiten Weltkrieg. Gleichzeitig gilt es auch als Musterbeispiel dafür, wie die Rechtsordnungen der Nachbarländer als Reformvorbild dienen können. Die kommunistischen Behörden verzichteten für viele Jahrzehnte auf eine echte Verwaltungskontrolle. Erst 1980 wurde das Hauptverwaltungsgericht als ein erstes Zeichen des kommenden Umbruchs ins Leben gerufen.

---

[34] Vgl. auch *Anna Tarnowska*, O niezależności sądów i niezawisłości sędziów Wojewódzkich Sądów Administracyjnych (1920–1939) [Über die Unabhängigkeit der Gerichte und die Selbstständigkeit der Richter an Woiwodschaftsverwaltungsgerichten (1920–1939)], Czasopismo Prawno-Historyczne [Rechtshistorische Zeitschrift] 58 (2006) H. 1, S. 119–143.

RECHTSHISTORISCHE REIHE

Die nachfolgende Liste führt die Titel der "Rechtshistorischen Reihe" ab Band 300 auf.
Eine vollständige Übersicht aller bisher in der Reihe erschienenen Bücher
finden Sie auf www.peterlang.de.

Band 300 Jan Kohlmann: Der Marsch zu den Gräbern von Karl und Rosa. Geschichte eines Gedenktages. 2004.

Band 301 Christian Rainer Schlicht: Die kumulative Schuldübernahme in der Rechtsprechung des Reichsgerichts und in der zeitgenössischen Literatur. 2004.

Band 302 Hans Peter Glöckner: Positive Vertragsverletzung. Die Geburt eines Rechtsinstituts. 2006.

Band 303 João Manuel Azevedo Alexandrino Fernandes: Die Theorie der Interpretation des Gesetzes bei Francisco Suárez. 2005.

Band 304 René Funk: Die Wahlprüfung der volksgewählten Abgeordneten der Volksvertretungen im Frühkonstitutionalismus. Eine Untersuchung der Wahlprüfung in den Kammern der Abgeordneten des Großherzogtums Baden, des Königreichs Württemberg und des Großherzogtums Hessen. 2005.

Band 305 Carolin O'Sullivan. Die Ahndung von Rechtsbrüchen der Seeleute im mittelalterlichen hamburgischen und hansischen Seerecht (1301-1482). 2005.

Band 306 Martin Jürgens: Staat und Reich bei Ernst Rudolf Huber. Sein Leben und Werk bis 1945 aus rechtsgeschichtlicher Sicht. 2005.

Band 307 Florian G. Dürselen: Franz Beyerle (1885-1977). Leben, Ära und Werk eines Rechtshistorikers. 2005.

Band 308 Kai Bandilla: Urheberrecht im Kaiserreich. Der Weg zum Gesetz betreffend das Urheberrecht an Werken der Literatur und Tonkunst vom 19. Juni 1901. 2005.

Band 309 Stefan Mieth: Die Entwicklung des Denkmalrechts in Preußen 1701-1947. 2005.

Band 310 Catharina Lodemann: Die Geschichte des französischen *acte de gouvernement.* 2005.

Band 311 Christina Wicke: Kodifikationsbestrebungen und Wissenschaft in Hessen-Darmstadt im vorkonstitutionellen Zeitalter. Zu der Beteiligung der Gießener Rechtsprofessoren an den Gesetzgebungsarbeiten in Hessen-Darmstadt in der Zeit zwischen 1769 und 1820. 2005.

Band 312 Christiane Chlosta: Nur dem Gesetz unterworfen? Eine rechtsgeschichtliche Untersuchung zu Idee und Wirklichkeit richterlicher Gesetzestreue unter besonderer Berücksichtigung der Aufwertungsrechtsprechung und des richterlichen Prüfungsrechts. 2005.

Band 313 Kathrin Dirr: Hoheitsrechtliche Streitigkeiten zwischen den Kölner Erzbischöfen und der Stadt Köln auf Grundlage reichskammergerichtlicher Verfahren des 16. und 17. Jahrhunderts. 2005.

Band 314 Michael Racky: Die Diskussion über Gewaltenteilung und Gewaltentrennung im Vormärz. 2005.

Band 315 Petra Thiemrodt: Die Entstehung des Staatshaftungsgesetzes der DDR. Eine Untersuchung auf der Grundlage von Materialien der DDR-Gesetzgebungsorgane mit zeitgeschichtlichen Bezügen. 2005.

Band 316 Julius F. Reiter: Entstehung und staatsrechtliche Theorie der italienischen *Carta del Lavoro.* 2005.

Band 317 André Book: Die Justizreform in der Frühzeit der Bundesrepublik. Die Beratungen der Kommission zur Vorbereitung einer Reform der Zivilgerichtsbarkeit in den Jahren 1955 bis 1961. 2005.

Band 318 Frank Zentz: Das amerikanische Strafverfahren als Element der Besatzungspolitik in Deutschland. Erziehung zur Demokratie durch den *Court of Appeals* 1948-1955. 2005.

Band 319 Friederike Quaisser: Mietrecht im 19. Jahrhundert. Ein Vergleich der mietrechtlichen Konzeptionen im Allgemeinen Landrecht für die Preußischen Staaten von 1794 und dem gemeinen Recht. 2005.

Band 320 Stefan Burghard: Professor Dr. Wilhelm Kahl – Leben zwischen Wissenschaft und Politik. 2005.

Band 321 Günter Baranowski: Die *Russkaja Pravda* – ein mittelalterliches Rechtsdenkmal. 2005.

Band 322 Christina Schneider: Die SS und das „Recht". Eine Untersuchung anhand ausgewählter Beispiele. 2005.

Band 323 Werner Schubert (Hrsg.): Zivilprozessreform in der Weimarer Zeit. Quellen zur Emminger-Zivilprozessverordnung vom 13.2.1924 und zu den Arbeiten der Zivilprozesskommission des Reichsjustizministeriums (1922-1930). Eingeleitet und herausgegeben von Werner Schubert. 2005.

Band 324 Felix Gaul: Der Jurist Rudolf Isay (1886-1956). Ein verantwortungsbewusster Vermittler im Spannungsfeld zwischen dynamischer Rechtsschöpfung, ökonomischem Wandel und technischem Fortschritt. 2005.

Band 325 Konstanze Braun: Dr. Otto Georg Thierack (1889-1946). 2005.

Band 326 Eckart Klein / Stefan Chr. Saar / Carola Schulze (Hrsg.): Zwischen Rechtsstaat und Diktatur. Deutsche Juristen im 20. Jahrhundert. 2006.

Band 327 Stefan Botor: Das *Berliner Sühneverfahren* – Die letzte Phase der Entnazifizierung. 2006.

Band 328 Andreas Köhler: Die Sorgerechtsregelungen bei Ehescheidung seit 1945. Scheidungsstrafe und verordnete Gemeinsamkeit. 2006

Band 329 Lars Düwel: Die Nichtigkeit und Anfechtbarkeit der Ehe in der Rechtsprechung des Reichsgerichts zwischen 1900 und 1945. 2006.

Band 330 Katalin Polgar: Das Oberappellationsgericht der vier freien Städte Deutschlands (1820-1879) und seine Richterpersönlichkeiten. 2007.

Band 331 Julia Schweitzer: Schiffer und Schiffsmann in den Rôles d'Oléron und im Llibre del Consolat de Mar. Ein Vergleich zweier mittelalterlicher Seerechtsquellen. 2007.

Band 332 Diana-Catharina Kurtz: Das Institut der Adoption im preußischen Allgemeinen Landrecht und im französischen Code civil zwischen Rezeption römisch-rechtlicher Prinzipien und verändertem Familienverständnis. 2006.

Band 333 Dino Joakim Duderstadt: Spiel, Wette und Differenzgeschäft (§§ 762-764 BGB) in der Rechtsprechung des Reichsgerichts und in der zeitgenössischen Literatur. 2007.

Band 334 Ronald Hoffmann: Die Domänenfrage in Thüringen. Über die vermögensrechtlichen Auseinandersetzungen mit den ehemaligen Landesherren in Thüringen nach dem Ersten Weltkrieg. 2006.

Band 335 Joachim Windmüller: *Ohne Zwang kann der Humanismus nicht existieren...* – „Asoziale" in der DDR. 2006.

Band 336 Sven Christian Gläser: Die Mediatisierung der Grafschaft Wertheim. Der juristische Kampf eines kleinen Reichsstandes gegen den Verlust der Landesherrschaft und seine Folgen. 2006.

Band 337 Benjamin Schleyer: Friedrich Wilhelm Bornemann (1798-1864). Eine Juristenkarriere im Preußen des 19. Jahrhunderts. 2006.

Band 338 Die Reform des Ehescheidungsrechts von 1976. Quellen zum Ersten Gesetz vom 14.6.1976 zur Reform des Ehe- und Familienrechts (Parlamentarische Ausschussprotokolle – Anglikanische Denkschrift von 1966 zur Scheidungsrechtsreform – Schlussabstimmung 1969 in der Eherechtskommission des Bundesministeriums der Justiz). Eingeleitet und herausgegeben von Werner Schubert. 2006.

Band 339 Andreas Feld: Das Bayerische Gesetz zum Schutz des Eigentums an Erzeugnissen der Literatur und Kunst gegen Nachdruck vom 15.04.1840. Vorgeschichte und Zustandekommen. 2007.

Band 340 Bernd Wörner: Adelbert Düringers Einfluß als Richter am Reichsgericht in Leipzig auf dem Gebiet des Personengesellschaftsrechts. 2007.

Band 341 Jan Jelle Kähler: Französisches Zivilrecht und französische Justizverfassung in den Hansestädten Hamburg, Lübeck und Bremen (1806-1815). 2007.

Band 342 Jörn Eckert / Pia Letto-Vanamo / Kjell Modéer (Hrsg.): Juristen im Ostseeraum. Dritter Rechtshistorikertag im Ostseeraum 20.-22. Mai 2004. 2007.

Band 343 Ferdinand von Weyhe: A.E. Wassermann. Eine rechtshistorische Fallstudie zur „Arisierung" zweier Privatbanken. 2007.

Band 344 Martin Klaus Römermann: Kündigungen und Kündigungsschutz im Franquismus. 2007.

Band 345 Thomas Hoffmann: Der Landrechtsentwurf David Hilchens von 1599. Ein livländisches Rechtszeugnis polnischer Herrschaft. 2007.

Band 346 Ingo Ullmann: Die rechtliche Behandlung holsteinischer Leibeigener um die Mitte des 18. Jahrhunderts. Dargestellt unter besonderer Berücksichtigung der Schmoeler Leibeigenschaftsprozesse von 1738 bis 1743 sowie von 1767 bis 1777. 2007.

Band 347 Petra Fischer-Langosch: Die Entstehungsgeschichte des Familiengesetzbuches der DDR von 1965. 2007.

Band 348 Lasse O. Johannsen: Die rechtliche Behandlung ausreisewilliger Staatsbürger in der DDR. 2007.

Band 349 Ralf Schlottau: Deutsche Kolonialrechtspflege. Strafrecht und Strafmacht in den deutschen Schutzgebieten 1884 bis 1914. 2007.

Band 350 Hartwig Brandt / Ewald Grothe (Hrsg.): Rheinbündischer Konstitutionalismus. 2007.

Band 351 Nora Lutze: Der Verwandtenunterhalt nach den §§ 1601 bis 1603 und §§ 1610 bis 1612 BGB in der Rechtsprechung des Reichsgerichts. Unter Berücksichtigung der Entstehung des BGB. 2007.

Band 352 Frank Thiäner: Das Verhältnis von Aufsichtsrat und Abschlussprüfern in der rechtshistorischen Entwicklung bis 1937. 2007.

Band 353 Britta Heymann: Ernst Melsheimer (1897-1960). Eine juristische Karriere in verschiedenen staatlichen Systemen. Mitarbeiter im Preußischen Justizministerium in der Weimarer Republik, im Justizministerium Preußens und des Reiches sowie Richter am Kammergericht in der NS-Zeit und Erster Generalstaatsanwalt der Deutschen Demokratischen Republik. 2007.

Band 354 Susanne Adlberger: Wilhelm Kisch – Leben und Wirken (1874-1952). Von der Kaiser-Wilhelms-Universität Straßburg bis zur nationalsozialistischen Akademie für Deutsches Recht. 2007.

Band 355 Moritz Waibel: Josef Berchtold (1833-1894). Ein Leben gegen den Ultramontanismus. 2007.

Band 356 Aline Levin: Erinnerung? Verantwortung? Zukunft? Die Beweggründe für die gemeinsame Entschädigung durch den deutschen Staat und die deutsche Industrie für historisches Unrecht. 2007.

Band 357 Ferdinand Krause: Die hergebrachten Grundsätze des Berufsbeamtentums. Eine rechtshistorische Analyse. 2008.

Band 358 André Tiebel: Die Entstehung der Schutztruppengesetze für die deutschen Schutzgebiete Deutsch-Ostafrika, Deutsch-Südwestafrika und Kamerun (1884-1898). 2008.

Band 359 Holger Ruff: Sittenwidrige Rechtsgeschäfte in der späten Kaiserzeit. Die Entwicklung der reichsgerichtlichen Rechtsprechung zu § 138 BGB von 1900 bis 1914. 2007.

Band 360 Frank Rohrer: Strafjustiz im Dritten Reich und in der SBZ/DDR. Die personelle und organisatorische Neuordnung des Justizapparates in den totalitären Diktaturen (1933-1955) mit ihren Auswirkungen auf die Rechtsprechung zum politischen Strafrecht. 2007.

Band 361 Hans-Georg Knothe / Marc Liebmann (Hrsg.): Gerichtskultur im Ostseeraum. Vierter Rechtshistorikertag im Ostseeraum. 18.-20. Mai 2006 in Greifswald. 2007.

Band 362 Christina Meß: Das Vertragsrecht bei Adam Smith. 2008.

Band 363 Quellen zur dänischen Rechts- und Verfassungsgeschichte (12.-20. Jahrhundert). Herausgegeben von Ditlev Tamm, Werner Schubert und Jens Ulf Jørgensen. 2008.

Band 364 Günter Baranowski: Die Gerichtsurkunde von Pskov. 2008.

Band 365 Mark Spengler: Die Entstehung des Scheckgesetzes vom 11. März 1908. 2008.

Band 366 Ivan Biliarsky / Radu G. Păun (eds./éds.): The Biblical Models of Power and Law. Les modèles bibliques du pouvoir et du droit. Papers of the International Conference, Bucharest, New Europe College 2005. Actes du colloque international, Bucarest, New Europe College 2005. 2008.

Band 367 Thomas A. Roth: Ausgestaltungen der Rechtsfähigkeit im 19. und 20. Jahrhundert. Zur Rechtspersönlichkeit natürlicher Personen in den bedeutenden deutschen Zivilrechtsordnungen. 2008.

Band 368 Björn Alexander Rautenberg: Der Fiskal am Reichskammergericht. Überblick und exemplarische Untersuchungen vorwiegend zum 16. Jahrhundert. 2008.

Band 369 Thorsten Miederhoff: *Man erspare es mir, mein Juristenherz auszuschütten.* Dr. iur. Kurt Tucholsky (1890-1935). Sein juristischer Werdegang und seine Auseinandersetzung mit der Weimarer Strafrechtsreformdebatte am Beispiel der Rechtsprechung durch Laienrichter. 2008.

Band 370 Philipp Nordloh: Kölner Zunftprozesse vor dem Reichskammergericht. 2008.

Band 371 Judith Freund: Die Wechselverpflichtung im 19. Jahrhundert. 2008.

Band 372 Hans-Michael Empell: Gutenberg vor Gericht. Der Mainzer Prozess um die erste gedruckte Bibel. 2008.

Band 373 Rainer Schröder: Die DDR-Ziviljustiz im Gespräch – 26 Zeitzeugeninterviews. 2008.

Band 374 Christian Neschwara: Ein österreichischer Jurist im Vormärz. „Selbstbiographische Skizzen" des Freiherrn Karl Josef Pratobevera (1769-1853). 2009.

Band 375 Stefan Ullrich: Untersuchungen zum Einfluss des lübischen Rechts auf die Rechte von Bergen, Stockholm und Visby. 2008.

Band 376 Johanna Gertrude Schmitzberger: Das nationalsozialistische Nebenstrafrecht 1933 bis 1945. 2008.

Band 377 Christian Brom: Urteilsbegründungen im „Hoge Raad van Holland, Zeeland en West-Friesland" am Beispiel des Kaufrechts im Zeitraum 1704-1787. 2008.

Band 378 Christian Böse: Die Entstehung und Fortbildung des Reichserbhofgesetzes. 2008.

Band 379 Tobias Röhnelt: Timm Kröger. Leben und Werk. 2009.

Band 380 Andrea Elisabeth Sebald: Der Kriminalbiologe Franz Exner (1881-1947). Gratwanderung eines Wissenschaftlers durch die Zeit des Nationalsozialismus. 2008.

Band 381 Angela Kriebisch: Die Spruchkörper Juristenfakultät und Schöppenstuhl zu Jena. Strukturen, Tätigkeit, Bedeutung und eine Analyse ausgewählter Spruchakten. 2008.

Band 382 Nana Ozawa: Louis Adolphe Bridel – Ein Schweizer Professor an der juristischen Fakultät der Tokyo Imperial University. Die geschichtliche Bedeutung der Yatoi zur späten Meijizeit. 2010.

Band 383 Christian Weißhuhn: Alfred Hueck 1889-1975. Sein Leben, sein Wirken, seine Zeit. 2009.

Band 384 Andreas Hunkel: Eduard Dietz (1866-1940) – Richter, Rechtsanwalt und Verfassungsschöpfer. 2009.

Band 385 Meike Guskow: Entstehung und Geschichte der Europäischen Charta der Regional- oder Minderheitensprachen. 2009.

Band 386 Markus J. Jahnel: Das Bodenrecht in „Neudeutschland über See". Erwerb, Vergabe und Nutzung von Land in der Kolonie Deutsch-Südwestafrika 1884-1915. 2009.

Band 387 Matthias Günter Steiner: Die Klöster und ihr Wirken – eine der Wurzeln des Stiftungswesens? 2009.

Band 388 Cornelia Staats: Die Entstehung des Bundes-Immissionsschutzgesetzes vom 15. März 1974. 2009.

Band 389 Cai Niklaas E. Harders: Das Bundesjagdgesetz von 1952 sowie die Novellen von 1961 und 1976. Vorgeschichte, Entstehung des Gesetzes sowie Problemfelder. 2009.

Band 390 Matthias Pohlkamp: Die Entstehung des modernen Wucherrechts und die Wucherrechtsprechung des Reichsgerichts zwischen 1880 und 1933. 2009.

Band 391 Sebastian Baur: *Vor vier Höllenrichtern...* Die Lizentiats- und Doktorpromotionen an der Juristischen Fakultät der Universität Heidelberg. 2009.

Band 392 Christoph Salmen-Everinghoff: Zur *cautio damni infecti*: Die Rückkehr eines römischrechtlichen Rechtsinstituts in das moderne Zivilrecht. 2009.

Band 393 Till Meno Sellschopp: Der Weg zum Revokationsrecht der Ehegatten nach § 1368 BGB. Zugleich ein Beitrag zur Geschichte des ehelichen Güterrechts. 2009.

Band 394 Marc Biermann: Das Staatseigentum an öffentlichen Sachen im Gemeingebrauch in der ersten Hälfte des 19. Jahrhunderts. Die Theorie des reinen Hoheitsrechts an den öffentlichen Sachen von Rudolph von Jhering und Friedrich Ludwig Keller im Zusammenhang mit dem Baseler Schanzenstreit von 1859/62. 2009.

Band 395 Markus Tüxen: Kollegialprinzip oder Einzelrichter. Die Entwicklung des zivilrechtlichen Spruchkörpers bei den Landgerichten sowie den Oberlandesgerichten seit 1879 unter besonderer Berücksichtigung der Reformen von 1974 und 1976. 2009.

Band 396 Adam Polkowski: Die polnische Zivilprozessordnung von 1930/33. Unter Berücksichtigung des deutschen, österreichischen, russischen und französischen Rechts. 2009.

Band 397 Barbara Riedi: Die Porten der Unteren Strasse, ihr Ladungsrecht und der Strassenunterhalt. Rechtshistorische Betrachtungen zur Verkehrs- und Wirtschaftsgeschichte Graubündens. 2009.

Band 398 Stefanie Jessica Loroch: Zeitungsrubrik: Gerichtssaal. Strafprozessberichterstattung in Münster im 19. Jahrhundert (1848-1890). 2009.

Band 399 Dirk Henning Hofer: Karl Konrad Werner Wedemeyer (1870-1934). Ein Juristen- und Gelehrtenleben in drei Reichen. Eine Biographie. 2010.

Band 400 Thomas Simon (Hrsg.): Hundert Jahre allgemeines und gleiches Wahlrecht in Österreich. Modernes Wahlrecht unter den Bedingungen eines Vielvölkerstaates. 2010.

Band 401 Dörte Mentz: Die Beweislastumkehr in der Rechtsprechung des Reichsgerichts. 2010.

Band 402 Werner Schubert (Hrsg.): Oberster Gerichtshof für die Britische Zone (1948-1950). Nachschlagewerk Strafsachen – Nachschlagewerk Zivilsachen. Präjudizienbuch der Zivilsenate. Eingeleitet und herausgegeben von Werner Schubert. 2010.

Band 403 Yong Lei: Auf der Suche nach dem modernen Staat. Die Einflüsse der allgemeinen Staatslehre Johann Caspar Bluntschlis auf das Staatsdenken Liang Qichaos. 2010.

Band 404 Andreas Schwenk: Die Formbestimmung des § 313 BGB a. F. (§ 311 b Abs. 1 BGB n. F.) bei Verträgen über Grundstücke in der Rechtsprechung des Reichsgerichts. 2010

Band 405 René Schorsch: Eberhard Georg Otto Freiherr von Künßberg (1881-1941). Vom Wirken eines Rechtshistorikers. 2010.

Band 406 Ulrike Köbler: Werden, Wandel und Wesen des deutschen Privatrechtswortschatzes. 2010.

Band 407 Björn Florian Faulenbach: Rolle und Bedeutung der Lehre in der Rechtsprechung der Internationalen Gerichtshöfe im zwanzigsten Jahrhundert. 2010.

Band 408 Guangyu Fu: Das Causaproblem im deutschen Bereicherungsrecht. Eine rechtshistorische Untersuchung. 2010.

Band 409 Andreas Kimmelmann: Die Folter im Beweisverfahren der Leges Visigothorum. Chindasvinths Gesetzgebung im Spiegel der westgotischen Rechtsentwicklung. 2010.

Band 410 Jacqueline Schmaltz: Die Entwicklung der Industrie- und Handelskammern. Zwischen Pflicht und Kür. 2010.

Band 411 Hermann Nehlsen: Bayerische Rechtsgeschichte vom frühen Mittelalter bis zum 20. Jahrhundert. 2011.

Band 412 Kathrin Spoerr: Recht und Revolution. Deutsche Ökonomen und ihr Einfluss auf das Recht der Weimarer Republik – eine Zeitschriftenschau 1917-1920. 2011.

Band 413 Moritz von Köckritz: Die deutschen Oberlandesgerichtspräsidenten im Nationalsozialismus (1933-1945). 2011.

Band 414 Annika Lillemor Lara Rabaa: Die Ehe als Rechtsinstitut im Badischen Landrecht von 1810. Unter besonderer Berücksichtigung der gesellschaftlichen Entwicklungen im 19. Jahrhundert. 2011.

Band 415 Christian Hattenhauer / Klaus-Peter Schroeder (Hrsg.): 200 Jahre Badisches Landrecht von 1809/1810. Jubiläumssymposium des Instituts für geschichtliche Rechtswissenschaft der Ruprechts-Karls-Universität Heidelberg und der Heidelberger Rechtshistorischen Gesellschaft vom 23. bis 26. September 2009. 2011.

Band 416 Tobias Alexander Krammerbauer: Die Ministerverantwortlichkeit und die Vorformen sonstiger Verfassungsgerichtsbarkeit in Württemberg zwischen 1815 und 1918. 2011.

Band 417 Werner Schubert (Hrsg.): Quellen zur GmbH-Reform von 1958 bis zum GmbH-Änderungsgesetz von 1980. Eingeleitet und herausgegeben von Werner Schubert. 2011.

Band 418 Gisela Emling: Johannes Heckel. Leben und Wirken (1889-1963). 2011.

Band 419 Jochen Kirschbaum: Die Etablierung der Historischen Rechtsschule an der Ludoviciana (1814-1824). 2011.

Band 420 Sören Koch: Unaufgeforderte Hilfeleistung in Notsituationen. Eine rechtshistorische und rechtsvergleichende Studie zu den zivilrechtlichen Aspekten der Nothilfe mit besonderer Berücksichtigung des Rechts der Geschäftsführung ohne Auftrag. 2011.

Band 421 Friedrich Carl von Savigny: Die Prinzipienfragen in Beziehung auf eine neue Strafprozeß-Ordnung. Ausgearbeitet im Justizministerium für die Gesetzrevision. Eingeleitet und herausgeben von Werner Schubert. 2011.

Band 422 Stephan Faulwetter: Von der Zunft zur Handelskammer. Zur Entwicklung des Gewerberechts in thüringischen Staaten. 2011.

Band 423 Moritz Eisenhardt: Sanierung statt Liquidation. Die Geschichte des Vergleichs zur Abwendung des Konkurses unter besonderer Berücksichtigung der Vergleichsordnung von 1927 und 1935. 2011.

Band 424 Gerd Kleinheyer: Beiträge zur Strafrechtsgeschichte. Herausgeben von Franz Dorn, Mathias Schmoeckel und Jan Schröder. 2011.

Band 425 Ralf Maertens: Das Landgericht Altona (1879-1937) und die Anfänge des Landgerichts Itzehoe (1937-1945). Unter besonderer Berücksichtigung ihrer Tätigkeitsberichte und rechtspolitischen Stellungnahmen. 2011.

Band 426 Mark Friedrich: Ferdinand von Martitz (1839-1921). Rechtshistoriker, Staatsrechtler und Völkerrechtler zwischen dem Ende des Deutschen Bundes und dem Beginn der Weimarer Republik. 2012.

Band 427 Sebastian Krusche: Die Bundesrechtsanwaltsordnung vom 1. August 1959. Vorgeschichte und Entstehung. 2012.

Band 428 Marju Luts-Sootak / Sanita Osipova / Frank L. Schäfer (Hrsg./eds.): Einheit und Vielfalt in der Rechtsgeschichte im Ostseeraum. Unity and Plurality in the Legal History of the Baltic Sea Area. Sechster Rechtshistorikertag im Ostseeraum, 3.-5. Juni 2010 in Tartu (Estland) / Riga (Lettland). 6th Conference in Legal History in the Baltic Sea Area, 3rd-5rd June 2010 Tartu (Estonia) / Riga (Latvia). 2012.

Band 429 Margret R. I. Bootz: Die Hamburger Rechtsprechung zum Arbeitsrecht im Nationalsozialismus bis zum Beginn des 2. Weltkriegs. 2012.

Band 430 Heiko Zech: Die soziale Frage im Konkursrecht 1879-1900. 2012.

Band 431 Jan C. Lorenzen: Das Bundesnaturschutzgesetz vom 20. Dezember 1976. Die Entwicklung des Naturschutzrechtes in Deutschland von den Anfängen bis zur Neukodifikation des Bundesnaturschutzgesetzes von 1976. 2012.

Band 432 Ulrike Ingrid Bernhardt: Geschichte des Weinrechts im Deutschen Kaiserreich (1871-1918). Mit einem Überblick zur Vorgeschichte und Weiterentwicklung bis zur Gegenwart. 2012.

Band 433 Elisabeth Otto: Das Verwaltungsrecht in der SBZ / DDR bis zur Verwaltungsneugliederung im Jahr 1952. 2012.

Band 434 Werner Schubert: Zur Geschichte der Justizverfassung in Schleswig-Holstein im 19. und 20. Jahrhundert. Quellen und Studien. 2012.

Band 435 Stefan Ellenberg: Herrschaft und Reform. Zur Diskussion um die Aktienrechtsreform und den Konzern in der Weimarer Zeit. 2012.

Band 436 Jasmin Sonntag: Gesetzgebung und Verwaltung im Dalbergstaat 1802-1810. 2012.

Band 437 Martin Komusiewicz: Die Diskussion um das Verhältnis von Rechtsanwaltschaft und Notariat seit dem Ende des 18. Jahrhunderts bis zum Erlass der Bundesnotarordnung. 2012.

Band 438 Henriette von Breitenbuch: Karl Neumeyer – Leben und Werk (1869-1941). 2013.

Band 439 Günter Baranowski: Russische Rechtsgeschichte: Texte und Erläuterungen. Teil 1: Von den Anfängen bis 1612/13. 2013.

Band 440 Werner Schubert (Hrsg.): Staatsanwaltschaftsrecht (1934-1982). Quellen zu den Reformprojekten (Organisation – Innerer Dienstbetrieb – Ermittlungsverfahren – Verhältnis der Staatsanwaltschaft zur Polizei) und zur Anordnung über Organisation und Dienstbetrieb der Staatsanwaltschaft (OrgStA). Eingeleitet und herausgegeben von Werner Schubert. 2013.

Band 441 York Zieren: Das Schiedsverfahrensrecht der ZPO (1877-1933) unter Berücksichtigung der Genfer Übereinkommen von 1923 und 1927 sowie der Rechtsprechung des Reichsgerichts. 2013.

Band 442 Stefan Wolf: Das Jenaer Studium der Rechte im Dritten Reich. Zwischen Tradition und nationalsozialistischer Ideologie. 2013.

Band 443 Bernhard Klose: Das Verblassen eines Makels. Das Nichtehelichenrecht der DDR als Teil der gesamtdeutschen Entwicklung. 2013.

Band 444 Peter Opitz-von Bardeleben: Das Generalgouvernement Niederrhein. 2013.

Band 445 Nadine Göppner: Vorgeschichte und Entstehung des Atomgesetzes vom 23.12.1959. 2013.

Band 446 Frank L. Schäfer / Werner Schubert (Hrsg./eds.): Justiz und Justizverfassung / Judiciary and Judical System. Siebter Rechtshistorikertag im Ostseeraum, 3.-5. Mai 2012 Schleswig-Holstein / 7th Conference in Legal History in the Baltic Sea Area, 3rd-5th May 2012 Schleswig-Holstein. 2013.

www.peterlang.de